W9-BBH-438

The Press in American Politics, 1787–2012

THE PRESS IN AMERICAN POLITICS, 1787–2012

Patrick Novotny

HUMBER LIBRARIES LAKESHORE CAMPUS
3199 Lakeshore Blvd West
TORONTO, ON. M8V 1K8

PRAEGER

AN IMPRINT OF ABC-CLIO, LLC
Santa Barbara, California • Denver, Colorado • Oxford, England

Copyright © 2014 by Patrick Novotny

All rights reserved. No part of this publication may be reproduced, stored in a retrieval system, or transmitted, in any form or by any means, electronic, mechanical, photocopying, recording, or otherwise, except for the inclusion of brief quotations in a review, without prior permission in writing from the publisher.

Library of Congress Cataloging-in-Publication Data

Novotny, Patrick.
  The press in American politics, 1787–2012 / Patrick Novotny.
    pages cm
  ISBN 978-1-4408-3289-5 (hardback) — ISBN 978-1-4408-3290-1 (ebook)
    1. Press and politics—United States—History.   2. Government and the press—
  United States—History. I. Title.
PN4888.P6N68 2014
071'.3—dc23   2014016904

ISBN: 978-1-4408-3289-5
EISBN: 978-1-4408-3290-1

18 17 16 15 14   1 2 3 4 5

This book is also available on the World Wide Web as an eBook.
Visit www.abc-clio.com for details.

Praeger
An Imprint of ABC-CLIO, LLC

ABC-CLIO, LLC
130 Cremona Drive, P.O. Box 1911
Santa Barbara, California 93116-1911

This book is printed on acid-free paper ∞

Manufactured in the United States of America

To my parents, John and Margaret Novotny

Contents

Preface   ix

1. The Press and American Politics, 1787–1800   1

2. The Nineteenth-Century Press and American Politics   24

3. Newspapers and Twentieth-Century American Politics   47

4. Radio and the Rise of Broadcast Politics   72

5. Television in the Early Twentieth Century   102

6. Television in the 1930s and in Wartime America   115

7. Television and the Transformation of Postwar American Politics   137

8. The Internet and Politics in the Digital Age   175

Notes   199

Index   227

Preface

The Press in American Politics, 1787–2012 is a work that spans almost two decades of my teaching and writing on the place of the press in American politics and its history in our country's campaigning and political parties. Having had my first e-mail address as a doctoral student at the University of Wisconsin-Madison in the late 1980s and watching the growth of the World Wide Web as a graduate student and then a young faculty member, I have always been drawn to telling the story of the impact of the latest technologies on campaigning and on the nation's political life. Having spent many days at the University of Wisconsin's Memorial Library and at the Wisconsin Historical Society as a doctoral student and in the years since in archives, historical societies, and university libraries across the country, I also wanted to tell the history of politics through the stories of campaigning, elections, and political parties in American life. Having always been fascinated with America's political past, especially the era of the Constitutional Convention of 1787 and the changes that shaped the political life of the nineteenth and twentieth centuries, I strive in my teaching and my writing to tell the story of the political present with an eye to the political past.

When *The Press in American Politics* began as a series of essays to accompany my course on the press in American political history, little could I have known that these writings might someday come together into a book. Never especially drawn to the theoretical frameworks developed by my colleagues in communications and journalism history, my interest—as with much of my scholarly writing——has always been focused on the descriptive details of events and how they unfolded in American history. I am fascinated by the people who made our history as well as by the events that unfolded in the pages of America's newspapers, that first rough draft of history too often missing from scholarly writing and teaching in my own field of political science. I hope I have brought my enthusiasm for the story of the press as it relates to the nation's political candidates, their political parties, and their campaigns to the pages of *The Press in American Politics*.

The Press in American Politics is a mosaic of the press's enduring place in America's political traditions. The chapters are set in chronological sequence and tell a story of the press from the days of hand-turned printing presses to the digital era. Newspapers and their long-established place in the American conversation begin this book's journey across the decades. No one part of this story is especially more noteworthy than another, but my own imagination is captured in the histories of those early pioneers of the printing press who brought their inks, tools, types, and other supplies by boats to the riverbanks of settlements in Illinois, Indiana, Missouri, and elsewhere. Theirs is a story worthy of greater recognition by Americans who want to learn the story of their nation's press. Their dedication and determination to bring their presses into the rough-hewn settlements of the Western territories is every bit the foundation for the telephone crews who crossed the same terrain with their earthmoving equipment in the 1940s and 1950s to lay the coaxial cables that made coast-to-coast live television a technical reality and a commercial success—as well as a political game-changer—in postwar America. Radio's earliest inventors and visionaries come to life in later pages of this book—their efforts so much a part of the twentieth-century's innovations in radio and television broadcasting. Television's three early eras—its invention in the 1920s; its Depression-era innovations, interrupted by economic collapse that nonetheless saw important television breakthroughs in workshops and in broadcast studios; and its third wave of invention and innovation in the 1940s that ended with the beginnings of television's modern era—are all described in detail. The Internet's emergence in the postwar era—from the pages of engineering and scientific journals to the corners of computer laboratories on college and university campuses to the once-familiar squeal of the dial-up telephone-based computer modems and the all-encompassing broadband technologies of the digital present—is discussed with a particular attentiveness to their adaption and use by political candidates and by the nation's political parties and their leaders.

Insight seemingly only appreciated after many years of research, teaching, and writing on the histories explored in *The Press in American Politics* is the importance of appreciating the people as well as the places where these histories are lived, made, and shaped. Lives of political figures from Thomas Jefferson and Abraham Lincoln to Theodore Roosevelt, Franklin Roosevelt, John F. Kennedy, Lyndon B. Johnson, and others bring a better understanding of the way they both shaped and were shaped by the press of their time. Telling the stories of the press through the lives of the women and men of our nation's political past and present is something I believe is one of the best ways to teach and write this part of our nation's story. I also am reminded of my own firm belief in the importance of place in learning about and studying and writing about the events of the political past and the present day. The newspaper newsrooms, the radio and television broadcast studios, and workshops where many of the stories told herein are a kind of civic sacred ground as important as any microfilmed documents or archival materials. Some still stand to this day, some are sadly destroyed, some have been painstakingly rebuilt by those with an eye to preserving their local histories, some are designated by bronze markers or historical plaques; all too many have no markers to tell their stories. These buildings and historic places across the United States were unnamed, silent co-authors while I was writing this book. I hope that readers of this book will come to feel something of the same connection I have to the importance of the physical places where these political contests and debates occurred and in the story of the press that covered these contests and debates. Taking time to travel to these places, to see them in their present state, and to imagine their place in our past, is something I will forever be drawn to. Our past is a story we write every day not merely in the pages of books but in our classrooms, in our conversations, and in our own backyards and communities. It is a story I hope to be a part of for many years to come—and a story I am grateful and humbled to share in the pages of this book.

Chapter 1

The Press and American Politics, 1787–1800

Through the hard-fought battles of the War of Independence and in the tumultuous years after the war, the printers of the North American colonies and their circulars, pamphlets, and printings denouncing British authorities—materials sometimes delivered at not inconsiderable difficulty—are remembered as an indispensable and irreplaceable part of the history of that war. Printers went to extraordinary lengths and showed remarkable resourcefulness during the war to ensure their papers reached their readers. Print shops suffered constant shortages of paper and supplies, and they faced the disruption caused by wartime's conflict. Some printers had their presses confiscated by the British while still others hid their presses or fled their homes with their families, taking their presses with them. Others closed their shops before the British could.

When finally ratified by all thirteen states, the Articles of Confederation and its unicameral legislature assumed the leadership of the nation in the final months of the war. Its governing structure remained intact and largely effective during the war; however, the ending of the war most certainly revealed some of the many flaws inherent in the Confederation as a governing body. With the failings of the Articles of Confederation well evident by the war's end, lively debates and sometimes heated discussions of the Confederation's ineffectiveness became commonplace in the pages of the nation's newspapers. By 1783, Philadelphia boasted eleven weekly papers, Boston had eight weekly newspapers, and New York City was home to six papers. It was in 1783, at the end of the War of Independence, however, that newspapers took a more prominent role in the life of the country.

The nation's first daily paper, the *Pennsylvania Evening Post and Daily Advertiser*, was first printed as a daily edition on or near Monday, May 5,

1783, by printer Benjamin Towne from his print shop in Philadephia's Pewter Platter Alley. "All the news for two coppers" young boys hired to sell Towne's paper in the afternoons told passersby on the sidewalks of Philadelphia during the paper's largely unheralded tenure at the country's 1st daily paper, a paper whose printer faced financial difficulties for its duration until finally closing his paper sometime in October 1784, this only days after the appearance of the country's second daily paper printed just blocks away in their Market Street print shop by John Dunlap and David C. Claypoole. Philadelphia's *Pennsylvania Packet and Daily Advertiser*, printed by Dunlap and Claypoole, became that city's and the nation's second daily paper on Tuesday, September 21, 1784. Dunlap and Claypoole's *Pennsylvania Packet and Daily Advertiser* would have the distinction of being the first paper to publish the text of the 1787 Constitution on Wednesday, September 19, 1787.

While well-established printers and print shops along the Eastern Seaboard catered to the public's growing enthusiasm for newspapers with the emergence of daily papers in the years after 1783, so too the public's enthusiasm for papers in the further expanses of the West led to the expansion of newspapers into the newly settled towns of the frontier. The *Pittsburgh Gazette*, its first issue on Saturday, July 29, 1786, by printers John Scull and Joseph Hall, was the first paper published in the more distant reaches of the Western territories. Pittsburgh, a small settlement near Fort Pitt at the confluence of the Allegheny and Monongahela Rivers, was a town of only three hundred inhabitants when Scull and Hall printed their first issue of the *Pittsburgh Gazette* using a printing press transported from Philadelphia across the rutted roads of Pennsylvania to Fort Pitt's settlement. Facing difficulties in shipping supplies of ink and paper for their print shop, Scull and Hall occasionally used cartridge paper obtained from the armaments maintained by Fort Pitt's soldiers to print their issues.

NEWSPAPERS AND THE CONSTITUTIONAL CONVENTION OF 1787

In the final weeks of April and in early May 1787, delegates from twelve of the thirteen states began their travels to Philadelphia, where the Constitutional Convention met in the Pennsylvania State House after that state's legislature adjourned from its session. As delegations began arriving in Philadelphia, they met at the inns, boarding houses, and gathering places of the city. With a sufficient number of delegates to constitute a quorum on Friday, May 25, 1787, delegates opened the session of the Convention in what some delegates believed would be a session that would last only a matter of several weeks. Having elected George Washington as the Convention's presiding officer, delegates then moved to discuss the proceedings of the

Convention. One of the first proposals was for the meetings to take place in closed-door sessions without a public gallery.

Philadelphia boasted no fewer than eleven newspapers at the time of the Convention, including the country's only daily paper, Dunlap and Claypoole's *Pennsylvania Packet and Daily Advertiser*, yet remarkably few if any details of the Convention made their way into the city's papers. While delegates were reminded by George Washington to avoid discussion of the day's proceedings when entertaining and dining with their guests in the evenings, little beyond speculation of the Convention's proceedings found its way into the pages of papers in Philadelphia. Instead, rumors and unsubstantiated items seem to have been the order of the day in many of the items printed in the newspapers—rumors that circulated more widely as the Convention in the Pennsylvania State House continued into July and then into August.

"From the day in May when that body began to sit with closed doors," John Bach McMaster tells us, "the anxiety of the multitude had been steadily increasing and had, long before August came, risen to fever heat. Boasts, idle conjectures, prophecies, and anxious letters filled the newspapers and poured in upon the delegates from all parts."[1] As the Convention extended far longer than the several weeks most delegates, their families, and their state legislatures anticipated, all manner of speculation arose. On Monday, August 20, 1787, South Carolina's Charles Pinckney proposed a list of thirteen enumerations, which were then referred to the members of the Committee of Detail, a committee of delegates established to deliberate in greater detail some of the Constitution's unfinished issues. Pinckney was the first of the Convention's delegates to endorse the idea of a declaration protecting the freedom of the press. With the Committee of Detail charged by the Convention to, in the words of one observer, "arrange and systematize the materials which that honorable body have collected," the committee became the first delegates at the Convention to formally consider Pinckney's proposal to protect the liberty of the press.

In the language recommended by Pinckney to the Committee of Detail on Monday, August 20, 1787, was a proposed clause in the Constitution that "the liberty of the Press shall be inviolably preserved." It is the first of several instances during the closing days of the 1787 Convention that the issue of the liberty of the press became a part of the discussion of the Convention's delegates. Well known is Virginia's George Mason's insistence on a Declaration of Rights to be incorporated into—or to even preface to—the Constitution.

When a motion to preface the Constitution with a "declaration" of rights was made by Mason on Wednesday, September 12, 1787, it was his insistence on including such a declaration—not to mention his stature as one of the most well-respected delegates from one of the largest states—that carried the debate forward by a Convention exhausted after months of debate and deliberation. "It would give great quiet to the people," Mason is recalled to have told the Convention's delegates, "and with the aid of the State Declarations, a bill might be prepared in a few hours."[2] Massachusetts's Elbridge Gerry is remembered as having made a motion for a committee to be chosen to write such a declaration to preface the Constitution, a motion seconded by Mason.

Mason's insistence on a Bill of Rights is one of the more remarkable stories of the Convention and it was still important in the months following the adjournment of the Philadelphia Convention into the debate in the states over ratification. Still another motion, this one introduced on Friday, September 14, 1787, by Pinckney and Gerry, "that the liberty of the press should be inviolably preserved" was discussed by the Convention's delegates and once again set aside, this time with just four of the state delegations expressing support for the motion. When one of the Convention's final days of work finished on Friday, September 14, 1787, the delegates still faced Mason's insistence on prefacing the Constitution with a Declaration of Rights, a proposition backed by Gerry and Virginia's Edmund Randolph, who by that Friday appeared all but certain to join Mason in withholding their signatures from the Constitution.

Few details of any kind are with us today of the statement appearing in the pages of Philadelphia's *Pennsylvania Packet and Daily Advertiser* on Monday, August 20, 1787, that assured the public that the delegates in Pennsylvania's State House were not establishing a monarchy: "We are informed that many letters have been written to the members of the federal convention from different quarters, respecting the reports idly circulating, that it is intended to establish a monarchical government, to send for the Bishop of Osnaburgh, etc., to which it has been uniformly answered, tho' we cannot, affirmatively, tell you what we are doing, we can, negatively, tell you what we are not doing: we never once thought of a king."[3] Speculation to this day persists that it was Philadelphia's Benjamin Franklin who took the lead in authoring the statement and releasing it to the Philadelphia newspaper in late August. Certainly, Franklin's relationships with the printers of Philadelphia (not to mention his lifetime's experience of authoring such unsigned items) would suggest the plausibility of his speculated role in passing along this statement. Other accounts speculate whether James Madison had a role in its authorship, although little if any record exists to confirm or substantiate any of these rumors.

The 1787 Convention came to an end in mid-September at a time when the nation's newspapers were growing in circulation and readership. Still emerging as an indispensable part of the lives of a growing number of Americans in the 1780s, newspapers were on the cusp of further expansion that September in Philadelphia as a Convention that yielded few stories of substance—because of their closed proceedings—now exploded with argument, debate, and discussion on the Constitution proposed by the Convention. A Convention closed to the public and without any newspaper coverage now became a national debate, one heatedly played out in all manner of essays, letters, and writings in the newspapers of the day. Newspapers, of course, were to be pivotal from the first moments of the debate over the Constitution's ratification beginning that Monday in September 1787 through the long months of the ratification conventions to follow.

NEWSPAPERS AND THE RATIFICATION DEBATE OF 1787 AND 1788

On Wednesday, September 19, 1787, Dunlap and Claypoole's *Pennsylvania Packet and Daily Advertiser* was the first paper in the country to publish the text of the Constitution. Days later it was printed in all eleven of Philadelphia's newspapers. Over the next three weeks, another fifty-five papers printed the full text of the Constitution for their readers. Week after week, newspapers took the lead in the long months of debate surrounding the Convention's work that summer as well as the conventions to be held in each of the states for the ratification of the Constitution.

With the 1787 Convention concluded and its delegates returning home to begin the debates over the ratification in their states, newspapers took an even greater prominence in the debates to unfold over the next ten months as people in all parts of the country read the text of the Constitution in their newspapers, debated it with each other in often anonymous, unsigned letters and items, and read the latest news and reports of the plans for the ratifying conventions being held in each state. "It seems fair to say," writes Charles L. Mee Jr. in the *Genius of the People*, "the majority of the people were completely against it."[4] Newspapers took center stage—and a great many newspapers took sides—in the debate regarding the ratification of the Constitution.

Of all the essays, items, and letters written on behalf of the Constitution's ratification, none is as enduring a part of the history of the Constitution and its ratification as a project undertaken in October 1787 in the newspapers of New York City. Alexander Hamilton's collaboration with Madison and with New York's John Jay is a remarkable story, a story that certainly speaks to the importance of newspapers to the ratification debate. Awaiting his own state's ratifying convention, Madison devoted his energies for several months to the difficult task of penning two to three essays a week with Hamilton and Jay.

"After an unequivocal experience of the inefficiency of the subsisting federal government, you are called upon to deliberate on a new Constitution for the United States of America," readers of New York City's *Independent Journal* were told on Saturday, October 27, 1787. This first essay in the series under the pseudonym *Publius* was penned by Alexander Hamilton. Within a matter of days, one of the most well known of the essays, the tenth essay in the series, was penned by James Madison for the Friday, November 23, 1787, issue of the *New York Packet*, explaining the proliferation of factions, in Madison's famous formulation, as a part of representative government. Nearly every two to three days, essays written by Hamilton, Jay, and Madison appeared in New York City's newspapers; essays that were circulated and reprinted widely in most of New York City's seven newspapers as well as papers throughout the state and in no fewer than sixteen of the nation's eighty-nine newspapers in circulation at the time.[5] New York City's *Independent Journal*, *New York Packet*, and *Daily Advertiser* ran the bulk of the essays, each addressed "To the People of the State of New York."

From the first essay in the *Independent Journal* on Saturday, October 27, 1787, through the eighty-fifth *Publius* published in New York City's *McLean's Edition* on Saturday, August 16, 1788, the enduring Constitutional concordance is still well recalled, in the words of Richard B. Morris, as "a masterly effort of advocacy written to persuade."[6] James Madison himself wrote years later, "It frequently happened that whilst the printer was putting into type the parts of a number, the following parts were under the pen and to be furnished in time for the press."[7] According to Ralph Ketcham, "Time was short, and the purpose was to promote ratification in New York and other states not to write dispassionately for posterity about the great questions of government."[8] That said, the essays by Hamilton, Jay, and Madison endure to this day as some of the definitive writings on the Convention, the Constitution, and its ratification. Line by line, paragraph by paragraph, in the pages of New York's newspapers, the authors explained the workings of the Constitution. Hamilton and Madison authored the largest number of essays in the series, with Madison finally completing his work in the series and returning home to Virginia in March. *McLean's Edition* published the final nine essays, all written by Hamilton, several specifically addressing the lack of a Bill of Rights in the Constitution.

The ratifying convention in New York in June 1788 was still months away when Delaware's delegates unanimously voted as the first state to ratify the Constitution on Friday, December 7, 1787, by a vote of 30 to 0. Pennsylvania's ratifying convention is remembered as a much more contentious affair, beginning in late November 1787 and finally adjourning on Wednesday, December 12, 1787, as the first convention to split its vote—with forty-six delegates in favor of ratification and twenty-three opposed to ratification. When delegates at Pennsylvania's convention voted by 46 to 23 to ratify the Constitution, twenty-one of the twenty-three delegates casting their votes against ratification took to their state's newspapers to pen a letter calling attention to their disagreements with the Constitution, including the lack of a Bill of Rights.

With a sharply divided vote of delegates in its Wednesday, February 6, 1788, ratification vote, with some 187 delegates casting their votes in favor of ratification and 168 delegates voting against ratification, Massachusetts is not only remembered as one of the most divided of the ratifying conventions but it is also the first state to ratify with the insistence by many of its state's delegates that the Constitution be amended to include specific enumerations for the liberties of citizens, including the press. Maryland, ratifying the Constitution on Saturday, April 26, 1788, and South Carolina, its convention adjourning after ratification on Friday, May 23, 1788, both saw a number of delegates cast their votes against ratification as did New Hampshire, the ninth state to ratify on Saturday, June 21, 1788, where some fifty-seven delegates cast votes in favor of ratification with forty-seven delegates casting votes against.

THE BILL OF RIGHTS, THE FIRST CONGRESS, AND THE FIRST AMENDMENT

With the ratification of the Constitution by New Hampshire on Saturday, June 21, 1788, and the ratification conventions unfolding in the following weeks, attention turned to the elections of members of the House of Representatives and the selection by the state legislatures of the Senate as well as the election of the first president. Newspapers continued to grow in circulation, in readership, and most certainly in influence among members of the First Congress and those taking a role in the new federal government. Papers also had expanded beyond the Atlantic Seaboard into the newly settled regions of the West as population grew steadily across the Appalachian Mountains. And few if any means aside from the newspapers of the day gave officials in the new federal government a way to explain their work in establishing the new government.

Printer John Bradford began publication of the *Kentucky Gazette* in Lexington, Kentucky, on Saturday, August 11, 1787. Bradford brought his press to Lexington by wagon from Philadelphia to Pittsburgh, then by flatboat on the Ohio River to Limestone (now the city of Maysville, Kentucky), then finally arriving in Lexington.[9] With the closest print shop more than five hundred miles away, Bradford hand carved some of the larger types and engravings from dogwood trees for his printing press. Difficulties in transportation to Lexington were such that in 1789, it took as long as four to five months for news to travel from London, across the Atlantic Ocean, to the riders who eventually carried these reports to Lexington.

The factionalism slowly simmering in the First Congress in New York City in the late spring and early summer of 1789 manifested itself in one of the first significant graftings of the nation's newspapers to its emerging political rivalries. Alexander Hamilton lent his financial assistance to the establishment of a New York City paper called the *Gazette of the United States*. With the First Congress convening only days earlier on Wednesday, April 1, 1789, the first issue of *The Gazette*, printed by John Fenno, established from the outset the link between newspapers and their political patrons in the earliest days of the new federal government.

With the first issue of *The Gazette of the United States* circulating on Saturday, May 2, 1789, in New York City, Hamilton's position as the secretary of the Treasury afforded him a unique vantage point to share items with Fenno's paper as well as to leverage his financial support for the paper. Hamilton arranged for Fenno to be the printer-of-record for the Department of the Treasury, the first of many such arrangements with newspaper editors and printers in the years to come. Hamilton almost immediately began penning his own unsigned items for the *Gazette* authoring items under a variety of pseudonyms, including "An American"—and soon after was joined by Vice President John Adams and others in printing anonymous essays, letters, and items within the pages of the *Gazette*.

James Madison took his seat as one of sixty-five members of the House of Representatives in April 1789, having narrowly won a seat in the House of Representatives in February 1789. Having spoken on behalf of amending the Constitution to include a Bill of Rights during his 1789 bid for the House, Madison brought a sense of urgency to this debate in the First Congress. Madison felt that the amendment of the Constitution, contrary to the inattention of some of his fellow members of the House of Representatives and the Senate in the First Congress, should not be postponed for an indeterminate time.

In his speech on Monday, June 8, 1789, Madison, fulfilling his pledge to his Virginia constituents in his race for the House of Representatives for amendments to the Constitution in the First Congress, introduced his amendments to the House of Representatives. Almost immediately, opponents of the amendments raised objections. Still, Madison told his fellow members of the House of Representatives that a "great number" of persons were, in Madison's own words, "dissatisfied" with the Constitution and reminded his fellow representatives of the unwillingness of North Carolina to ratify without a Bill of Rights. Amendments, he explained, would be "important in the eyes of many" as a "safeguard" against the newly established federal government "to limit and qualify the powers of Government, by excepting out of the grant of power those cases in which the Government ought not to act, or to act only in a particular mode."[10] "It is certainly proper for Congress to consider the subject in order to quiet that anxiety which prevails in the public mind," Madison told his fellow members of the House. Madison urged his fellow Representatives to work on the Constitution's amendments for "the safeguards," the "securities for liberty," and "the security of rights."

"I am of the opinion," Representative James Jackson of Georgia began in his remarks that Monday, "that we ought not to be in a hurry with respect to altering the Constitution."[11] Jackson told the members of the House of Representatives, "If I agree to alterations in the mode of administering this Government, I shall like to stand on the sure ground of experience and not be treading air. What experience have we had of the good or bad qualities of the Constitution?"[12] Jackson urged his colleagues not to hastily amend the Constitution. "Our Constitution, sir," Jackson explained in his remarks, "is like a vessel just launched, and lying at the wharf, she is untried and you can hardly discover any one of her properties. It is not known how she will answer her helm or lay her course, whether she will bear with safety the precious freight to be deposited in her hold. But, in this state, will the prudent merchant attempt alterations? Will he employ workmen to tear off the planking and take asunder the frame? He certainly will not."[13] In urging postponement of a discussion of the amendments, Jackson told the House of Representatives, "I am against taking up the subject at present and shall therefore be totally against the amendments, if the Government is not organized, that I may see whether it is grievous or not."[14] Jackson finished in his remarks to the members of the House of Representatives, "Let the Constitution have a fair trial, let it be examined by experience, discover by that test what its errors are, and then talk of amending, but to attempt it now is doing it at risk, which is certainly imprudent."[15]

The Monday, June 8, 1789, debate in the House of Representatives on the proposed Bill of Rights took a sometimes dismissive and skeptical tone from Representative Jackson's remarks through those of some of his colleagues. South Carolina's William Smith explained it was improper to amend the Constitution before the federal government had been given time to establish itself. Aedanus Burke characterized the debate on the proposed amendments to the Constitution as "frothy and full of wind" and as "a waste of time."[16] Georgia's Jackson spoke yet again at the end of the day's debate on the amendments, telling members of the House of Representatives, "If such an addition is not dangerous or improper, it is at least unnecessary."[17] Jackson added, "The more I consider the subject of amendments, the more I am convinced it is improper."[18] Representative George Clymer of Pennsylvania also spoke unfavorably of the amendments, joining his colleagues from Georgia, South Carolina, and elsewhere in calling for a postponement of the amendments.

Weeks later, the House of Representatives had still not returned to the amendments. It was not until later in the summer on Tuesday, July 21, 1789—some six weeks after Madison initially introduced his amendments—when Madison "begged the House to indulge him" in returning to a discussion of the amendments. Days of postponements and motions to reconsider the amendments left Madison seeing, "the real possibility that the amendments would not be proposed during this first session of Congress," a disappointing turn for Madison and those members of the House of Representatives favoring the amendments.[19]

Finally, on Thursday, August 13, 1789, members of the House of Representatives took up the wording of the amendments. And on Monday, August 24, 1789, members of the House of Representatives finished most of its work on the language and wording of the proposed amendments, sending some seventeen proposed amendments to the Senate, which, in the words of one account at the time, treated the amendments "contemptuously" with several unsuccessful motions made to postpone any consideration of the amendments. All meetings and sessions of the Senate were still closed to the public, but work began on the amendments in the Senate sometime around Wednesday, September 2, 1789, until the seventeen amendments were, after some three weeks of deliberations, combined into twelve amendments. After weeks of deliberations, motions to postpone or reconsider, parliamentary maneuvers, speeches, and various other legislative workings, the House of Representatives agreed to the Senate's revised language of the amendments on Thursday, September 24, 1789. Final approval of the amendments in the Senate came the next day, Friday, September 25, 1789.

Ratification of the amendments went to the states on Friday, October 2, 1789, and almost immediately led to outpourings of debate and discussion in the newspapers of the day. In North Carolina, the Constitution and the Bill of Rights were soon ratified. With Virginia's ratification of the amendments on Thursday, December 15, 1791, a long chapter in the protection of the liberty and freedom of the press was brought to a close, ending one significant chapter in the history of the relationship between the press and the government, yet also opening up what would be decades of debate surrounding the interpretation of the First Amendment, the extent of its protection of the press, those moments where the Constitution's protections were ignored or rendered inoperative by the indifference of state and federal officials, and ultimately a debate unfolding in the early years of the twentieth century on the extent to which the First Amendment, in a Constitutional provision, which began with the words "Congress shall make no law," also would be interpreted to incorporate and extend to state governments as well.

NEWSPAPERS IN THE 1790s

Weekly and daily newspapers grew in circulation and readership in the 1790s and were ever more caught up with the electoral rivalries of the day. Newspapers carried all manner of editorial items in support of and against candidates for elected office. Unsigned editorials were especially entwined with the partisan and personal rivalries of elected officials and lawmakers during this time. Written by some of the most prominent lawmakers in the nation—figures no less than the vice president of the United States, the secretary of the Treasury, members of the House of Representatives and the Senate—some of these anonymously authored items that appeared in the newspapers of the day did much to express the rifts and rivalries of the era. Classical Greek and Roman pseudonyms blunted, to some extent, the sharper edges of the rivalries of the authors who might sit together in President George Washington's cabinet, serve with each other as members of the House of Representatives or the Senate, or otherwise have to meet regularly in the newly established government.

Even as the nation's capital moved to Philadelphia for the next decade, New York City grew in stature in the 1790s in part because of its newspapers and publishing and print shops, which produced the largest number of daily papers. Newspapers also spread farther into the Western settlements and territories in the 1790s. On Saturday, November 5, 1791, George Roulstone printed the first issue of the *Knoxville Gazette*, the first paper printed in the Tennessee territory. Ohio's first paper, Cincinnati's *Centinel of the Northwestern Territory*, published its first issue on Saturday, November 9, 1793.

"Largely without tradition, often without welcome," Thomas C. Leonard explains, "the commercial press found itself at the center of government in the young republic."[20] The *Gazette of the United States* moved from New York City to Philadelphia when the capital moved to that city in 1790, making it still the most important paper for the members of Congress and the executive branch. Vice President Adams is known to have written unsigned essays for the pages of Fenno's *Gazette* using the pseudonym "An American Citizen." Vice President Adams's son, John Quincy Adams, penned his own letters in the pages of that same newspaper, using the pseudonym *Publicola*.

In 1790 and after, Secretary of the Treasury Hamilton continued to assist Fenno in editing and financing the *Gazette* and he sometimes wrote using the pseudonym T.L. He also wrote under the pseudonyms "An American," *Amicus*, *Catulus*, *Civis*, *Metellus*, and "A Plain Honest Man." Hamilton took up his pen to defend himself against the charges that he advocated a monarchy, a defense mounted yet again against charges he was fashioning his role as a sort of prime minister under Washington. Hamilton's combustible relationship with some members of the House of Representatives in the First Congress proved to be a significant rift manifesting itself in unsigned letters in the *Gazette* and other papers. Not only did Hamilton personally loan his own money to the *Gazette* and assist in finding subscribers for the paper in 1790 and in 1791, he also saw to it that Fenno's Philadelphia print shop was given most of the Senate's official printing contracts as well as most of the Department of the Treasury's print contracts.

President Washington, establishing the first workings of the executive branch and presiding over the founding of the new federal government as the capital moved from New York City to Philadelphia, settled into his home at 6th and Market Streets just a block away from the Pennsylvania State House and Congress Hall and soon thereafter was swept into the tumults of the newspapers of the day. Washington was, as Joseph Ellis describes him, "an obsessive reader of newspapers."[21] Washington is remembered to have regularly read with great interest the *Gazette of the*

United States, Philadelphia's *American Daily Advertiser*, the *Pennsylvania Gazette*, and Benjamin Franklin Bache's *General Advertiser*. In addition, some newspapers he did not regularly read were delivered to him from time to time with the compliments of their printers.

When Congress adjourned in April 1791, Representative James Madison and his fellow Virginian, Secretary of State Thomas Jefferson, left New York City for a trip through New England. Traveling into New England, the Virginians visited with several printers, including the *Vermont Gazette*'s Anthony Haswell. Traveling from Vermont to New Jersey, the Virginians spent time with Madison's former classmate from the College of New Jersey, Philip Freneau. During this visit with Freneau at his home in April 1791, it is all but certain that Jefferson and Madison explained their suspicions of Hamilton and his hand in the *Gazette of the United States*.

"We have been trying to get another weekly or half-weekly paper set up so that it might hope to go through the states and furnish a Whig vehicle of intelligence," Thomas Jefferson wrote his son-in-law in May 1791, shortly after returning to Philadelphia from his trip to New England.[22] Soon thereafter, Freneau informed Madison that he was moving to Philadelphia to begin printing such a newspaper, a paper that almost immediately rose to national prominence and that drew the ire of no less than President George Washington.

Freneau's *National Gazette*, bearing the masthead "By Philip Freneau," printed its first issue in Philadelphia on Monday, October 31, 1791. From his seat in the House of Representatives, Madison circulated appeals for financial contributions and subscriptions to the *National Gazette* from his friends in Virginia and elsewhere. Lending their prestige to this newspaper, Jefferson and Madison corresponded with their fellow Virginians to solicit subscribers. "The Virginia leaders became so closely involved in Freneau's operations, . . . that several subscribers wrote to Madison rather than the editor with complaints about delivery problems."[23] John Hancock and Samuel Adams sought contributions and subscribers for the *National Gazette* in Massachusetts and across New England. From his post as secretary of state, Jefferson lent his own support for Freneau, offering him a job as a translator in the department.

Within months, the *National Gazette* became widely circulated among those following the debates in Philadelphia's Congress Hall, located near the intersection of 6th Street and Chestnut Street. With encouragement from Madison and others, the *National Gazette* was to become the voice of an emerging group of figures soon to adopt the name "Democratic Republicans" or simply "Republicans," as many took to calling themselves. In the fall of 1791, Madison penned a series of unsigned essays in the *National Gazette* covering a wide range of topics from the proceedings of the House of Representatives to his writings on political parties. The *National Gazette* grew as influential as the *Gazette of the United States* as its pages filled with the latest news and reports of the executive branch and Congress as well as with the writings of anonymous essayists.

When Washington contemplated whether or not to seek a second term as president in 1792, his concerns with the contemporary press weighed heavily on his mind. Washington's first term as president had been marked by a fracturing in his administration and in the halls of Congress. Washington's critics struck a nerve and after some reflection, the president told his family and friends of his decision to not seek a second term. At the urging of friends and lawmakers, including Secretary of the Treasury and Representative James Madison, Washington reluctantly reconsidered his decision not to run for a second term.

Still, the ever more caustic rifts expressed in the pages of the newspapers Washington read every day left him angered and discouraged at the state of affairs even after his decision to stand for a second term as president. Privately, Washington fumed at the editors of several newspapers, not least of whom was Benjamin Franklin Bache, editor of the *General Advertiser*. Washington complained about newspaper editors by name, some of whom he took to calling "discontented characters."[24] In fact, Freneau regularly sent copies of the *National Gazette* to President Washington, a gesture that, in private, left Washington furious. From the very first days of the First Congress in New York City's Federal Hall, the Senate was not open to the public and allowed no reporters to sit in its sessions. The House of Representatives allowed journalists to attend its sessions beginning on Wednesday, April 8, 1789, just days after the first quorums in both the House of Representatives and in the Senate.[25] New York City's Federal Hall and its chamber for the House of Representatives bustled with crowds in the visitors' galleries on Wednesday, April 8, 1789, and in the weeks and months to come.

The Senate's closed doors stood sealed in striking contrast to the crowds visiting the chamber of the House of Representatives in New York City's Federal Hall. The Senate, Philip Freneau wrote in the Wednesday, February 13, 1793, *National Gazette*, was closed "in defiance of every principle which gives security to free men." Writing of what Freneau decried as "the secret privileges of the House of Lords," the *National Gazette* insisted in issue after issue that the Senate open a public gallery and admit visitors to watch its proceedings.[26] Members of the Senate and the House of Representatives as well as the legislatures in several of the states seeking to open the sessions of the Senate found no more untiring and unyielding champion of their cause than Freneau. Finally, on Wednesday, December 9, 1795, having considered a motion to open the doors of its chambers to visitors in a public gallery, the Senate (in a motion introduced by Senator Alexander Martin of North Carolina and seconded by Senator Pierce Butler of South Carolina) agreed to open its sessions to the public, allowing visitors—and editors of newspapers—to sit in a public gallery for the first time.

Newspapers were intricately bound with the emergence of various caucuses, committees, meetings, and societies that together comprised the stirring of early political parties in the 1790s. Elected officials and government officers did not hesitate to pitch the disagreement of the moment to the readers of the nation's newspapers. As always, however, they remained hidden behind their pseudonyms. This practice is not unlike the twenty-first-century variant that cites "sources close to the White House," "unnamed senior White House aides," "senior Congressional staff speaking on condition of anonymity," or any of the off-the-record and background comments uttered to and circulated by reporters in contemporary news reporting in and around the capital.

BENJAMIN FRANKLIN BACHE AND PHILADELPHIA'S *AURORA AND GENERAL ADVERTISER*

On Friday, October 1, 1790, Benjamin Franklin Bache, the grandson of Benjamin Franklin and the oldest son of Franklin's only daughter, Sally, and her husband, Richard Bache, printed the first issue of Philadelphia's *General Advertiser and Political, Commercial, Agricultural, and Literary Journal*, later known as the *General Advertiser*, then renamed yet again in its Saturday, November 8, 1794, issue as the *Aurora and General Advertiser*, which was often simply known as the *Aurora*. At the age of twenty-six, Bache, following in the footsteps of his grandfather, began his own paper. In 1790, with an inheritance from his grandfather, Bache opened his Philadelphia print shop, publishing his paper six days a week.

With its first issue on Friday, October 1, 1790, the *Philadelphia General Advertiser and Political, Commercial, Agricultural, and Literary Journal* branded Secretary of the Treasury Alexander Hamilton and his supporters in Congress a "monarchic and aristocratic junto." Shortening its name to the *General Advertiser* in August 1791, Bache's paper became well known for its attacks on President Washington and Vice President Adams.[27] With a nod to his grandfather's experiments with electricity and his own willingness to throw himself into the controversial issues of the day, Bache earned the nickname Lightning Rod Junior.

John Fenno's *Gazette of the United States*, William Cobbett's *Porcupine's Gazette*, and other papers sympathetic to President Adams spared no effort in rebuking Bache's *Aurora and General Advertiser*. Jefferson in his private correspondence urged his friends to subscribe to Bache's paper. Bache's vilification by his ever more infuriated critics mounted not only in the pages of newspapers sympathetic to Adams and his supporters in Congress but also in several assaults on Bache's print shop and even attacks on Bache himself.

When President Washington made the decision to retire at the end of his second term, his historic letter, published on Monday, September 19, 1796, on the front page of Claypoole's *American Daily Advertiser*—with the banner proclaiming "The Address of General Washington to the People of America"—omitted in its final published version a passage in which he was especially sharp in his criticism of the press.

"As some of the Gazettes," Washington's first draft of his remarks began, "have teemed with all the Invective that disappointment, ignorance of facts, and malicious falsehoods could invent, to misrepresent my politics and affections, to wound my reputation and feelings, and to weaken, if not entirely destroy, the confidence you have been pleased to repose in me; it might be expected at the parting scene of my public life that I should take some notice of such virulent abuse. But, as heretofore, I shall pass them over in utter silence, never having myself nor by any other with my participation or knowledge, written or published a Scrap in answer to any of them."[28] Washington's published letter left out his sharply worded statement against the newspapers of the day, sentiments no doubt weighing heavily on Washington's private thoughts as he stepped off of the national stage in a time of partisan fracturing and political fissuring.

1798 AND THE SEDITION ACT CONTROVERSY

Wartime's uncertainties far from the shores of the United States in the late 1790s set the stage for yet another chapter in the history of the freedom and liberty of the press in the young republic. France's war with Great Britain in the mid-1790s plunged the United States into unease. When reports of American ships having hostile confrontations with the French reached the United States, tensions with France escalated still further, plunging the nation into even greater unease. "The passions of our citizens have been artfully inflamed by war speeches and addresses," the *Aurora and General Advertiser* told its readers on Thursday, May 10, 1798. "Perhaps," James Madison wrote to Vice President Thomas Jefferson three days later on Sunday, May 13, 1798, "it is a universal truth that the loss of liberty at home is to be charged to provisions against danger, real or pretended, from abroad." Madison added as a final note in his letter to the vice president, "I received no paper by last mail but Fenno's, I hope the bridle is not yet put on the press," a telling remark coming just days before the House of Representatives and the Senate met to debate just such legislation.[29]

On Thursday, May 17, 1798, President Adams delivered what would be known as his War Speech just two days into a session of Congress convened to deal with the relations between France and the United States. In the days following the president's speech, Bache's *Aurora and General Advertiser* expressed doubts of the impending hostilities with the French, accusing the president and his supporters in Congress of being swept up in "war fever" with the French.

"Wild rumors swept [Philadelphia]," historian David McCullough reminds us. "It was said France had already declared war on the United States, that the French were moving to take possession of Florida and Louisiana."[30] People acted "as though a French army might land at any moment." "Everybody was suspicious of everybody else," McCullough recalls. "Everyone saw murderous glances."[31] Fears of sabotage and sedition mingled with denunciations of any writings or utterances that were critical of Congress or the president. "Whatever American opposes the Administration is an Anarchist, a Jacobin, and a Traitor," the *Boston Centinel* told its readers. In the early weeks of the summer of 1798, a wave of suspicion and unease swept across the nation, as Americans heard rumors of an impending war with the French.

"He that is not for us is against us," stated Fenno's *Gazette of the United States*' front-page masthead on Wednesday, June 20, 1798. This was an unsettling proposition for those newspaper editors and even those members of Congress who believed the rumors of an imminent declaration of war by the French to be exaggerated and used as pretext for suppressing the publication of newspapers critical of President Adams and his supporters in Congress. "The publication of false, scandalous, and malicious matter against the Government tends to produce insurrection and total disrespect for its authority," one newspaper sympathetic to Adams told readers, "and that, without the power of preventing these, no government can exist."

Meeting in the summer of 1798, leaders in the House of Representatives and the Senate enacted several federal statutes, including a statute sanctioning those writing or speaking out against the government. Imprisonment and fines for any "false, scandalous and malicious statement against the Government of the United States or either House of the Congress of the United States" became the centerpiece of what Congress in late June and early July enacted, including the 1798 Sedition Act.

The 1798 Sedition Act was passed in a two-week period of deliberations beginning in the Senate on Monday, June 18, 1798. Debate over the Sedition Act was largely a subdued affair, with only a few sitting members of the Senate or the House of Representatives taking a stand against the legislation. "Bache's [paper] has been particularly named," Vice President Jefferson later wrote James Madison as the deliberations unfolded in the Senate. When the debate on the Sedition Act moved to the House of Representatives, one member of the House, Representative John Allen of Connecticut, read aloud editorials from Bache's *Aurora and General Advertiser* on the floor of the House.

Pennsylvania's Albert Gallatin told the House of Representatives on Thursday, July 5, 1798, "This bill must be considered only as a weapon used by a party now in power in order to perpetuate their authority and preserve their present places."[32] On Wednesday, July 4, 1798, just one day before Gallatin's remarks, supporters of the Sedition Act publicly burned copies of

Boston's *Independent Chronicle*, leaving little doubt of the unease felt by the act's opponents that it would silence any newspapers critical of Congress and the president.

The Sedition Act was signed by President Adams on Saturday, July 14, 1798. Defiantly, Bache's *Aurora and General Advertiser*—a paper printed just blocks away from Philadelphia's Congress Hall—printed the entire Declaration of Independence in its first issue the day after President Adams signed the Sedition Act. "For my own part," Vice President Jefferson wrote his fellow Virginian, Senator Stevens Thomson Mason, on Thursday, October 11, 1798, "I consider those laws as merely an experiment on the American mind to see how far it will bear an avowed violation of the Constitution."[33] The vice president wrote from his home in Monticello, "If this goes down, we shall immediately see attempted another act of Congress, declaring that the President shall continue in office during life, reserving to another occasion the transfer of the succession to his heirs, and the establishment of the Senate for life."[34] Days later, the first indictments were issued under the Sedition Act, including a sitting member of the House of Representatives known for his outspokenness against the president.

"The real and obvious intent was to stifle the [anti-Adams] Republican press," McCullough tells us of President Adam's signing the bill; this became obvious in the months to follow as federal authorities issued their first arrest warrants under the Sedition Act.[35] The day after the passage of the 1798 Sedition Act, the *New York Commercial Advertiser* declared any person or persons speaking out against the Sedition Act "deserves to be suspected." Having been arrested on charges of libel by federal authorities on Tuesday, June 26, 1798—weeks before President Adams signed the Sedition Act— Benjamin Franklin Bache remained an unwavering opponent of Adams and one of the editors most likely to face indictment under the act. Indictments of newspaper printers (not to mention a sitting member of the House of Representatives) began within weeks of its enactment.

Beginning in October 1798, approximately twenty-five persons would be arrested by federal authorities under the 1798 Sedition Act, ten of whom were brought to trial with presiding justices of the Supreme Court. All ten of those brought to trial were found guilty and sentenced to some prison time (with a maximum of two years under the statute) as well as fines (with a maximum fine of $2,000). Four newspaper editors were found guilty and convicted to serve sentences under the Sedition Act.

William Durrell, editor and publisher of the *Mount Pleasant Register* in Mount Pleasant, New York, was the first newspaper editor indicted under the Sedition Act. Durrell's newspaper was brought onto the national stage for reprinting a paragraph from a story originally printed in Connecticut's *New Windsor Gazette*. The offending paragraph, republished in the *Mount Pleasant Register* on Tuesday, June 5, 1798, was a rebuke of President Adams. It caught the attention of then–secretary of state Timothy Pickering, who instructed authorities to investigate the New York editor. Durrell was arrested just three days after the president signed the Sedition Act into law, taken into custody by federal authorities, and released on bail pending his trial. Durrell then closed the newspaper fearing continued publication might violate the terms of his release.

On Thursday, September 5, 1799, Durrell entered a plea of not guilty in New York's federal Circuit Court, a plea that began nearly two years of legal proceedings and postponements as prosecutors assembled the criminal charges against the editor. Finally, in the fall of 1799, Durrell was brought to trial by authorities for publishing "false, scandalous, malicious, and defamatory Libel of and concerning John Adams." In a trial presided over by Associate Supreme Court Justice Bushrod Washington, Durrell was sentenced to four months in prison and fined $50 for his reprinting a paragraph from a story in the *New Windsor Gazette*. The day after his sentence began, New York's District Attorney Richard Harison appealed to then–secretary of state Pickering to commute Durrell's prison term, "[Durrell] appears to be very poor at present, has a large family to maintain, and has a considerable Time since [Durrell] discontinued his newspaper."[36] Serving only two weeks of his four-month sentence, Durrell was granted a pardon by President Adams on Tuesday, April 22, 1800, the only person sentenced under the 1798 Sedition Act to be pardoned by the president.

Thomas Adams, editor and publisher of Boston's *Independent Chronicle*, was another well-known newspaper editor indicted under the Sedition Act. Adams was arrested on Tuesday, October 23, 1798, pleading not guilty to a charge of "sundry libelous and seditious publications tending to defame the government of the United States." Released on bail because of his poor health, Adams remained too ill to appear in court and his trial was postponed by authorities. Still, state prosecutors in Massachusetts filed their own indictment for libel against Thomas Adams and his older brother, Abijah.

On Thursday, February 28, 1799, with Thomas Adams's trial still pending, Adams and his older brother Abijah were indicted by Massachusetts authorities for their alleged libel of members of the Massachusetts General Court, charged with "contriving falsely and maliciously to bring the Government into disrespect, hatred, and contempt among the good and liege citizens of the Commonwealth." Abijah Adams eventually appeared before the Massachusetts magistrate but his younger brother remained too ill to appear. Abijah was found guilty, sentenced to thirty days in jail, and ordered to pay a $500 bond. With his own illness and the imprisonment of his older brother, Thomas Adams sold the *Independent Chronicle*. Just days later, on Monday, May 13, 1799, Thomas Adams passed away. In Philadelphia, attorney and editor Thomas Cooper was indicted on Saturday, November 2, 1799 (his indictment noted that Cooper was "a person of wicked and turbulent disposition") under the Sedition Act. Serving for several months as the acting editor of Pennsylvania's *Sunbury and*

Northumberland Gazette, Cooper had written a series of editorial items critical of President Adams, including one calling the president a "power mad despot" and still another declaring Adams "incompetent" and an "enemy" of the "rights of man."[37] Cooper's writings in the *Sunbury and Northumberland Gazette* reached a much larger audience when reprinted in Philadelphia's *Aurora and General Advertiser*.

In April 1800, Cooper's trial began in the federal Circuit Court for the District of Pennsylvania in Philadelphia. He was charged "with having published a false, scandalous, and malicious attack on the character of the President of the United States, with an intent to excite the hatred and contempt of the people of this country against the man of their choice." Found guilty on all counts, Cooper was sentenced to six months in prison and fined $400. Cooper's sentence also required he post a $2,000 bond.

Years later, Cooper went on to serve as a federal judge in northern Pennsylvania and still later as counselor to President James Madison. Cooper's writings included *A Treatise on the Law of Libel and the Liberty of the Press*, published in 1980. In it, Cooper called the 1798 Sedition Act "the favorite act of Mr. J. Adams and his coadjutors," calling it "clearly and indisputably un-Constitutional." Cooper told his readers, "As the Constitution of the United States had prohibited Congress from passing any law whatever abridging the freedom of speech or of the press, it was so clearly and indisputably un-Constitutional that nothing could account for this usurpation of prohibited authority but the rancor of party politicians who felt that they had power and forgot that they wanted right."[38] "The law," Cooper observed decades after his own trial and sentence under the 1798 act, "became so obnoxious to the people that it was the main cause, if not the chief, of Mr. J. Adams losing his re-election as President."[39] Cooper's career as an educator eventually led him to a teaching position at Dickinson College and then at the University of Pennsylvania, before becoming the president of South Carolina's Columbia College in 1820.

Having written for years as an essayist in Philadelphia, James T. Callender had moved in 1798 to Richmond, Virginia, following a series of misfortunes, including the death of his wife in Philadelphia and threats to his physical safety when a rival Philadelphia essayist revealed Callender to be the author of several items critical of any number of figures, including Secretary of the Treasury Hamilton. Callender's essays in the *Richmond Examiner* called President Adams "repulsive," "a tempest of malignant passions," and "a strange compound of ignorance and ferocity, of deceit and weakness," all writings entered into his indictment by federal authorities.

Indicted in May 1800 as "a person of wicked, depraved, evil disposed, disquiet, and turbulent mind and disposition" under 1798's Sedition Act, Callender was sentenced in June 1800 to nine-months imprisonment and levied a $200 fine. During his imprisonment, Callender was given the privilege of having paper, pen, and ink, as well as having visitors meet him at the prison. Callender wrote during his incarceration, he passed his writings along to friends who visited him. Few papers, however, dared print these writings from prison, fearful of prosecution under the act. Still, several of Callender's essays written during this time were published in the *Richmond Examiner*, including one essay describing President Adams as "a gross hypocrite and an unprincipled oppressor."[40] Callender also spoke against Supreme Court Justice Samuel Chase, calling him "the most detestable and detested rascal in the state of Maryland" and expressing disapproval for his sitting as the presiding judge in Callender's trial.

Charles Holt, the twenty-eight-year-old editor of the *New London Bee* of New London, Connecticut, was indicted in October 1799 for printing an item commenting on the long-rumored extramarital affairs of former secretary of the treasury Hamilton. Holt was indicted in October 1799 as "a wicked, malicious, seditious, and ill-disposed person greatly disaffected to the government of the United States." Supreme Court Justice Bushrod Washington presided over the April 1800 trial and handed down its guilty verdict—with Holt found guilty and sentenced to a three-month imprisonment and a $200 fine.

Some of the country's most widely circulated newspapers and their printers rallied to the cause of President John Adams and defended the arrests, indictments, and prosecutions of their fellow printers under the Sedition Act. The *Gazette of the United States* defended the Sedition Act and the *Columbian Centinel*, Hartford's *Connecticut Courant and Weekly Intelligencer*, the *New York Gazette and General Advertiser*, and the *New York Commercial Advertiser* all stood by President Adams's enforcement of the Sedition Act. William Cobbett's *Porcupine's Gazette* printed its own list of "seditious" papers. The *Albany Register*, the *Baltimore American*, and the *Richmond Examiner* all took a stand against the 1798 Sedition Act. Still, few of the arrests and trials under the Sedition Act left as many Americans uneasy with the enforcement of the 1798 statute as the arrest, trial, and sentence of a well-known sitting member of the House of Representatives.

MATTHEW LYON AND THE SEDITION ACT

Born in Dublin, Ireland, in 1750, a young Matthew Lyon had shown early signs of interest in becoming a printer, having apprenticed at the age of thirteen in a print shop in Dublin before leaving for the colonies in 1764. Lyon lived in Connecticut where he eventually gained his freedom after three years of indentured servitude. For a time, Lyon worked at an iron works in Salisbury, Connecticut, where he married the niece of Ethan Allen and soon after, in 1884, moved with his wife to Vermont.

During the war, Lyon took up arms with the Green Mountain Boys, a Vermont militia formed in 1770, and rose to the rank of colonel. At the end of the war, Lyon returned to his home and settled into a comfortable life as a successful business owner. Working with his son James, Lyon printed his first newspaper, the *Farmer's Library*, a small-circulation weekly paper later known as the *Fair Haven Gazette*. Lyon's son James assisted him in printing the *Farmer's Library*—the younger Lyon having learned the print trade years earlier in an apprenticeship in Benjamin Franklin's Philadelphia print shop. Lyon saw the *Farmer's Library* as, in his words, "a means of saving the district from being deluged by the overpowering flood of anti-Republicanism."[41] Soon thereafter, Lyon won a seat in the House of Representatives.

In June 1798—days before the passage of the Sedition Act—Representative Lyon penned a sharply worded essay for the pages of the *Vermont Journal* accusing Adams of having, in Lyon's words, "a continual grasp for power" and "an unbounded thirst for ridiculous pomp. Whenever I shall, on the part of the Executive, see every consideration of public welfare swallowed up in a continual grasp for power, in an unbounded thirst for ridiculous pomp, foolish adulation, or selfish avarice," Lyon wrote, "I shall not be their humble advocate."[42] Rival printers of Vermont's newspapers, including *Spooner's Vermont Journal* and the *Rutland Herald*, leapt to the defense of the president and attacked Lyon for his writings—attacks, in turn, replied to by Lyon in a series of items and letters published just after the enactment of the Sedition Act.

Lyon was indicted by a federal grand jury, presided over by Associate Justice of the Supreme Court William Paterson. Indicted for his "scurrilous, scandalous, malicious, and defamatory language" in writing about President Adams, Lyon's indictment drew attention from across the country. Facing a grand jury selected by federal prosecutors for their sympathies to the president, the jury on the evening of Monday, October 8, 1798, returned a verdict of guilty on all three counts in the indictment against Lyon. Lyon was sentenced to four months in jail and fined $1,000—as well as the court costs for his trial totaling some $60.

Imprisoned on the morning of Wednesday, October 10, 1798, in the city prison in Vergennes, Vermont, Lyon faced hardships during the four months of his incarceration and, as a sitting member of the House of Representatives, his imprisonment drew widespread attention from around the country. His sentence proved at times to be difficult, especially with the inclement weather of the late fall and winter. Lyon was refused both writing materials as well as a stove—until his family interceded and brought him one.

"Matthew Lyon of Vermont has had the honor of being the first victim of a law framed directly in the teeth of the Constitution of this Federal Republic," the *Aurora and General Advertiser* told its readers on Thursday, November 1, 1798. "The ancients were wont to bestow particular honor on the first citizen who suffered in resisting tyranny."[43] Weeks earlier, Lyon ran for reelection from his jail cell—an election decided some weeks later in a December runoff in which Lyon won his reelection.[44]

When Lyon was released from jail on Saturday, February 9, 1799, his constituents celebrated with a procession that made its way across parts of rural Vermont—what biographer James Fairfax McLaughlin exclaimed as "a triumphal journey from a prison to Congress."[45] "The very schoolhouses," one observer enthused, "poured forth their children to swell the ovation which welcomed the valiant Democrat to liberty."[46] Lyon traveled along the ice-covered roads and through the snow-bound towns of Vermont with his constituents—while his supporters delivered speeches along the way.

Having settled in Bennington shortly after his apprenticeship with Boston's Isaiah Thomas, printer Anthony Haswell established his own shop and newspaper, which was to eventually bring him an indictment under the Sedition Act. Haswell printed the first issue of the *Vermont Gazette* on Thursday, June 5, 1783. The *Vermont Gazette* is remembered as one of the few papers in New England opposed to President Adams and his supporters in Congress. According to Smith, "it stood out like a fire in the Green Mountains on a dark night."[47]

When Matthew Lyon was found guilty and sentenced on Monday, October 8, 1798, the *Vermont Gazette* printed a series of editorials and items sympathizing with Lyon during his incarceration in Vergennes, Vermont. "Week after week, [Haswell] had denounced the prosecution and imprisonment of Lyon," biographer John Spargo reveals. "Again and again," Spargo recounts of Haswell, "he had published the news of Lyon's ill-treatment."[48] Additionally, the *Vermont Gazette* reprinted items from the *Aurora and General Advertiser* rebuking President Adams.

On Tuesday evening, October 8, 1799, Haswell was arrested by two federal marshals in the middle of the night, forced to ride almost sixty miles on horseback, and refused dry clothing when finally placed in his jail cell to await his hearing before the court. Appearing before the Circuit Court in Rutland, Vermont, presided by Supreme Court Justice William Cushing that next morning, Wednesday, October 9, 1799, Haswell was charged with "false, malicious, wicked, and seditious libel." Items printed in the *Vermont Gazette*, including several items critical of President Adams reprinted from the *Aurora and General Advertiser*, were part of the indictment against Haswell.

Months later, on Friday, May 9, 1800, after a trial lasting five days, Haswell was found guilty and sentenced to two-months imprisonment and fined $200 in a trial presided over by Associate Supreme Court Justice William Patterson. Days later, on Tuesday, May 13, 1800, Haswell began his sentence at the city jail in Bennington, Vermont. Located a short distance from Haswell's home, he was able to receive visitors in his jail cell as well as correspond and write from his cell. "He carried on spirited controversies with the editors of other newspapers while he was in prison," Spargo recounts of Haswell's penning essays and letters against rival editors of the Brattleborough, Vermont, *Federal Galaxy* and *Vergennes Gazette*.[49]

Nearly two thousand people gathered to meet Haswell when he ended his two-month sentence. Released on the morning of Wednesday, July 9, 1800, Haswell's neighbors in Bennington had postponed their Fourth of July festivities until the printer's release from jail—celebrating with Haswell upon his release on Wednesday, July 9. In the end, Haswell, Lyon, indeed all of those arrested or even threatened with arrest under 1798's Sedition Act, not to mention the many Americans fearful and frustrated by the arrests and trials of their fellow citizens for exercising their most fundamental rights of expression, speech, and writing in the press, all emerged even more resilient and resolute in the wake of the controversy.

"We were then at War with France," President John Adams wrote in his correspondence some years later, by way of explaining 1798's Sedition Act. Writing his recollections, Adams insisted that the legislation had been necessary because "French Spies then swarmed in our cities and in the Country. To check them," Adams insisted, "was the design of this law."[50] The end of the War of Independence, the debate and ratification of the Constitution, and the ratification of the Bill of Rights with its First Amendment had done much to establish the vibrancy and vitality of newspapers and the freedom of the press, yet it is also well recalled as a prologue to one of the most unforgivable chapters in the history of America's press, a chapter that saw no less a figure than the president of the United States enforce restrictions upon the same newspapers and printers whose cause he had championed just years earlier during colonial rule. Newspaper printers had been imprisoned, harassed, and intimidated, and a handful of printers were imprisoned for brief sentences, all under the tenure of a president who as a young man celebrated the freedom of the press at the height of the movement for independence from Great Britain. Printers imprisoned during his administration, Adams wrote years later, had been "intolerably turbulent, impudent and seditious." That this champion of the liberty of the press who spent days as a young man in the print shop of the *Boston Gazette* found himself later presiding over the arrest, trial, and incarceration of printers—his presidency's legacy defined in no small measure by his defeat as the first sitting president in the nation's history not to win reelection—is a part of a fascinating era in the late eighteenth century's history of America's press in the young nation's political life.

Chapter 2

The Nineteenth-Century Press and American Politics

"The history of the American press is the history of the United States," write Olga G. Hoyt and Edwin P. Hoyt, a history nowhere more apparent than in the press of the early nineteenth century and after.[1] In the early nineteenth century, the press saw a widening circulation of newspapers, books, magazines, and circulars. Editors, their writers, their printing presses, and their newsstands and delivery men barely kept up with the demand for coverage of the nation's candidates for elected office, especially in the years during and after the Civil War. Newspapers, books, and even sheet music and songs were all part of the nineteenth-century culture of partisanship unfolding across a nation physically expanding into the West and expanding politically in demands for greater involvement and participation.

When President Thomas Jefferson was elected in 1800, America's newspapers and their editors gained prominence in the nation's political life. The years after 1801 marked a closer connection between newspapers and the nation's elected officials than in the preceding years. "The papers are overrunning with election essays, squibs, and invectives," one observer noted as elections for office became more boisterous and boldly fought affairs and as partisan loyalties and sympathies grew more blatant in the newspapers of the day.[2] Jefferson's inaugural speech, delivered on Wednesday, March 4, 1801, offered a reaffirmation of the freedoms and the rights of the American people, including, in the president's words, "the diffusion of information" and the freedom of the press.

By the time Jefferson was elected, the United States had more than 235 weekly papers and some twenty-four daily papers. Philadelphia boasted six daily papers and New York City had five daily papers in 1800, growing to seven daily papers in 1810 and eight daily papers in New York City by

1820. Improvements in printing presses and in the delivery of newspapers—not to mention the declining cost of the manufacture of paper—soon led to even larger circulations. "The omnipresence of the American newspaper was a continual wonder to visitors from abroad," writes Frank Luther Mott.[3]

With the sometimes bitter campaigning for elected office between Democratic Republicans and Federalists in the early years of the nineteenth century, newspapers devoted ever more pages to the speeches and public remarks of candidates for office and to editorials either praising or scorning officeholders or those candidates seeking elected office. "Although mid-nineteenth-century readers realized the press twisted the news, they seemed to believe that distortion was natural and proper," writes Michael E. McGerr.[4] The partisan texture of America's newspapers in the early nineteenth century coincided with the improvements of the printing press and the manufacture of paper, allowing newspapers to expand their circulation. By 1810, more than 195 paper mills were operating in the United States, producing tens of thousands of pounds of newsprint annually.

The *National Intelligencer and Washington Advertiser*, a newspaper founded soon after President Jefferson's election, became one of the most influential papers in the nation's capital in the early years of the nineteenth century, building close connections with presidential administrations over the next several decades. The *National Intelligencer* remained among the most influential newspapers in Washington, D.C., until Andrew Jackson's supporters founded the *United States Telegraph* in 1826, which took the place of prominence from the *National Intelligencer*.

Years later, the 1830 inaugural issue of the *Washington Globe*, edited and published by Francis Preston Blair, underscored the closeness of the connections between the nation's elected officials and its newspapers in the early decades of the nineteenth century. According to Lynn L. Marshall, "the Jackson party organization, . . ." saw to it that special electioneering [*Washington*] *Globe* extras and copies of the veto message papered taverns and public places throughout the land."[5] Through the middle and even into the end of the nineteenth century, editors enjoyed a close proximity to presidents, their cabinets, and leaders in both the House of Representatives and the Senate that only grew as the party battles of the era intensified in both the halls of government and in the pages of the nation's newspapers.

"Newspapers could move freely between commerce and politics in the early decades of the century," Judith R. Blau and Cheryl Elman explain, "and were thereby valuable as brokers in the fledgling central government."[6] Tens of thousands of dollars of what today would be called no-bid government contracts for printing official documents flowed to those papers sympathetic to elected officials. "There was nothing deceptive about this," writes Michael Schudson. "It was standard practice and common knowledge."[7] Newspaper editors saw themselves as partial in nearly every election contest, looking askance upon their competitors who were unwilling to commit themselves to a particular slate of candidates or a party ticket. Newspaper circulation steadily grew in the early to midcentury because of the growing readership and improvements in the printing press—but also because of the tight relationship between newspapers and America's elected officials.

THOMAS JEFFERSON, NEWSPAPERS, AND POLITICAL PARTIES AFTER 1800

Beginning almost immediately in his first term as president, Jefferson maintained his close counsel with several of the nation's newspaper editors, including Samuel Harrison Smith, the editor of the *National Intelligencer*. Jefferson worked to ensure that the new capital had a newspaper closely associated with his new administration. At the urging of Jefferson, the twenty-eight-year-old Smith moved his *Universal Gazette* to Washington and began publication of his paper under its new name, the *National Intelligencer and Washington Advertiser* on Friday, October 31, 1800. Smith's friendship with Jefferson established his paper as the most influential of the several newspapers established that summer and fall of 1800 in the new capital. By the end of 1800, Washington had four newspapers, yet none enjoyed the closeness to Jefferson and his administration's supporters in Congress as the *National Intelligencer*, a paper Jefferson himself is known to have written anonymously for during his tenure as president.

The establishment of the *New York Evening Post* in 1801 by Alexander Hamilton and his supporters in New York City soon took its place as the leading paper to circulate items in opposition to President Jefferson. Months before the printing of the first issue of the *New York Evening Post*, Hamilton corresponded with his friends and political supporters in New York and elsewhere, urging their assistance by whatever financial investments they might contribute to the paper. Hamilton himself is thought to have contributed more than $1,000 to its first issue.

New York City's *New York Evening Post* published its first issue on Monday, November 16, 1801, from its offices on New York City's William Street. William Coleman is remembered as the first editor of the *New York Evening Post*, yet it is recalled that Hamilton had an important hand not just in securing investors and subscribers for the paper but also in authoring any number of unsigned items for publication. Hamilton lent his writing talents to the paper in its earliest issues, including an eighteen-part rebuttal of Jefferson's first message to Congress.

"It is the Press which has corrupted our political morals and it is to the Press we must look for the means of our political regeneration," the *New York Evening Post* offered in its first issue on Monday, November 16, 1801. "We openly profess our attachment to that system of politics denominated

Federal," the *New York Evening Post* informed its readers, and called for letters and essays written by "honest and virtuous men," pledging it would offer a forum for debate of all issues. Hamilton contributed editorial items to the paper—contributions easily and frequently exaggerated in some accounts—yet his patronage, prestige, and prolific writing all most certainly contributed to the well-deserved reputation of the *New York Evening Post*.

Jefferson took the step at the end of his first term as president to assist Thomas Ritchie with the founding of the *Richmond Enquirer*, a paper that printed its first issue on Wednesday, May 9, 1804. The *Richmond Enquirer* remained close to Jefferson in the years to come. Ritchie ended his forty-one-year association with the *Richmond Enquirer* only when President Polk convinced him to move to Washington, D.C., in March 1845 to edit the *Washington Union*, where he finally closed out his career when he retired in 1851.

On Friday, January 1, 1813, the *National Intelligencer and Washington Advertiser*, a newspaper known for its close affiliations with Jefferson (and later with his friend and fellow Virginian, James Madison) changed its name and became a daily. The *Daily National Intelligencer*, as the paper in its daily edition was now named, boasted of its close association with President Madison and his supporters in Congress. The *Daily National Intelligencer*'s editors Joseph Gales Jr. and his brother-in-law, William Winston Seaton, became so close to the leadership in the Congress that the editors reportedly took part in closed-door meetings with congressional leaders. Seaton and Gales were part of Washington society in the nation's capital, entertaining members of Congress, visiting dignitaries, and various federal officials. Seaton served for years as the mayor of Washington, further establishing the *Daily National Intelligencer* as the newspaper of record unrivaled for its proximity to those in positions of influence and power in the nation's capital for much of the early nineteenth century.

THE RISE OF NEWSPAPERS, THE RISE OF THE WESTERN TERRITORIES, AND THE WAR OF 1812

"The purchase of the Louisiana territory in 1803 stimulated the expansion of the press West of the great river," writes Frank Luther Mott.[8] In the early years of the nineteenth century, America's most influential newspapers were still published in the nation's coastal cities and towns, yet this preeminence of newspapers and publishing in the East was slowly but most certainly challenged as papers and their printers began expanding their circulation and their business interests into the expanses of the West. As wagons and horse-drawn carts loaded with settlers and their belongings moved across the Appalachian Mountains and into the plains to the west of the great Mississippi River, America's frontier saw itself forging its own identity in the settlements and prairie towns a world apart from the cities of the East.

"With the purchase of Louisiana and the migration to the Western states and territories," Hoyt and Hoyt tell us, "the press followed and flourished almost everywhere without constraint."[9] As America's population expanded and grew in the West and as territories of the country opened up to commercial settlement, the nation's newspapers followed into the newly settled regions of the country; Illinois, Indiana, Kentucky, Louisiana, and Ohio all saw newspapers established in these early years.

The rise of newspapers in the West is one of the most remarkable chapters in the early-nineteenth-century history of newspapers. Supplies, transportation difficulties, and uncertainty in the delivery of the mail were but a few of the many obstacles faced and almost always surmounted by the printers of the West; their papers opening almost every week in some ever-farther flung corner of the territories. "The belated arrival of paper from the East," Reuben Gold Thwaites observed, "often necessitated borrowing from more fortunate contemporaries. Even stocks of government cartridge paper were occasionally loaned from the forts to tide over the difficulty, and now and then the famine was so complete that publication must be suspended for weeks at a time."[10] The printers in the territories not only dealt with the difficulty and the distance of the mail delivery of news from the East but also with the impediments of delivering their papers to their subscribers and their readers.

By the end of Jefferson's second term, printer Joseph Charless began publication of the *Missouri Gazette* on Tuesday, July 12, 1808, in the territory along the Mississippi River. The *Missouri Gazette* was published in St. Louis, which at that time was a settlement of some one thousand inhabitants. Charless published some news items and ads in both English and in French for a time in the pages of the *Gazette*, given the large French-speaking population settled in the territory around St. Louis. And, for a time, he had to ship paper for the *Gazette* hundreds of miles from the closest paper mill in Pennsylvania.

The federal purchase of the Louisiana Territories in 1803 also brought newspapers into the towns and settlements of the newly acquired territories, with the son of Vermont's Matthew Lyon, James Lyon—who had learned the print trade as an apprentice in Benjamin Franklin's Philadelphia print shop—publishing the first issue of New Orleans's early newspaper, the *Union or New Orleans Advertiser and Price Current*, on Tuesday, December 13, 1803. Jefferson praised James Lyon in his correspondence as "a young man of bold Republicanism in the worst of times, son of the persecuted Matthew Lyon" and took an interest in following the younger Lyon's printing ventures throughout the country.[11]

As settlements steadily moved closer to the Mississippi River and then into the territories to the Western plains across the Mississippi River, newspapers and their editors accompanied the settlement of population into these territories. Cumbersome and difficult as these printing presses were to transport given the conditions of travel, the printing of these newspapers by these publishers is nothing less than testimony to their determination to bring the circulation of news to their often isolated settlements. For example, the *Indiana Gazette*, published by Elihu Stout in Vincennes, Indiana, began publication on Wednesday, July 4, 1804. Material for Stout's printing press, including the paper, had to be brought from Louisville down the Ohio River, then on the Wabash River, and finally on pack horses to his shop in Vincennes.

Matthew Duncan's *Illinois Herald* began publication as Illinois's first newspaper in June 1814. A native of Kentucky, Duncan settled in Kaskaskia, Illinois, about fifty miles south of St. Louis. When Henry Eddy and Peter Kimmel established Illinois's second paper, the *Illinois Emigrant*, in the summer of 1818 in Shawneetown on the banks of the Ohio River, they did so after their boat became stranded on a sandbar in the river and local Shawneetown residents convinced them to stay and establish their paper.

In the largest Eastern cities and in newly settled Western towns alike, Americans by the end of the nineteenth century's second decade found themselves immersed in newspapers. The *Cincinnati Advertiser*, the *Cincinnati Enquirer*, Lexington's *Kentucky Reporter*, the *Louisville Public Advertiser*, the *Pittsburgh Gazette*, and the *Pittsburgh Statesman* were but a few of the papers in circulation in this era. Even with the expansion of population (and eventually papers) into the ever more distant settlements in the West, the importance of papers to the nation's political battles being waged in Washington took center stage yet again with the 1820 presidential race and then most especially in the 1824 race. The capital city boasted newspapers whose influence now stretched far beyond the lawmakers and their immediate environs to extend into the public in nearly all parts of the country. Improvements in postal delivery and in roads, not to mention the growth of railroads, allowed Washington's papers to circulate farther and farther away from the capital.

By 1820, 512 newspapers were in circulation in the United States, the bulk of which openly expressed their partisan affiliations and loyalties, from their editorial pages to their mastheads to their very names themselves. Newspaper circulation grew in this period of time as improvements in printing and in transportation made newspapers more readily circulated and as the political affairs of the nation continued to be of interest to many Americans. Yet, in so many ways, America's newspapers and especially its political life would be forever changed by the historic events of the 1824 election.

Secretary of State John Quincy Adams, Speaker of the House Henry Clay, Georgia's William H. Crawford, and Jackson of Tennessee all emerged as the candidates in the 1824 race for president. Each carried a portion of that year's vote. Jackson led the field with ninety-nine Electoral College votes. Adams garnered the second largest number of votes, winning some eighty-four Electoral College votes. Crawford carried forty-one Electoral College votes and Clay thirty-seven. With this, it was the second time in the nation's history that no candidate running for the presidency carried the largest number of Electoral College votes, forcing the House of Representatives to select the president from Jackson, Adams, and Crawford.

When a Philadelphia newspaper in January 1825 published some of the first allegations of collusion in a purported deal struck between Secretary of State Adams and Speaker of the House Clay to deprive Jackson of the presidency, it lit the fuse of what would be many months if not years of rumors regarding the events that unfolded in 1825 in the nation's capital. On Friday, January 28, 1825, Philadelphia's *Columbian Observer* published a letter charging that Clay had offered his endorsement to Adams in return for Clay's nomination as secretary of state. The *Columbian Observer*'s anonymous author disclaimed the rumored deal as "one of the most disgraceful transactions that ever covered with infamy the Republican Ranks." Clay himself took to the pages of Washington's *Daily National Intelligencer* to renounce the allegations made in the *Columbian Observer*.

On Wednesday, February 9, 1825, members of the House of Representatives met at noon, for its second time in the nation's history, to elect a president. "Every lodging place, hotel, and boarding house in Washington was filled with visitors to the city," J. E. D. Shipp recalls in his account of that day's events in the capital.[12] Expectations grew outside of the chamber in the hallways of the Capitol Building that the election of the president by the House of Representatives might take several days or even weeks. Yet when the time arrived for the state-by-state balloting by the twenty-four state delegations in the house, a calm seemed to take hold in the chamber, a calm certainly belying the controversy to ensue. Adams carried the majority of the House of Representatives on Wednesday, February 9, 1825, winning the presidency with the votes of thirteen of the twenty-four states.

Days later when President Adams announced his nomination of Clay as his selection for secretary of state and, only a few days later, when Clay accepted the nomination, the rumors swirling in the newspapers of the day took on a much more indelible part of the nation's political landscape. Newspapers filled their pages with allegations of collusion in the House of Representatives' vote for Adams—allegations that damaged the reputation of Clay and probably sealed Adams's fate as a one-term president.

In 1825, the *New York Daily Advertiser* installed the first steam-driven printing press in the United States. It cost approximately $5,000 to install and was capable of printing more than two thousand newspapers an hour. The installation of this press paved the way for the *New York Daily Advertiser* to experience an historic growth in the circulation, readership, and sale of papers at a time when the fever-pitch of campaigning for elected office and the commercial expansion and population growth of both the nation's cities as well as its Western settlements increased continued to increase the demand for daily papers. By 1832, improvements to the *New York Daily Advertiser*'s steam-driven press allowed it to print more than four thousand papers an hour.

NEWSPAPERS IN THE 1830s

"Its [newspapers] influence in America is immense," Alexis de Tocqueville wrote in the first volume of his *Democracy in America*. Tocqueville traveled throughout the United States from May 1831 through February 1832 and wrote his impressions of the civic, commercial, and political life of the American people, including the attachments of most Americans to the nation's newspapers: "Its eye is constantly open to detect the secret springs of political designs and to summon the leaders of all parties in turn to the bar of public opinion. It rallies the interests of the community around certain principles and draws up the creed of every party, for it affords a means of intercourse between those who hear and address each other without ever coming into immediate contact."[13] Tocqueville also observed that "the sovereignty of the people and the liberty of the press may therefore be looked upon as correlative institutions."[14] Additionally, he explained that "in order to enjoy the inestimable benefits that the liberty of the press ensures, it is necessary to submit to the inevitable evils that it creates."[15]

In 1830, at that moment when de Tocqueville saw firsthand the importance of newspapers to the commerce and the civic lives of most Americans, the United States had 650 weekly papers and 65 daily papers. Within a decade's time, the United States had 1,141 weekly papers and 138 daily papers, papers that, by 1840, were becoming increasingly affiliated with candidates and political parties.

The business of America's newspapers in the nineteenth century was, to put it bluntly, to make money, and while the affiliations of newspapers with candidates for elected office may have increased sales, it may also have lost some advertisers or readers. Newspapers and printed materials distributed during the campaigns of the late 1820s and the early 1830s were used by elected officials on both sides of the aisle. Newspaper editors committed to Jackson in the 1828 election were rewarded with printing and other government contracts. Editors sympathetic to Jackson built a system of patronage, government contracts, and subsidies from those in elected office at the local, state, and national levels. From their posts as customs collectors, administrators in the public land offices of the West, and even as the librarian of Congress, editors held positions of some influence when appointed by President Jackson and his supporters. "Before dawn and then again in the late afternoon," Charles G. Steffen recalls, "every day of the year except

Sundays and holidays, newspaper carriers swarmed the streets and alleys of American cities, depositing their papers at the doors of subscribers."[16] By 1830, in the middle of Jackson's first term, America boasted sixty-five daily papers that reached thousands of readers every day. Newspapers in the nation's larger cities were a part of the bustling life that took place on its sidewalks and streets, their deliverymen and vendors often calling out the headlines of the day as they delivered and sold their papers.

Travel in most of the United States in the 1920s and early 1930s was excruciatingly slow—even with the continued growth of railroads and with the improvements of roads—and the news in the nation's papers took days and even weeks to be delivered. With the advent of the telegraph still well over a decade away, news of Jackson's 1829 inaugural took more than a week to travel by carriage or by horseback from Washington, D.C., to St. Louis, Missouri. In the early 1830s, news traveling by horse, by men known as express riders, from New York City to Cleveland, Ohio, still took as long as ten days depending on the conditions of the roads and the weather.

In the years after the 1828 presidential race, newspapers took on an even greater prominence in the nation's political life. The press galleries in the House of Representatives and Senate chambers grew ever busier as newspapers outside of Washington increasingly sent their reporters to cover the proceedings on Capitol Hill. Newspaper editors were in the innermost circles of Jackson's closest advisors, serving both informal and formal posts within the government. In fact, as many as fifty editors or publishers were appointed to various official government posts by Jackson.

By the early 1830s, America's cities and towns boasted approximately 1,200 newspapers, many of which associated themselves with either President Jackson or with the growing ranks of his opponents, a group who called themselves Whigs. In 1830, sixty-five daily papers were in circulation, growing to 138 daily papers by 1840. With the often controversial administration of President Jackson and with the ever-growing ranks of his opponents, many papers wedded themselves to the nation's political figures and its candidates for elected office. "For an established newspaper to change political faith would have marked it as a Judas," Frank Luther Mott notes.[17] "American newspapers were expected to present a partisan viewpoint not a neutral one," agrees Michael Schudson.[18] Little pretense of impartiality was found in the pages of many of the papers in this era, where one surmises that their editors might even have disagreed in their coverage of the weather itself.

Editors such as the *United States Telegraph*'s Duff Green and the *Washington Globe*'s Francis Preston Blair were as influential as the officeholders they associated themselves with. The *United States Telegraph* published its first issue in 1826 and played an important role in Jackson's 1828 presidential race. Green met Jackson while traveling on a keelboat on the Ohio River, befriending the Tennessean and eventually moving to Washington in 1825 where he purchased the *United States Telegraph*. The *United States Telegraph* soon became one of Washington's most influential papers. The *Washington Globe*, first published on Tuesday, December 7, 1830, became important to Jackson, replacing the *Telegraph* in the spring of 1831 as the newspaper of record for his administration.

"I expect you all to patronize *The Globe*," President Jackson told his associates in his administration, lending still further prestige to that paper. Blair's influence through his editorship of the *Washington Globe* led to his purchase of a mansion across the street from the Executive Mansion, which is known today as the Blair House. Years later, still an influential figure in the nation's capital even after his falling out with President Polk and his sale of the *Washington Globe* in 1845, Blair lent his prestige and his powerful connections to the formation of the Republican Party in the early and mid-1850s, especially when he backed that party's first presidential nominee, California's John C. Fremont.

"We can endure a thousand convulsions" with newspapers, Martin Van Buren famously explained to his fellow Democrats. "Without them, we might as well hang our harps on willows."[19] Newspapers not only provided their editorial voice and pages for the defense of their patrons in elective office but offered the essential workings of campaigns themselves, printing not just handbills and circulars but also the ballots used by voters in most parts of the country until the end of the nineteenth century. In many smaller towns and even in larger cities, newspaper offices sometimes served as the meeting places for party leaders. Newspapers also served as the gathering place on election days and especially the evening after polls closed.

Newspaper editors and publishers certainly sought positions and offices in all levels of government and most certainly benefitted not only from their proximity to the powerful figures of the day but also benefitted financially from contracts as well as outright financial subsidies and payments from party leaders. "The wages of political journalism," Donald A. Ritchie writes, "were patronage."[20] Newspapers stirred and stoked the electorate in the months before elections—their editorials, news items, and various writings and cartoons slanted in favor of their particular slate of candidates. Newspapers in the nineteenth century frequently received contracts for government printing not only at the federal level but also in state and local governments.

"Newspapers of the Jacksonian era were opinionated, politically biased, one-sided, argumentative, and frequently strident," writes Gerald J. Baldasty.[21] In some instances, smaller-circulation papers might be bought and sold between elections, a changing-of-hands invariably weakening the editorial and journalistic quality of these papers. Subsidies for sympathetic editors and government contracts for printing jobs certainly attracted people to the newspaper publishing business with little or no interest whatsoever in journalism or reporting. The sharp exchanges between editors affiliated with rival candidates for elective office became such that fistfights, threats of violence, and even attacks on newspaper offices themselves were all too commonplace in the 1830s and the years after.

NEWSPAPERS AND THE RISE OF THE WHIGS

In the early 1830s and into the 1840s, the newspapers of the day witnessed a number of far-reaching changes, as newspaper publishers and their editors in the nation's larger cities and towns began to appeal to wider audiences, in part, by distancing themselves from the nation's partisan battles. Improvements in printing presses, especially the steam-powered cylindrical presses, set the stage for a new era of a less costly, more widely circulated newspaper known as the "penny press." The *New York Sun* led the way as the first paper to cost just .01 cent an issue. First published on Tuesday, September 3, 1833, it was a breakthrough made possible by the declining cost of paper, the growing efficiency of steam-driven printing, and the greater reliance of papers on commercial advertising, the latter an especially important force over the next century in dislodging a growing number of papers from their solidly partisan allegiances.

Innovations in the printing press in the early and mid-1840s most certainly and most indelibly changed the business of publishing. The installation of a steam-driven printing press in 1846 that was capable of printing more than eight thousand pages an hour at the *Philadelphia Public Ledger* offered a glimpse of the future of large-circulation newspapers that came to dominate much of the nation's political life at the end of the nineteenth century. Still another glimpse of that future came in the mid-1840s with the invention of the telegraph. The arrival of the telegraph in the 1840s soon improved the circulation of news and reports between newspapers. Samuel F. B. Morse's demonstration of the telegraph in the Capital Building in 1844 offered newspapers an astonishing new way for their reporters covering Washington to file their stories with their newsrooms. By June 1846, the first direct telegraph line from Washington to New York City brought the latest news from the nation's capital to the largest newspaper publishers in the country.

Innovative as the technology of low-cost newspapers, high-speed printing presses, and leading-edge telegraphs were for the newspapers of the 1840s, few forces were as indelibly a part of the nation's newspapers in this era as the blistering campaigns for offices by rival elected officials of the day. With the fracturing of the nation's politics in the mid-1830s in the second term of Jackson's administration, the opponents of the president came together to form the Whig Party, a ticket that brought together the disparate vestiges of the often fractured, sectionally divided groups against President Jackson.

Whatever else the Whigs did to organize the public and to effectively establish themselves as the opponents of Jackson and the Democratic Party, their relationships with the newspapers in this era, especially in the 1840s when the Whigs experienced their widest influence and popular support, was clear. "Every crossroads town claimed a Jacksonian paper and an opposition Whig sheet," Ritchie writes.[22] The *New York Express*, the *New York American*, the *Louisville Journal*, the *Cincinnati Gazette*, and the *Pittsburgh Daily American* were some of the many papers aligned with the Whigs in the 1840s.

New York's Horace Greeley is one of the most well-known figures to emerge from this era, beginning with his work with some of the earliest campaigns by candidates running on the Whig ticket in the mid- to late 1830s. Greeley's work as an editor began in 1837 when he was hired by Thurlow Weed to assist in editing the *Albany Evening Journal*. In 1840, Greeley lent his talents to several publications on behalf of Whigs running in that year's election, including editing New York City's Whig paper, the *Log Cabin*, a paper that published its first issue on Saturday, May 2, 1840. Also in 1840 the Whigs' rustic iconography was written into the names of some of that campaign's papers including the *Log Cabin Advocate*, the *Log Cabin Farmer*, and Indiana's *Whig Rifle*.

Newspapers by the early to mid-1840s saw continued increases in their circulation and readership, exercising greater influence when candidates and their platforms clamored for space in the pages of these papers. New York City's typical daily paper in 1810, for instance, had a circulation of some nine hundred copies. Improvements in printing presses by 1820 allowed many of these same New York City papers to see their circulation double to almost two thousand copies printed daily. Still, even further improvements in printing presses saw that number grow to as many as 4,000 papers daily by 1830 and as many as twenty thousand by 1845. "You meet newspaper readers everywhere," a European observer recounted in 1850, "and in the evening the whole city knows what lay twenty-four hours ago on newswriters' desks."[23] In short, papers were reaching an ever-expanding, ever-widening readership at exactly that time when the ever-sharpening rivalries between candidates for elective office still dominated the pages (not to mention the editorial boards) of most newspapers.

Improvements in transportation, especially with the dense latticework of well-traveled railroads extending over most parts of the country and ever further into the West, where new territories were opening up in the 1840s to increases in population, also led to the expansion of newspapers in these new territories. California's first newspaper, the *Californian*, published its first issue on Saturday, August 15, 1846. "This is the first paper ever published in California, and though issued upon a small sheet, is intended it shall contain matter that will be read with interest," the *Californian* announced in its Saturday, August 15, 1846, issue. Published in English and in Spanish, the *Californian*'s first issue included reports from throughout the territory as well as news from Washington, D.C.

Even as the establishment in 1849 of what would become the Associated Press in New York City formed to adopt a more impartial, unbiased source of news and reporting for newspapers, most of America's newspapers and their editors still had either formal or informal affiliations with Democratic or Whig leaders. By 1850, the Bureau of the Census reported the nation had 2,302 papers, most of which were weekly papers, making the United States, in the words of David M. Ryfe, "the newspaper capital of the world."[24] Of that, well over half of these papers, some 1,597, had a partisan affiliation. As many as 855 papers reported an affiliation with the Whigs in the Census of 1850 while 742 papers reported affiliation with the Democratic Party. Literally incorporating the names of their patron political parties into their own names, newspapers in the mid-nineteenth century and some well into the twenty-first century still have "Democrat" or "Republican" in their names, a nod to this bygone era when some of the nation's newspapers were actively aligned with political parties.

THE FORMATION OF THE REPUBLICAN PARTY, THE PARTY NEWSPAPERS OF THE 1850s, AND THE 1860 ELECTION

With the steam-driven printing presses of the 1850s expanding the circulation and the readership of some larger newspapers, editors and especially publishers carefully balanced their well-established partisan loyalties with the larger circulation and readership of their papers. Nicknamed "lightning presses," the steam-powered cylindrical presses first introduced as prototypes in the 1840s and engineered to higher efficiency by the early 1850s could print as many as 12,000 impressions an hour in their larger models by this time, a remarkable accomplishment for an era where editors and publishers were poised to reach a nation riveted by each issue of their papers for the latest news and reports of the day. Even with the improvements in high-speed printing and in lowered costs for the manufacture of paper and for the distribution of newspapers to the public, a substantial number of papers in the mid- and late 1850s were still heavily subsidized by elected officials, their publishers regularly awarded printing contracts and appointments to government posts, and their editorial columns and reporting tilted in favor of their patrons in their races for elective office. "The press and parties worked well together because they needed each other," Michael E. McGerr writes of the high-water mark of partisan ferment in the nation's newspapers in the mid- and late 1850s—most especially in the early days of the Republican Party's founding.[25]

In the winter of 1854, the Republican Party emerged from meetings in churches, schools, and gathering places of all kinds where former Whigs, members of the anti-slavery Liberty Party, supporters of the Free Soil Party, and others gathered in meetings to debate the issues of slavery and sectionalism facing the United States. Newspapers and their editors were certainly a part of this early history of the Republican Party. From his Ohio offices where he edited the *Cleveland Leader*, Joseph Medill was especially active in his correspondence with those forming this new party in the winter of 1854. "Like so many young men in the Middle West at that time," George Henry Payne recalls of Medill, "he burned with indignation over the arrogance of the South and in his little paper the editorials were so bitter that on one occasion sundry Democrats waylaid him and answered his editorial attacks with cuts and bruises."[26] Medill brought a fierce belief in the need for a new party to replace the Whigs when he moved to Cleveland, where his stature as editor of *The Cleveland Leader* grew.

In March 1854, Medill hosted a meeting of leading figures of the varied parties at the offices of his Ohio paper to discuss the future of the anti-slavery Whigs, the Free Soilers, and the growing number of anti-slavery Democrats in the northern states. Medill and the representatives from these varied groups worked up a statement of principle for those calling themselves Republicans to circulate among the various groups beginning to coalesce around that name. In April 1855, Medill and his family moved to Chicago where he purchased the *Chicago Daily Tribune* in May 1855, which would merge on Thursday, July 1, 1858, with the *Daily Democratic Press* to become the *Chicago Press and Tribune*. By the fall of 1856, Medill met at his offices at 51 Clark Street with Abraham Lincoln, the first of many such meetings to take place in Medill's Chicago office. Lincoln personally took out a subscription for the *Chicago Press and Tribune* in their first meeting in Medill's office.

Newspaper editors, including Joseph Medill and Horace Greeley, played a significant role in corresponding with local residents in the winter of 1854 as meetings in Michigan, Wisconsin, and elsewhere began to come together to form what would become the Republican Party. Editors sympathetic to the newly formed Republican Party carried news of the party far and wide giving it far more circulation than it might otherwise have had at this time.

On Thursday, September 18, 1851, the *New York Daily Times* circulated its first issue, a newspaper whose legacy of excellence in journalism is still regarded more than 150 years later as one of the most important media institutions in the world. "We publish today the first issue of *The New York Daily Times*, and we intend to issue it every morning (Sundays excepted) for an indefinite number of years to come." The *New York Daily Times* promised its readers the highest standards of reporting. By the late 1890s, the *New York Times* (it removed "Daily" from its name on Monday, September 14, 1857) under the editorship of Adolph S. Ochs took pride in its commitment to "pure information," with the masthead "All the News That's Fit to Print." This newspaper has earned more than 110 Pulitzer Prizes for its reporting, and it remains undiminished in its influence and its reputation from its first issue that Thursday in 1851.

In 1860, 387 daily papers were in circulation, reaching tens of millions of Americans with the latest news and stories from that year's national party conventions, carrying extensive coverage of the speeches and remarks of the candidates themselves. Chicago, Kansas City, New Orleans, and St. Louis now had papers that rivalled many cities in the eastern United States. St. Louis boasted six daily papers by 1850, a number that grew to ten daily papers by 1860. Los Angeles's first newspaper, the *Los Angeles Star*, published its first issue on Saturday, May 17, 1851, beginning the rise of that city's newspaper publishing over the next decade. Not to be outdone, New York City boasted seventeen major daily papers by 1861. Improvements in photography and high-speed rotary printing, improvements in paper manufacturing in the 1850s, and the widespread use of the typewriter in the 1860s all opened exciting opportunities for the newspapers of the mid-nineteenth century.

"Editors unabashedly shaped the news and their editorial comment to partisan purposes," William F. Gienapp writes of the newspapers of the mid- and late 1850s. "They sought," Gienapp explains, "to convert the doubters, recover the wavering, and hold the committed."[27] "Partisanship was extreme on both sides," Richard Allen Heckman recalls of a great many of the papers in this day, as, in Heckman's words, "Republican and Democratic papers often arrived at opposite conclusions after witnessing the same event."[28] With the seeming irreversibility of the growing partisan and sectional rifts in the late 1850s, readers of newspapers on both sides of the political aisle took to the pages of their papers as never before to read the latest news, commentary, and editorials of various events and speeches.

No figure in the 1860 presidential race is as much at the intersection of newspapers and the campaigning of his day as Illinois's Abraham Lincoln, an attorney and former lawmaker in Illinois's General Assembly and former Whig officeholder in the House of Representatives. Lincoln was an avid reader of newspapers and had close friendships with several newspaper editors, especially Chicago's Medill who played a significant role in lining up support for Lincoln's bid for the Republican presidential nomination in 1860.

By 1860, Lincoln's home state of Illinois had four hundred newspapers, including eleven daily papers in Chicago. Lincoln not only read newspapers, he often found himself writing short editorial items and letters to his state's newspapers on the topics of the day. As a well-known attorney with terms in both Illinois's General Assembly and in the House of Representatives, Lincoln's signed items were frequently of some public interest. As often as not, Lincoln also anonymously authored items to the papers of his state, not unlike many of those drafters of the Constitution whose legacies Lincoln himself grappled with in his tenure years later as the sixteenth president of the United States.

As a young man in the New Salem settlement outside of his later home in Springfield, Illinois, Lincoln's work as New Salem's postmaster allowed him to read papers as he sorted and delivered the mail to residents of the town. Later, as an attorney, a member of the state's General Assembly, and eventually a member of the House of Representatives, Lincoln always kept up with the day's news, editorials, and stories in the paper. Lincoln read the *Chicago Press and Tribune*, the *New York Tribune*, the *Louisville Journal*, and the *St. Louis Republican*, scouring their pages for the latest news and reports.

In the 1830s and the 1840s, as a lawmaker in Illinois's General Assembly, Lincoln wrote unsigned items for Springfield's *Illinois Daily State Journal*, known in its early years (when Lincoln contributed items to it) as the *Sangamo Journal* when the paper was founded in 1831. In Lincoln's Springfield of the mid- to late 1850s, as his prominence grew, the *Illinois Daily State Journal* took up Lincoln's cause and that of the Republican Party, while the city's other paper, the *Illinois State Register*, known for its Democratic leanings, wrote editorials against the Republican Party. Lincoln is known to have written items for the *Illinois Daily State Journal*. And in his historic 1858 bid for the Illinois Senate, Lincoln understood, as did most candidates of his day, the importance of working closely with reporters to ensure the most sympathetic account of his remarks and speeches in the pages of their newspapers. "He never overlooked a newspaper man who had it in his power to say a good or bad thing of him," William Herndon later wrote of his friend and former law partner.

On Monday, May 30, 1859, Lincoln invested $400 in a set of German-language type and printing presses to publish Springfield's German-language weekly newspaper, the *Illinois Staats Anzeiger*, writing up a contract with printer Theodore Canisius, who moved to Springfield from the river town of Alton to produce his paper. It is unclear whether or to what extent Lincoln penned any editorials or unsigned items for his paper during the time he co-owned it, though members of the Illinois state House of Representatives and the state Senate were thought to have received copies of the paper in the state capital.[29] In early December 1860, President-elect Lincoln arranged for the transfer of sole ownership of the *Illinois Staats Anzeiger* back to Canisius.

"Men gathered around the cracker barrels of grocery stores at thousands of crossroads every day to discuss what 'Uncle Horace' said in *The Tribune*," Robert S. Harper recalled of the *New York Tribune*'s Greeley and his editorials in the 1860s presidential race.[30] Greeley was one of a group of influential editors in that year's contest, a group later nicknamed the "Newspaper Generals," all of whom were admired by Lincoln, who himself regularly learned the latest news, reports, and updates of local issues in the campaign from these editors. Lincoln, however, adhering to a well-worn tradition, remained at his home in Illinois for the long months of the campaign. The *Chicago Press and Tribune*'s Medill was especially invaluable in arranging convention delegates to support Lincoln's nomination at the 1860 Republican convention. "Lincoln trusted no newspapermen more," Harold Holzer writes of Medill and the *Chicago Press and Tribune*.[31] Its offices in

Chicago became the setting of many meetings of Lincoln's supporters during the 1860 convention. Months earlier, the *Chicago Press and Tribune* editorialized on behalf of Lincoln during the 1858 Senate race in Illinois, which pitted Stephen Douglas against Lincoln.

In New York City, Printing House Square became one of the most important locations for newspaper publishing in the United States in the long months from Lincoln's election on Tuesday, November 6, 1860, through his inauguration on the Capitol's steps on Monday, March 4, 1861. Telegraph wires into the buildings and offices on Printing House Square crackled with hourly updates sent to the editorial offices and newsrooms. These newsrooms would take an even more significant role of the events of the difficult years to come.

Within hours of the hostilities in Charleston, South Carolina, federal officials assumed control of all telegraph wires leading into and out of Washington, effectively exercising control over the most important means for disseminating the latest news and reports. Newspaper editors complained of "telegraphic censorship of the press" and some editors came to rely on the Postal Service or even private couriers for transmission of potentially sensitive stories. Yet newspaper editors and especially their journalists reporting in some of the most dangerous and difficult wartime circumstances imaginable persisted in delivering their latest stories—by whatever means available—to their newsrooms.

"The Civil War," according to Richard Carwardine, "created an unprecedented demand for news and commentary."[32] In the difficult years of the war, newspapers and their editors and publishers moved to a position of almost unrivaled importance in the nation. Newspaper readers were able to read detailed accounts of the war, while reporters came into sharp conflict with officials over coverage of everything from the treatment of prisoners of war to alleged corruption among wartime's private contractors. Battlefield photography—not to mention the exceptionally detailed maps by a skilled generation of artists and engravers—accompanied by news updated throughout the day in the multiple editions of some larger papers, made papers an important if not irreplaceable part of the lives of many Americans during the years of the Civil War.

The inevitable clashes between newspapers, their editors, and their reporters and government and military authorities fill volumes on the history of the Civil War, with accounts of everything from the suspension of the circulation of newspapers in the Postal Service to the closure of newspapers due to boycotts to the heavy-handed dealing of military officers and government authorities with journalists wanting to accompany and report on the military and the field of battle. Closures of newspapers by military officials, the arrest of their editors by authorities, even the confiscation of scarce printing supplies and paper all certainly deeply affected these newspapers, yet their editors, publishers, printers, deliverymen, and most especially their reporters and photographers were resilient in the face of such difficulties. Whether it was editorial cartoons mocking President Lincoln, his Cabinet, or his generals, or commentary and letters critical of President Jefferson Davis, little effort was spared by the papers, their editors, reporters, and readers to carry on the tradition of debate in the papers.

In Washington, Lincoln kept his close relationships with newspaper editors and publishers and followed their newspapers throughout his days as a wartime commander-in-chief. Lincoln maintained his reputation for being accessible to reporters—even taking their written questions during private meetings, which were often written on their business cards. The president, in turn, either wrote brief answers in reply to the questions or excused himself momentarily from his meeting to briefly talk with the waiting reporter.

"Atlanta is ours and fairly won," stated Major General William T. Sherman's Sunday, September 3, 1864, telegraph, which informed President Lincoln of one of the war's most decisive moments. From the first moments in the 1864 presidential race when Lincoln faced mounting doubts and uncertainties among many in his own party through the moment of Atlanta's capture by the Union Army, the editors of some of the nation's most influential newspapers played an important role in Lincoln's 1864 reelection. When the time came, the *Chicago Tribune*, the *Philadelphia Evening Bulletin*, and the *Philadelphia News* all editorialized for Lincoln's reelection.

With Appomattox's peace overshadowed by the assassination of President Lincoln in Washington, D.C., on Friday, April 14, 1865, newspapers yet again played their part in sharing the news of the nation's tragedy. The *New York Herald* printed a 2:00, 3:00, 8:45, and 10:00 edition of its paper in the early morning hours of Saturday, April 15, 1865, providing the latest news of the president's condition. Newspapers endured, survived, even thrived during wartime's difficult days—and now held the nation together through its grief and mourning after the death of President Lincoln, much as television did in the tragic days after the death of President John F. Kennedy in Dallas, Texas, on Friday, November 22, 1963. Publishers saw for themselves a place of influence (not to mention profitability) in their reporting of the news of the war, an influence that continued to thrive even after the lingering sectional tensions of the war. These tensions were compounded by the hard-fought electoral contests that were too often marred by some of the nation's worst instances of fraud and corruption, which, in turn, provided headlines that brought in even larger circulations and readership for those newspapers.

NEWSPAPERS AND POLITICS IN THE LATE NINETEENTH CENTURY

Newspapers emerged after the war with larger circulations driven by the demands of a public hungry for the latest news of the day. Newly expanded printing presses allowed many newspapers to have daily circulations of as many as 77,000 issues or more. Newspapers like Joseph Pulitzer's *St. Louis Post Dispatch* or E. W. Scripp's *Cleveland Press* were some of the great newspapers of the late nineteenth century. Pulitzer's 1883 purchase of the *New York World* and expansion of its circulation in the mid- and late 1880s built on his work with the *St. Louis Post Dispatch*, where his paper had advocated railroad and utility regulation, public works, and the reform of corporations. In the West, papers like the *San Francisco Examiner* published upward of three or four daily editions, its editions hitting the newsstands and the sidewalks throughout the day; their headlines sometimes yelled aloud by their deliverymen.

By 1870, the United States boasted some 574 daily papers. Newspapers reached millions of readers each day, with an ever larger number of cities and towns boasting two or more competing newspapers. Newspaper readers in New York City had twenty-nine daily papers in circulation by 1870 while Philadelphia had twenty-four daily papers and San Francisco twenty-one. Some two hundred new daily papers were in circulation by the end of 1880, bringing the total of general circulation daily papers in 1880 to more than 850. In 1880, about 239 of America's cities or towns had two or more competing daily papers. Chicago produced about eighteen daily papers, including some eight or more foreign-language dailies in 1880. San Francisco—whose population numbered approximately 230,000 in 1880 had twenty-one daily papers for its readers. In 1881, Cincinnati had some twelve daily papers, including seven in English and five in German. By 1890, New York City's fifty-five daily papers enlivened the life of that city—and most certainly solidified its ranks as the capital of the nation's newspaper publishing.

Hundreds of thousands of miles of telegraph wire was strung from wooden pole to wooden pole between 1850—when the country had some 16,000 miles of telegraph wire—and 1900, when more than 237,000 miles of telegraph wire crisscrossed the country. Improvements in high-speed printing allowed the circulation of newspapers to keep pace with the growth in their circulation and readership, as papers printed from as many as 85,000 copies per issue daily in 1870 to as many as 147,000 daily by 1880. Sunday, December 4, 1881, saw the publication of the first issue of the *Los Angeles Times*, a paper that grew in the coming years to become one of the most prominent papers in the country. Improved typesetting machines, first introduced in 1886, allowed type to be much more quickly set for printing presses while allowing several large presses to print the same paper simultaneously. By the early 1890s, improvements in the printing presses of some of the nation's larger newspapers—including continuous-roll presses for printing on both sides of a sheet of paper simultaneously and then automatically cutting, folding, sorting, and stacking the papers once printed—allowed for printing as many as 300,000 copies or more a day at some larger papers.

"The old traditional battling for the party was supplanted in some instances by the emphasis of the New Journalism on crusades to correct local abuses and to promote certain phases of social welfare," Frank Luther Mott writes of the late nineteenth century's shift of most of the nation's newspapers toward a different form of news coverage and editorials, one still frequently encompassing the nation's political debates but also driven by coverage of business and financial news, civic and municipal reform, and numerous other issues.[33] The partisan newspapers so important to America's campaigning in the nineteenth century showed some signs of waning in the early years of the twentieth century as a rise in newspaper circulation and readership brought more pressure to move away from their partisan patrons.

Newspaper editors at the end of the nineteenth century, long accustomed to speaking out against election corruption, fraud, or irregularities only when undertaken by the candidates of rival parties, now took up the cause of much more far-reaching electoral reform, especially the state-printed ballot, allowing voters to look at the candidates for all offices and all party tickets on the same ballot as well as cast their votes for different parties. So-called split ticket voting was all but impossible with the party tickets of the nineteenth century. The *Chicago Tribune*, the *Cleveland Press*, the *New York Times*, the *New York Tribune*, and the *St. Louis Post Dispatch* all engaged in investigations and crusades for civic improvement and electoral reform.

Ever-growing circulations of the nation's major metropolitan daily papers coupled with the changing standards of journalism and the larger place of advertising revenue for the balance sheet of the business side of newspapers combined to open a new chapter for America's newspapers. In everything from their coverage of entertainment and popular culture to their reporting on international affairs and the latest debates in Washington, D.C., America's late nineteenth-century newspapers were filled with stories covering virtually every issue of the day. Heightened competition in securing advertising revenues and the investments of a new generation of financial patrons had the effect of pushing most larger newspapers away from overtly partisan sympathies. "Newspapers that had once peddled advertisers to readers," George Juergens tells us, "now lived or died by their success in delivering readers to advertisers."[34] Strengthening of laws mandating the competitive bidding for most government printing contracts and the expansion of government printing offices still further weakened the subsidies that once flowed to newspaper editors and publishers. Professional expectations emphasizing the craft of editorial and journalistic writing certainly changed by the end of the nineteenth century, leading most editors and their reporters to more impartial, unbiased journalistic reporting.

At the end of the nineteenth century, journalism's professional emphasis on the craft of reporting was accompanied by the growing prestige and stature of individual reporters themselves. Unlike the anonymous news stories and items that filled the pages of most newspapers in the nineteenth century, individual reporters now saw their names in the bylines of their stories, giving them a professional stature and earning them the respect and the trust of their readers.

Washington, D.C.,'s most widely read daily papers, the *Washington Evening Star* and the *Washington Post*, were an important part of the growth of professional independent journalism at the end of the nineteenth century. When the *Washington Post* began publication on Thursday, December 6, 1877, the capital had a population of some 130,000 and five daily papers in circulation. Years earlier, the *Washington Post*'s chief rival, the *Washington Evening Star*, published its first issue on Thursday, December 16, 1852. Both these papers set a high standard for news reporting in the nation's capital.

The 14th Street newspaper offices and the nearby buildings of Pennsylvania Avenue in Washington, D.C.—where the *Washington Evening Star* and some of the city's smaller circulation papers, as well as some telegraph services, had their offices—was a neighborhood nicknamed "Newspaper Row" in the 1870s, its sidewalks often bustling with passers-by hoping to catch the latest news. From the hotels and the rented rooms near 14th Street to the offices of Western Union and other telegraph services, the words of the reporters carried out into the country across the wires and over the telegraph lines to their news editors, who waited eagerly for the latest news from the nation's capital to be printed in the predawn hours for the millions of newspapers left on doorsteps, lawns, and porches reaching even the smallest towns thousands of miles from Washington, D.C.

The impartiality, objectivity, and investigative reporting done by newspapers by the end of the nineteenth century were a result of the larger subscriptions and readership and the greater advertising revenues generated. The continued success of newspapers was a testimony to the professionalism of editors, journalists, and reporters by the century's end. The *Kansas City Star*, the *New York Times*, the *Washington Evening Star*, and the *Washington Post* were some of the many papers moving toward objectivity in reporting. When, by the end of the nineteenth century, the *New York Times* promised its readers would remain dedicated as ever to the reporting of "pure information," as the paper's editors termed it, importance of impartiality in its reporting the news expressed the trend already evident across any number of newspapers and their editors and publishers at the turn-of-the-century.

The bustling of the high-ceilinged, desk-filled newsrooms of America's great newspapers in the late nineteenth and early twentieth century were a place of reinvention for newspapers at this important time in the country's history, as the changing professional expectations of impartiality and objectivity increasingly held sway. "It took nearly 40 years for the old style to completely recede," David M. Ryfe writes of the changes in the nation's newsrooms and editorial meeting rooms at the end of the century.[35] Newfound emphasis on investigative reporting and the larger typeface for front-page headlines—not to mention the expansion of such popular features such as cartoons, crossword puzzles, weather reports, and sporting news—generated greater circulation and larger profits from subscription and newsstand sales. With the rise of the telegraph and wire services to distribute columns, stories, and articles, owners and publishers of many of the nation's newspapers increasingly encouraged the quality of the work of their individual reporters and columnists, whose syndicated columns, editorial commentary, and stories were reprinted in other newspapers, bringing both revenues from the fees for republishing these stories as well as greater prestige and prominence for the papers themselves. Investigative, in-depth reporting played an important part in the competition for readers by papers as they took on some of the same elected officials who might have only years earlier been able to steer subsidies and government contracts to loyal newspaper editors. As the growth in readership and circulation brought in greater subscription and sales revenues to these papers, editors and their reporters once tempted by the lure of government employment or needing to rely on whatever patronage was available to improve their bottom line now found their work admired by the public for their objectivity and for investigative reporting. Editors faced growing competition with syndicated periodicals and news magazines, prompting many papers to expand their special weekly newspaper editions, especially the Sunday editions that many had started during the Civil War.

Washington's newspaper reporters slowly became more of a presence on Capitol Hill, the Executive Mansion, and elsewhere in the years after the Civil War. Capitol Hill hallways and offices, during times of significant debate, were more often than not crowded with reporters looking for the latest news to telegraph to their editors. The *Washington Evening Star*'s William W. Price, regarded by many historians as the first reporter to regularly cover the Executive Mansion at the end of the nineteenth century, began his career interviewing visitors as they left meetings with President Grover Cleveland.

By 1900, improvements in the design of high-speed, cylindrical printing presses rather than the more conventional flat-bed presses allowed newspapers to increase circulations to as many as 1,000,000 daily copies, an astonishing figure for a century that had begun with hand-operated printing presses and ink rolled onto metal plates by hand in print shops. As early as 1893, larger rotary printing presses could print as many as 96,000 eight-page papers an hour. Huge rolls of paper came in to the loading docks of some of the great newspapers around the clock as some papers put out three, four, or even more editions throughout the day. By the end of the nineteenth century, having endured all manner of change and controversy and now competition in the delivery and circulation of news, newspapers still remained as important, influential, and relevant as ever. Fiercely competitive and amassing ever larger profits, publishers pushed their editors, reporters, and staff to increase readership and to increase advertising revenues. Pursuing investigative stories rather than the partisan politics of decades earlier, newspapers were now poised to have far-reaching impacts on the change and reform of America's political institutions. Declining costs of newsprint at the end of the nineteenth century allowed publishers to print larger and longer papers with greatly expanded space for advertising. This commercial growth ensured that newspapers would remain vital, vibrant, and voluble players in America's political life.

Chapter 3

Newspapers and Twentieth-Century American Politics

Newspapers continued to grow in circulation and readership in the early years of the twentieth century. Newspapers also saw their political influence grow as the nation's elected officials sometimes witnessed their careers either roused or routed because of a newspaper's headline or editorial. Americans in all parts of the country were accustomed to being able to read several newspapers each day, often reading papers not only published in their city but also papers brought in by railroad or by truck from cities sometimes hundreds of miles away. Readers delighted in everything from the pages of full-color comic strips in the Sunday paper to the growing number of photographs featured to the nationally syndicated columnists to crossword puzzles and all other manner of games.

Newspapers were a familiar part of the daily lives of most Americans at this time, many of whom began their mornings at home reading a paper delivered to their front door. Others would purchase a paper at a newsstand on their way to work or on their way home at the end of the day. Midday and late-afternoon editions of papers, with some papers publishing multiple daily editions, allowed people to read several editions of the same paper throughout the day. According to Peter Benjaminson, "the relatively primitive presses of the time could barely keep up with the demand for afternoon newspapers in America's big cities."[1]

Readers in larger cities with sometimes a dozen or more competing daily papers and multiple editions of the same paper might find themselves reading three or four of them a day. Railroads, telegraphs, teletypes, and telephones allowed for the latest news and coverage of events to be distributed to even the farthest reaches of the country as it was breaking. The rapid-fire clatter of the teletype machine in newsrooms was emblematic of the fast-paced circulation of news taking place at the beginning of the twentieth century.

America's early-twentieth-century newspapers gave their readers everything from cartoons and comic strips, court and legal proceedings, and criminal and police reports to editorials, obituaries, sports, and weather. Newspaper delivery trucks were some of the most familiar vehicles in busy neighborhoods—their drivers and delivery men sometimes yelling out the paper's headlines throughout the day and into the afternoons and evenings. Newsrooms bustled with the comings and goings of reporters, many of whom used the telephone from their news desks to track down material for their stories and to report their news back to their editors. Teletype machines rattled at all hours of the day and night with the latest news and wire reports. Enormous presses ran with the deafening roar of a factory. Delivery trucks rolled up to the back of huge printing plants at all hours of the day and late into the night to load newspapers for later delivery.

In the early years of the twentieth century, improvements in transportation allowed easy delivery of papers to the doorsteps of apartment and tenement buildings, front porches of suburban homes, and lawns of houses across the country. Delivery trucks and railroads allowed for greater circulation and sales of newspapers, especially as automobiles led more and more Americans to live outside the city. In most cities, newspapers also led the way in operating and owning some of the first radio broadcast stations. By 1933, over 220 papers owned or were affiliated with radio stations and they led the way in investment in broadcasting during the early years of the twentieth century. Forever changed by the arrival of radio broadcasting and by growing competition from weekly news magazines, newspapers remained as important in the early years of the twentieth century as they had a century earlier.

By 1900, America's cities and towns boasted some 1,967 daily papers. New York City published approximately fourteen major papers in 1900, with smaller foreign-language and weekly papers published in many of its boroughs. Newspaper circulation grew as a public eagerly read the latest investigative reporting or followed the scores of their popular professional sports teams. Newspapers in the early twentieth century expanded both in readership and in sales of ads to the nation's department stores, retail chains, and other businesses. Increased ad revenues, newsstand sales, and subscriptions made newspapers a profitable investment for some of America's wealthiest investors.

Newsstands in railroad stations, office buildings, and on street corners were a familiar part of the landscape in the early years of the twentieth century. Trolley stops, street car lines, and bus stops often saw newspaper vendors on the sidewalks—sometimes yelling out the news headlines while passengers waited for their busses, streetcars, trains, or trolleys. "Editors competed to attract readers in the split second it took to make a decision,"

George Juergens writes of the headlines in papers being sold by vendors to those waiting in lines at newsstands, on subway and trolley platforms, and at bus stops.[2] "The big modern newspaper is made with a speed that is almost bewildering," Chester S. Lord observed in his 1922 book *The Young Man and Journalism*, a speed nowhere more evident than the newsstands of America's cities where vendors offered their customers a large selection of newspapers, each with seemingly ever-larger typeface heralding the headlines of the hour.[3] William Randolph Hearst's *Los Angeles Examiner* is remembered to have printed as many as twelve editions a day and published almost 1,000,000 individual copies a day.

Newspaper editors, owners, and publishers wielded vast influence in America's political life at the beginning of the twentieth century. *New York Times*' Adolph S. Ochs, *New York Journal*'s William Randolph Hearst, *Chicago Tribune*'s Robert R. McCormick, *New York World*'s Joseph Pulitzer, and other publishers were engaged with the highest levels of the nation's elected officials. Well into the twentieth century, candidates for president counted newspaper editors and publishers as some of their closest advisors. Editors and especially publishers of some of the great papers of the day also were known to throw their own hat in the ring, so to speak, as candidates for elective office.

"Publicity is one of the purifying elements of politics," then-governor Woodrow Wilson of New Jersey told audiences in the 1912 presidential race. "The best thing that you can do with anything that is crooked is to lift it up where people can see that it is crooked, and then it will either straighten itself out or disappear. Nothing checks all the bad practices of politics like public exposure. You can't be crooked in the light. To open doors, pull up blinds, drag sick things into the open air and into the light of the sun," that Wilson said in his 1912 race for the White House, "is the importance of the press."[4] His relationship with the press raised the prominence and the proximity of newspapers to elected officials, a relationship established earlier in the century by another of the three candidates running for the White House that year.

WILLIAM MCKINLEY, WILLIAM HOWARD TAFT, WOODROW WILSON, AND EARLY-TWENTIETH-CENTURY NEWSPAPERS

While newspapers no longer had the especially close relationships with America's elected officials and its political parties they had enjoyed in the early and mid-nineteenth century, newspapers and their editors still played a decisive part in the nation's elections. Newspaper editors, publishers, and especially the reporters covering their speeches, were especially sought-after by candidates for elected office.

President McKinley's relationships with journalists in the years after the 1896 presidential race marked an important chapter in the bond between

the nation's newspapers and its elected officials. Regular briefings of reporters, sometimes on the sidewalk just outside of the gates of the White House
by members of the president's staff, began under McKinley. McKinley also
saw to it that a large table on the second floor of the White House was
cleared so that reporters might have some room to work. Early in his first
term, McKinley hired John Addison Porter, an editor with years of work
with newspapers, including the *Hartford Evening Post*, the *New York
Observer*, and the *New York Tribune*, as a special assistant to the president.
Unfortunately, Porter failed to build close relationships with many of
Washington's reporters in his time in the White House. Porter's assistant,
George Cortelyou, was promoted by McKinley in 1900, and forged closer
relationships between the president and the reporters covering the White
House.

McKinley's death on Saturday, September 14, 1901—days after his
shooting in Buffalo, New York, on Friday September 6, 1901—led his suc-
cessor, Theodore Roosevelt, to change still further the relationship between
the president and journalists. As New York City's police commissioner and
later as governor, Roosevelt cultivated close relationships with the reporters and editors of his state. New York City alone boasted some fourteen
daily papers in 1900, allowing Roosevelt to cultivate numerous friendships
with prominent editors, publishers, and reporters. His prominence rose still
further in the early years of the twentieth century as he embraced many of
the reforms growing popular with many Americans—reforms popular with
the editorial boards and reporters of many of the nation's newspapers as
well.

While overseeing the October 1902 renovations of the White House,
Roosevelt specifically instructed that the renovations include a room set
aside for reporters to work in the White House. With congressional appro-
priations of some $540,000 to renovate the main building of the White
House and to build much-needed office space, the White House press room
became one of the busiest, most crowded rooms in an already crowded
building. "The room the newsmen moved into in October 1902 was more
than just a convenience," George Juergens writes. "By conferring a sort of
legitimacy on their presence, it suggested they were no longer there just as
guests of the President." "They were filling a public function." This room off
the main lobby in the White House, built more than one hundred years ago,
is perhaps the most important nexus between governance and the press in
the United States today.[5]

Knowing well the challenges and the pressures of reporters, Roosevelt
worked with them to meet their deadlines. Roosevelt supported reporters,
who often had insufficient newsworthy materials on Sunday for their
Monday editions, by sharing items with them on Sunday evenings, thereby
assuring that his remarks would more often than not make front-page headlines in their Monday morning editions.

"Fundamental to all of Roosevelt's other accomplishments," George Juergens tells us, "was his recognition that American journalism had entered the age of the reporter."[6] Roosevelt did much to improve the relationship between the president, his cabinet, and the reporters covering the White House, yet those reporters who cast the president in what he saw as an unfair light or who quoted him without his permission found themselves cooly received in the White House. "Reporters had to toe the line to remain insiders which caused some editors to grouse that their men in the White House often seemed to be working for the President rather than their newspapers," Nathan Miller recounts.[7]

Writing an essay of some length in the *Washington Evening Star* on Tuesday, December 16, 1902, William W. Price offered some insights into the workings of the early White House press corps. "Newspaper men nowadays have access to the President, but they do not intrude upon his privacy except in cases of absolute necessity," Price explained. "All newspapermen in Washington fully realize the immense amount of work devolving upon the President and the fact that he has few spare minutes. When, however, they need to reach the fountainhead of news," Price noted of Roosevelt, "he is most accessible to newspapermen." "The needs of the newspaper staff assigned to the White House have been recognized in a satisfactory manner in the new office building just completed for the President," Price wrote of the room for the press in the newly expanded West Wing.[8] When Roosevelt traveled as president—including the first trip overseas in history taken by a sitting president—he invited reporters to join him and directed his staff to assist reporters with their travel arrangements. Roosevelt also mingled with reporters on the train when he traveled across the United States, providing them with summaries of his remarks prior to delivering his speeches.

On the evening of Tuesday, November 8, 1904, having just won reelection, Roosevelt released the following statement to the press announcing his decision not to run for another term. "Under no circumstances will I be a candidate for or accept another nomination for President." In the celebrations of the hour, Roosevelt surprised even his closest aides with a statement, which he later privately expressed some regret for releasing to reporters that night. "I would cut my hand off right there if I could recall that written statement," Roosevelt told his friends, gesturing to his own wrist.[9] Roosevelt's announcement that he would not seek another term marked a moment when the White House press corps came into its own, with reporters immediately able to relay news of the president's statement to their editors, some of whom rushed early-morning editions of their papers into print with the news.

Years after his second term, from October 1917 until his death in January 1919, Roosevelt wrote editorial columns for the *Kansas City Star*, columns that were syndicated in more than fifty newspapers across the country. William R. Nelson, editor of the *Kansas City Star*, had followed Roosevelt's career from his days as a lawmaker in New York. He became much closer to the then-vice president during the 1900 presidential race. When Roosevelt began writing his editorials for the *Kansas City Star* in September 1917, he took to calling himself a cub reporter, visiting the paper's newsroom on more than one occasion.

The former president wrote most of his editorials for the *Kansas City Star* while at his home in New York's Oyster Bay or while traveling, having them telegraphed to the Kansas City paper. Wartime controversy surrounded some of Roosevelt's editorials, especially those columns critical of President Wilson's willingness to back legislation in Congress in the spring of 1918 that made it a crime to speak out against the president and congress during wartime.[10] As in all things, Roosevelt expressed himself bluntly and boldly in these columns.

On Friday, January 3, 1919, Roosevelt dictated his final column for the *Kansas City Star* from his home at Oyster Bay. He had made arrangements to correct some proofs of a column that weekend. He passed away the following Monday, January 6, 1919, at his Oyster Bay home. Few presidents left as lasting a mark on the press of their era as Roosevelt—a figure whose familiarity with and fondness for reporters covering the White House literally brought them into the West Wing. The presence of the press in the White House—from the network television crews along the White House driveway to the rows of reporters seated in the White House press briefing room—is an enduring legacy of the Roosevelt years.

On Sunday, March 29, 1908, in a meeting of a small group of reporters at the city's Chamber of Commerce, the National Press Club was established in Washington, D.C., launching the most well-known organization for the capital's growing ranks of journalists. The club gathered at several different locations over the next several years until 1926, when the National Press Building was built on the location of the city's Ebbitt House Hotel, a short walk from the White House and Capitol Building.

As a young man, William Howard Taft worked as a reporter in Cincinnati, first with his family's newspaper, the *Cincinnati Times Star*, and then with the *Cincinnati Commercial Gazette*. The Taft family owned several papers in Ohio, ownership that continued during President Taft's son Robert's bid for the 1952 Republican nomination. Despite his personal history with newspapers, President Taft expressed little of the enthusiasm his predecessor felt toward the reporters who were now settled in the West Wing's press room. Reporters found Taft to be more measured in his relationships with the press than Roosevelt. He delivered fewer public remarks as president and declined most interviews with reporters.

Woodrow Wilson's first press conference on Saturday, March 15, 1913, saw almost 125 reporters assemble in the East Room to meet with him. "I feel that a large part of the success of public affairs depends on the news-paperman," Wilson told the reporters gathered for his first press conference. "Not so much on the editorial writers because we can live down what they say, as upon the news writers, because the news is the atmosphere of public affairs." "Wilson Wins Newspapermen," "Amazed to Have 125 Call, He Makes a Hit by His Frank Talk," the *New York Times'* headlines reported on Sunday, March 16, 1913. Wilson did not have the close relationship with the press that President Roosevelt had but he stood as a welcome break with the arms-length relationship that President Taft had with reporters.

Because of the growing number of reporters in the West Wing in the early years of the Wilson White House, a group of reporters, led by the *Washington Evening Star*'s William W. Price, founded the White House Correspondents Association (WHCA) in 1914. Announcing that "our primary objective shall be the promotion of the interests of those reporters and correspondents assigned to cover the White House," the WHCA held its first meeting on Wednesday, February 25, 1914. The WHCA would grow steadily over the next century in influence and prominence in Washington, D.C. It would work on White House pool-reports for reporters who accompanied the president when traveling as well as the credentialing of those journalists who traveled with the president and presidential candidates during their campaigns. It also continues to host its annual dinner at Washington, D.C.'s Hilton Hotel.

By the beginning of Wilson's second term, with World War I taking up much of the president and his staff's time, reporters enjoyed fewer press conferences and less contact with the president and his staff. "What Wilson promised never came to pass," explains Oswald Garrison Villard of the decline of the president's pledge to regularly hold press conferences with journalists. "Gradually," Villard recalls, "the press conferences became more irregular and took place at greater intervals."[11] By the end of Wilson's second term in the White House, the newspapers whose reporters remained a part of the day-to-day routines in the halls of the West Wing were themselves on the cusp of a new day. The birth of radio broadcasting and the growing popularity of motion pictures and the motion-picture newsreels shown in the nation's theaters changed the way news reached millions of Americans.

Financial difficulties in the early years of the twentieth century began for many newspapers a long century of financial challenges. By 1910, daily papers in the nation's cities and towns had grown to some 2,200 English-language general circulation daily papers, a slight increase from the 1,967 in circulation in 1900. Total daily circulation of these papers grew from 15,100,000 daily in 1900 to 22,400,000 by 1910. By the second decade of the twentieth century, however, a number of papers either closed their doors or were purchased by rival publishers in a wave of acquisitions, consolidations, and mergers that marked the beginning of a century-long trend in America's publishing business.

Newspapers ended the second decade of the twentieth century with new-found prominence in Washington, D.C., their pages now featuring a growing array of stories of domestic and international news, stories featuring the ever-popular motion picture industry, as well as the coverage of financial and legal news, fashion, real estate, sports, and weather. Newspapers well aware of their competition for readers pushed their reporters to pursue more investigative journalism. Newspapers now chased every possible story regarding the unethical behavior or wrongdoing of elected officials and public figures. "The World Has No Friends," a sign in the *New York World*'s newsroom reminded its reporters—a sentiment likely shared by more than a few editors and newspaper publishers as growing circulation and readership boosted competition between rival papers.

Newspaper investigations of business malfeasance, government corruption, and even the growth of financial contributions to the nation's candidates for elective office most certainly increased the circulation and readership of Joseph Pulitzer's *New York World* and any number of newspapers during this time. Newspaper investigations of the Senate in the early twentieth century likely did a great deal to further the ratification of the Seventeen Amendment. Suffrage for women was similarly championed by many newspapers in the early twentieth century. Investigative journalism, in short, was assisting in reshaping not only the issues and the terms of the debate in Washington, D.C., but the very institutions established in the Constitution itself.

HARDING, HEARST, HOOVER: NEWSPAPERS AND POLITICS IN THE 1920s

With some 2,042 daily papers in circulation in 1920, millions of Americans lived in cities with two, three, or more rival, separately owned daily papers whose competition for readership increased the circulation of papers in 1920 to an estimated 27,800,000 daily papers—papers whose pages were filled with reporting on the financial, political, and sporting news of the day as well as, in the years to follow, of stories following the growing popularity of radio broadcasting and motion pictures. Newspaper publishers were larger-than-life figures who boasted of their friendships with presidents, senators, and governors—and whose editorials and investigative stories sometimes reverberated from city halls and state legislatures all the way to the White House and Capitol Hill. Newspapers certainly faced some of their most difficult years at the end of the 1920s with the Depression-driven wave of bankruptcies, closures, and layoffs; yet newspapers still defined much of the news and the reporting of the nation's cultural, financial, and political life. Their buildings—which were sometimes some of the most recognizable buildings on the skylines of America's largest cities—and delivery trucks were a familiar presence on streets ever more crowded with automobiles, busses, streetcars, and trolleys. Even with the arrival of competition in the form of weekly news magazines—with *Time* magazine publishing its first issue on Saturday, March 3, 1923, and *Newsweek* printing its first issue on Friday, February 17, 1933—papers retained far-reaching and wide-ranging influence at every level of the nation's campaigning and governing of its elected officials.

The race between Republican Warren Harding and Democrat James M. Cox in 1920 inaugurated many innovations in twentieth-century campaigning, including the first broadcast of election night returns on Tuesday, November 2, 1920. What is less often remembered about this race is that it was a contest between two well-known publishers with long careers in the newspaper business who were challenging each other for the nation's highest office. Cox began working with his hometown paper in Dayton, Ohio, and then for a time with the *Middletown Signal*, an Ohio paper published by his brother-in-law, before moving to Cincinnati to work as a reporter for the *Cincinnati Enquirer*. In 1898, at the age of twenty-eight, Cox returned to his hometown and—with his own savings and with a loan of $6,000— purchased the *Dayton Evening News*. Years later, in the predawn hours of Tuesday, July 6, 1920, Cox learned of his nomination as the Democratic Party's presidential nominee on the telegraph in his paper's newsroom at the *Dayton Evening News*. "There was no radio in those days," Cox later recalled.[12] In 1903, Cox purchased his second paper, Ohio's *Springfield News*. Elected as the three-term governor of Ohio as well as a member of Congress, Cox won the Democratic Party's 1920 presidential nomination, running with his fellow Democrat, New York's Franklin D. Roosevelt.

Ohio's Warren Harding began his work in journalism at the age of nineteen, as a printer's apprentice and a young reporter prior to purchasing the *Marion Daily Star* in 1884. As a small Ohio town already boasting two papers, Marion seems an unlikely setting for yet another daily paper to prosper; Harding, however, succeeded in enlivening the reporting of the *Marion Daily Star*, purchasing the paper for some $300 when, in the words of one observer, "it was head over heels in debt and could be had for a mere song."[13] By 1920, the *Marion Daily Star* boasted a circulation of some 15,000, with its business offices and a print shop in downtown Marion.

His "home campaign," as Harding called it, commenced just after Notification Day on Thursday, July 22, 1920, from his family's home in Marion. Harding built a three-room bungalow near a small apple orchard behind the family home. With telephones and desks for visiting reporters, Harding's small backyard bungalow was a gathering place for the reporters. At least once a day, W.G.—as he was known by reporters—wandered in and met with the press, greeting many of the journalists by name. "Once each day and not infrequently twice, the presidential candidate, bareheaded, visited the boys in what they called their 'shed,'" Sherman A. Cuneo recalls.

"Usually he seated himself on the rail of the porch and after lighting a stogie or cigarette (more often the former, which was his favorite smoke), or 'bumming' a chew of fine cut, he'd say 'Shoot!'"[14] Harding's sympathetic disposition to the press is known to have continued in the White House after and included regular visits to gatherings of the National Press Club.

"These talks did not end with the election," biographer Sherman A. Cuneo explains of Harding's willingness to regularly meet with reporters in the White House much like he had during the 1920 presidential race. Harding's own background as a newspaper publisher is certainly one of several factors in strengthening the relationship between the White House and reporters during his tenure. Weekly press conferences and briefings by the president's staff took place in the White House and Harding attended dinners and even played cards with reporters on occasion at the National Press Club.

Three years after losing his bid for the White House, Ohio's James M. Cox began the expansion of his newspaper, purchasing Florida's *Miami Metropolis* in April 1923 for $1,000,000. The paper was renamed the *Miami Daily News* by Cox and was published until December 1988. Cox also founded WHIO, Dayton's first broadcast station. Expanding his influence into the South, Cox purchased the *Atlanta Journal* in December 1939. "Journal, WSB Sold to James M. Cox," the *Atlanta Constitution*'s morning headlines on Wednesday, December 13, 1939, reported.

"This was not," Cox recalled years later of his December 1939 purchase of the *Atlanta Journal*, "the mere acquiring of another newspaper property. Atlanta fitted perfectly into the picture of our operations between Dayton and Springfield in Ohio and Miami in Florida."[15] Cox also purchased the *Atlanta Georgian*, a paper owned by William Randolph Hearst since February 1912. Cox closed its doors shortly after the purchase. By May 1950, Cox purchased the *Atlanta Constitution*, owning both the *Atlanta Constitution*—its first issue under Cox ownership with editor Ralph McGill published on Monday, May 15, 1950—and the *Atlanta Journal*.

Broadcasting's growth after 1920 brought new challenges to newspapers, especially as the owners and publishers of America's newspapers began to invest large amounts of their fortunes into radio stations, investments that at times complemented their papers and at other times increased competition between their own papers and those of their competitors not only for advertising dollars but also for the attention and interest of the public. Still, the longer-form reporting style that newspapers did well by the 1920s kept newspaper circulation and readership at historic levels. In-depth, long-form investigations, including the *Wall Street Journal*'s investigation of the leasing of oil lands in Wyoming, known as the Teapot Dome scandal, invigorated the reputation and especially the relevance of newspapers at a time when some observers began to predict newspaper's demise.

With the headline-making, scandal-driven reporting of his newspapers as well as his acquisition of radio stations beginning in the mid-1920s, William

Randolph Hearst extended his influence over nearly every part of America's life as a nation—and most especially its campaigns for political office. Whatever the city and whatever the paper, Hearst's editors and writers stirred up the local issues of the day and participated in cutthroat competition with rival papers, setting their headlines in ever-larger boldface type to catch the attention of even the most inattentive passers-by at newsstands.

Having been elected to the House of Representatives as a Democrat in 1902 and reelected in 1904, Hearst's own political ambition was fueled still further in 1904 when seeking the Democratic Party's presidential nomination. Defeated in his bid for the Democratic Party's 1904 presidential nomination, Hearst lost his bid for New York's governor in 1906. By this time, Hearst's papers now included the *Chicago American*, the *Chicago Examiner*, the *Boston American*, and the *Los Angeles Examiner*.

Hearst's purchase of papers in some of America's largest cities grew under President Wilson and still further in the years after World War I. Hearst's 1912 purchase of the *Atlanta Georgian*, his 1917 purchase of the *Boston Daily Advertiser* and the *Washington Times*, his 1918 acquisition of the *Chicago Herald and Examiner*, and his 1921 purchase of the *Detroit Times* and the *Seattle Post Intelligencer* all were a prelude to his most lucrative year of acquisitions in 1922, when Hearst purchased the *New York Mirror*, the *Oakland Post Enquirer*, the *Rochester Journal*, the *Rochester Post Express*, the *Syracuse Telegram*, and the *Washington Herald*, the second of his two daily papers in the nation's capital. By 1923, Hearst owned twenty-two papers in fifteen cities, not to mention his purchase of news magazines and periodicals, his investment in motion picture newsreels, and his growing interest in commercial broadcasting, first in radio broadcasting and then later, after World War II, in television.

In the midst of his career's most remarkable chapter of newspaper acquisitions and purchases in the early 1920s, Hearst again briefly considered the possibility of running for the Democratic Party's presidential nomination in 1920, but postponed his race for the nomination until 1924. In yet another unsuccessful bid for the nation's highest office, Hearst's 1924 race for his party's nomination for the White House seemed to be ill-thought and short-lived. Finally, on Thursday, February 14, 1924, after weeks of working to build popular support for his bid for the Democratic nomination, Hearst withdrew his name from the race. Unsuccessful in his bids for elective office, Hearst turned his attention back to his newspapers, his acquisition of radio stations, and his later investment in some of the first commercial television stations. His life story was so remarkable that its fictionalized account in Orson Welles's classic 1941 motion picture *Citizen Kane* is still popular decades later.

In 1929, the United States had some 1,944 daily papers—with a combined daily circulation of some 39,000,000 or more—in a year when the nation's papers faced the same financial difficulties as every business in

America. Bankruptcies, layoffs, and mergers were the watchwords of newspaper publishers even before the collapse of the New York Stock Exchange on Tuesday, October 29, 1929, that began the Great Depression. Yet, in the face of financial challenges, newspapers still remained at the end of the 1930s an irreplaceable part of the lives of Americans who faced the most dire financial difficulties in their lives and who sought the most accurate and up-to-date news in their newspapers.

NEWSPAPERS AND THE NEW DEAL

With the Great Depression's financial dislocation, even America's wealthiest newspaper publishers faced declining ad sales from even their most well-established customers. They also saw the decline in circulation and sales of papers at newsstands and in home subscriptions. By 1936, the total number of daily papers had dwindled to 1,457 daily papers, with only 251 cities having competing, separately owned daily papers. Newfound competition from radio broadcasting brought still further woes to the business offices of papers as Americans spent longer hours of their day listening to radio programming and to the commercial advertising of its sponsors. In 1935—for the first time in the history of newspaper publishing—papers received less than half of the money spent in the country on advertising.

The *Washington Post* nearly closed due to financial difficulties in July 1931 and was almost purchased by William Randolph Hearst, whose own acquisition of papers had slowed during the Depression years. Washington, D.C.'s papers in 1931—the *Washington Post*, the *Washington Evening Star*, the *Washington Daily News*, and Hearst's *Washington Herald* and *Washington Times*—were all struggling financially. Of the five papers in the city, the *Washington Post* faced some of the most significant financial difficulties.

With Hearst already owning two of Washington, D.C.'s papers, it certainly seemed likely that he would purchase the *Washington Post* either to merge it with his papers or close it outright. "Hearst would, no doubt, merge *The Post* with his *Herald*," *Time* magazine reported on Monday, June 6, 1931.[16] Instead, however, the *Washington Post* remained under the publishership of Edward Beale McLean, who kept the paper's doors open. The *Washington Post* is currently the capital's leading daily paper and continues to be one of the most important papers for political reporting.

In the early days of President Franklin D. Roosevelt's first term in the White House, the president's masterful use of America's radio airwaves in the difficult days of the Depression is certainly some of the most well recalled of his administration, yet his relationship with newspaper reporters covering the White House remains an important part of this legacy. Shortly after his election, Roosevelt spoke at a dinner for members of the National

Press Club. The president also frequently sparred with some of the most well-known publishers of his day. New York's Frank E. Gannett, Chicago's Robert McCormick, and William Randolph Hearst all saw their papers set some of the largest typeface available for their front-page headlines exclaiming the latest defeats or setbacks of Roosevelt's White House.

Roosevelt frequently expressed his irritation—both in private and sometimes in public—with the editorials of the day, yet Roosevelt enjoyed close relationships with many of the reporters who covered the White House and who wrote those editorials. Reporters who traveled regularly with the president found him as accessible on his trips away from Washington, D.C., as he was in the White House. Roosevelt also hired a number of journalists to work as liaisons with the press in various administration posts, where, in the words of Graham J. White, "party hacks in press agents' jobs were replaced by experienced newsmen."[17] White House Press Secretary Stephen T. Early is a remarkable figure during the four terms of Roosevelt's White House. Early's familiarity with the demands placed upon reporters by their editors; his ease in working with reporters to meet their deadlines; his willingness to be accessible to reporters when their reporting on breaking news stories demanded it; and his willingness to press Cabinet members to pass along information in a timely manner when requested by reporters working on a deadline earned him the respect of newspaper reporters working the White House.

"President Enjoys First Conference with Correspondents," the *New York Times'* Thursday, March 9, 1933, headline told its readers the day after the president's first of almost one thousand such meetings with the press over the next twelve years. "Roosevelt at Ease in Chat with Press," another *New York Times'* headline enthused. "Roosevelt Meets His Problems, and the Press, with a Smile," read the caption beneath a photograph of a smiling president surrounded by reporters at his desk at that first press conference. In fact, Roosevelt's twice-weekly press conferences in the Oval Office became a crucial part of his work with reporters covering his White House. To this day, photographs of these Oval Office press conferences capture in black-and-white images the crowds of reporters standing with their pens and their notebooks in front of Roosevelt's desk. The president's ease and enjoyment of these sessions is evident in many of these photos. The expressions on the faces of many of the reporters standing in front of the president's desk seem to show that reporters also enjoyed these back-and-forth sessions with the president. Reporters later remarked on the president's grasp of even the smallest details of pending legislation in Congress, in the latest financial or economic reports, or in the matters of international diplomacy when war came during his third term in the White House.

First Lady Eleanor Roosevelt began her own conferences with reporters who covered the White House and Capitol Hill on Monday, March 6, 1933. These press conferences continued well into her husband's tenure in the

White House. Years later, Roosevelt wrote her own newspaper column, "My Day," which was syndicated in papers across the country. The First Lady held more than three hundred of her own press conferences, which included members of the Newspaper Women's Club of Washington, D.C. The president and his wife not only hosted receptions for reporters at the White House—as well as their home in New York when reporters traveled there—but also expanded the press room in the West Wing to allow for greater space for the reporters to write and to telephone their newspapers when filing their stories.

Day after day, the *Chicago Tribune*, the *New York Herald Tribune*, and other papers in some of the nation's largest cities published editorial items opposed to the president—especially during his first campaign for reelection in 1936. Hearst's papers frequently ran editorials denouncing Roosevelt's "Raw Deal." Still, no publisher had as unique a vantage to express himself in the 1936 race as Chicago publisher Frank Knox—running-mate with the Republican nominee, Governor Alfred Landon of Kansas. Knox—a former general manager of Hearst's newspaper division and publisher of his city's largest circulation afternoon paper, the *Chicago Daily News*—had years of experience in the newspaper business, beginning his career as a young reporter in Grand Rapids, Michigan, then later serving as founding editor of New Hampshire's *Manchester Leader*. As Landon's running mate, Knox's place on his party's ticket evidenced yet again the commingling of newspaper publishing and the nation's candidates for political office.

Between Roosevelt's reelection for his second term on Tuesday, November 3, 1936, and his successful third-term bid on Tuesday, November 5, 1940, the clashes between the White House and some of the nation's most outspoken newspaper publishers by no means subsided. Yet these disagreements were eventually overwhelmed by the front-page headlines covering the war in Europe and, eventually, America's entry into World War II after the attack at Pearl Harbor on Sunday, December 7, 1941. Newspaper circulation and readership held steady during the war—much as it had during the financial difficulties of the Depression—even as radio broadcasting took a larger place in the lives of most Americans. Newspaper circulation, especially the multiple-edition papers whose headlines and stories might be updated on the hour in some cities, grew during wartime even as more and more American households spent more time listening to the radio. Newspapers—not only the larger city metropolitan papers but also many of the smaller town daily and weekly papers—were heroic in their efforts to bring the news of the day to Americans during World War II, facing wartime shortages in everything from the reporters who wrote the stories to the scarcity of ink, paper, and supplies needed to put out a paper.

In 1944, one of America's most well-regarded journalists expressed his concern with changes in the ownership of newspapers, as rival newspapers continued to acquire, consolidate, and merge with their competitors' newspapers in many cities, sometimes purchasing rival papers only to close them down. In the 1944 book *The Disappearing Daily*, Oswald Garrison Villard expressed concern with the trends in ownership of newspapers, especially given that hundreds of daily newspapers had been closed through consolidation or merger since 1909. "The outstanding fact in any survey of the American press is the steady and alarming decrease in the number of dailies," Villard told his readers.[18] "Consolidation, suppression, and a strong drift toward monopoly are taking their toll," Villard warned. "To establish a press monopoly in a locality is to restrict the field of public information or to narrow its vision."[19] Once-thriving papers closed their doors, sometimes merging with their one-time rivals, at other times closed by their owners due to financial bankruptcy. By war's end in 1945, only 117 cities and towns had two or more competing daily papers in circulation, a continued decline in the circulation and readership of afternoon and early evening papers accounted for much of this decline.

Well into the twentieth century, reporters were a familiar presence on the campaign trail, especially as candidates for elected office traveled more extensively beginning in the 1920s by railroad (and later by airplane) rather than remain at their homes for much of their campaigns as was the customary practice in much of the nineteenth century. Elaborately outfitted private railroad cars (and later chartered airplanes) became a familiar setting for reporters who traveled with the candidates, a scene well documented in the accounts (and photographs) of reporters who traveled by train with President Truman during his 1948 reelection bid. Newspaper reporters riding the rails with the president, the vice president, the rival ticket of New York's governor Thomas E. Dewey and California's governor Earl Warren, the families of the candidates, and their staff—and boarding and re-boarding the train at every stop and at every speech of the candidates along the way—spent much of their day in specially outfitted railroad cars. These railroad cars were equipped with window-facing wooden tables that ran the full length of the cars. Reporters' backs were to one another facing the windows as mile after mile of the countryside rolled by and as they typed their bylines and stories of the campaign. Black-and-white photographs survive that show reporters traveling with Truman and Dewey on their trains in the 1948 race.

A single evening's headline from the final hours of that year's race is forever remembered as not only an important historical moment in the history of 1948 but also as one of the most iconographic images in the history of twentieth-century presidential campaigns. Photographs of President Truman in the hours after his reelection taken by photographers accompanying the president to Washington, D.C., from Missouri, where the president spent the day of the election, show the president holding aloft one of the twentieth century's most famous newspaper headlines: "Dewey Defeats Truman." This photograph of Truman in St. Louis's Union Station taken by photographer

Pete Hangge of the *St. Louis Globe Democrat* is an iconographic image in the history of political campaigning.

As famous as the *Chicago Tribune*'s headline: "Dewey Defeats Truman" is to the history of twentieth-century papers, a much less-noticed headline in that paper some weeks earlier drew the attention of readers to a business investment by the *Tribune*'s owners that marked the beginning of yet another challenge to the nation's papers. The Monday, April 5, 1948, headline announced: "WGN TV Makes Debut Tonight with Big Show, 2 Hour Salute Begins at 7:45 P.M." The *Tribune*-owned television station, WGN-TV, would be the first post-war television station in Chicago and would grow larger after the arrival of the coaxial cable made coast-to-coast commercial television possible. The *Chicago Tribune*'s ownership of WGN-TV a station owned and operated by the *Chicago Tribune* as a radio station since 1924, led the way for commercial television broadcasting and was a significant challenge to the circulation, readership, and sales of newspapers.

NEWSPAPERS IN THE NEW CENTURY

Newspapers in the second half of the twentieth century saw some of their most serious financial challenges to date, yet they also remained a vital, vibrant part of the lives of millions of Americans, especially in the nation's political campaigns. By the beginning of the 1960s, newspapers saw themselves facing the challenge of the first major period of growth of television broadcasting that began in the mid- to late 1940s and culminated in 1960 when almost 90 percent of American households owned televisions.

Newspapers were familiar parts of the daily life of Americans by the end of the World War II and into the postwar years. Historians and archivists working with the microfilm records of America's newspapers in the 1950s and even still in the 1960s bring from that experience a sense of the reporting of newspapers well into the second half of the twentieth century. "A good newspaper is a nation talking to itself," wrote playwright Arthur Miller.[20] In the 1940s and even well into the 1950s for many of America's larger circulation and even its smaller circulation papers, the conversation, to use Miller's phrase, is remembered as being as lively and robust as almost any time in the history of twentieth-century newspapers.

Newspapers by the end of the 1950s and the early 1960s boasted a number of widely read columnists, whose writings remained some of the most influential reporting of their day. Walter Lippmann, Ralph McGill, Drew Pearson, Walter Winchell, and other columnists penned a seemingly endless array of columns, many of which were nationally syndicated, that reached from their newspaper offices to the White House and Capitol Hill.

Newspapers proved very influential with political campaigns and with party leaders in the mid-twentieth century. Editors and publishers remained figures of influence within the parties and were well accustomed to meeting with elected officials at the highest levels. James M. Cox's ownership of newspapers and broadcast stations made him a prominent figure in the Democratic Party, with several of his senior employees regularly assisting candidates for office, including Truman's 1948 reelection and Senator John F. Kennedy's 1960 race for president.[21] Eugene Meyer of the *Washington Post* held influence within the Republican Party well after World War II, including advising then-governor Earl Warren of California in his decision to accept the vice presidential nomination for the 1948 Republican ticket. The Taft family and their paper, the *Cincinnati Times Star*, carried their influence in Ohio politics and throughout the country influencing Republican leaders well into the 1950s.

In the years after World War II and into the early years of commercial television broadcasting, Washington, D.C., was a city where newspaper reporters and their news bureaus were considered the nexus of the world of campaigning and publishing. Newspapers with large circulations like the *Boston Post*, the *Chicago Daily News*, the *Cleveland Plain Dealer*, the *Dallas Times Herald*, the *Dayton Journal Herald*, the *Detroit Free Press*, the *Louisville Courier Journal*, the *New York Herald Tribune*, the *New York World*, the *St. Louis Post Dispatch*, and others wielded influence through their editorials and their reporting, some maintaining Washington, D.C., bureaus with as many as twenty or more reporters stationed in the nation's capital. "These reporters," Douglass Cater writes in his 1959 book *The Fourth Branch of Government*, "are the most direct spiritual heirs of the long tradition of the Washington correspondent."[22]

"In the years immediately after World War II," James L. Baughman writes, "the typical American family took one, sometimes two, daily papers." "Nationally," Baughman adds, "newspaper circulation per households had remained relatively constant between 1923 and 1953."[23] Still, by 1960, the number of daily papers had fallen to fewer than 1,800 papers, with the closure of once-thriving city papers even as the country's fast-growing suburban areas saw their own local daily and weekly papers begin to grow in this same period. The *Cincinnati Times Star*, an afternoon paper owned by the Taft family, was purchased in August 1958 by its longtime rival, the *Cincinnati Post*. The *Cleveland News*, the *Pittsburgh Sun Telegraph*, and the *Detroit Times* all closed their doors in 1960. The Thursday, January 4, 1962, closing of the *Los Angeles Evening Mirror* and the purchase of the *Houston Press* by the *Houston Chronicle* on Friday, March 20, 1964, ceased the publication of still more evening newspapers. The closing of the *New York Herald Tribune* on Monday, August 15, 1966, after years of financial difficulties was felt throughout the publishing industry as yet another once-thriving paper closed its doors.

"Freedom of the press is guaranteed only to those who own one," journalist Abbott Joseph Liebling penned in the Saturday, May 14, 1960, issue of the *New Yorker*. This essay, titled "Do You Belong in Journalism?," is remembered for its attention to the closure of some of America's great twentieth-century metropolitan papers and the decline of cities with competing, independently owned papers.[24] "Mortality among newspapers has been high from the twenties on," Liebling writes in his oft-cited essay, "but the last years have brought a quickening of decimation. The worst of it is that each newspaper disappearing below the horizon carries with it, if not a point of view, at least a potential emplacement for one."[25] Competing, independently owned daily papers in sixty-five cities in 1960, declining to sixty-one cities in 1961, and still further to fifty-three in 1962, is the backdrop for A. J. Liebling's oft-cited memorable phrase about the decline of competitive, independently owned newspapers, to "a monovocal, monopolistic, monocular press" evident in the early to mid-1960s.

The suburbanization of the nation's population outside major cities contributed to the difficulties of newspapers, especially afternoon papers that thrived in the era prior to the growth of the automobile commuter's late-afternoon rush-hour drive. "The increased sprawl of communities, coupled with the astronomical growth of automobile traffic, has compounded the task of distributing the newspaper's daily edition," writes Jack Lyle in *The News in Megalopolis*.[26] By 1968, only forty-five cities had locally owned, competing daily papers, a trend continuing with the closure of daily papers in cities that mirrored the continuing exodus of residents to the suburbs where weekly papers and television news broadcasts served to replace the reading of the daily paper.

The suburbanization of America made it costly for most of the nation's largest papers to continue to circulate their newspapers and the time spent by commuters in their automobiles made it difficult to maintain newspaper circulation. Figures at this time indicate a decline from 34 percent of Americans reading two or more daily papers in 1961 to 32 percent in 1970, falling still further to just 20 percent of Americans reading two or more daily papers in 1979.[27] Television's reach by the early 1970s combined with the introduction of cable television—and the rise by the end of the decade of dedicated, twenty-four-hour cable news channels—certainly posed a challenge to newspapers, not least of which was the increased cost to households for both newspaper subscriptions and cable television bills.

In the years after World War II, candidates for elective office continued to keep their relationships with newspaper publishers, editors, and with individual reporters close. California's Richard M. Nixon, while running for the House of Representatives in 1946, enjoyed a close relationship with the *Los Angeles Times*. President Eisenhower's friendships with William E. Robinson of the *New York Herald Tribune* and Roy A. Roberts of the *Kansas City Star* are remembered as exceptionally strong. Reporters on Capitol Hill, who were still predominantly newspaper-affiliated reporters, extended their influence over groups such as the National Press Club and the WHCA.

President John F. Kennedy, known for his skillful use of commercial television broadcasting, is remembered as having close friendships with a number of newspaper editors and publishers. Kennedy, who worked for a time as a correspondent for Hearst's *Chicago Herald Examiner* covering elections in Great Britain as well as the 1945 charter conference of the United Nations, famously sparred with and complained to editors, publishers, and individual reporters about their papers' coverage of his administration. When Kennedy held his first live televised press conference on Wednesday, January 25, 1961, he told reporters that he read several papers every day, including the *Baltimore Sun*, the *Chicago Tribune*, the *New York Herald Tribune*, the *New York Times*, the *St. Louis Post Dispatch*, the *Washington Evening Star*, and the *Washington Post*. *New York Times* photographer George Tames, who shot an iconic image of Kennedy in the Oval Office, related that at the moment that photograph was taken the president was complaining about a news story in the pages of Tames's own *New York Times*.

Newspapers figured prominently in the nation's political life in the late 1960s and early 1970s. The investigative reporting by the *New York Times*, the *Washington Post*, and other papers uncovered the involvement of Nixon's White House in obstructing the federal investigation of a break-in at the Democratic National Committee offices in Washington, D.C. Newspapers were often the recipients of sharp rebukes by President Nixon during and after the 1972 campaign as reporters with the *Washington Post* and other papers detailed allegations of White House connections with the Watergate break-in. Even so, and in spite of his strained relations with many journalists and reporters as well as their editors and editorial boards, Nixon carefully kept his relationships with newspaper owners and publishers close—relationships initially formed with the *Los Angeles Times* early in Nixon's political career. Publication of large portions of a classified Department of Defense history of the Vietnam War in the *New York Times*, the *Washington Post*, and other papers made newspapers central to the leading stories of the day.

On Thursday, August 8, 1974, President Nixon, in a televised address to the nation, announced his resignation from office effective Friday, August 9, 1974, at 12:00 noon. The investigative reporting by the *Washington Post*'s Carl Bernstein and Bob Woodward was one of the highest profiled journalistic event to date. The story began months earlier with the pair's first of many front-page headlines, "G.O.P. Security Aide among 5 Arrested in Bugging Affair," published in the Monday, June 19, 1972, issue of the *Washington Post*. Black-and-white photographs of the *Washington Post*'s executive editor, Benjamin C. Bradlee, the paper's owner and publisher, Katharine Graham, and the editorial and reporting staff conferring on the investigations of the Nixon administration in the paper's newsroom remain some of the twentieth century's most iconographic images of journalism and newspaper publishing. Well remembered, too, is the photograph of Bernstein sitting in a chair and Woodward sitting on the floor of a small newsroom office at the *Washington Post* watching a televised image of one of Nixon's televised addresses.

That same Sunday morning, June 18, 1972, as newspaper readers in the nation's capital awoke to see the first story to appear in the *Washington Post* reporting on the five men arrested at the Democratic National Committee offices ("5 Held in Plot to Bug Democrats' Office Here")—is also the day the *Boston Herald Traveler* went to press with its last run after 125 years of publication. Weeks later, the Wednesday, July 12, 1972, headlines—and the accompanying photographs of pressmen examining the final run of the *Washington Daily News*—announced the news of the closing of the Washington, D.C., afternoon paper after fifty years of publication. Closings of the *Boston Herald Traveler* and the *Washington Daily News* left Chicago and New York City as the only cities in the United States with more than two separately owned, general circulation daily papers.

Newspapers, owners, reporters, and most certainly readers of newspapers—especially those in the broadcast media that often begin their days with newspapers and have much of their own broadcast coverage and reporting shaped by stories in newspapers—remained a familiar part of the nation's political landscape in the 1970s and in the years to follow. Candidates for elected office began their careers by cultivating their own relationships with papers, their editorial boards, their reporters, and the owners and publishers of these newspapers. With the beginning of regularly televised presidential and vice presidential debates during the 1976 presidential race, newspaper editors and reporters were called upon to moderate these debates, a reminder of newspapers' continued importance to political candidates.

"Newspapers Challenged as Never Before," the Friday, November 26, 1976, *Los Angeles Times* headline announced; a headline that reported yet again the all-too-familiar story of the fading financial fortunes of newspapers facing another decade of acquisitions, closures, and consolidations. The closing of the *Chicago Daily News* on Saturday, March 4, 1978, left that city with just two daily papers, the *Chicago Tribune* and the *Chicago Sun Times*—and left New York City as the last city in the United States with three or more separately owned daily papers. The closure of the *Washington Evening Star* on Friday, August 7, 1981, long the home to a number of nationally recognized columnists and reporters, marked a significant departure of journalism from the nation's capital. As its editorial and reporting staff shared their final day together and as its final issue went to press on the afternoon of Friday, August 7, 1981, the *Washington Evening Star* drew bipartisan praise from President Ronald Reagan and Speaker of the House Thomas P. "Tip" O'Neill as well as from numerous other figures in the capital and from its publishing rival, the *Washington Post*.

Newspaper closures continued well into the 1980s, bringing still more difficult news to the once-thriving publishing industry—an industry, in the words of *New York Times*' Alex S. Jones, "that is being steadily transformed by decades of pressure from rival media and a national lifestyle that has altered reading habits."[28] Newspapers featured stories of these closings—stories frequently accompanied by black-and-white photographs of newsrooms crowded with reporters as they listened to the announcements of their papers' closures or sometimes by photographs showing their printing presses and printing press workers holding copies of the paper's final run. The *Philadelphia Bulletin*, a 134-year-old paper and once the nation's largest circulating afternoon newspaper, closed its doors on Friday, January 29, 1982. The *Minneapolis Star*—at one time the largest circulation paper in the Twin Cities—closed its doors on Friday, April 2, 1982. The *Des Moines Tribune* closed its doors on Wednesday, June 2, 1982. The *Cleveland Press*, carrying the headline "Press Halts Production," closed its doors on Thursday, June 17, 1982. It was purchased by its rival, the *Cleveland Plain Dealer*. The *Baltimore News American* published its last issue running the front-page headline "So Long, Baltimore" on Tuesday, May 27, 1986, leaving the *Baltimore Sun* as that city's only daily newspaper. The *St. Louis Globe-Democrat* closed its doors on Wednesday, October 29, 1986. The closure of the *Los Angeles Herald Examiner* on Thursday, November 2, 1989—an afternoon paper with a daily circulation of some 238,000 with an estimated monthly loss of approximately $2,000,000 at the time of its closing—meant that the nation's second-largest and most diverse city had only a single major daily paper, the *Los Angeles Times*. The purchase of the *Dallas Times Herald* on Monday, December 9, 1991, by its rival, the *Dallas Morning News*, led to the closing of yet another well-known metropolitan newspaper, after some 112 years of competition. Weeks earlier, the closing of Little Rock's *Arkansas Gazette* on Friday, October 18, 1991, which had been in circulation for 172 years, left the historic Gazette Building vacant in downtown Little Rock, a building that once served as the national offices for the 1992 presidential campaign of then-governor Bill Clinton.

The decline in the number of cities in the United States with two or more competitive, independently owned and independently published daily papers is a remarkable—and not often enough remarked upon—story of the twentieth century's history of the press. After the storied heyday of America's newspaper publishing and its legendary rivalries between the publishers of some of the great newspapers in the nation's larger cities at the end of the nineteen century, America began the twentieth century with some 559 cities and towns with separately owned, competing daily papers in 1900. By 1910, that number grew to some 689 cities and towns in the United States boasting two or more competing, separately owned papers. That number declined to 552 cities or towns with two or more competing, independently owned rival papers in 1920, beginning a sudden and startling decline in the early decades of the twentieth century. "Only a few dozen American cities can observe freedom of the press lifted in the daily newspaper field above the realms of academic discussion and made vital," wrote Alfred McClung Lee in July 1939, well before the postwar disappearance of even more cities home to two or more competing daily papers.[29]

"Perhaps the greatest industry transformation," writes James L. Baughman of the twentieth century, "[is] the decline of, indeed, the disappearance of, local competition."[30] From some 502 cities with two or more separately owned daily papers in 1923, America's cities with independently owned, competitive papers declined steadily in the twentieth century—a disappearance in town after town, which deprived once-loyal readers of the papers they had read and relied on for so many years and a disappearance of once-thriving rivalries between papers, their owners, and their reporters.

New York City's *New York Times*, *New York Post*, *New York Daily News*, and *Wall Street Journal* as well as its suburban dailies offer the largest number of competing, separately owned daily papers in any metropolitan area in the United States today. Boston, Chicago, Los Angeles (with *The Los Angeles Times* and San Fernando Valley's *The Los Angeles Daily News* offering the largest circulation of a dozen or more daily papers in the surrounding metropolitan area), and Washington, D.C., all boast two competing, separately owned daily papers, not including the suburban daily papers in these cities and in the metropolitan areas of most of the country's larger cities. Colorado's *Aspen Daily News* and *Aspen Times* and New Jersey's *Trenton Times* and *Trentonian*, are among the towns with separately owned, competing daily papers still in circulation.

The Arkansas Gazette. The Brooklyn Eagle. The Chicago Daily News. The Cincinnati Times Star. The Cleveland News. The Dallas Times Herald. The Houston Press. The Houston Post. The Indianapolis Times. The Kansas City Journal Post. The Kansas City Times. The Los Angeles Daily News. The Los Angeles Evening Mirror. The Los Angeles Herald Examiner. The New York Herald Tribune. The Newark Evening News. The Philadelphia Bulletin. The Pittsburgh Press. The St. Louis Globe Democrat. The St. Louis Times Star. The Washington Daily News. The Washington Evening Star. The Washington Herald. Not so much as even a bronze marker or plaque on the buildings of these now-defunct, all-but-forgotten papers recalls the hundreds upon hundreds of men and women who once worked there. These papers and others were once thriving newsrooms and were at the forefront of the nation's political life.

In the early years of the twenty-first century some of the nation's largest, once-thriving papers—among them the *Baltimore Sun*, the *Boston Globe*, the *Chicago Sun Times*, the *Minneapolis Star Tribune*, the *Philadelphia Inquirer*, and the *San Francisco Chronicle*—have all faced fiscal setbacks and strains. The *Cincinnati Post*, one of the last large circulation afternoon daily newspapers in the country, closed its doors on Thursday, December 31,

2007. The closing of Denver's *Rocky Mountain News* on Friday, February 27, 2009, ended a long tradition of competitive daily newspapers in that city, as did the Tuesday, March 17, 2009, closure of the print edition of the *Seattle Post Intelligencer* just days later. In a city known for its cutting-edge, high-tech innovations, the *Seattle Post Intelligencer* was the first large circulation newspaper in the United States to entirely shift its publication to an online-only version. "Wounded but not slain," James L. Baughman calls the late-twentieth-century newspaper, a profitable enterprise for those publishers remaining in the business even with the decline in circulation and readership, and a still-robust business for publishers in what essentially are monopoly marketplaces in all but a handful of America's cities today.[31] It is certainly clear that fewer reporting staff in newsrooms at the beginning of the twenty-first century leaves fewer reporters to do in-depth investigative reporting. In Washington, D.C., it is certainly clear that fewer reporters represent their papers in the nation's capital.

"Big News in Washington, but Far Fewer Cover It," the *New York Times* reported on Thursday, December 18, 2008.[32] At the state level, the downward trend in reporters covering state capitals is even more evident. And at the local level—where in-depth investigations and the kind of long-form reporting on municipal governance is possible only with the financial assets, staff time, and reputations available to newspapers—reporting is even more infrequent. This is a far cry from the time in many cities when newspapers, their editors, and the stories covered by their reporters were once as feared and as formidable for their headlines as any judicial proceedings or official investigations.

Well established as this trend is, newspapers still wield considerable influence and prominence with political candidacies currently seeking office. Editorial boards and reporters remain close to the campaigns and provide wide-spread coverage, especially in states with early primaries or with crucially close elections. Iowa's *Des Moines Register* and New Hampshire's *New Hampshire Union Leader* (formerly the *Manchester Union Leader*) exert significant influence in the coverage and reporting of the nation's presidential nomination campaigns. Their editors, publishers, and reporters remain well-known figures during the race for the White House. Well represented, also, is the presence of newspaper editors, columnists, and reporters in the corridors of power and on the campaign trail. Figures such as MSNBC's Chris Matthews, after leaving his Capitol Hill post as an aide to then-Speaker of the House Thomas P. "Tip" O'Neill Jr., became the Washington, D.C., bureau chief for the *San Francisco Examiner*. Al Gore began his career, after graduating from Harvard University and completing military service in Vietnam, as a reporter with Nashville's *Tennessean*, working for the paper for five years prior to his election to serve in the House of Representatives in 1977 at the age of twenty-eight. David Axelrod's tenure at the *Chicago Tribune* in the 1980s preceded his work advising candidates for elective office, working first with then-senator Paul Simon in his 1984 reelection bid, then Chicago's mayor Harold L. Washington, and eventually advising then-senator Barack Obama in the 2008 presidential race. He eventually worked in the White House as senior advisor to the president.

Weekly and daily print publications, including the *Hill*, *Roll Call*, and *Politico*—the latter published in a printed edition in Washington, D.C., with some 34,000 free copies distributed in locations throughout the city and a familiar publication in the hallways of office buildings on Capitol Hill—all shape the reporting of legislative debate on the nation's broadcast and digital media in far-reaching ways. The press galleries in the House of Representatives and the Senate and the flash of cameras in hearing rooms across Capitol Hill serve as reminders of the presence of newspaper reporters and their colleagues in television and radio broadcasting. Many of the forty-nine seats for the reporters who assemble daily in the James S. Brady Press Briefing Room are set aside for White House reporters representing newspapers and wire services. In all, some one thousand reporters are credentialed by the White House to attend press conferences, special press briefings, bill signing ceremonies, and other events, with one hundred or so reporters, many of them affiliated with the nation's papers, working in the White House on any typical day when the president is in Washington, D.C. Hundreds of reporters—of the approximately six thousand credentialed journalists who cover the work of the House of Representatives and the Senate—work the hallways of the Capitol and its nearby office buildings. Members of the House of Representatives and the Senate have press secretaries who issue a steady stream of press releases and hold press conferences and conference calls where reporters, especially with papers located in their home districts and states, are briefed on the latest news from Capitol Hill.

Newspapers from across the United States, their front pages prominently displayed daily in glass cases in front of Washington, D.C.'s Newseum located on Pennsylvania Avenue, just blocks from both the White House and Capitol Hill, stand as testimony to the continued vitality of papers in the daily life of the nation. The Newseum's seventy-four-foot-high engraving of the First Amendment on the front of their building facing Pennsylvania Avenue reminds thousands of passers-by each day that the spirit that protects free speech is alive and well. The Newseum's display of the nation's newspapers on the sidewalk of Pennsylvania Avenue is a remarkable reminder of the relevance and the resilience of America's grand and great tradition of newspapers beginning with Benjamin Harris's first and only issue of *Publick Occurrences Both Foreign and Domestick* sold from his Boston print shop on Thursday, September 25, 1690, through the current day's headlines found displayed in the Newseum's glass cases.

Newspaper circulation and readership in the United States at the beginning of the twenty-first century clearly face innumerable challenges in a time of declining circulation and readership, yet newspapers play an irreplaceable role in holding elected officials accountable, in educating and informing the nation's electorate, in providing a conduit for elected officials to bring sustained discussion on policy to the public, in bringing the enduring importance of newspapers to television and the Internet in the hosting of nearly all major broadcast debates by newspaper reporters, and still producing a profit for their investors and owners. This last achievement, however, is one that is becoming more and more difficult for newspapers. The cost of newsprint, the expenses for fuel for delivery trucks and the labor costs for their drivers, and the costs of editorial and reporting staff continue to pose financial difficulties for newspapers—even as newspapers generate billions of dollars in advertising revenue and remain profitable investments for Warren Buffet and other such investors. Beset as they are, newspapers remain as vital to the nation in the twenty-first century as they were in the nineteenth.

Chapter 4

Radio and the Rise of Broadcast Politics

The history of radio in the early years of the twentieth century is the history of America's politics in the twentieth century. America's homes, apartment buildings, department stores, and businesses in the mid-1920s crackled to life with the voices of radio broadcasts, and the nation's political life was transformed in ways unimaginable to that first generation of electrical engineers whose experiments pioneered broadcasting in the early twentieth century. During this remarkable period of time, America's airwaves buzzed with everything from operas and weather reports to college basketball games and presidential nominating conventions. Financial news, sporting events in distant cities, and entertainment programs of all kinds became a familiar part of American life. Newspaper's greatest publishers, including William Randolph Hearst, Frank E. Gannett, and James M. Cox, invested a portion of their fortunes in radio broadcasting.

The early twentieth century saw the federal government begin a century-long effort to commercially regulate radio broadcasting. As America entered into World War I, government officials restricted all private wireless transmitters and experimental radio stations. America's wireless enthusiasts and hobbyists closed down their transmitters, and backyard engineers and basement enthusiasts packed away their wireless equipment when federal authorities issued a closure order in April 1917. Some tried to argue that their stations might be put to wartime use in surveillance of German telegraph transmissions.

At the end of World War I, the federal government relaxed its wartime ban on wireless transmitters while introducing still more federal regulations of the nation's airwaves. With America's airwaves a bedlam in the early 1920s, radio's innovators and especially its business investors soon backed calls for tighter regulation of the airwaves. Informal agreements between some stations to honor "silent nights"—times in the evening when smaller transmitters lowered their signals to allow larger commercial transmitters to broadcast a clearer signal without interference—were ignored, and, as radio stations popped up around the country, chaos ensued.

The growth of commercial radio broadcasting in the early and mid-1920s had a significant impact not only as an investment opportunity and entertainment vehicle but also as a force that helped reshape the nation's political life. It no doubt strengthened the roots of America's national identity and lifted the public's attention in ways never before seen by lawmakers in Washington, D.C. Radio broadcasting of politicians' speeches as well as the campaign speeches of candidates seeking offices redefined the geography of the nation's electoral politics, carrying nominating conventions, speeches, and news coverage into isolated areas where it was once all but impossible for Americans to hear.

The early years of radio broadcasting were transformative for the nation's political parties and its candidates for elected office. A candidate's speech could now be carried across entire regions and eventually the whole country. Tried-and-true stem-winding stump speeches by candidates gave way to the more conversational cadences of radio broadcasts. Conversational forms of speech delivery—the most familiar of which are found in the recordings of President Franklin D. Roosevelt's broadcasts from the White House, which began on the evening of Sunday, March 12, 1933—took hold for a new generation of candidates and elected officials.

"The time is forever past when party leaders speak for their candidate," New York's Governor Alfred E. Smith explained in July 1928. "Radio has made the candidate speak for himself directly to the citizens," Smith observed.[1] Elected officials and the candidates campaigning for office became familiar presences in the homes of the millions of American families who owned radios, families that might live at a distance from campaign rallies or speeches, families that might, indeed, never see a candidate face-to-face were now able to hear their words over their radios.

RADIO IN THE EARLY 1900s

The earliest history of the transmission of wireless signals is a story bound together by some of the most well-known European inventors and electrical pioneers as well as a group of American inventors whose own accomplishments were not insignificant. Guglielmo Marconi's 1895 experiments with "wireless telegraphy"—as he called it—and his incorporation of the Wireless Telegraph and Signal Company in July 1897 were acclaimed on both sides of the Atlantic Ocean. Marconi's experiments had been publicized in the United States as early as March 1897 in *McClure's Magazine* and *Telegraph*

Age, both of which heralded Marconi telegraphy as "telegraphy without wires."

Eager to foster the expansion of wireless innovation in the United States, both the Weather Bureau and later the U.S. Navy financed portions of the work done by the Canadian scientist Reginald Aubrey Fessenden. Fessenden—who settled with his family on the shoreline of the Maryland coast—and his assistants built a small wooden shack for their laboratory and erected two large wooden towers for their experiments on Maryland's Cobb Island, located forty-five miles southeast of Washington, D.C. Fessenden's work on Cobb Island continued for the next two years as he and his staff erected towers and built shacks for their experiments with wireless transmissions along the Atlantic coastline in Maryland, North Carolina, and Virginia.

On Sunday, December 23, 1900, Fessenden transmitted the sound of his voice by wireless transmission from his Cobb Island experimental station to his assistant, Alfred H. Theiessen, a meteorologist with years of service in the Weather Bureau, fifty yards away. After sending an inaudible transmission some hours earlier that same day, Fessenden sent the voice message, "One, two, three, four. Is it snowing where you are, Mr. Thiessen? If it is, would you telegraph me back?" This message was the first voice ever transmitted by wireless and heard by another person.

"It is a success," the Weather Bureau's Willis S. Moore told reporters in February 1901 of the wireless telegraphy experiment on Maryland's Cobb Island. "We have been experimenting for a year at Cobb Island in the Potomac River, 70 miles below Washington," Moore explained. "We have completed an apparatus that we expect will enable us to signal ships 500 miles or more out at sea," Moore added; he went on to announce the Weather Bureau's building of stations for wireless experiments on North Carolina's Roanoke Island and at Virginia's Cape Henry.[2]

Having successfully experimented with their transmissions on Cobb Island, Fessenden and his assistants disassembled their two wooden towers and packed up the equipment in their wooden shack in January 1901 and moved it to a larger station on Roanoke Island, North Carolina. The move proved difficult and the towers were nearly lost in the rough seas of the Outer Banks. They were ultimately successful, however, and brought their equipment to the docks at Manteo on North Carolina's Roanoke Island.

Weather Bureau buildings on North Carolina's Outer Banks offered a much larger setting for Fessenden and his staff who reassembled their equipment and expanded their stations to several locations on the Outer Banks and at Virginia's Cape Henry. Fessenden and his family, accompanied by his assistants, took up residence along the North Carolina coastline. They worked out of houses built by the Weather Bureau and constructed several large wooden towers on the beaches of Cape Hatteras and on the shores of Roanoke Island. One of the towers brought from Cobb Island was raised on the northeastern shoreline of Roanoke Island at Weir Point near what is today the Croatian Sound Bridge. The second mast brought from Cobb Island was raised on Hatteras Island near the town of Buxton. This site is operated today by the Dare County Parks and Recreation Department. Sometime later, a third tower was erected 104 miles away at Cape Henry, Virginia.

By the summer of 1901, Fessenden and his staff, at their main transmitting station on the shoreline of Roanoke Island, were experimenting on a regular basis with wireless signals transmitted a distance of fifty-three miles to their station in Buxton on Cape Hatteras as well as with transmissions a distance of 104 miles to a station on Virginia's Cape Henry. From Roanoke Island, Fessenden and his assistants traveled back and forth by ship to the Cape Henry station and by horseback to their station in Buxton. In April 1902, performances on violins and other instruments by Fessenden and his assistants were transmitted for the first time from Cape Hatteras to Roanoke on what Fessenden called his "Hatteras-Roanoke line." "Very loud and plain" is how Fessenden described those April's transmissions. "The new receiver is a wonder," Fessenden wrote of his transmissions between Cape Hatteras and his main station on Roanoke Island's shoreline.

"The age of the cable has passed," Fessenden told newspaper reporters, who were accompanying officials from the navy on a visit to North Carolina's Roanoke Island on Saturday, April 26, 1902.[3] "Government Test of Wireless Telegraphy," the New York Times, Sunday, April 27, 1902, front-page headline read. "Extraordinary Results of a System Said to Be New," another New York Times headline told its readers. "Wireless work speeded up to an almost frenzied tempo," Fessenden's wife, Helen Fessenden, wrote in 1902 as her husband and his assistants experimented with their wireless transmissions on North Carolina's Outer Banks through the fall of 1902.[4]

Fessenden's experiments with wireless transmissions on North Carolina's Outer Banks came to an end when he resigned from the Weather Bureau on Monday, September 1, 1902. Weather Bureau officials closed the three stations in North Carolina and Virginia, eventually auctioning some of the equipment from these coastal experiments. Historical markers along the Maryland and North Carolina shorelines are reminders of the contributions Fessenden made to twentieth-century broadcasting. The North Carolina shoreline is still scattered with long-abandoned concrete pilings that were once the foundations and footings for the wooden shacks where Fessenden and his assistants spent two years working.

In 1904, President Theodore Roosevelt established the Inter-Departmental Board of Wireless Telegraphy, the first commission by the federal government to study the breakthroughs and innovations in wireless transmissions. The 1905 Wireless Telegraphy: Report of the Inter-Departmental Board Appointed By the President to Consider the Entire Question of Wireless Telegraphy in Service of the National Government is the Inter-Departmental

Board's report of the experiments with wireless transmissions in the first decade of the twentieth century—experiments closely followed by the navy, the Weather Bureau, the Army Signal Corps, and other government agencies. Within months of Fessenden's experiments with the Weather Bureau on North Carolina's Cape Hatteras, other electrical engineers began their own wireless experiments. New York City's Lee DeForest, a former Yale University professor, built a wireless telegraphy station for the Army Signal Corps at Fort Hancock in Sandy Hook, New Jersey, and another one twenty-two miles away at Staten Island's Fort Wadsworth.

Scientific American published what is possibly the first ad for a "wireless telegraph receiver" to be sold in the United States on Saturday, November 25, 1905. Telimco's Wireless Telegraph Outfit ("Guaranteed to work up to 1 mile") went on sale to the public at a cost of $8.50. With a small transmitter and receiver run off of dry-cell batteries, Telimco's Wireless Telegraph could send and receive low-strength, short-distance wireless Morse code signals. Attic amateurs and backyard hobbyists purchased the Telimco Wireless Telegraph and other similar apparatuses sold in the classifieds of scientific magazines. Others shared their own homemade designs for inventions used to transmit and receive messages over short distances.

When Reginald Fessenden made his first publicly announced voice broadcast on Christmas Eve, Monday, December 24, 1906, from his station at Brant Rock, Massachusetts, wireless telegraph operators in the eastern United States and on ships in the Atlantic Ocean heard, through the static of their headphones, the sound of a woman's voice followed by a violin being played. Fessenden's Christmas Eve broadcast had been publicized to the wireless telegraph operators in the navy, on the ships of the United Fruit Company, and others with wireless telegraphs. Reception of this Christmas Eve transmission—and a second broadcast that New Year's Eve—was reported as far away as Norfolk, Virginia.

By the spring of 1907, with the success of Fessenden's Brant Rock broadcasts, hobbyists were assembling their own crystal sets for listening in on signals transmitted from wireless stations up and down the eastern United States. Fessenden's transmissions were heard by wireless operators as far away as Brooklyn, New York, on a regular basis by the end of 1907. Lee DeForest—working from his own transmitter atop New York City's Parker Building—founded the Radio Telephone Company in 1906. DeForest and other wireless firms contracted with commercial shipping lines, passenger ships, and even the federal government to build wireless transmitters and receiving equipment, which were sometimes called "radiotelegraphs."

The outfitting in 1907 of all navy ships sailing out of Brooklyn's Navy Yard with DeForest's Wireless Telephones increased the visibility of wireless experiments. The navy's wireless telephones often malfunctioned in their early days and were typically less reliable than standard wireless telegraphs. Improvements by navy servicemen who installed and operated these wireless telephones, however, saw success as the sounds of human voices more regularly could be heard through the static of the airwaves in the vicinity of New York City. Initially reliable at a distance of as far as twenty-two miles, DeForest's wireless telephones and their transmissions grew in strength, allowing conversations to be heard by those with only the most rudimentary scratch-built receivers.

The engineering and commercial success of wireless receivers and transmitters in 1907, especially their successful installation on the navy's fleet in the Atlantic, brought a new chapter to America's early-twentieth-century broadcasting as wireless experiments grew in popularity with amateur hobbyists and attic enthusiasts. The publication of *Wireless Telegraphy for Amateurs* in 1908 ushered in a new wave of wireless experiments with "radiotelegraphy" or "radiotelephony," as it was variously known. Inexpensive wireless receivers were available for purchase from mail-order catalogs and classified ads while scratch-built, homemade receivers were easy to build with simple instructions.

The nation's first wireless club—the Junior Wireless Club, later incorporated as the Radio Club of America—was founded in 1909 in New York City. Lee DeForest became one of the first to use wireless telephony to broadcast news items and to play phonograph records for his listeners—an audience largely comprised of young wireless enthusiasts, or "hams," as they became known. These young enthusiasts labored away over tables filled with electronic parts in attics, bedrooms, basements, and garages often working for hours on their rudimentary receivers and wearing their headphones to make out the distant sounds of Morse code, music, and the occasional voice.

DeForest's Wednesday, January 12, 1910, wireless transmission from the New York City Metropolitan Opera is remembered as one of the more widely publicized transmissions at this time and was heard hundreds of miles out on the Atlantic Ocean. Most large cities in the United States by this time had wireless clubs, especially as a growing number of enthusiasts built not only their own wireless receivers but also their own transmitters. The creation of the Department of Commerce's Radio Division in 1911 reflected the growing interest of the federal government in the transmission of wireless signals. Wireless operators for the navy complained about "amateur chatter" on the nation's airwaves, prompting calls for the first federal regulations of wireless transmissions.

Simple receivers—built from coils of wire wound around empty Quaker Oats containers, a battery, and a pair of headphones—became familiar to tens of thousands of self-taught hobbyists and backyard and basement enthusiasts listening and searching for hours on end to hear the faint signals of Morse code transmissions and the occasional voices and music. The sales of improved, less-costly circuits and amplifiers in 1912 made wireless receivers even more affordable. In 1912, Congress took up the issue of regulating the nation's radio airwaves, the first legislation to deal with the regulation of broadcasting.

Modern Electrics (first published in 1908 by Hugo Gernsback), *Radio Amateur News*, *Radio Broadcast*, *Radio News*, *Electronic World*, *Radio Digest*, *Radio Age*, *The Wireless World and Radio Review*, *Telephony*, *Wireless World*, and the Marconi Publishing Company's *Wireless Age* were but a few of the magazines that encouraged a new generation of enthusiasts to experiment with wireless receivers and transmitters. Well-publicized stories of wireless hobbyists relaying Morse code news updates during flooding in the Midwest in April 1913 fueled the imaginations of basement and backyard enthusiasts. *American Boy*, *Scientific American*, *Boy's Life*, and other magazines filled page after page with news of the latest inventions in wireless experiments.

The American Radio Relay League (ARRL) was established in 1914, connecting more than two hundred wireless radio clubs in cities and towns across the United States. Formed on Wednesday, January 14, 1914, in Hartford, Connecticut, the ARRL brought wireless operators together to share news. The ARRL, the Radio League of America, the National Amateur Wireless Association, and other groups built relays across the Midwest—and eventually across the country—for transmitting wireless messages from amateur transmitter to transmitter. Large antennae and their signature rigging of wiring hung outside of these attics and atop of rooftops soon became the symbol of wireless broadcasting.

In 1916, Lee DeForest again led in one of the first wireless transmitters to air a full schedule of nightly programming using the call letters 2XG from a transmitter in Highbridge, New York. Incorporated as the DeForest Radio Telephone and Telegraph Company, DeForest built an assembly plant in New Jersey to manufacture wireless receivers. DeForest also envisioned what he called the "wireless newspaper." Wireless "news and music has the further great advantage that it can be delivered instantly and without the nerve-racking cry of 'extra,' in the quiet of your home, without opening the door or even ringing your bell," he told *Telephony* magazine in December 1916.[5]

For six hours on the evening of Tuesday, November 7, 1916, DeForest transmitted from Highbridge, New York, the latest news and updates of the presidential election, which was heard by a listening audience of an estimated 7,000 to 8,000 wireless receivers and crystal set owners. That evening, DeForest transmitted news updates and reports, including the latest election returns and news telephoned in from the newsroom of the *New York American*. While DeForest is known for mistakenly announcing Wilson's defeat at the close of his broadcast that night, he is more famously remembered for this historic transmission and the excitement it built among wireless enthusiasts. That evening's transmission would be a prelude to even greater historic events in broadcasting that would begin to unfold in the coming weeks.

WIRELESS AND WORLD WAR I

World War I ushered in a new chapter in the history of America's development of wireless and the growth of transmitters and crystal receiver sets. By 1917, amateur radio transmitters and their clubs were relaying wireless signals from one station to the next, playing records on the air, updating their listeners on the current weather, and even selling ads. By March of that year, newspapers were regularly reporting on the nation's amateur wireless operators as many listened through headphones over either large, table-sized wireless receivers or much smaller, sometimes homemade wireless receivers for the occasional voice or, more often, musical recording. *The New York Times* built a large antennae on top of its building to receive wireless from Europe and was one of the first newspapers with a wireless receiver to listen to the latest news of the war happening abroad.

In August 1914, months before America's entry into the war—President Wilson issued a directive to cease all private wireless transmissions. The order established federal monitors at the nation's larger wireless transmitters on the East Coast to prohibit "transmitting or receiving for delivery messages of an unneutral nature and from any way rendering to any one of the belligerents any unneutral service during the continuance of the hostilities."[6] Enforcement of Wilson's order led to the closing "of the small stations of amateur radio operators on roof tops along the coast."[7] In California, where a number of the amateur transmitters were closed by government authorities, the *San Francisco Chronicle* and other papers took up their cause.

"20,000 American Watchdogs," the *San Francisco Chronicle*'s headline reported on Sunday, January 30, 1916. "How Our Boy Wireless Operators Are Forming a Great Army of Defense," read another headline. The *San Francisco Chronicle* told its readers, "The wireless man seems to be omnipresent. He is found in every part of the country. The delicate antennae are strung above the skylines of every city, and there are few persons who are not acquainted with some enthusiastic amateur." The *San Francisco Chronicle* related the formation of the Radio League of America to its readers by reprinting portions of its editorial from the *Electrical Experimenter*.[8] Still, some of these amateur wireless enthusiasts and their transmitters were allowed to continue operations, a circumstance that led the Radio League of America and other enthusiasts to press federal officials to allow them to transmit and receive wireless in the event of America's entry into the European war.

In the months leading up to America's declaration of war against Germany on Friday, April 6, 1917, the ARRL, the Radio League of America, and other enthusiasts petitioned Congress to allow amateur transmitters to continue to operate so that stations might act as "a thousand pair of listening ears" to monitor wireless transmissions from Germany. Months earlier, the league expressed its eagerness to assist in wartime preparedness. In the December

1915 issue of Gernsback's *Electrical Experimenter*, the Radio League of America made its own appeal to federal authorities not to suspend amateur wireless transmitters in the event of a declaration of war. The *New York Times* headline, "Wireless Owners Band for Defense," heralded the plea the Radio League of America had made to federal authorities.[9]

"There exists today a formidable defense weapon which up to now has not been exploited by Uncle Sam," the *Electrical Experimenter* explained in its December 1915 issue. "We refer to the tens of thousands of amateur radio stations scattered through the entire length and breadth of this fair land. There is hardly a hamlet which does not boast several amateur wireless stations and their number is increasing by hundreds every day." "It is thus of the utmost importance that every patriotic radio amateur should offer his station to his country."[10] Still, the pleas of the ARRL, the Radio League of America, and other wireless enthusiasts fell on deaf ears. From the White House, President Wilson ordered the immediate closure of all private wireless and radio transmitters on Saturday, April 7, 1917. The navy moved to close the nation's wireless transmitters, especially the trans-Atlantic commercial transmitters (and their large towers) along the coastline of the eastern United States.

"Government Seizes Whole Radio System," the *New York Times* headline reported on Sunday, April 8, 1917. "Navy Take Over All Wireless Plants It Needs and Closes All Others." "Under orders issued by the president," the *New York Times* reported, "the Navy took over the control and operation of all commercial radio stations that are considered useful to the Government and closed all other stations, commercial and amateur, the operation of which is considered dangerous to the nation."[11] "Wilson Orders All Radios Seized," "Amateur Stations Will Be Closed," the *Washington Post* headlines reported on the morning of Saturday, April 7, 1917.[12] In a statement, the navy explained that the closure of all commercial and amateur wireless transmitters was the only way to ensure "non-interference" with "naval and military signals."[13] Municipal authorities and police in New York City assisted federal authorities and were reported to have seized as many as eight hundred amateur wireless receivers and transmitters.

"Federal Agents Seek All Wireless Outfits," the *Atlanta Constitution*'s Wednesday, April 11, 1917, headline reported. Similar headlines appeared in newspapers in cities and towns across the United States over the next several days. "We think we have them all," one official noted.[14]

"War!" the ARRL's headline heralded in the May 1917 issue of *QST*. "The aerials of tens of thousands of us are being lowered to earth and our instruments disconnected," *QST* observed that May. "We have been ordered to do this by the Navy Department. Every amateur station is closed down. The lid is on and clamped tightly for a period of time, the duration of which no man knows." "All amateur traffic is halted where it happened to stand. All plans for improvements are cancelled. All the plans of our manufacturers are in mid-air." "In short," *QST* told its readers, "the great amateur wireless advance in these United States is stopped."[15] That summer, the nation's airwaves fell silent. Wireless transmitters throughout the country were shuttered by federal authorities. A special seal was placed on some of these transmitters and steep penalties were set for anyone unsealing these transmitters for the duration of the war.

Dozens of large transatlantic wireless commercial transmitters along the Atlantic coastline were closed by the navy on Saturday, April 7, 1917. Newspapers as well as wireless magazines described in sometimes vivid detail these closings. "Heavy wire is wrapped around the poles of the spark gap and the ends of this wire are joined with wax bearing the great seal of the United States of America," the *Electrical Experimenter* reported in its July 1917 issue.[16] "We are all anxiously awaiting the word that will give us permission to again reopen our stations, and we hope that it will be soon. Meantime, let us fly Old Glory at the top of our masts in place of the aerial and patiently await the outcome of Uncle Sam's entry into this Great War," *QST* told its readers in its July 1917 issue.[17]

"Not a single amateur aerial is in the air from the Atlantic to the Pacific," *QST* observed in September 1917. "The little buzzing spark is gone and dust covers the once-shining apparatus. How long this condition will last is a guess," *QST* explained. "But," *QST* added, "like most sad tales, it is not without a big ray of hope. This hope is that present conditions cannot go on forever and that the spirit of amateur wireless is just as much alive in these dead days as it ever was."[18] In that same issue of *QST* another headline, "More Stringent Than Supposed," expressed some uncertainty with regard to the wireless airwaves. "The lid is on tighter than we supposed," *QST* reported to its readers. "The facts are that we must not touch any radio apparatus." "All we can do is to read radio books and think radio thoughts. We hope they will not hold us in our present uncomfortable position any longer than is actually necessary."[19]

"Wilson Approves Making Wireless a Navy Monopoly," "Administration Plans Permanent Purchase and Operation of All Plants," Plans Permanent Purchase and Operations of All Plants," the *New York Times* front-page headlines reported on Monday, November 25, 1918. "Permanent Government control of all radio communication through the acquisition and operation by the Navy Department of all shore wireless stations in the United States used for commercial purposes is planned by the Administration under a bill now before Congress," the *New York Times* reported of President Wilson's backing of the proposal for government ownership of all radio broadcasting and wireless transmitters.[20] "Federal Control of Radio Stations Sought by Wilson," the *Atlanta Constitution*'s front-page headline reported on Monday, November 25, 1918, about the "permanent government control of all radio communications" being considered by the president and his cabinet.[21]

The Merchant Marine and Fisheries Committee in the House of Representatives formally convened its hearings in December 1918 just weeks after the November announcement by the White House of the president's support for federal regulation. The navy announced its support for the proposal insisting that "a complete monopoly is necessary" in wireless. "The United States Government is the only concern able to obtain and maintain such a monopoly," the navy report insisted, calling wireless a "public utility." The navy's statement declared, "Stations formerly operated commercially have been found to be unnecessary for either commercial or war purposes." In the same November 25, 1918, issue of the *New York Times*, which announced the White House's backing of the proposal for federal wireless ownership, also included the headline "Griggs Doubts Passage,"—a story that quoted John W. Griggs, president of the Marconi Wireless Telegraph and Cable Company, who expressed doubts about the passage of the bill and pointed out what he insisted was disagreement within the ranks of both the Congress and the navy as to the ownership of the airwaves by the government.

In December 1918, Secretary Daniels, Postmaster General Burleson, Secretary of Commerce William C. Redfield, and others in the cabinet backed the federal government retaining its control of the nation's airwaves after the war. "Radio communications stands apart because the air cannot be controlled and the safe thing is that only one concern should control and own it," Daniels testified before the House of Representatives, advocating "permanent government control of all radio communication" through "acquisition by the Navy Department" of all wireless stations. Calling it "good business" for "either war or peace," Secretary Daniels and other members of the cabinet estimated that some $5,000,000 in federal appropriations might purchase all privately owned wireless transmitters in the United States.[22]

Weeks after the Tuesday, November 5, 1918, elections, the House of Representatives seemed unreceptive to proposals for a federal government monopoly of the airwaves. The ARRL's Hiram Percy Maxim and others objected to the government's retaining control over the airwaves after the war. Executives with the Marconi Wireless Telegraph and Cable Company, members of the National Wireless Association, and other business executives spoke against federal ownership, which included testimony in the December 1918 hearings of the Merchant Marine and Fisheries Committee.[23]

Testifying before Congress in December 1918, Postmaster Burleson advocated government ownership of all telegraph and wireless systems. "The principle which justified government control of the Postal Service applies equally to all electrical means of communication," Burleson told members of the House of Representatives. "To establish and maintain means of communication is as much the function of the government as is the provision of national defense," he explained. He urged a federal government "monopoly"—what he also called a "unified system"—of wireless as the only means of serving the entire public. "To get the best result, the common control of this unified system should extend to the furthest possible limits [and] should cover our nation and the international communications to the boundaries of all other nations with which we have existing or potential relations," Burleson urged. His testimony and that of his fellow cabinet members was not persuasive to a skeptical House of Representatives and his proposal ended with no floor vote.[24]

On Monday, April 14, 1919, the Naval Communication Service in Washington, D.C., released a statement authorizing the resumption of wireless receivers for listening to wireless transmissions and signals on the nation's airwaves. Commander E. B. Woodworth, the assistant director for Naval Communications, authorized the resumption of wireless receivers: "The Acting Secretary of the Navy authorizes the announcement that effective April 15, 1919, all restrictions are removed on the use of radio receiving stations other than those used for the reception of commercial radio traffic. This applies to amateur stations, technical and experimental stations at schools and colleges, receiving stations maintained by jewelers or others desirous of receiving time signals, receiving stations maintained by manufacturers of radio apparatus, etc."[25] Within days of the navy's announcement, meetings of wireless enthusiasts and hobbyists resumed in cities and towns across the country.

"Amateur Radio Restored," the Radio League of America's president Hugo Gernsback reported in a front-page story in the June 1919 issue of the *Electrical Experimenter*. "As soon as the newspapers published the welcome tidings on April 15th that the ban on receiving was off," Gernsback wrote, "hundreds of thousands of amateurs began dusting off their sets and aerials blossomed forth overnight by the thousands to resume their former activities once more."[26] Headlines in cities and towns across the country expressed similar excitement among hobbyists and wireless enthusiasts.

On Friday, September 26, 1919, the president ended months of debate in his cabinet by announcing that privately owned wireless transmissions and broadcasting would resume effective Wednesday, October 1, 1919. In a statement from Washington, D.C.'s Naval Communication Service, Commander E. B. Woodworth authorized the resumption of wireless transmission and amateur broadcasting: "In so far as amateurs are concerned, radio resumes its pre-war status under the Department of Commerce." All wireless and experimental transmitters were able to resume their transmissions; however, "those used for the purpose of transmitting or receiving commercial traffic of any character including the business owners of the stations" were instructed that the wartime restrictions remained in effect "until the President proclaims that a state of peace exists."[27] "Lift Ban on Private Radios," "Navy Announces Restrictions Will Be Removed Next Wednesday," the *Washington Post*'s Saturday, September 27, 1919, headlines reported.[28]

With this, America's wireless and broadcasting again resumed as a part of American life.

"Ban Off!" proclaimed the ARRL in the October 1919 issue of its monthly magazine, *QST*. "The Job Is Done and the A.R.R.L. Did It!" *QST* enthused. "Coming! The Biggest Boom in Amateur Radio History!" "Amateurs: Order Your Apparatus and Get Your Licenses!" To electronics retailers and suppliers, the ARRL exclaimed, "Manufacturers and Dealers, Tell Us What You Have! At Once! Immediately! Today! Now! We're Off!" Wireless transmitters resumed their broadcasts and the airwaves were once again filled with conversation, music, and transmissions of all kinds.

THE EMERGENCE OF COMMERCIAL RADIO BROADCASTING AND AMERICAN POLITICS IN THE 1920s

"The antennae of the wireless telegraph are the symbols of our age," President Wilson told an audience in Des Moines, Iowa, on Saturday, September 6, 1919, just days before his announcement of the resumption of privately owned wireless transmissions and experimental broadcasts. "All the impulses of mankind," the president told his Des Moines audience, "are thrown out upon the air and reach to the end of the earth, quietly upon steamships, silently under the cover of the Postal Service, with the tongue of the wireless and the tongue of the telegraph."[29] With the end of World War I and the lifting of the federal government's restrictions on amateur wireless broadcasting, radio once again regained its growing presence in America's life.

The resumption of wireless transmitting in 1919 required that all amateurs complete licensing paperwork with the federal government. Within a year, more than six thousand Americans had applied for amateur wireless licenses. Front-page headlines and feature stories, as well as mail-order sales of wireless receivers in *Boy's Life* and other magazines, drove the postwar enthusiasm for wireless broadcasting. By the end of 1920, radio enthusiasts were relaying the news, weather, music, and other information to one another via their own transmitters.

In the months after World War I, Frank Conrad, an electrical engineer with the Westinghouse Company, began to air a regular program of recorded music from a transmitter he built in his Wilkinsburg, Pennsylvania, garage. Conrad was among those wireless experts who had assisted the federal government in its experiments with wireless during World War I. At the end of the war, Conrad returned to his home just outside of Pittsburgh to continue his own experiments. "Phonograph's Music Heard on Radiophones," "400 Pittsburgers Listen to Selections Transmitted by Local Inventor," the *New York Times* headlines reported from Pittsburgh in December 1919, letting its readers know of the popular transmissions of musical recordings by "wireless telephone" on Saturday evenings.[30] Conrad's employers at Westinghouse realized the popularity of the broadcasts and the company's vice president Harry P. Davis made arrangements for Conrad to assemble a transmitter on the roof of the Westinghouse factory in East Pittsburgh. The company financed its assembly in a shack on the top of its factory in September 1920, applied for a commercial license with the Department of Commerce, and established what today is regarded as the first broadcast schedule for a commercial radio station in the United States under the call letters KDKA. In late September, Pittsburgh's Horne department store began selling an inexpensive crystal receiver set for listening to KDKA's broadcasts with regularly scheduled broadcasting hours and programming slated by Westinghouse to begin sometime in late October. Westinghouse also advertised its own sales of wireless receivers—or "wireless telephones"—in Pittsburgh newspapers for sale in the city's department stores and retailers.

At 8:00 PM on the evening of Tuesday, November 2, 1920, as millions of Americans were settling in after their day at work and after voting at the polls, Conrad's assistant, Donald Little, worked at a hurried pace in a small room atop Westinghouse Company's East Pittsburgh building finishing the preparations for that evening's broadcast. Miles away, Westinghouse executives gathered at the Edgewood Country Club where a special receiver had been installed to hear the evening's broadcast. Throughout the Pittsburgh area, hundreds of wireless owners tuned in for the evening's broadcast as well; some awaited Conrad's regularly scheduled popular program of classical and contemporary music. While Westinghouse executives and their families toasted the evening's broadcast at the Edgewood Country Club, the scene on the roof of the Westinghouse building in East Pittsburgh was far more frenetic. In the hours and even minutes before the broadcast was scheduled to begin, Westinghouse employees were still finishing their tuning of the transmitter from the building's rooftop.

"This is KDKA of the Westinghouse Electric and Manufacturing Company in East Pittsburgh, Pennsylvania," were Westinghouse employee Leo Rosenberg's first words that evening, as KDKA's transmitter sparked to life: "We shall now broadcast the election returns. We would appreciate if anyone hearing this would communicate with us, as we are very anxious to know how far the broadcast is reaching and how it is being received." For the next three hours, Westinghouse employees frantically broadcast the latest news and updates of the day's election returns from the newsroom of the *Pittsburgh Post* to the rooftop of the Westinghouse building. Westinghouse's broadcast that evening reached an estimated ten thousand radio owners in the Pittsburgh area with later reports arriving that confirmed that the evening's broadcast had been heard by listeners as far away as Manchester, New Hampshire, and Wheeling, West Virginia.

The sales of radio receivers to American households grew between 1921 and 1924, with an increase of sales from $2,000,000 in 1921 to more than $400,000,000 in the space of just three years. Sales of radio sets went from 100,000 receivers sold in 1922 to as many as 550,000 sold in 1923, in what some observers described at the time as a "radio boom." That same year saw Chicago's Sears Roebuck Company offer the first radio receivers for sale in the pages of its catalog. "Radio," Catherine L. Covert writes, "appeared gradually to inhabit the living room, not the garage." She explains, "Installed in a modishly designed cabinet, it was transformed from a laboratory apparatus into a piece of furniture."[31] Farmers in particular were sold on the popularity of radio, most likely to relieve the isolation of rural life and to receive crucial weather reports and news updates.

Newspapers in many cities began regularly listing radio broadcast shows and times while magazines, including *Radio Broadcast* and *Boy's Life*, offered more coverage of new stations and their broadcast schedules as they became available. Department stores and electronics retailers in some of the nation's larger cities were some of the earliest businesses to recognize the potential for radio broadcasting. In city after city, some of the largest papers invested in broadcasting by applying for commercial licenses, hiring electricians and engineers to build their transmitters, opening their broadcast studios, and promoting their broadcasts in the pages of their newspapers. The *Atlanta Journal*'s WSB, the *Chicago Tribune*'s WGN, the *Dallas News*' WFAA, the *Kansas City Star*'s WDAF, and the *Louisville Courier Journal*'s WHAS were among some of the first newspapers to license their own radio broadcast stations.

The first radio receiver—known then as a "wireless telephone receiver"—was installed in the White House on Wednesday, February 8, 1922. On that day, White House staff set up a radio for the president; it consisted of a simple receiver and amplifier installed in a bookcase in the White House. "Wireless Telephone Receiver Installed in Harding's Study," the *New York Times* reported in a front-page headline on Thursday, February 9, 1922.[32] The *Washington Post* also reported "Harding Has Radio Telephone in Study," in a headline on Thursday, February 9, 1922.[33] Harding learned how to operate the receiver and is recalled as having shown considerable interest in listening to the White House radio.

In 1922, thousands of low-power radio transmitters and many thousands of wireless broadcast receivers were set up in cities and smaller towns across the country by amateur enthusiasts and hobbyists. Newspapers, electronics retailers, department stores, college and university campuses, and radio manufacturers licensed and set up their own transmitters by the hundreds. Applications for new commercial broadcasting licenses to the Department of Commerce in Washington, D.C., arrived at the rate of some three a day, as reported by the *New York Times* on Sunday, September 3, 1922. Distant stations often crackled through the airwaves in the evening hours from faraway cities as Americans clamored to the businesses, stores, or homes and apartments of their neighbors to hear musical performances, news, and reports coming over the airwaves by the fall of 1922.

"Radio Is the Gift of Providence to the Democratic Party," William Jennings Bryan told *New York Times* readers in its Sunday, September 3, 1922, headline. Anticipating radio broadcasts to be "a boon to the Democrats" and to "work in favor of the Democrats," Bryan told the *New York Times*, "My first experience was with an instrument installed by the Westinghouse plant at Pittsburgh." The *New York Times* also reported Bryan's enthusiasm for candidates to "talk to the entire nation." This statement was made just two years before Bryan's own largely uninspiring performance on a coast-to-coast radio broadcast from the Democratic National Convention in Madison Square Garden and underscored the potential perils and pitfalls of radio broadcasting for candidates unaccustomed to its microphones.[34]

"Early radio reception," Randall Patnode reminds us, "was fraught with interference."[35] Head phones were still familiar for most wireless listeners, especially those living in rural areas away from transmitters in larger cities and towns. Nighttime listening was advised for wireless owners as some smaller stations ended their broadcasts earlier in the evenings. Lightning, rain, thunderstorms—even the passing of streetcars and trolleys—played havoc on those tuning in to the radio. Seasonal circumstances and atmospheric conditions impacted the reception of signals by wireless owners as did the interference of many low-frequency, smaller transmitters operated by radio enthusiasts and amateur broadcasters. With broadcast stations reporting difficulty for their listeners to have a clear reception of their signals because of the interference of smaller transmitters on the air, federal authorities with the Department of Commerce—and later the Federal Radio Commission (FRC)—grew more aware of pleas by broadcasters for the regulation of frequencies, bandwidth, and signal strength of the crowded radio airwaves.

Investments and innovation in commercial radio broadcasting stations and in the manufacture of wireless receivers exploded at an astonishing pace between 1922 and 1924. The annual sales of radio receivers grew from $60,000,000 in 1922 to more than $350,000,000 by the end of 1924. The nation's sixty licensed commercial broadcast stations in January 1923 grew to some 588 commercial stations by December 1923 with some estimates placing the number of radio receivers sold by department stores, mail-order catalogs, and retailers that year at as many as 550,000. The founding in 1923 of the National Association of Broadcasters (NAB) began the rise of commercial broadcasting as a permanent and powerful presence in Washington, D.C. These commercial broadcast stations reached an estimated 1,000,000 households that owned radios by the end of 1923, a year when Americans became more aware of the changes in the nation's campaigning methods because of the increased presence of radios in kitchens, living rooms, parlors, and workplaces.

1924, 1928, AND RADIO'S TRANSFORMATION OF AMERICAN POLITICS

More than 1,250,000 American households bought radio receivers in 1924, a year when commercial radio broadcasting had its first major impact on the nation's politic landscape. In 1924, businesses invested larger sums in the nation's radio stations, especially as "chain broadcasting," as it became known, allowed transmissions between stations in different cities, eventually allowing for coast-to-coast broadcasting. By December 1924, almost 1,000 commercial stations were on the air and sales of radio receivers and radio-related equipment averaged an estimated $1,000,000 each day.

Financially, 1924 is remembered as a year when as many as two thousand manufacturers were assembling their own radios and selling them in thirty or more radio magazines and periodicals, driving an estimated $450,000,000 in radio-related sales in that year alone. Politically, the commercial success and astonishing growth of the radio industry in 1924 led candidates and their advisors—especially those managing the nominating conventions—to devote significant efforts to reach out on the airwaves. Staff with the Democratic National Committee (DNC) and the Republican National Committee (RNC) as well as the candidates for elective office and their own staffs saw radio's possibilities in reaching out to more and more constituents.

On Thursday, December 6, 1923, President Coolidge delivered the first State of the Union Address to be broadcast on the radio from the chamber of the House of Representatives. Thanks to the work of engineers with AT&T who installed temporary telephone lines in the House of Representatives, the president's remarks were carried to a transmitter at Washington, D.C.'s WCAP station on 13th Street near Capitol Hill. Standing before members of the House of Representatives and Senate, President Coolidge spoke into several microphones at the podium. The president's speech was transmitted to six different radio stations, including stations in Dallas, Kansas City, and St. Louis. "So clearly was President Coolidge's message broadcast by radio through half of the nation today that while he was speaking, KSD, the radio station in St. Louis, telephoned the Capitol and asked, 'What's that grating noise?'" The transmission experts at the Capitol promptly replied: "That's the rustling of the paper as he turns the pages of his message."[36] Shortly after the president's radio broadcast, politicians began to grasp radio's potential to reach a massive, unseen audience far larger than any assembled before them or indeed larger than any newspapers would reach the next morning.

On Tuesday, June 24, 1924, the Democratic National Convention opened in New York City's Madison Square Garden, with thousands of Democratic Party delegates, elected officials, and party leaders gathering from across the country. The 1924 convention offered a historic opportunity for the nation's radio broadcasters to carry the first live radio broadcasts of a presidential nominating convention to one of the largest, most populous cities and one of the largest radio markets in the entire country. Nineteen radio stations aired broadcasts of the convention, some stations broadcast only in the New York City metropolitan area and others broadcast to distant stations via specially installed telephone lines. WEAF and WJZ were two of the eighteen stations airing portions of the 1924 Democratic National Convention. WEAF technicians assembled a glass-windowed radio booth on the side of the main stage to house its station's broadcasters.

The 1924 DNC stretched on for several weeks in the most famously deadlocked nominating convention in the nation's history. Democratic Party delegates were unable to decide between New York's governor Alfred E. Smith and California's William Gibbs McAdoo. For two weeks and with an extraordinary 102 ballots taken by the convention, delegates, their families, journalists, and radio broadcasters watched as convention delegates hotly debated their party's 1924 platform. In vote after vote their nomination of their party's presidential ticket remained undecided. Franklin D. Roosevelt offered one of the most stirring speeches of the 1924 convention on Thursday, June 26, 1924, advocating in favor of Governor Alfred E. Smith. In contrast, William Jennings Bryan's speech was regarded as one of the most disappointing of the convention. Bryan wandered around the convention's main stage addressing the hall's assembled delegates but walked away from the radio microphones, making it almost impossible for the audiences at home to hear the Democratic Party stalwart.

Weeks after the 1924 Democratic National Convention, exhausted delegates finally backed West Virginia's John W. Davis as the Democratic nominee. Radio broadcasters in Madison Square Garden carried the news of Davis's nomination. For the first time in the nation's history, a major news story from a national party convention was reported within minutes of its breaking.

In contrast, President Coolidge and the Republican National Committee, by all accounts, used the airwaves to reach the nation far more effectively than their counterparts in the Democratic Party. When President Coolidge's campaign manager, William M. Butler, announced in July 1924 that the president would, "campaign by radio from the Capitol," broadcast executives and party leaders alike expressed their enthusiasm. Broadcast executives also expressed concern that speeches by President Coolidge and John W. Davis would be difficult to broadcast given the limited capacity of long-distance telephone wires to relay the signal across the country. AT&T's

engineers, however, were able to assemble a sixteen-station network to cover the RNC in Cleveland.

As was still customary at the time, candidates accepted their nominations from their respective nominating conventions by receiving delegations of party leaders at their homes, a custom that in 1924 was broadcast over the airwaves to a number of stations. John W. Davis accepted the Democratic Party's nomination at his home in Clarksburg, West Virginia, on Monday, August 11, 1924, in a speech carried on a fifteen-station radio network. A rainstorm during the broadcast from Clarksburg, however, made it difficult for most radio listeners to hear Davis's speech. Days later, on Friday, August 15, 1924, President Coolidge delivered his acceptance speech from the White House over a fifteen-station radio network heard by an estimated 25,000,000 listeners.

The campaign in 1924 saw both the DNC and the RNC not only advertised their candidates on the airwaves of the nation's radio stations and worked to accommodate radio broadcasts in the speeches of the candidates, but also either temporarily leased or operated for a time their own radio stations in New York City. On Tuesday, October 21, 1924, just weeks before election day, RNC leaders and local Republican officials opened their own radio studio on West 46th Street in New York City. They aired broadcasts of the president's supporters and testimonials by New Yorkers over airtime leased on Long Island's WAHG and Providence, Rhode Island's WBHF. From its temporary studio the RNC featured broadcasts several times a day in the final days of the race. Not to be outdone by the RNC, the DNC paid New York City's WJZ to lease a transmitter and display it in a special studio in a Manhattan department store window, where pedestrians on the sidewalks might see the Democratic Party's broadcast.

Radio's far-reaching influence in the 1924 race between Coolidge and Davis led many observers, as well as the candidates themselves, to favor crisp diction, clear enunciation and pronunciation, and concise and succinct speeches or remarks. Radio, Davis remarked in the midst of the 1924 presidential race, "will make the long speech impossible or inadvisable." "The short speech will be in vogue," Davis explained. "Almost everyone has a good radio voice if he remembers to speak slowly and does not shout," Davis added.[37] Broadcast executives urged candidates to shorten their messages and to avoid whenever possible the long-winded speech. "Unless the broadcasting of politics is kept within reasonable bounds," explained one broadcast executive in July 1924 to *Time* magazine, "the public will tire of it as soon as the novelty wears off."[38] Remembering to speak into the radio microphones posed a challenge to candidates. After decades of having to speak loudly and pace from one side of a stage or platform to another to reach their audiences, candidates had to learn to stand still in front of the microphone for the duration of their speech and to speak in the calm, conversational, well-measured tones that were well suited for radio broadcasts heard in the quiet of kitchens, living rooms, and parlors.

"The old-fashioned spellbinder climbed down off the stump in this campaign of 1924," the editors of the December 1924 issue of *Popular Mechanics* observed, "and settled himself in front of a microphone, and incidentally, some of the political speakers had to fit themselves to an entirely new form of public speaking. Picturesque and vivid personalities are lost on the radio audience." *Popular Mechanics* editors observed, "The speaker's individuality counts for nothing, and what he says for everything when the listener is sitting a hundred or a thousand miles away. Words have displaced gestures as vote getters." Impatience with long-winded speeches, *Popular Mechanics* editors cautioned, meant candidates had to work even harder to hold the attention of listeners who easily might turn the dial "a fraction of an inch."[39]

After President Coolidge's reelection, radio's influence in Washington, D.C., whether in the hallways and offices of Capitol Hill, or in the president's speeches from the White House or on his travels around the country, was well established. Election-eve radio broadcasts that Monday evening, November 3, 1924, reached millions of listeners—an audience unprecedented in the nation's history. Weeks later, on Wednesday, March 4, 1925, some twenty-one radio stations carried President Coolidge's Inauguration from the Capitol. It was heard by an estimated 15,000,000 listeners. Yet still, in speaking with newspaper reporters in February 1925, the president expressed his hesitance to speak regularly on the radio. "I don't think that it is necessary for the President periodically to address the country by radio," Coolidge told reporters. "The newspaper reporters do very well for me in that direction," Coolidge explained.[40] Even so, one estimate suggests that the president's speeches were broadcast on the radio as often as once a month during his second term in the White House.[41]

"New Stations Bring Total Up to 733," the *New York Times* Sunday, March 6, 1927, headline announced, as the airwaves and broadcast wavelengths filled out its programming. The sales of radio receivers by 1928 topped a remarkable $843,000,000 with more than 8,000,000 households owning a radio by the time of the 1928 election; 3,000,000 of which had purchased their radios in that year. By the eve of the 1928 presidential race, the radio audience in the United States was estimated to total 40,000,000 listeners, millions of whom turned in on a regular basis to the programming now carried coast to coast. "That radio will play a major role in the forthcoming campaign is anticipated by both parties," the *New York Times* reported in July 1928 and noted that "this year will see [radio] come of age."[42] Improvements in the reception of aerials, in the clarity and crispness of microphones, and in the reliability of circuits in the latest radio models sold in 1928—some of which were now powered by electricity rather than dry-cell batteries—made radio even more desirable to American households in that election year.

According to David G. Clark, the year 1928 saw the emergence of radio as a "full-grown campaign device," a year remembered as one in which both the Republican Party nominee, Secretary of Commerce Herbert Hoover, and the Democratic Party nominee, Governor Alfred E. Smith, were adept in broadcasting and in which both the DNC and the RNC devoted greater attention and made larger financial investments in radio.[43] The 1928 Republican and Democratic conventions were carried in their entirety by the nation's radio broadcasters, including the newly established National Broadcasting Company (NBC) and the Columbia Broadcasting System (CBS). Both preempted other programming while the conventions were being held. The Democratic convention in 1928 was broadcast by forty-two stations while forty-four stations carried the Republican convention. These broadcasts reached tens of millions of listeners on the approximately 12,000,000 radio receivers located in America's homes. Weeks later, when Secretary Hoover and Governor Smith formally accepted their nominations, their addresses (from, respectively, Palo Alto, California, and the statehouse in Albany, New York) were broadcast over fifty-five station affiliates of the National Broadcasting Corporation (NBC) and some nineteen stations affiliated with Columbia Broadcasting System (CBS). Weeks later, the campaigns of Secretary Hoover and Governor Smith took to the nation's railways to crisscross the country in private railroad cars specially outfitted with the latest radio receivers, which allowed them to broadcast throughout the day.

"Smith Hails Microphone as Mouthpiece of Nation," read one of the *New York Times* headlines in July 1928, a reminder of the coast-to-coast listening audience now tuning in to hear the latest news, speeches, and updates from presidential candidates. Weeks later, on Wednesday, August 22, 1928, when Smith formally accepted his nomination in a speech in the Albany, New York, statehouse, a nationwide network of more than one hundred radio stations broadcast to millions of Americans the governor's comments. The *New York Times* reported this network was "the largest network ever assembled in the 8 year history of broadcasting."[44] While several dozen viewers watched as General Electric's experimental television station 2XAF and WGY in nearby Schenectady carried the first televised live images of a candidate for the White House, it was in the millions of homes and through the more than one hundred stations across the United States that radio's power and presence was established.

When Secretary Hoover and Governor Smith faced off in the fall of 1928, the DNC and the RNC were poised to reach out to the American electorate through the nation's commercial broadcasting stations and their growing coast-to-coast networks. DNC and RNC leaders established well-funded Radio Divisions in the 1928 race—the RNC Radio Division was headed by Paul Gascoigne and the DNC's Radio Division by Joseph Israels. Working with their respective candidates as they crisscrossed the country in their railroad cars, Gascoigne and Israels fought a fever-pitch battle of the airwaves.

"There was a time when the views of the candidate for national office were made to fit the locality he was speaking in but that time has passed," Governor Smith told the *New York Times* in the early weeks of the 1928 race. "It passed," the Democratic Party's presidential nominee observed, "when the radio audience linked the country into one huge audience."[45] "The successful political speaker on the radio," the *New York Times* advised weeks earlier, "must bear in mind that he is not addressing a meeting of his own supporters only but is speaking into the homes of many people hostile to him, scattered to the remotest corners of the nation. Appeals should be national in scope. Radio waves, especially those of the more powerful transmitters, recognize no local or state boundaries. Arguments that may placate one section of the country may irritate another. Thus votes are lost."[46] Radio, it seems, made the nation's politics national.

"All America will know who the choice of the party is as soon as those who nominate him know," "Radio has banished distance and time, . . . and has built the convention walls around the entire country."[47] The party nominating conventions in their typical all-night sessions that carried on in boisterous proceedings well into the early morning hours proved to be a challenge in 1924 and after to the candidates, their managers, and their staffs as they sought to reach the largest listening audiences earlier in the evenings with their larger listening audiences on the nation's radio airwaves.

Because radio was able to reach a large and growing audience, businesses saw a financial opportunity to advertise their products on the nation's airwaves, and the cost of purchasing airtime for candidate advertisements became a much greater strain on the coffers of the DNC and the RNC. In 1928, the DNC and RNC combined spent some $1,000,000 in broadcast-related expenses and ads, still well under half of the budgets for both parties in that year's race. The RNC spent roughly $435,000 on radio ads while the DNC is thought to have spent some $550,000 for its own radio broadcasts, with the DNC's spending on radio ads constituting some 18 percent of the expenses in that year's race compared to some 10 percent of the expenses of the RNC's budget that year.[48]

The Democratic Party's defeat in 1928 brought changes to the DNC. On Saturday, June 15, 1929, Charles Michelson, the former Washington, D.C., bureau chief of the *New York World* and a well-known figure in DNC publicity work over the years was hired. Michelson's charge was to revive the DNC advertising program, especially in regard to commercial radio broadcasting. Because of the debacle of the 1924 Democratic convention at Madison Square Garden and the defeat of Governor Smith in 1928, the DNC and its publicity bureau led by Michelson set out to improve their use of radio broadcasting. It marked the recognition of radio's growing impact and importance for the national parties and their candidates at a time when radio reached further than ever into the homes and lives of Americans.

RADIO, ROOSEVELT, AND THE 1930s

By 1932, 18,500,000 American homes had a radio. Radio broadcasts could rivet the listener's attention with breaking news bulletins or interruptions of regularly scheduled programs. Radio broadcast compelled millions of Americans to stop whatever they were doing, to lean in, to listen, to pay attention, to hang on the broadcaster's every word. It was a medium of shared moments—moments found in quiet hours when family members and friends gathered close to hear the broadcast, to listen to the faraway sounds and voices. Of course, radio still allowed Americans to do other things while listening. They could clean, cook, read, and attend to their chores and routines and work around the household without having to pause or stop to read a newspaper or sit still in one place, as the sounds and voices of the news or of musical performances carried from room to room.

The 1930s is remembered as commercial radio broadcasting's moment—a time when the radio receiver was the most prominent piece of furniture in the kitchen, living room, or parlor of a family's home, a place where families came together to listen to the news or the popular broadcast programs of the day. Newspapers in the nation's largest cities and even in its smaller towns boasted ever larger schedules of radio broadcasts while newspapers themselves invested in broadcast stations. Radio broadcasting is remembered as a source of comfort and connection to the world for many millions of American families in the grip of the Great Depression. Families stretched their budgets to purchase radios and to pay for their vacuum tubes and other equipment and parts. Those who could not afford a radio sought out radios at their neighbors' homes. The 1932 presidential race pitted President Hoover against New York's governor Franklin D. Roosevelt, a race that once again established radio's prominence in national elections. When radio broadcasters and their network chains covered the Democratic and Republican conventions that summer, tens of millions of American households listened by radio, accustomed by this time to this kind of coverage of the conventions. Governor Roosevelt's acceptance of his nomination is one that is well remembered. Roosevelt traveled from his home in Hyde Park, New York, by airplane to Chicago to accept his nomination in a break from well-established precedent. The hour-by-hour details of the governor's flight were covered by the nation's radio broadcasters as he made his way to the convention hall in Chicago.

News of Governor Roosevelt's flight from his home in New York to the Chicago Democratic convention quickly riveted the attention of radio broadcasters at the convention, their networks provided updates throughout the day while technicians worked to prepare the microphones in the Chicago stadium. For the first time, radio broadcasters and their networks prepared to carry a presidential nominee's acceptance speech live. Radio listening audiences grew throughout the day as stations interrupted their programming with updates on Roosevelt's New York–Chicago flight. These interruptions and updates throughout the day peaked the audience's interest and there were tens of millions of listeners by the time Roosevelt steadied himself at the Chicago stadium podium to accept his party's nomination and deliver his historic remarks.

"I pledge to you, I pledge to myself, a New Deal for the American people," Roosevelt told the delegates assembled in Chicago and the many millions listening to the radio in their homes on the evening of Saturday, July 2, 1932. "This is more than a political campaign," he told the delegates. "It is a call to arms. I have started out on the tasks that lie ahead by breaking the absurd traditions that the candidate should remain in professed ignorance of what has happened for weeks until he is formally notified." "Let it be from now on," Roosevelt added, "the task of our party to break foolish traditions." In the months to come, radio audiences listened as President Hoover and Governor Roosevelt took to the airwaves with their appeals to voters, with their endorsements and testimonials from their supporters carried on the airwaves, and their speeches.

In the wake of the Tuesday, November 8, 1932, election, radio broadcasters told president-elect Roosevelt they were prepared to assist him when speaking on the nation's airwaves to the American public. In March 1933, Alfred McCosker, the president of the National Association of Broadcasters (NAB), promised Roosevelt his industry's assistance in the work before the new administration. NBC, CBS, and the Mutual Broadcasting Company all offered the president-elect their assistance if he needed to address the nation at a moment's notice. Within weeks, Roosevelt aired the first in a series of historic broadcasts that set records for some of the largest audiences in the history of commercial radio broadcasting.

"When a man can stand on the White House lawn or in the Capitol and talk without wire connections through compact devices, empowering his words to fly to Europe in a split-second," wrote *New York Times*' Orrin E. Dunlap Jr. about his observations of radio's prominence at the Saturday, March 3, 1933, Inaugural, "it represents a miracle of wireless little dreamed of when Marconi began his experiments in the days of Grover Cleveland." "The drama and romance of wireless in the pioneer days," Dunlap explained, "were intensified by the deafening spark as it crackled across a wide gap, or while a rotary arm whirled past a circular line-up of metallic points to create a flame that looked like a Fourth of July pin-wheel. But times have changed," Dunlap continued. "Radio is so silent in operation through the faint glow of the vacuum tubes that it is difficult to realize that a man in an automobile traveling down Pennsylvania Avenue is being heard in the twinkle of an eye in Berlin, Paris, London, Tokyo, and other cities thousands of miles away." Dunlap wrote this just days before President Roosevelt's radio broadcast from a basement room in the White House upended forever the way elected officials connected with the public.[49]

No figure was as well suited to the stillness of the radio's quiet hours in the evening's broadcasting than President Franklin D. Roosevelt, a president whose historic words from the steps of the Capitol Building in his Inaugural speech, "The only thing we have to fear is fear itself," were soon supplanted by his simple, conversational words from the Diplomatic Reception Room of the White House. Within days of Roosevelt's Inauguration, he had already begun preparations to address the nation's radio audience in remarks broadcast from the White House. Roosevelt's first radio address to the nation, an address famously christened the "Fireside Chat" by CBS's Washington, D.C., bureau chief Harry Butcher and soon widely repeated by newspaper reporters, dealt with the crisis in the nation's banking industry.

"My friends," the president's speech began that Sunday evening at 10:00, "I want to talk for a few minutes with the people of the United States about banking." With these words, the president began a broadcast, lasting only fifteen minutes, explaining the steps to be taken to deal with the nation's banking crisis. "I want to tell you what has been done in the last few days and why it was done and what the next steps are going to be," the president explained in his soon-to-be-familiar conversational style. Delivered at 10:00 PM EST on Sunday, March 12, 1933, President Roosevelt's broadcast from the White House was carried on hundreds of stations and changed forever the office of the presidency. To an estimated 60,000,000 Americans listening that Sunday evening, in clear, comforting, conversational words, the president urged his listeners to feel safe when depositing their money in their local banks and promised that Congress would enact legislation to protect their savings accounts. "Let us unite in banishing fear," he told his audience, reprising his famous remarks weeks earlier in his Inaugural Address. "It is your problem no less than it is mine." "Together we cannot fail," the president finished, expressing conviction and determination as well as compassion. This tone was to become a signature of Roosevelt's White House radio broadcasts in the years to come.

"Roosevelt Appeals on the Radio for Full Confidence," a *New York Times* front-page headline heralded on Monday, March 13, 1933, side by side with the headline, "Many Banks in the City and Nation Re-Open for Normal Operations." What President Roosevelt did, in that brief fifteen-minute broadcast on Sunday evening from the White House, was a defining moment in the relationship between the presidency and the radio listening audience, who were invited to lean into their radios in the quiet of a Sunday evening and listen to the words of their leader. "My fellow Americans," the president's remarks to the nation began—a familiar greeting, comforting in its warmth and sincerity, that he used in almost all of his subsequent radio broadcasts. The president's conversational tone, ease of delivery, and optimism ("Together we cannot fail") carried with it a certain steadiness and a solemnity befitting the late hour of the Sunday evening broadcast.

Nearly all of the president's close advisors and staff recall his extensive preparations for these broadcasts. He prepared many drafts of his remarks and carefully re-reread and rehearsed his remarks before each broadcast. White House staff and cabinet members attending that first broadcast and subsequent radio broadcasts remarked on his ability to connect with and relate to his unseen audience. His opening salutation, "My fellow Americans" carried weight across the country over farms and fields and factories.

Most of those who spoke into the radio microphone had the habit of reading their remarks hastily from the page in rapid-fire staccato. The president, however, deliberately drew out his words, slowed down his speaking, and delivered his remarks in relatable terms. "This unusually deliberate pace," Lawrence W. Levine and Cornelia R. Levine tell us, "allowed [President Roosevelt] to pay attention to his phrasing, his pauses, and his vocal pacing, all of which he became a master at, elongating and prolonging his vowels and consonants, using silences effectively, varying his emphases and the modulations of his tenor voice."[50] His ability to envision the "quiet of the home," as the president himself liked to call it, informed his delivery of these historic broadcasts. "It was as if sitting in the studio he could visualize his audience sitting around their radios in their homes," David Halberstam writes, "and he spoke not to the microphone but to those homes."[51] Even when the president paused during his live broadcasts from the White House to ask one of his staff for a glass of water, it served to further establish his own sincerity and spontaneity in what were, in fact, well-scripted and well-timed performances that allowed for little or no improvisation.

"Most Americans in the previous 160 years had never even seen a President," David Halberstam writes. "Now almost all of them were hearing him *in their own homes*. It was literally and figuratively electrifying."[52] "I never forget that I live in a house owned by all of the American people and that I have been given their trust," President Roosevelt told his listeners in a Thursday, April 14, 1938, broadcast from the White House. Anecdotal reports of radio listeners placing the president's photograph next to their radio sets underscore the president's physical connection with some of his listeners.

From 1933 until 1944, Roosevelt made as many as thirty-one radio addresses from a basement room in the White House that, in fact, had no fireplace. He had delivered only four such radio addresses in the first year of his first term in the White House. Writing to his staff aides, Roosevelt wanted to allow at least six weeks between his radio broadcasts so that his remarks would remain fresh and that the many millions of people listening to his broadcasts would not tire and possibly not tune in if they thought his remarks too regular or routine. "Scheduling" and "timing" remained the watchwords of these White House broadcasts, which were carefully scheduled for either Saturday or Sunday evenings when the White House believed most Americans would be in their homes with their families.[53]

"More than any other individual," Francis Chase Jr. writes, "Mr. Roosevelt has a feel for audiences, a feel for the microphone which has made the vital core of the nation's activities not the formal reception rooms of the White House, the Blue, Red, Green, and East Rooms, but the Oval Room, which, oddly enough, doesn't have a fireside."[54] Roosevelt's remarks from a basement room in the White House—formally known as the Diplomatic Reception Room but forever associated with Roosevelt—is without parallel in the history of radio broadcasting and America's political life. Not without miscues and missteps—and certainly not without his detractors and critics eager to pounce on his every utterance when he took to the airwaves—President Roosevelt spoke into the microphone from a small desk in the basement of the White House and lifted up a nation in despair.

In the early months of America's entry into World War II, on the evening of Monday, February 23, 1942, President Roosevelt spoke on the occasion of George Washington's birthday, invoking the words from Thomas Paine's *The Crisis*. Speaking to a radio audience of some 61,365,000 Americans that Monday evening, President Roosevelt's broadcast is famously remembered decades later as a striking example of America's resoluteness in times of war. His broadcast was later nicknamed the "Map Speech" because Americans were asked to purchase a world map for reference during the president's radio broadcast. Looking back we are reminded of radio's pervasive and powerful presence in the lives of nearly every American in one of the most despairing and difficult times in the twentieth century. It irreversibly transformed the relationship between the presidency if not the entirety of the government itself with the American people by bringing government to the people in the Depression's most difficult days and in so doing elevated the presidency to a voice unanticipated by the drafters of the Constitution and most certainly unparalleled in the history of the office itself.

ROOSEVELT, REAGAN, AND THE RADIO

"The simplest way for each of you to judge recovery lies in the plain facts of your own individual situation," President Roosevelt told the nation from his desk in the Diplomatic Reception Room in the White House during his Thursday, June 28, 1934, broadcast—the fifth of his historic Fireside Chats. "Are you better off now than you were last year? Are your debts less burdensome? Is your bank account more secure?" Hundreds of miles away in Des Moines, Iowa, a young Ronald Reagan is likely to have heard the president's words. His votes cast in 1932, 1936, 1940, and 1944 for President Roosevelt is a well-known fact; we can assume that Reagan most certainly leaned in, learned from, and listened closely to his radio when the president spoke. Echoes of Roosevelt's "Are you better off now than you were last year?" radio broadcast morphed into Reagan's "It might be well if you would ask yourself, are you better off than you were four years ago?" question asked during his televised debate with President Jimmy Carter on Tuesday, October 28, 1980, before an audience estimated at some 80,000,000 viewers.

With the growth of radio's listening audiences and with households spending more hours each day tuning into broadcasts and programming, it is little wonder that when President Roosevelt stood for a second term in the Tuesday, November 3, 1936, election, radio took a place of prominence in that year's race. Well over 70 percent of the nation's households owned a radio by the time Kansas's governor Alfred M. Landon won his party's nomination to face President Roosevelt. By the end of the 1930s, America's households for the first time were more likely to have a radio than they were a telephone.

Nearly 6,500,000 American automobiles on the road in 1939 were equipped with radios, an important trend that grew steadily in the second half of the twentieth century as larger numbers of Americans commuted in their automobiles in the early mornings and late afternoons in many cities. Radio listenership grew as Americans drove longer distances each day in their automobiles, especially after the federal government's interstate highways were constructed after World War II. The year 1939 is also when radio broadcasting took on a larger part not only in covering political campaigns but also covering politicians and lawmakers at work in the nation's capital. The approval by the House of Representatives on Thursday, April 20, 1939, of a bill reserving "such portion of the gallery of the House of Representatives as may be necessary to accommodate reporters of news to be disseminated by radio, wireless, and similar means of transmission, wishing to report debates and proceedings" laid the ground for the eventual construction and opening of the gallery for radio broadcasters in August 1939.

"By states," William C. Ackerman wrote of figures estimating radio ownership as of Monday, April 1, 1940, "the percentages of radio-equipped occupied dwellings ranged from 39.9% in Mississippi to a high of 96.2% in Massachusetts."[55] Efficiencies in the assembly, manufacturing, and sales of radios led to even less expensive sets so that by the end of the decade, it was affordable to all but the poorest households. Well-known newspaper columnists emerged by the beginning of World War II as popular newscasters on the nation's airwaves. Hans V. Kaltenborn, known for his work as a newspaper reporter, gained prestige as a radio newscaster and was featured in a cameo appearance in Frank Capra's 1939 movie *Mr. Smith Goes to Washington*. Edward R. Murrow, Elmer Davis, and Howard K. Smith were also well-known newspaper reporters who emerged as several of the most well-regarded and respected radio newscasters. And when nearly 80,000,000

Americans heard Roosevelt's historic broadcast announcing the United States' entry into World War II ("A date which will live in infamy") at 12:30 PM on Monday, December 8, 1941, radio's presence in the lives of Americans was solidified.

On the evening of Tuesday, November 7, 1944, less than twenty-five years since several hundred listeners tuned in via their headphones and rudimentary radio receivers in the Pittsburgh metropolitan area listening to KDKA's report on the 1920 presidential race, 100,000,000 persons were estimated to have heard broadcasts of President Roosevelt's reelection to a fourth term defeating New York's governor Thomas Dewey. With radio personalities from Groucho Marx to Frank Sinatra to Orson Welles appearing in radio broadcasts by the Democratic ticket in the 1944 race for the White House, audiences became more accustomed to radio's presence in the coverage of the nation's campaigning for elective office four years later when Governor Dewey faced President Harry S. Truman. The 1948 presidential race is still remembered as one of the last presidential races in which the candidates spent a larger percentage of their campaign budgets on radio advertising than on television ads—a race whose commercials that fall included an October 1948 radio commercial featuring actor Ronald Reagan speaking on behalf of President Truman's reelection. Truman even took the time to prepare for some of his radio broadcasts with J. Leonard Reinsch, a Cox radio executive and general manager of that company's stations in Florida, Georgia, and Ohio.

"I don't give a damn whether there's nobody there but you and me," President Truman told his associates before a Saturday, June 5, 1948, speech in Omaha, Nebraska, to what the *St. Louis Post Dispatch* later called a "nearly empty auditorium." Newspaper reporters with the president in Omaha mocked the small attendance at the speech, with one reporter calling it a "floperoo," even as Truman himself, as David McCullough writes, "did not seem to mind" and "went on stage as if speaking to a packed political house," insisting his intended audience were those at home in the radio listening audience.[56] "I am making a speech on the radio to the farmers," Truman explained to his staff at the Nebraska speech. "They won't be there. They'll be at home listening to that radio." "They're the ones I'm going to talk to."[57]

Even after World War II and the growth of television receivers and an increase in commercial television stations, radio's familiar presence in the household, the office, the store, and the workplace remained a defining part of the lives of most Americans. As of Saturday, January 1, 1944, the Bureau of the Census estimated that some 89 percent of the more than 36,544,000 American households owned a radio, compared to 55 percent of households that owned an automobile and 45 percent that owned a telephone. By 1945, that figure would push to approximately 31,100,000 American households, or 90 percent of the nation's households that owned a radio.

Radio's immediacy challenged newspaper readership while its intimacy in the familiar settings of the kitchen or the living room or the office allowed Americans to do their chores, straighten their houses, or work and still be able to listen to the radio. The difficulties of the Depression and the hardships of World War II combined to cement radio broadcasting's place in the history of the twentieth century, a place still important in the imaginations and in the lives of Americans today.

Chapter 5

Television in the Early Twentieth Century

"The idea of television," Gary R. Edgerton tells us, "existed long before its realization as a technology."[1] "Television was an idea that existed long before its realization," Michael Winship continues, it was "a natural progression in a world that had seen the birth of telephones, radio, and motion pictures."[2] Its history is not a history of a singular moment of invention as it is a history of steady innovation and sometimes rival efforts to transmit images over a distance. It is a story of venturers and visionaries, some famous, most unknown. While science fiction's essayists and magazine illustrators fueled the imaginations of a generation at the dawn of the twentieth century with the promise of the transmission of images and voices over futuristic screens, with pulp magazine stories of "radioscopes," "radiovisors," "radiovisor receivers," "sight radio," and "telephonoscopes," inventors working in makeshift apartment laboratories and in basement workshops in France, Germany, Great Britain, the United States, and elsewhere labored on the much more rudimentary transmission of blurred, often-flickering black-and-white silhouettes and imagery as television's early realization eluded the pace of its practical innovations.

Constantin Perskyi's delivery of a paper titled *Télévision au Moyen de L'électricité* at the International Electricity Congress on Friday, August 25, 1900, is remembered over a century later as one of the first uses of the word "television" well before the scientific achievements and inventions that made that word a reality. Perskyi's paper coined the word "television" to define the transmission of images over a distance. It gave language to a dream already in the minds of some visionaries at the turn of the century. In the early years of the twentieth century, inventors in Europe and the United

States working to perfect the wireless transmission of the human voice also imagined a time when images might also be transmitted by wireless. These visionaries likely had little idea where their experiments might take them.

"There was no sudden flash of inspiration that came to a single lone inventor," Michael Winship tells us.[3] When Perskyi offered his term *television* at the 1900 International Electricity Congress, it built upon the work of years of inventions well underway. Experiments with "vision by radio" captured the imagination of inventors in Great Britain, France, Russia, Japan, Germany, the United States, and elsewhere. Visionaries imagined what they variously called "distant electric vision," "radio movies," "radio vision," "visual radio," or "visual wireless" while artistic renderings of the transmission of images appeared in pulp fiction and even cartoons and comic books of the day.[4] Experimenting with inventions variously called "radioscopes," "telephonoscopes," "televisors," and then, simply, "television," however, was a far cry from the works of science fiction and futuristic illustrators in the mid-1920s. AT&T experimented with the transmission of images over telephone lines while General Electric, Westinghouse Electric and Manufacturing Company, and other companies invested in their own experimental transmissions of imagery. It was two separate public demonstrations, one in a London department store displaying the experimental work of John Logie Baird and another weeks later in a demonstration in the Washington, D.C., laboratory of Charles Francis Jenkins, however, that the earliest and most successful exhibits of this new technology were seen.

TELEVISION IN THE 1920s

Wednesday, March 25, 1925. London, England. 400 Oxford Street. Selfridge and Company's First Floor Electrical Section. A low-ceilinged, dimly lit room. A large apparatus with a "DANGER" sign warning of the apparatus's electrical current. John Logie Baird is demonstrating what, at that time, he called "shadowgraphs" to the shoppers at Selfridge's department store. Baird worked for months in his second floor flat on London's Frith Street, experimenting with the transmission of images by wire over a short distance.

"Selfridge's Presents the 1st Public Demonstration of Television in the Electrical Section (1st Floor)," the London retailer's flyers announced to its customers at its 400 Oxford Street location. The flyer stated:

Television is to light what telephony is to sound—it means the INSTANTANEOUS transmission of a picture, so that the observer at the 'receiving' end can see, to all intents and purposes, what is a cinematographic view of what is happening at the "sending" end. For many years, experiments have been conducted with this end in view:

the apparatus that is here being demonstrated is the 1st to be successful and is as different to the apparatus that transmits pictures (that are from time to time printed in the newspapers) as the telephone is to the telegraph. The apparatus here demonstrated is, of course, absolutely "in the rough"—the question of finance is always an important one for the inventor. But it does, undoubtedly, transmit an instantaneous picture. The picture is flickering and defective and at present only simple pictures can be sent successfully.[5]

Unquestionably the present experimental apparatus can be similarly perfected and refined. It has never before been shown to the public. Mr. J. L. Baird, the sole inventor and owner of the patent rights, will be present daily while the apparatus is working in the Electrical Section at 11:30 A.M., 2:30 P.M., and 3:15 P.M. He will be glad to explain to those interested in details.[6]

Crowded into a small, low-ceilinged room, Selfridge's shoppers visiting the store's electrical section on Wednesday, March 25, 1925, saw the silhouette of a small figurine transmitted on a two-by-four-inch screen. This was Baird's first of three weeks of demonstrations in which hundreds of shoppers and visitors to the department store caught a glimpse of Baird's still-experimental transmissions.

On Tuesday, January 27, 1926, after months of work in his Frith Street flat to improve the clarity and the resolution of his transmissions, Baird demonstrated for the first time his transmission of much higher-resolution images. In a well-publicized demonstration before fifty invited guests and members of the Royal Institute, Baird transmitted the images of human faces and objects, with much higher resolution and with much more shading and detail than he was able to show in his shadowgraphs. "The scientists," O. G. Hutchinson of the *New York Times* reported of Baird's Tuesday, January 27, 1926, demonstration in London, "saw each other in the receiver from electrical impulses transmitted over a wire from one room to another."[7] What Baird called his "Televisor" transmitted an image described by one observer as "faint and often blurred," yet it remained clearer and far more recognizable than his earlier shadowgraphs. "Mr. Baird has definitely and indisputably given a demonstration of real television," *Radio News* reported in its September 1926 issue.

With the successful demonstration of his Televisor transmissions, Baird capitalized on his international acclaim and newspaper headlines on both sides of the Atlantic by securing financial investments from several investors, hiring his first assistants, and constructing an antennae for transmitting his images. Sending transmissions from his London workshop to a receiver in Harrow, a distance of some nine miles, Baird's London experiments took hold on the public's imagination at almost exactly the same moment as similar transmissions in the United States were making headlines of their own.

In Washington, D.C., Charles Francis Jenkins demonstrated his own apparatus for the transmission of images at almost the same time as Baird's London demonstrations. Jenkins, in his workshop on Connecticut Avenue, achieved breakthroughs with what he called "visual radio" or "radio movies" in the spring of 1925. Weeks after Baird's demonstration of his shadowgraphs in London, Jenkins prepared for his own demonstration of a transmission of black-and-white silhouetted images before an audience of government officials and newspaper reporters.

On Saturday morning, June 13, 1925, just days after Baird's London demonstrations, Jenkins showed a ten-minute film of a rotating windmill. The transmission was sent from the Naval Station in Anacostia, Virginia, to Jenkins's laboratory, a distance of five-and-one-half miles. Secretary of the Navy Curtis D. Wilbur, Acting Secretary of Commerce Stephen B. Davis, Navy Admiral David W. Tayl, and Dr. George K. Burgess, the head of the Bureau of Standards, were among the dignitaries at the demonstration. Representatives from the Department of Commerce and other federal agencies, as well as reporters from the *New York Times*, the *Washington Post*, the *Washington Evening Star*, and other papers were in attendance and watched "the first public demonstration of radiovision," in the form of a flickering image of the rotating windmill on a ten-by-eight-inch screen. "It would be just as easy to reproduce the picture 100 miles away if we had the apparatus necessary," Jenkins told his audience.[8] Jenkins's demonstration was one of the most widely publicized and successful early demonstrations of an experimental television transmission in the United States.

The following morning, the *New York Times* headline read: "Radio Shows Far Away Objects in Motion." This headline was one of many such headlines in the morning newspapers that next day across the country. "Radio Vision Shown First time in History by Capital Inventor," the Washington, D.C., *Sunday Star* front-page headline heralded on Sunday, June 14, 1925. "First Motion Pictures Transmitted by Radio Are Shown in Capital," the *Washington Post* reported in a front-page headline on Sunday, June 14, 1925. In its front-page story that Sunday morning, the *Washington Post* reported, "The machine has not been christened, but it has been suggested that it be called the 'telerama,' which means 'distant viewing,' and it is possible [Jenkins] will make it 'telaramaphone,' 'distant viewing and hearing.'"[9] Writing weeks later in *Popular Radio*, Jenkins christened the transmission of motion pictures the "ether waves."

These 1925 headlines built on the enthusiasm shown after Baird's and Jenkins's successful demonstrations. A handful of "advanced amateurs"—as Jenkins termed them—worked in 1925 and 1926 to assemble the first scratch-built television receivers in Great Britain and in the United States. Some of these receivers were built by hobbyists using diagrams mailed to them by Baird or Jenkins. Jenkins sent out dozens of these hand-written instructions to hobbyists so they could build their own radio vision receiving sets or, simply, Radio Visors. Jenkins sold these Radio Visor schematics for as little as $7.50. This was only months before Jenkins and his assistants began to assemble some of the first Radio Visors to be sold fully assembled. Those purchasing these Radio Visors could look-in (much the way that wireless enthusiasts just several years earlier began to listen-in) to the transmissions from Jenkins's own Maryland station as well as the signals of a small number of other transmitters soon with their own signals on the airwaves.

The transmission of a visual moving image by AT&T engineers on Thursday, April 7, 1927, from Washington, D.C., to New York City, featuring the Secretary of Commerce Herbert Hoover, marked another historic moment in the development of television: it was the first demonstration of television by one of the largest and most well-established companies in the world.

"What its practical uses shall be I leave to your imagination," AT&T president Walter F. Gifford told those assembled in New York City at the Thursday, April 7, 1927, demonstration. That same day, AT&T engineers transmitted a television signal ("by radio") from its station 3XN in Whippany, New Jersey, a distance of twenty-two miles to the company's laboratories in New York City. The AT&T transmission—what the company's executives called "television applied to radio" or "radiotelephonic television"—was a broadcast featuring several actors and actresses performing vaudeville skits.

"Far Off Speakers Seen as Well as Heard in a Test of Television, Like a Photo Come to Life," "The First Time in History, Pictures Are Flashed by Wire and Radio Synchronizing with Speaker's Voice," read *New York Times* headlines on Friday morning, April 8, 1927. That morning's front-page story of the AT&T transmission as well as the remarks made by Secretary of Commerce Hoover from the AT&T Washington, D.C., laboratory observed that the AT&T demonstration of television coincided with the screening of the German film, *Metropolis*, and likened the AT&T demonstration to the futuristic screens used by the actors and actresses in the German film, stating "a case of a prophecy being fulfilled about as soon as it started."[10] On Friday, April 8, 1927, the *Washington Post* front-page headline reported, "New York Gets Likeness and Voice by Telephone When Hoover Talks Here." Weeks later, on Monday, May 23, 1927, AT&T executives demonstrated its television transmissions to a meeting of some six hundred electrical engineers and radio engineers, generating further excitement for the company's breakthrough.

Widely read scientific and popular magazines as well as some of the nation's largest circulation newspapers ran even more stories on the experiments with television in the days after the Thursday, April 7, 1927, AT&T demonstration as television's inventors and investors alike stood on the cusp of one of television's exciting and most important years of its early history.

Radio magazines featured ads for inexpensive kits for the assembly of receivers to look in on the television transmissions. Charles Francis Jenkins, for example, sold his Radio Visors both as an assembly required kit or as a fully assembled receiver. On Friday, January 13, 1928, after years of its own innovations and investments in television transmissions, General Electric began transmitting television signals to receivers installed in the Schenectady homes of its company engineers and some of its company executives. Under the direction of Ernst Frederik Werner Alexanderson, pictures were transmitted by the company's 2XAF transmitter while sound was transmitted from the radio studio of Schenectady's WGY. General Electric executives estimated that the transmissions had a range of about twenty to thirty miles—a distance comparable to the roughly fifty miles of the transmissions of London's John Logie Baird in his experiments at the same time.

On Friday, January 13, 1928, Alexanderson demonstrated General Electric's television receiver, consisting of a three-by-three-inch screen in a large wooden cabinet, from his living room. Headlines in the *New York Times*, the *Boston Post*, and newspapers across the country that next day reported: "Radio Television to Home Receivers Is Shown in Tests." "The apparently simple instruments gave no hint of the years of experimenting and the tedious process of trial and error."[11] Under the headline "Radio Vision Takes Another Step Toward the Home, the *New York Times* reported only days later, on Sunday, January 22, 1928, "Those who have seen the machine in action do not find that it requires a long stretch of the imagination to foresee the day when every home equipped with a receiving set will get pictures along with the sound."[12] On the cover of its April 1928 issue, *Popular Mechanics* featured the headline "Television for the Home" with a photograph of the Alexanderson family watching the small screen on the television receiver in the living room of their Schenectady home.

On Friday, July 20, 1928, the Federal Radio Commission (FRC) granted its first broadcasting license to Jenkins Laboratories for its Washington, D.C., station, W3XK. Licenses for the construction and operation of nine visual broadcasting transmitters "for development and experimentation in the work of sending pictures through the air" were issued by the commission, including licenses for three transmitters in New York City for the Radio Corporation of America (RCA), a license for the Westinghouse Electric and Manufacturing Company, and licenses for smaller operators in Beacon, New York, Lexington, Massachusetts, Los Angeles, and Memphis.[13] In the days that followed, still more licenses were issued by the commission, including General Electric's 2XAF in Schenectady, New York, while headlines continued to report the latest improvements and successes of television transmissions.

As experimental signals and intermittent transmissions regularly aired across the East Coast, executives with some of the nation's largest electronics manufacturers expressed their enthusiasm for the commercial potential of home television receivers in the early months of 1928. RCA began a regular test signal from its W2XBS transmitter in New York City. On Thursday, May 10, 1928, General Electric announced it would begin a regular broadcast of television from its 2XAF transmitter, which was operating from Schenectady WGY radio station studios. Programming was aired by General Electric on 2XAF on a weekly schedule on Tuesday, Thursday, and Friday afternoons, typically from 1:30 to 3:30.

"Broadcasting of television images by WGY has stimulated a great overnight interest in neon lamps," the *New York Times* reported on Sunday, June 24, 1928.[14] Thousands of specially built neon lamps, similar to those used in General Electric's television receivers demonstrated in Schenectady, were sold by mail-order to hobbyists building their own receivers. Sales of sheet-aluminum, used to construct some of the receivers being built at the time, saw shortages by suppliers in Boston, while General Electric engineers announced the successful "quite clear" transmission of images "about one inch square" at a distance of some 163 miles from the Schenectady WGY station to its receivers in New York City.[15] "Scientists are working long-hours in an effort to perfect the radio moving picture," the *Atlanta Constitution* reported on Sunday, June 3, 1928, "aided to a certain extent by amateur experimenters."[16] RCA's W2XBS in New York City, RCA's W2XBW in Bound Brook, New Jersey, Westinghouse's W2XAV in Pittsburgh, Pennsylvania, and transmitters in Beacon, New York, and Los Angeles were all airing their own transmissions by that June. Schenectady's 2XAF and Charles Francis Jenkins's W3XK also aired their own transmissions.

On Friday, June 22, 1928, Jenkins announced that his transmitter W3XK would air its regular "radiomovie" broadcasts for the public. "Broadcast of Movies by Radio Here July 2," the *Washington Post* headline reported on Saturday, June 23, 1928. "The radiomovie broadcasts would begin at 8:00 PM on the evening of Monday, July 2, 1928, and would air the same time every Monday, Wednesday, and Friday evening. This was the first regular schedule of broadcast radiomovies," Jenkins later wrote in his 1929 book *Radiomovies, Radiovision, Television.*[17] Jenkins called his broadcasts "Picture Stories by Radio," and word soon spread of the broadcasts from Jenkins's studios in Washington, D.C.

Experimental television stations by the end of 1928 were in some of the nation's larger cities, including Boston, Los Angeles, Pittsburgh, and Washington, D.C., and in smaller cities such as Lexington, Massachusetts, and Schenectady, New York. Transmissions oftentimes came on the air and then abruptly stopped as technicians worked to improve their frequencies and signals. "Owners of sets unequipped for television," "heard television [transmissions] as an intermittent high-pitched whir" on their radios—no doubt stirring the public's interest in television still further for those who had not yet seen its demonstrations.[18] *New York Times* short-feature items, such as "How to Tune In on a Televisor," reflected the growing interest in television by the end of 1928.

On Wednesday, August 22, 1928, a historic transmission was carried from the Albany, New York, statehouse to viewers in Schenectady on General Electric 2XAF. It was the first time in the nation's history that a presidential candidate appeared in a television broadcast. The occasion for the General Electric transmission from Albany was New York governor Alfred E. Smith's acceptance of the Democratic Party presidential nomination. After having been nominated on Thursday, June 28, 1928, by the Democratic Party at its convention in Houston, Texas, Governor Smith formally accepted his nomination when a delegation of Democratic Party leaders arrived in Albany to present him with official notification of his nomination.

Governor Smith's Notification Day speech at the Albany, New York, statehouse was heard on the radio by millions of Americans across the United States. From its station a distance of some eighteen miles away in Schenectady, the WGY transmission of the governor's remarks was heard by thousands of listeners across the area. For the smaller Schenectady audience, the governor's remarks from Albany were not only heard on their radios but were also seen as a television broadcast on the General Electric 2XAF transmitter.

"Smith Rehearses for Camera Men," the *New York Times* headline reported about Governor Smith's Tuesday, August 21, 1928, preparations for the filming of a broadcast by the motion picture newsreel crews that would be shown in national motion picture theaters as well as for the governor's broadcast aired on the General Electric 2XAF transmitter. "As Accommodation, He Gives Gestures in Advance on Nomination Platform," read the headline reporting on the governor's Tuesday rehearsal. "His practice appearance in the speaker's stand on the capitol steps," the *New York Times* wrote on Wednesday, August 22, 1928, "was made noteworthy by the television broadcasting of his image over WGY, the General Electric station, which for the first time demonstrated the transmission of an outdoor television pickup. The light from a 1,000 watt lamp broken up by the scanning disk played on the Governor's face." "The photo-electric cells, which respond to the slightest changes in light intensity, caught the changing lights as the Governor moved his head and these light changes, converted into electrical current by the photo-electrical cells, were amplified and flashed to the WGY transmitter 18 miles from the capitol. The electrical signals were then impressed on the antenna as in the case of speech and were flung out in all directions."[19]

The Wednesday, August 22, 1928, speech by Governor Smith was an important moment in the history of early-twentieth-century television. 2XAF's transmission of the governor's remarks from Albany to the small Schenectady viewing audience is remembered as a mostly disappointing broadcast due to technical complications. That afternoon, a thunderstorm forced officials to move the ceremony inside the statehouse. Large banks of lights were set up to illuminate the platform for photographers, motion picture newsreel cameras, and the General Electric 2XAF television cameras, but the hastily assembled lighting inside New York's statehouse resulted in a dimly lit podium that only allowed the Schenectady viewers to see a blurred, barely recognizable image of the governor.

On Monday, August 27, 1928, less than a week after the 2XAF transmission, *Time* magazine offered its most comprehensive story to date on the experiments taking place in the work with "visual broadcasting," noting the nation's seven stations that were experimenting with the transmission of images and sound over the airwaves.[20] "These stations, one or another, are sending out still photographs, moving pictures," the *Time* magazine article continued.[21] This same issue also covered AT&T's work with television: "In Manhattan, Dr. Herbert E. Ives and Dr. Frank Gray of the Bell Telephone Laboratories operated a machine which directly broadcasts vast outdoor scenes a fair distance from their lens." "Heretofore," *Time* magazine continued, "only small studio scenes could be transmitted."[22] Headline-making demonstrations of experimental television by General Electric and other firms stirred public interest.

December 1928's *Radio News*, billed as "Radio's Greatest Magazine" by editor and publisher Hugo Gernsback, offered one of the most stirring images yet of television's future as its cover illustration that December. Below the headline, "Multiple Television," was a picture of a family seated in front of an elaborate television receiver. The large device featured three different screens, one in color and the remaining two in black and white. Each was several inches wide. A boxing match and a musical performance were depicted on the slightly smaller black-and-white screens while the larger, full-color screen featured a theatrical production. The "multiple television," as *Radio News* depicted it, allowed for the simultaneous viewing of three different stations and included three sets of knobs and controls presumably for tuning into each of the different broadcasts.

"Twenty-Six Transmitters Are Now Sending Images into Space," was the *New York Times* headline on Sunday, June 9, 1929. By 1929, these twenty-six licensees, including the Radio Corporation of America (RCA), the General Electric Company, the Jenkins Television Corporation, and the Westinghouse Electric and Manufacturing Company, held licenses from the Department of Commerce. RCA had five licenses for its transmitters, including three (W2XBS, W2XBV, and W2XCO) in New York City and two (W2XBW and W3XL) in Bound Brook, New Jersey. Westinghouse had two licenses for its transmitters: W1XAE in Springfield, Massachusetts, and W8XAV in Pittsburgh. General Electric's 2XAF and W2XCW were licensed in Schenectady. The Jenkins Television Corporation had two licensed transmitters, W2XCR in Jersey City, New Jersey, and W3XK at Jenkins Laboratories. Jenkins's W3XK's broadcasts were so popular that when, in

April 1929, the station temporarily suspended its transmissions for several days due to maintenance, the outpouring of letters and telephone calls for the broadcasts to resume was so great it made newspaper headlines.

The collapse of the New York Stock Exchange on Tuesday, October 29, 1929, and the ensuing months of headlines covering unemployment, evictions, and foreclosures, ended the first chapter of experimental television and visual broadcasting stations in the United States. Halting efforts by the Jenkins Television Corporation and the handful of manufacturers, electronics retailers, and mail-order catalogs to advertise the sales of television receivers in 1929 reflected what was essentially a collapse of the already small market for television receivers that existed prior to 1929. While some "advanced amateurs," as Charles Francis Jenkins called them, still spent hours working the dials of their receivers for the intermittently aired programming and test signals from the handful of transmitters in some of the nation's larger cities such as Chicago, Los Angeles, New York City, and Washington, D.C., as well as Pittsburgh and Schenectady, the era of experimental television essentially had come to an end.

Wary business executives and investors were still unconvinced of the commercial possibilities of television, and its decade-long, headline-making days of breakthroughs in broadcasting of sight and sound were coming to an end. The American public's imagination had been stirred after the first demonstrations in Jenkins's Washington, D.C., workshop on Saturday, June 13, 1925. The public's enthusiastic response continued through headlines reporting the boom in visual broadcasting stations by 1929, as well as the innumerable illustrations and drawings of futuristic television receivers on the covers of popular wireless and radio magazines. But it took nearly another ten years for television's technical feasibility and its commercial and investment potential to become once again evident to the American public.

TELEVISION AND THE DEPRESSION

On Monday, September 30, 1929, the British Broadcast Corporation (BBC) began its regular transmissions with Baird's television system just weeks before the world's attention was gripped with headlines of the Wall Street financial collapse, which all but ended television's commercial prospects over the next decade. London department stores installed their displays of Baird's Televisors, which, over the next ten years, sold at a somewhat modest pace in London but sold quickly everywhere else in the world. Television broadcasting during the Depression essentially disappeared. Its transmissions were less frequent. Its test patterns were gone from the airwaves. The Depression was to be radio's moment. Sales of radios grew as sales of television receivers fell. Still, 1930 saw television's entrepreneurial spirit very much alive in the work of a handful of inventors and investors as well as in the workshops of companies such as General Electric, AT&T, and RCA, whose executives still backed their engineers who were working with promising new breakthroughs in cathode rays.

Federal licenses for visual broadcast transmitters in the United States continued in 1930 as electronics manufacturers, retailers, and smaller firms pursued their own work in television transmission. Some twenty-five licenses had been approved by the Federal Radio Commission by June 1930, including Boston's W1XAV (owned by the Shortwave and Television Laboratory Incorporated), Lexington's W1XAY, Lawrence's W1XY (owned by Pilot Laboratories), Jersey City's W2XAP, Newark's W2XBA, Long Island's W2XBO (owned by the United Research Corporation), New York City's W2XBS, Beacon, New York's W2XBU, Passaic's W2XCD (owned by the De Forest Radio Company), New York City's W2XCO, W2XCP in Allwood, New Jersey (owned by the Freed Eisenmann Radio Corporation), Jersey City's W2XCR (owned by the Jenkins Television Corporation), Schenectady's W2XCW, Long Island City's W2XR, Ossining, New York's W2XX, RCA's W3XAD in Camden, New Jersey, W3XAK and W3XL in Bound Brook, New Jersey, Maryland's W3XK, Oregon's W7XAO, Westinghouse's W8XAV and its W8XT in Pittsburgh, Pennsylvania, Aero Products Incorporated's W9XAG in Chicago, W9XAO (owned by the Western Television Corporation) in Chicago, and W9XR in Downers Grove, Illinois (owned by the Great Lakes Broadcasting Company).

Chicago's W9XAP took to the airwaves on Wednesday, August 27, 1930, with its own television transmitter, which was licensed, owned, and operated by the *Chicago Daily News*. "More than 300 television receivers placed in the hands of dealers throughout Chicago and its suburbs demonstrated to thousands of curious spectators that there was something to this thing referred to as talking pictures of the air," the *Chicago Daily News* reported on the day after its own station's first evening broadcast. Sets received a signal transmitted from the twenty-fifth floor of the newly opened *Chicago Daily News* building.[23] Large crowds watched W9XAP's first broadcast that Wednesday evening, including a large crowd watching a receiver on display at Sears Roebuck Company. Weeks later, on the evening of Tuesday, November 4, 1930, election returns were broadcast on W9XAP from its studios in the *Chicago Daily News* building. Within a matter of months, the W9XAP signal is reported to have been received by viewers at a distance as far as four hundred miles from Chicago, then still farther at a distance of some five hundred miles away by January 1932.

In 1931, electronics retailers and manufacturers put on the market additional television receiver models and still more assembly required television sets built with the blueprints in circulation among hobbyists and radio enthusiasts. "Radio Dealers Foresee Harvest in Television," the *New York Times* headline reported on Saturday, March 22, 1931. "Radio retailers are expecting a rich harvest to grow from the seeds of television now being planted by the research laboratories and by the activities of the television outfits now on the air," the *New York Times* reported, telling its readers of the widespread interest in New York City's W2XBS, a transmitter licensed, owned, and operated by RCA, which was airing nightly broadcasts from a studio atop the New Amsterdam Theater.[24] New York City's second transmitter, W2XCR, a Jersey City–based transmitter licensed, owned, and operated by Charles Francis Jenkins in partnership with radio station WGBS, began airing broadcasts from its studios on 5th Avenue in April 1931, generating even further excitement and interest.

On Tuesday, July 21, 1931, the CBS transmitter W2XAB began airing a regular schedule of programming as the city's third television transmitter—a station that led the way in early television programming as well as broadcasting some of the first election night returns in television history on the evening of Tuesday, November 8, 1932. CBS installed the W2XAB transmitter on the Chrysler Building that rivaled that of RCA, which had installed its own transmitter on the Empire State Building's eighty-fifth floor. NBC's early broadcasts in October 1931 from the Empire State Building marked the beginnings of their innovations in pioneering some of that company's most popular and successful broadcasts in the early years of its television.

"Six Visual Stations on the New York Air," the *New York Times* headline reported on July 19, 1931, about RCA's W2XBS, Jenkins's W2XCR, and CBS's W2XAB as well as Long Island City's W2XR, all owned and operated by Radio Pictures, Inc., W2XBO licensed and operated by United Research Corp, and Passaic, New Jersey's W2XCD, licensed and operated by the DeForest Radio Company. "Television plans to climb above the sidewalks of New York in hopes that dreams will come true," the *New York Times* reported of the television boom in the city: "Printed signs, images of people, engineers making funny faces to see if observers at outposts can see them, images of Felix the Cat as he revolves on a turntable, photographs of motion picture stars and prominent men held in front of electric eyes, all fly through the homes at the speed of light."[25]

The grand opening of NBC studios on Tuesday, December 27, 1932, dubbed the "Broadcast Metropolis" by *Radio News*, at the Radio City complex marked the decade's astonishing growth in commercial radio broadcasting as well as the still-unfolding transmissions of television. Radio City in New York City was emblematic of the promise and of the prosperity of one of the country's largest, most well-established businesses not only in the financial success of radio but also its early and continuing investments in television. Featuring some thirty-five smaller studios as well as a large auditorium seating as many as one thousand audience members, some Radio City's studios were constructed with special glass "curtains" to be installed when needed between the audience and the performers being broadcast in their studios. Special lighting in some Radio City studios, the kind of lighting that would be a familiar part of television's early broadcasting, was also constructed in some of the building's studios to further accommodate television's production in the years to come.

"Television," Erik Barnouw writes of the end of the 1940s, "seemed indeed to be about ready."[26] "The often delayed promise of television's 'imminent' arrival teased most would-be viewers in the 1930s," Ray Barfield tells us, is "nowhere perhaps more evident than in the air-conditioned, glass-walled quiet of RCA's Radio City and its modern studios."[27] In keeping with the millions spent by RCA in the construction of New York City's Radio City, in 1930 some of the largest companies in the United States invested substantial sums in television's still-emerging technology. Television still had little regular programming and there were few sales of television receivers, but the promise anticipated by business executives, investors, and innovators working to improve the quality of television's transmissions as well as the reliability of receivers to be sold to the public remained strong. Some department stores and retailers continued to display televisions in their stores through the end of the 1930s. *Popular Mechanics* and other magazines featured ads for television sets and even for training in television installation and repair ("Be a Television Expert!" "Learn Television with Radio—Now!")—ads complete with the familiar Depression-era symbol of the National Recovery Administration (NRA) eagle.[28] AT&T engineers completed their installation of the first high-capacity coaxial cable between New York and Philadelphia by the end of 1936. This specially designed cable was capable of carrying the signals of television broadcasts from city to city for the first time. With RCA's Radio City and its transmitter atop the New York City Empire State Building beaming its signals a distance of some fifty miles or farther across the New York City metropolitan area, television's promise seemed to have finally or at least partially fulfilled its prophecy; its boom and bust and boom in the early years of the twentieth century was a prelude to television's ascendancy in 1939.

Chapter 6

Television in the 1930s and in Wartime America

Sunday, April 30, 1939. Flushing Meadows, Queens. President Franklin D. Roosevelt becomes the first U.S. president to appear on a live television broadcast, speaking before a crowd of spectators at a large outdoor ceremony at the World's Fair. Breakthroughs in the RCA laboratories continued well into the end of the 1930s and RCA was one of the few companies with the financial assets to invest a sizeable amount in television's innovation through the decade of the Depression. RCA operated its television transmitter from the eighty-fifth floor of the Empire State Building, from which its broadcast signals were transmitted a distance of some fifty miles across the New York City metropolitan area, transmissions that by June 1940 included the first broadcast of a national party convention to New York City television viewers. RCA's Vladimir Zworykin and his assistants brought television into the modern era with his innovation of an electronic beam for scanning images and objects. Working from the Camden, New Jersey, RCA laboratories, Zworykin and his assistants perfected what was soon touted by RCA executives as "all-electronic television."

Months of preparation went into the unveiling of RCA's new television receivers at the 1939 World's Fair in Queens, New York. RCA's construction of a large exhibit building, with its futuristic architecture and its large transmitting tower built over a two-story glass-walled entrance to the building, took center stage with the debut of their latest television receivers. RCA partnered with some of New York City's department stores and retailers to display the company's newest receivers on their store floors and in their display windows, but few of these displays matched the excitement felt by the thousands of visitors to the World's Fair who crowded into the RCA exhibit building to catch a glimpse of the flickering images on the televisions displayed there. With RCA's regular transmissions aired to viewers throughout New York City and with the newspaper ads and displays of its newest line of televisions in the city's department stores, RCA's Sarnoff told the press that his company would sell 100,000 or more television sets in 1939.

On the morning of Thursday, April 20, 1939, Sarnoff formally opened the RCA exhibit featuring its newest television sets at the company's building at the World's Fair. That morning's ceremonies, broadcast on television live by RCA, began with a musical performance at the company's Radio City studios. With the broadcast moving from Radio City to a small garden, nicknamed the "Television Garden" by RCA employees, next to the RCA building at the World's Fair, Sarnoff spoke from behind a small podium with his company's logo on its front, his image and voice transmitted across the airwaves of New York City. "Now we add radio sight to sound," Sarnoff told his audience at the garden and those watching any one of the one hundred or more television receivers either a few feet away inside the RCA exhibition hall or those on display at New York City department stores and retailers. "It is with a feeling of humbleness that I come to this moment of announcing the birth in this country of a new art so important in its implications that it is bound to affect all society," Sarnoff explained. "It is a creative force which we must learn to utilize for the benefit of all mankind." His remarks finished, Sarnoff then gave the signal to technicians at the fairgrounds who switched the broadcast to an RCA studio in Manhattan where an exhibition boxing match was being televised as part of that day's ceremonies.

The RCA building at the World's Fair featured more than a dozen display models of the company's newest receiver, the TRK-12. A translucent Lucite TRK-12, dubbed the "Phantom Teleceiver" by reporters, stood at the entrance of the RCA pavilion. It was seen by tens of thousands of visitors who walked through the company's exhibition hall, and its photographs were widely reprinted in newspapers and magazines covering the World's Fair and the RCA exhibit. The picture tubes of the RCA TRK-12 receivers ranged in size from five inches to twelve inches and their screens faced upward on the top of their cabinets, which were typically four to five feet in size. The wooden cabinets featured mirrors under their tops that tilted upward to reflect the screen's image from the tube, which faced upward in the cabinet. While some RCA models were priced as low as $200, most of RCA's TRK-12 models with their distinctive Art Deco styling cost as much as $600 or more.

On an overcast Sunday, on April 30, 1939—coincidentally, also the one hundred and fiftieth anniversary of President Washington's inauguration in New York City—RCA's Sarnoff opened the ceremonies from a platform in front of the World's Fair's Federal Building, a $3,000,000 U.S. exhibit that featured displays and murals depicting the country's history. With an audience of several thousand visitors to the fairgrounds assembled in front of the Federal Building, Sarnoff looked across the crowd at the scaffolding built for the photographers who were covering the day's ceremonies, scaffolding that included the RCA television cameras with two specially equipped vans located just yards away to transmit the signal to the company's Empire State Building transmitter. They were preparing to broadcast the first live televised speech of a president in the nation's history.

President Roosevelt arrived at the World's Fair shortly after a fairgrounds parade opened that day's ceremonies. He was accompanied by RCA executives and other fair officials to the podium where he delivered his remarks to the assembled crowd. More than 200,000 attendees were at the fair that Sunday and many thousands of those visitors gathered in front of the stage to witness the remarks of the president and other dignitaries. Thousands of visitors crowded into the plaza between the stage and the scaffolding.

"The eyes of the United States are fixed on the future," President Roosevelt told the crowd in front of his podium as well as the radio listeners and those watching the RCA broadcast on television receivers at some of the one hundred stores, retailers, and special displays located throughout the city. More than a dozen receivers were set up at RCA's Radio City, where hundreds of viewers watched the president's speech taking place some eight miles away at the fairgrounds. The RCA TRK-12 television receivers, nine in all, were on display in the company's exhibit building for visitors to the fairgrounds wanting to watch the ceremony on television. Another hundred or so RCA receivers were in operation in department stores, retailers, and other locations. Viewers of that Sunday's television broadcast recall the picture as clear and steady, and photographs from that day clearly show the president as well as images of the fair's Perisphere and Trylon.

Against the backdrop of the World's Fair's Federal Building, President Roosevelt stood at a podium carrying the 1939 World's Fair Trylon and Perisphere emblem and looked across at the scaffolding holding dozens of journalists and RCA television cameras that were broadcasting him across the airwaves a distance of some fifty miles to those watching in department stores and elsewhere throughout the metropolitan area. While only several thousand viewers likely saw the president's black-and-white image broadcast on television that Sunday, an audience of some 600,000 or more heard the event broadcast on the radio. Millions more read about it in their papers in the days that followed, and many saw photographs of the president, the television cameras on their scaffolding, and the specially equipped NBC vans that transmitted the broadcast. Millions of Americans certainly saw excerpts from the president's remarks at the World's Fair in the black-and-white motion picture newsreels in their local movie theaters.

"Telecast of President at the World's Fair to Start Wheels of New Industry," "Television Now Drops Mantle of Mystery and Public Becomes Its Judge" read the *New York Times* headlines on Sunday, April 30, 1939, regarding the paper's coverage of the events that day. "For weeks," the *New York Times*' Orrin E. Dunlap Jr. reported of NBC's employees, "the mobile vans, television stations on wheels, have been practicing at the fairgrounds. They have been tossing pictures from Flushing to Radio City, and even in the rain and through low-hanging Long Island fogs, they have flashed remarkably clear scenes over the eight mile bee-line. Hopes run high because the preview tests have been successful." Many read his account of the preparations for the inaugural television broadcast just hours before the president took the stage at the World's Fair.[1]

"Ceremony Is Carried by Television as Industry Makes Its Formal Bow," the *New York Times* headline reported on Monday, May 1, 1939. "Science presented television as a new deal in communication yesterday as President Roosevelt spoke in the Court of Peace at the opening of the World's Fair," Dunlap reported. "Sight-seeing by radio," with crowds gathered in front of the one hundred or so television receivers on display at department stores and at locations throughout the city, was reported as "highly successful."[2] Crowds, who were watching any of the nine TRK-12 receivers on display in the RCA building yards away from where the president delivered his remarks, watched a signal carried from the fairgrounds through the RCA cameras, then through the specially equipped vans where technicians worked to transmit the signal to the transmitter on the Empire State Building, then through that building's antenna that transmitted the signal back to the TRK-12 receivers at the World's Fair RCA building.

The exhibition of the latest RCA television receivers at the 1939 World's Fair did little to drive the sales of RCA television sets. Tens of thousands of visitors to the fair went through the RCA building in the first week of May alone, but these displays and exhibits yielded few sales, and sales of RCA televisions at Bloomingdale's, Macy's, and other department stores were slow. Macy's displayed four different models on the floor of its largest store, yet few of these receivers sold. By June, a total of ten television models were on sale at Macy's, including sets manufactured by DuMont, RCA, and Westinghouse. RCA TRK-12 was one of the most costly televisions on the market at this time with a price tag of almost $600 for some of its larger models, a pricetag that approached that of a new 1939 automobile. RCA's TRK-12 featured a twelve-by-twelve-inch screen, the largest in any retail television receiver sold to that date, with RCA's signature mirror appearing from an opening on the top of the wooden cabinet. The RCA TRK-9 and TRK-5 models were less costly, the latter a tabletop set priced at $199, which could be connected by a short electrical cord to a family's radio to receive the television's audio signal.

In 1939, RCA brought its television sets to well-publicized exhibits, not just to the viewers in New York City but also across the United States, including the Illinois and Indiana State Fairs. In Illinois, Indiana, Minnesota, Ohio, and elsewhere in the Midwest, RCA's cameras and its television sets were displayed, sometimes in tents. Visitors were charged an admission fee of 10 cents apiece; these visitors might see their state's governor, prominent public figures, or motion picture and radio personalities taking part in special demonstration broadcasts. In September 1939, thousands of visitors attending the Indiana State Fair visited the RCA television exhibit. The RCA traveling television unit also visited Minnesota, including a special exhibition at the Minneapolis Radisson Hotel where four TRK-12 receivers were displayed to large numbers of visitors throughout the Twin Cities as well as Chicago's Marshall Field and Company and St. Louis's Famous-Barr department store. Musical performers and variety acts of all kinds participated in some of these television demonstrations that summer as RCA and its employees brought the marvel of modern television to the Midwest and elsewhere.

"Television Reaches Capital and What Seemed Magic Becomes a Fact," a *Washington Post* headline reported on Sunday, January 29, 1939, two days after the Friday, January 27, 1939, television demonstration on the National Mall in the nation's capital. Weeks before President Roosevelt's speech at the World's Fair, a television demonstration at the National Press Club and on the National Mall marked the arrival of television cameras to that city. "Several distinguished members of Congress, including a Congresswoman, went nearly a mile, from Capitol Hill to the Washington Monument Grounds, to be interviewed Friday," *Washington Post*'s John Cabot Smith reported on Sunday, January 29, 1939, "making more spectacular history than they could have by staying at their legislative desks" by taking part in "the 1st demonstration of America's 1st mobile television outfit." "Hundreds of Washingtonians learned that the device so long dreamed about is now fact," Smith reported, as curious onlookers crowded into the upper floors of the National Press Building to watch the transmissions from almost a half-mile away, while lawmakers and other notable figures stood on the National Mall and spoke into the "iconoscope camera" for the "telecast."[3]

"Television is only now about to emerge from the experimental stage," *Washington Post*'s Cabot Smith explained of the first demonstration of RCA's television in Washington, D.C., on Friday, January 27, 1939, weeks before the unveiling of the company's television broadcasting and its receivers at the New York World's Fair. "For years, we have heard about it, and during the last two days, many Washingtonians for the first time have seen it." "It works," Smith reported, "it is no longer just a dream." "But," he added, "how long will it be before we all have television sets, before programs are something more than sidewalk interviews or studio experiments? That, like everything about the future of television, is a question. With the opening of the World's Fair in New York on April 30," Smith continued, "commercial telecasting will begin but how far television will have advanced by then from its present position or how far and how rapidly it will change thereafter, one can only guess." "Contrasted with the flickering silhouettes produced by Jenkins in 1928," Smith explained, referring to Charles Francis Jenkins whose experiments were made only a decade earlier from his

Connecticut Avenue workshop, "the modern television is, though small, virtually perfect. Nation-wide hook-ups of telecasting stations are impractical," Smith continued, noting that the signals transmitted by RCA in New York City traveled no farther than a distance of some forty-five to fifty miles. "What will become of television? Will it ever be more than an experiment? Will it ever reach all the homes of the nation? Will it ever pay its own way? And if so, how soon? Television is a great question mark," Smith reported. RCA's television demonstrations in Washington, D.C., a city whose place in the history of television as the home of its early innovator Charles Francis Jenkins and a city that, within a decade, would forever be fixated on television broadcasting and the coverage of the city's lawmakers and their debates, is a central part of the television's story in the second half of the twentieth century.

"Mobile Television Unit Brings New Magic to Washington," Washington, D.C.'s *Evening Star* reported on the evening of Friday, January 27, 1939, the day of the television demonstration in the National Mall. Photographs of the "notables from Capitol Hill gathered today at 14th Street and the Mall" as well as of viewers and visitors one-half mile away at the National Press Club accompanied the *Evening Star*'s reporting of that day's exhibit. "This was Washington's 1st demonstration of America's 1st and only mobile television outfit," *Evening Star*'s Carter Brooke Jones reported, noting the two RCA trucks ("telemobiles") adjacent to the National Mall "parked rather far apart alongside the Agriculture Building. The lights in the receiving room flashed off, and the screens [in] back of the receiving sets began to reflect what the cameras and microphone in front of the East Wing of the Agriculture Department Administration Building were picking up. The televised image comes in upside down on a flat screen at the top but is mirrored right-side up on a 2nd perpendicular screen at the back."[4] Standing in the rooms of the National Press Club where the TRK-12 receivers flashed their flickering images of Capitol Hill's lawmakers, the buildings and historical monuments on the National Mall, and even the automobiles and the pedestrians passing by in the background, Jones and his fellow reporters became some of the first in the country to witness a device that dramatically changed the work and world of elected officials and lawmakers in Washington, D.C.

"Televisions 1st Roadshow Proves a Hit," *Broadcasting*'s Martin Codel reported in his Wednesday, February 15, 1939, coverage of the RCA's demonstration in Washington, D.C., a demonstration on the National Mall just blocks from the White House and Capitol Hill and weeks before New York City's broadcast by President Roosevelt at the World's Fair on Sunday, April 30, 1939. "Federal Officials Much Impressed by NBC-RCA," the headline reported, complete with photographs of the cameras on the National Mall and of viewers watching on five of RCA's TRK-12 receivers blocks away at the National Press Club. Codel reported, "The pictures shown in the National Press Club were extremely clear, even during the several days of cold and rain, so clear, in fact, that they drew excited 'oh's' and 'ah's' from the viewers as they saw persons they knew step before the microphones to be interviewed and as they saw clear panoramas of Washington's famed Mall, the Washington Monument, and passing automobiles."[5] Cabinet members, congressional leaders, FCC commissioners, newspaper reporters, and visitors to the National Press Club watched the images from in front of the Department of Agriculture building on the National Mall where two of the RCA mobile units transmitted their images the half-mile necessary to be received on five of the RCA TRK-12 receivers on display at the press club.

With some of RCA's most expensive receivers costing almost as much as a new automobile and with the limited availability of broadcasting and programing in most parts of the country, 1939 proved a year not only of promise but of only partial commercial success. Television displays at department stores and at retailers across the country spurred some of the first sales of television sets, and regular RCA broadcasts in New York City and elsewhere certainly made headlines in cities across the country. In 1939, *Broadcasting*'s summer issues featured stories of RCA's demonstrations and its traveling units across the country from Pennsylvania's Allegheny County Fair to San Francisco, California, to Seattle, Washington, as well as a similar short-distance, portable television unit exhibited by Philco. In Atlanta, Rich's department store premiered "the miracle of the modern age" in an RCA television display at its store in early August 1939 as thousands of customers visited the store for a glimpse of the televisions, which were being well publicized in magazines and newspapers.

Few of television's most enthusiastic and far-sighted financial investors were prepared for the cost of the installation of coaxial cables, with some estimates placing its construction and installation from $4,000 to as much as $6,000 per mile between cities and television transmitters in those cities as well as what some called "booster relay stations" to transmit television signals from city to city. Compounding the expense of constructing the city-to-city networks for transmitting television signals, challenges in the transmission of television signals in 1939 involved everything from atmospheric conditions interfering with television signals to the construction of taller buildings that interfered with television signals. When high-rise apartment and office buildings were constructed in 1939 and afterward in the vicinity of the Empire State Building, where RCA had its transmitter for broadcasting its signal in the New York City metropolitan area, RCA engineers worried that the newly constructed skyscrapers would interfere with their television signal.

"Too Early for Television?" *Time* magazine questioned in the headline accompanying its Monday, April 15, 1940, story—a story detailing the thicket of technical issues still being resolved by authorities almost a year after the April 1939 debut of the RCA television system at the World's Fair. Licensing the construction and operation of new transmitters continued as electronics manufacturers, radio stations, and newspapers invested in television operations. Receiver sales, however, were essentially stalled for all but the most well-to-do households in New York City, Philadelphia, and other cities with stations, with just a scattering of sets sold outside of these areas until broadcasters aired a more regular schedule of programming. The RCA factory in Camden, New Jersey, averaged production of only seven television receivers a day in February 1940, a measure of the slower-than-anticipated sales of its receivers almost a year after the New York World's Fair.[6] Fewer than 10,000 televisions were estimated to have been sold by 1940, with some 3,000 of these thought to have been purchased in New York City, a figure estimated to grow to only some 4,000 sets in New York City by July 1941 when broadcasters began airing their first regular transmissions with a full broadcast schedule in the city that summer.

TELEVISION AND THE 1940 REPUBLICAN NATIONAL CONVENTION

The 1940 Republican National Convention offered an opportunity for stations in Philadelphia and New York City to air the first televised coverage of a national party convention. On Tuesday, June 25, 1940, Philadelphia's W3XE—later known as WPTZ-TV—transmitted the first live television coverage of a national party convention, coverage carried by the newly constructed coaxial cable from Philadelphia to New York City, allowing viewers in New York City and Schenectady to watch the Philadelphia convention.

"The latest television apparatus, including portable equipment and four cameras, will be utilized to electrify the scene and relay the pictures over coaxial cable to New York," *New York Times'* Orrin E. Dunlap Jr. reported of the 1940 coverage of the Republican convention. "From the NBC transmitter atop the Empire State Building, the pictures will be flashed to the estimated 3,000 tele-radio receivers within a 50-mile radius."[7] Hundreds of visitors to the RCA exhibition hall at the World's Fair fairgrounds watched parts of the telecast from Philadelphia on the first day of its broadcast by New York City's W2XBS. W3XE producers built specially constructed lighting in Philadelphia's Municipal Auditorium for its cameras; the lighting was so intense during broadcasts, however, that some convention delegates complained of the brightness.

Reporting from Philadelphia, *Time* magazine, in its Monday, July 8, 1940, issue told readers, "Individual close ups of speakers showed up well on the screen. Long shots were fuzzy . . . as television backers gave their product its 1st big play."[8] RCA engineers worked with Philco's W3XE to transmit some sixty hours of the convention from Philadelphia to New York City stations and—by a new relay transmitter—still farther to General Electric's viewers in Schenectady. General Electric's newly constructed relay transmitter near Schenectady in the Helderberg Mountains first successfully tested in February 1940 ("Success of Television Relay Experiments Announced," the *Los Angeles Times*, Friday, February 23, 1940, headline reported), carried the signal from New York City's W2XBS to General Electric's Schenectady station.

"Roosevelt Rally Sent by Television," the *New York Times'* Tuesday, October 29, 1940, headline announced of a television broadcast by NBC's W2XBS, which carried the remarks of President Roosevelt to a rally of some 20,000 supporters in New York City's Madison Square Garden just days before the November election. "First Use of New Medium as 'Vote Getter' Is Made at Gathering in Garden," a *New York Times* headline added, noting the complaints of the poor quality and difficulties in seeing the dark images on many of the "sight-sound receivers" throughout New York City. An audience of approximately 40,000 "long-distance viewers," watched the forty-five-minute speech by President Roosevelt, the president's second time to appear in a television broadcast. "Television's peculiar power [is] transmitting not only the scene and the sound of an event that is still unfolding but also much of its inherent excitement," NBC Vice President Alfred H. Morton explained. Still, the clarity of the images broadcast that October evening was reportedly worse than the Philadelphia television transmission of the Republican convention in June 1940.[9]

On Friday, May 2, 1941, after months of deliberations, hearings, and testimony, the Federal Communications Commission (FCC) granted the nation's first commercial broadcast licenses to television stations and licensing became effective on Tuesday, July 1, 1941. With an estimated 5,000 to 7,000 television sets in operation in the country at this time, 4,000 of those thought to be owned by households in New York City, commercial television's introduction into a war-torn world stirred little enthusiasm. On the first day of federally licensed commercial broadcasting, WNBT-TV broadcast a ballgame between the Brooklyn Dodgers and the Philadelphia Phillies. During that game the country's first televised commercial—an ad for Bulova Watches—was aired. Few of those watching that afternoon's game knew they were part of another historical moment in twentieth-century television.

TELEVISION AND WORLD WAR II

President Roosevelt's radio broadcast from the chamber of the House of Representatives brought tens of millions of Americans together at 12:23 PM EST on Monday, December 8, 1941, to hear his historic speech—"Yesterday, December 7, 1941, a day which will live in infamy"—from a shaken but steadfast Capitol Hill. Only thirty-three minutes after President Roosevelt's speech, the House of Representatives and Senate declared war on Japan. Radio broadcasts washed across the nation from coast to coast with up-to-the-minute news of the latest developments from the opening hours of the war, a war already well underway for America's European allies whose own prewar broadcasting had come to an abrupt end some months earlier when Germany invaded Poland. Within a matter of hours of the invasion, Great Britain's television went off the air and did not resume until the end of the war.

In the United States, television broadcasts by some stations continued through World War II, only stirring the public's interest by the end of 1944 as some larger manufacturers detailed their plans for expanding production of receivers and for extending their broadcast schedules after the war. Few American households owned television sets, and wartime shortages made it impossible for most households to keep their televisions in service. Radio broadcasting grew as never before, and newspaper readership kept millions of Americans informed of the latest news and stories of the day, but television itself largely exited wartime America. Only a handful of television stations aired their signals and stayed on the air for the duration of the war even as retail sales of receivers stopped, manufacturers of receivers suspended their production, and scheduling of broadcasts cut back for these few stations on the air until the mid-1940s.

"Making of Radios and Phonographs to End April 22," "Nelson Orders That Plants Then Devote Entire Time to War Production," *New York Times* front-page headlines reported on Sunday, March 8, 1942. With what the *New York Times* that Sunday reported as a "complete switch" to wartime production for these plants expected by Tuesday, June 30, 1942, the story marked the suspension of all manufacturing of television receivers for the duration of the war. Stations in Chicago, Los Angeles, New York City, Philadelphia, and Schenectady stayed on the air with a reduced broadcast schedule, oftentimes in the evenings for only one or two days a week.

New York City's WABD-TV, licensed, owned, and operated by Allen B. DuMont, was one of the few television stations that remained on the air for almost the entirety of the war, broadcasting to the estimated 2,000 households in New York City who owned an operating television receiver during that time. DuMont's WABD-TV aired its programming just two or three days a week for only one to two hours in the evenings. New York City's WNBT-TV limited its transmissions to typically four or five hours of broadcasts a week for the war's duration. RCA executives had television receivers installed in more than one hundred New York City police precincts; these receivers were used to view wartime broadcasts from WNBT-TV and included special training broadcasts for the city's 148,000 volunteer air raid wardens. Executives with General Electric, DuMont Laboratories, and RCA worked together to air these instructional broadcasts for New York City public safety officials. NBC's "Air Raid Warden's Basic Course" was first televised to New York City's viewers on WNBT-TV on Monday, February 23, 1942, and later aired by special arrangement on General Electric's WRGB-TV in Schenectady and Philco's WPTZ-TV in Philadelphia. In Chicago, Paramount's WBKB-TV, still known as W9XBK until receiving its call letters in 1943, was the only station on the air in that city, airing only a limited schedule of programming with one of the lowest transmitting wattage of any television station in the country at the time.

General Electric's WRGB-TV in Schenectady was one of the only commercial stations in the United States to offer a regular broadcast schedule for the duration of the war, reaching an estimated three hundred or so Schenectady households with television sets. Washington Avenue WRGB-TV studios opened their doors on Friday, December 19, 1941, just days after the attack on Pearl Harbor. Newspaper headlines across the country reported on Schenectady's WRGB-TV and its broadcasts, a rare success story for television's wartime broadcasting and a station that introduced any number of entertainment, theatrical, and even news programming during the war. General Electric's own wartime ads, complete with "For Victory, Buy and Hold War Bonds," heralded its Schenectady station ("G.E. has already produced over 900 television shows over its station, WRGB, in Schenectady") and reported WRGB-TV as one of nine wartime stations that updated its programming, its relay of signal transmission, and its new products and services.

On Monday, May 7, 1945, New York City's celebrations of Germany's surrender were aired in a broadcast on WNBT-TV. WNBT-TV sent its television camera to New York City's Times Square to air their street celebration. That next day, New York City's three television stations all aired live broadcasts of the official announcements marking the end of war in Europe, including WNBT-TV's interview of former First Lady Eleanor Roosevelt. That Tuesday morning beginning at 8:45 AM, WNBT-TV aired its broadcast, starting its coverage with remarks by President Truman. WNBT-TV's television coverage continued until 10:45 PM that evening.

In the final days of World War II, television was well positioned for its postwar return to the aisles and display windows of the nation's department stores as well as to the airwaves of America's cities with more regular broadcasts. With the cancellation of wartime controls on most manufacturing by the War Production Board on Monday, August 20, 1945, manufacturers and retailers of television receivers stepped up the pace of their production and sales plans. Within a matter of weeks, RCA, General Electric, and Philco announced plans to produce television sets again, while months earlier, smaller manufacturers such as New York's Western Electric Company and others had announced their plans to begin manufacture of television sets immediately after the war.

On Friday, January 3, 1947, television cameras were allowed into the House of Representatives chamber to air portions of the opening session of the Eightieth Congress, the first time in history that television audiences were able to see "the radio picturization" of the proceedings of the Congress.[10] Leaders in the House of Representatives allowed television cameras to air a live telecast of the floor vote for the Speaker of the House, with the newly elected Republican majority in the House of Representatives electing Representative Joseph W. Martin Jr. (R-Massachusetts) as the nation's forty-fifth Speaker of the House. Martin represented his party's newly elected majority in the House of Representatives, and television broadcasters aired the image of outgoing Speaker of the House Samuel T. Rayburn handing the speaker's gavel to speaker-elect Martin, a broadcast carried by coaxial cable from Washington, D.C., for transmission by New York City and Philadelphia stations. In all, the first televised broadcast from the House of Representatives aired for some two hours during the opening session and included among its viewers President Truman, who watched the Capitol Hill proceedings on a television set installed in the Oval Office that same Friday morning by RCA technicians. Days later, on Monday, January 6, 1947, President Truman delivered the State of the Union address from the same chamber to a joint session of Congress, the first time that the State of the Union address was televised to a viewing audience; in this instance, it was carried on New York City and Philadelphia stations along with Washington, D.C.'s WTTG-TV Channel 5. The president's address aired over hundreds of radio stations and, for the first time, by television with an estimated viewing audience of as many as 10,000,000, watching the address in appliance retailers, department stores, and other businesses where television sets had been displayed for the occasion.

"The pictures from the House chamber were received in New York by means of a coaxial cable and for the most part were of acceptable clarity," the *New York Times* reported on Tuesday, January 7, 1947, of the televised images aired on New York City's WNBT-TV, WABD-TV, and WCBS-TV from Capitol Hill in Washington, D.C. "Clearly visible," the *New York Times* added, was "the President's smile when he commented on the House's revised seating arrangements in the wake of the Republican election victory and his turning of the pages of the prepared text of his speech."[11] Months later, on the evening of Sunday, October 5, 1947, President Truman became the first U.S. president to air a live television broadcast from the White House. His thirty-minute remarks were aired on the nation's radio networks and carried on television, the first of many such televised White House addresses in the decades to come.

With as many as 5,000 new television receivers being manufactured and sold every month by January 1947, new stations licensed, owned, and operated by newspapers, radio stations, and other businesses in Cleveland, Detroit, Los Angeles, Milwaukee, and St. Louis soon after the war's end showed the growing audience and commercial potential for television. St. Louis's first television station, KSD-TV, licensed, owned, and operated by the *St. Louis Post-Dispatch*, went on the air at 2:30 PM on Saturday, February 8, 1947. In Detroit, WWJ-TV went on the air with its first broadcast on Tuesday, March 4, 1947, a station licensed, owned, and operated by the *Detroit News*. Milwaukee's WTMJ-T, licensed, owned, and operated by the *Milwaukee Journal*, aired its first broadcast on the evening of Wednesday, December 3, 1947, as that state's first television station. In Cleveland, the first Ohio television station, WEWS-TV, a CBS affiliate, aired its inaugural broadcast on Wednesday, December 17, 1947. The broadcast, a Christmas special sponsored by that station's owners, Scripps-Howard and the *Cleveland Press*, was hosted by actor Jimmy Stewart.

TELEVISION AND THE 1948 ELECTION

"Television towers [are] going up," *Time* magazine told its readers in their Monday, May 24, 1948, issue. Some twenty-seven television stations were on the air and as many as 325,000 "tele-sets" were in the country's households, half of them estimated to be "clustered" in New York City. "The chances are," *Time* told its readers, "that it will change the American way of life more than anything since the Model T."[12] With AT&T construction crews "closing the last gap" in the coast-to-coast coaxial network and with as many as 1,000,000 sets anticipated to be in households by the end of the year, 1948 is remembered as the year of television's arrival in the United States as a pervasive and powerful presence. Construction of the AT&T coaxial cable, or "Co Ax," as it was nicknamed, and the building in some distant parts of the country of microwave towers to relay television signals from tower to tower marked a significant chapter in transmitting television broadcasts across much of the country. And, with as many as sixty manufacturers assembling and advertising the sales of their television sets, families as often purchased their first television sets from their neighborhood furniture stores or appliance retailers as from larger department stores. Excited crowds stood on the sidewalks in front of appliance stores, electronics retailers, and large department stores to watch televisions on display in the store windows. Television's arrival in millions of American households after World War II not only brought the nation's campaigning for elective office into the living rooms of American homes, it also changed the way candidates campaigned—from the length of their speeches and the staging of important events to the time spent fundraising to pay for the larger expense budgets associated with campaigning, especially the increased expense of television coverage.

T Days—the days of the first broadcasts of television stations as they went on the air in cities across the country—became major events: newspapers printed special T Day sections welcoming stations to the air, large crowds gathered outside of businesses and other locations displaying television sets, and families and their friends gathered in homes with their newly purchased televisions to watch that early programming. The arrival of television in cities across the country brought excitement to the pages of newspapers in these cities as page after page of ads welcoming stations, announcing televisions for sale, and scheduling programming and special broadcasts became a familiar part of life in the years after World War II. Mayors and even governors—along with station owners, well-known celebrities, local performers, and other figures—often were on the inaugural T Day broadcasts as stations went live across the country.

"WGN-TV Makes Debut Tonight with Big Show," announced the *Chicago Daily Tribune* headline on Monday, April 5, 1948, on the debut of the Windy City's second postwar station; its transmitter reached a distance of some forty-five miles across the metropolitan area.[13] The Sunday, April 4, 1948, issue of the *Chicago Daily Tribune* featured a special section for its readers of more than twenty pages highlighting the station's debut to Chicago's airwaves and running dozens of ads from department stores and retailers in Chicago selling all makes and models of sets. Days later, on Wednesday, April 14, 1948, the *Washington Post* published its own special "Television Section," heralding the arrival of television broadcasting for what the paper estimated to be some 8,600 sets operating in the Washington, D.C., area. WMAL-TV, NBC's WNBW-TV, and DuMont's WTTG-TV each saw in-depth coverage and reporting of their programming by the *Washington Post* in that Wednesday's special section of the newspaper. "Washington, D.C. has unlimited resources as a television origination point," *Washington Post*'s Sonia Stein told readers in that Wednesday's special section, which included a front-page photograph of Senator Robert Taft in a guest appearance on NBC's *Meet the Press*.[14]

The Democratic National Convention and the Republican National Convention, both held in Philadelphia's 15,000-seat Municipal Auditorium in 1948, were remembered as a time when television brought the nation's viewers the largest and most extensive coverage to date of both parties' nominating conventions. Viewership for both conventions is estimated to have been some 10,000,000, a figure that by the 1952 national conventions would grow to an audience estimated at some 50,000,000. Network executives, producers, and technicians—some eight hundred persons in all—worked for weeks installing the wiring and constructing the studios built for that summer's broadcasts from Philadelphia's Municipal Auditorium.

When President Truman won his party's nomination for a second term at the Philadelphia convention on Thursday, July 15, 1948, the nomination process was completed sometime around 12:45 AM. The president took to the podium almost an hour later at 1:45 AM and spoke until almost 2:30 AM, a time when few viewers were watching and when all but a handful of businesses with televisions for their customers had closed for the evening. As rousing as President Truman's acceptance speech was, few of the many millions of viewers who had watched television broadcasts were likely still awake to hear it.

"Midwest TV Net Makes Intercity Shows Possible," the *Chicago Daily Tribune* headline told readers on Sunday, October 31, 1948. "This video network," Larry Wolters reported that Sunday, "makes possible the linking of stations in Chicago, St. Louis, Cleveland, Toledo, Detroit, Buffalo, and Milwaukee."[15] Two days later, on the evening of election day, Tuesday, November 2, 1948, AT&T technicians threw the switch completing a portion of the coaxial cable stretching from the Atlantic Seaboard to several of these stations in the Midwest. With that link opened by AT&T, newscasters with ABC, CBS, DuMont, and NBC and their affiliated stations in several cities were able to broadcast the latest news and election returns, which lasted well into the early morning hours of Wednesday, November 3, 1948. As many as 10,000,000 Americans are estimated to have watched some part of that evening's broadcasts and a portent of headlines in the weeks to come as still more "Golden Spikes" were anchored as the opening of more portions of AT&T coaxial cable and microwave relay tower networks brought the nation's television audiences ever closer to coast-to-coast television.

"Coaxial Cable, Linking East and Midwest Video Outlets, Will Be Opened Tonight," a *New York Times* headline reported on Tuesday, January 11, 1949. "East Joined to Midwest by Television," another *Washington Post* headline reported on Wednesday, January 12, 1949. "Video Network of 14 Cities to Open Tomorrow," *Chicago Daily Tribune*'s headline reported on Monday, January 10, 1949, confirming the live transmissions to be aired beginning the next evening on Chicago's four television stations, WGN-TV, WNBQ-TV, WERN-TV, and WBKB-TV. "TV Networks Join Tonight," the *Milwaukee Journal* headlined on Tuesday, January 11, 1949, reporting on WTMJ-TV's broadcast that evening beginning at 8:30 PM as part of that station's connection to the East and Midwest coaxial and microwave-tower networks. In what *Billboard* editors christened "C Day," the coaxial cables and microwave towers connected together on the evening of Tuesday, January 11, 1949, and brought live transmissions of television broadcasts to still more stations in cities in the East and in the Midwest. These transmissions meant that these stations no longer had to wait hours or even days for taped film of programs to be flown in by airplane.[16]

"Pending further consideration of the technical problems involved," Winifred Mallon of the *New York Times* reported on Friday, October 1, 1948, "the Federal Communications Commission (FCC) today announced suspension temporarily of action on pending or prospective applications for television authorizations." That previous day, Thursday, September 30, 1948, FCC officials surprised most observers by announcing effective immediately its suspension of all pending and new applications. Over three hundred pending applications were suspended for what FCC officials said might be "possibly 6 months." Mallon reported that "operation of the

37 television stations now on the air, including seven in the New York and New Jersey area, will continue unaffected by today's order." FCC chairman Wayne Coy told the *New York Times*, "What we are doing is seeking to improve the present service and perhaps obtain a larger service area for stations." He added, "Our belief is that television is going to be a terrific service."[17] Far from lasting "possibly 6 months," the FCC's suspension of all pending and new applications lasted almost four years—what Erik Barnouw describes as "a strange television period"—until Monday, April 14, 1952, in another election year when television was poised to play a still greater role in the nation's political campaigns.[18]

TELEVISION AND 1952

"The industry's growth has staggered even those close to it," Los Angeles's *Billboard* magazine observed of the country's television stations and their emerging city-to-city networks in their Saturday, January 15, 1949, issue, a story published just days after Los Angeles's KTTV-TV, a CBS affiliate owned by the *Los Angeles Times*, went on the air. "Statistically," *Billboard* reported, "virtually any published report becomes out-of-date almost as soon as it appears and there is no sign of any abatement for years to come."[19] NBC's vice president for Planning and Development William S. Hedges observed in January 1949, "Television is moving forward with a force as inexorable as a river in flood,"—this at a time when sales of television receivers reached 1,000,000 sets with analysts forecasting sales at an even more brisk pace.[20] Sales of television sets grew steadily in 1949, in the words of William J. Bird Jr., "as Americans displayed their first set as the centerpiece of their home."[21] Ownership of television sets grew from an estimated 175,000 in 1947 to some 1,000,000 in January 1949 to some 2,000,000 sets by November 1949 to more than 5,000,000 television sets in 1950.[22] With some 9 percent of America's households purchasing a television set by 1950—an increase from the approximately 3 percent of households owning a television in 1949—it most certainly poised postwar television sales for even larger growth as more cities saw not just one, but two, three, and sometimes even more television stations on the air.

The inauguration of President Truman on Thursday, January 20, 1949, indicated the further growth of the cross-country network that brought together audiences and viewers of television broadcasts in an expanding number of cities. Television stations in the Midwest as well as in the East carried some five hours of live television coverage from Capitol Hill on Thursday, January 20, 1949, with coverage beginning around 11:30 AM EST and continuing with televised coverage of the Inaugural Parade until almost 4:30 PM EST for some stations. "The cameras of television covering an Inauguration for the 1st time caught both the solemnity and pageantry of the occasion with such startling detail and realism that the sense of 'being there' was inescapable," *New York Times* journalist Jack Gould reported.[23] An estimated 10,000,000 viewers watched the inaugural ceremonies, which were carried on television stations in some seventeen cities, a figure much larger than the estimated crowd of some 1,000,000 attendees who stood on the sidewalk along the Inaugural Parade route and on the steps of the Capitol.

Television's growing popularity in 1950 coincided with another of postwar America's most far-reaching innovations: air conditioning and central heating systems. Tens of millions of households purchased central heating and air conditioning in their homes at the moment when most of these same households purchased their first television sets, allowing families to spend longer hours watching television in the comfort and quiet of their homes. Weekly magazines that listed television programming were widely popular in the years after 1950, and their popularity grew as television's broadcasts and programming grew. The first issue of *TV Guide* on Friday, April 3, 1953, brought television's growing prominence in the nation's life to supermarket check-out counters and newsstands of the country while C. A. Swanson and Sons' marketing and sales of its first frozen TV dinners brought the country's fascination with television together with the time-saving convenience of electronic appliances and especially the affordability of refrigeration and freezers in the postwar American home. Manufacturers and retailers of television receivers "went to great lengths to merchandise television as a way to draw families together."[24] In the day of America's postwar suburbanization, families owning televisions at some distance from the towers broadcasting their stations' television signals found themselves on their rooftops sometimes adjusting (or heightening) their antennas to bring an ever-growing array of entertainment and programming into their homes.

"President on New Coast-to-Coast Video Hook-Up," a *New York Times* headline reported to its readers on the morning of Wednesday, September 5, 1951. "Television Spans United States for the 1st Time as President Talks at Parley," another *New York Times* headline reported from San Francisco. "The images reproduced on the screens in the New York area, nearly 3,000 miles from the scene, had excellent clarity and compared favorably with programs of local origin," *Times* correspondent Jack Gould reported. The nation's first coast-to-coast transmission was broadcast from San Francisco to New York City on Tuesday, September 4, 1951, the signal connected through Omaha, Nebraska, which had only recently been connected by AT&T to the nation's coaxial cable and microwave relay network.[25] AT&T had invested years of work and some $40,000,000 in a system that carried images from and back to the network studios in New York City across the Midwest to Omaha and Denver and then over the Rocky Mountains to Salt Lake City and then finally to San Francisco and Los Angeles. As many as 1,000,000 households with television sets in California now saw live broadcasts from New York City and from other cities across the United States while the television audiences east of the Mississippi River were able to watch television programming being produced by the nation's motion picture studios and movie production companies in Los Angeles.

An announcement on Monday, April 14, 1952, by the FCC of the resumption of its licensing of new stations ended the federal government's restrictions on television and brought renewed excitement and growth to television on the eve of that year's election. This announcement also brought about a historic moment for the candidates and their strategists in that year's race for the White House as the first presidential race of the television era.[26] New York City's Madison Avenue, the Los Angeles motion picture studios, party leaders in both the DNC and the RNC, and even some of the professional animators and cartoonists with some of Hollywood's largest motion picture studios, all converged on the 1952 race for the White House in what is remembered as television's first presidential election.

The Democratic and Republican 1952 conventions, both held in Chicago's International Amphitheater that July, took on different tones from the traditionally boisterous national gatherings of years past as Democratic and Republican strategists devoted more attention to the always-present cameras from the nation's television networks covering that year's conventions; coverage that was carried live coast-to-coast for the first time. The 1952 television broadcasts from the Republican convention, held from July 7 to July 11, and the Democratic convention, meeting from July 21 to July 26, saw an estimated 50,000,000 Americans watch the first coast-to-coast broadcasts of the nominating conventions in the nation's history. "The International Amphitheater," *Time* reported in its Monday, July 14, 1952, issue, "chosen chiefly because it has more room for TV coverage than the otherwise more convenient Chicago Stadium, was one vast TV studio."[27] The convention addresses by prominent party speakers and the acceptance speech by Republican nominee Dwight D. Eisenhower were well timed, although Adlai E. Stevenson accepted his nomination and delivered his own address well after midnight, recalling earlier broadcasts by radio when these remarks were delivered late into the night.

The official program for the 1952 Democratic convention in the Chicago International Amphitheater reminded convention delegates, "At any moment, long-distance lenses of television cameras may center upon you personally, subjecting your every expression and casual gesture to the appraising scrutiny of a million eyes!" Hotel rooms for convention delegates had placards left by convention staff on their doors reading "YOU'RE BEING WATCHED! Be in your seat tonight at 8!" "Dull or not," David Culbert tells us of television's viewing audience looking in on the Democratic and Republican conventions that summer, "seeing a convention was new. Viewers were forming visual images of candidates and television let them see things the candidates did not wish seen."[28] Among the television-inspired

innovations unveiled at the 1952 Republican convention was the Tele-
Prompter, which allowed convention speakers at the podium to read from
their prepared text while looking into the television cameras.

Eisenhower's television commercials became an especially memorable
part of the 1952 presidential race with the candidate himself speaking directly to the camera in a series of ads airing on stations across the country.
His campaign purchased a series of one-minute commercials from stations
across the country. Stevenson's commercials airing in the 1952 race featured
testimonials on behalf of Stevenson, including animated cartoons featuring
one of several songs written for the Democratic ticket in that year's race.
Still, it was Eisenhower's plain-spoken ads in which the candidate looked
directly into the camera and answered questions posed to him by women
and men appearing in these ads, that television's presence and its prominence was felt for the first time in a presidential race.

Headlines in the *New York Post*, appearing on newsstands on Thursday,
September 18, 1952, weeks after one of the most successful national conventions for his party and in the midst of the first major purchase of television ads by his party's ticket, unexpectedly brought vice presidential nominee
Richard Nixon into the nation's headlines and more important into the nation's family rooms and living rooms through their televisions. Having en-
dorsed the Republican ticket only weeks earlier, the *New York Post* broke a
story on Thursday, September 18, 1952, complete with headlines of an
$18,000 fund maintained in Senator Nixon's name and financed by a group
of businessmen in California, Texas, and elsewhere. "Secret Rich Men's
Trust Fund Keeps Nixon in Style Far beyond His Salary," read the headline.[29] The *New York Post*'s story of Nixon's account, an account maintained for his campaign-related expenses, led some of the nation's largest,
most influential newspapers and their editorial boards to urge Eisenhower
to reconsider Nixon as his running mate on that year's ticket.

"My fellow Americans, I come before you tonight as a candidate for the
vice presidency and as a man whose honesty and integrity has been questioned," Nixon told his viewers. While sitting behind a desk on a set in Los
Angeles's El Capitan Theatre, he began his historic broadcast at 9:30 PM
EST on the evening of Tuesday, September 23, 1952. "Now the usual political thing to do when charges are made against you is to either ignore them
or to deny them without giving details. I believe we have had enough of that
in the United States, particularly with the present administration in
Washington, D.C." The vice presidential nominee delivered an at times unsteady and seemingly unscripted thirty minutes of remarks while looking
directly into the television camera.

The Tuesday, September 23, 1952, televised broadcast by the California
senator saw the thirty-nine-year-old Nixon apologize to his television audience and express his regret for the appearance of impropriety in the contributions from wealthy donors to a private fund that he and his family had

accepted, a fund for campaign-related expenses, Nixon told his viewers. Nixon is seen decades later in the footage from that Tuesday evening broadcast, unsteady at times in his delivery to the camera as he goes to some length to detail his family's modest financial means, and then famously tells of his family's having received several smaller gifts from their benefactors, including a small puppy given to the Nixon family by a supporter in Texas. "It was a little cocker spaniel dog in a crate that he'd sent all the way from Texas. Black and white spotted. And our little girl Tricia, the six year old, named it Checkers. And you know, the kids, like all kids, love the dog. And I just want to say this right now, that regardless of what they say about it, we're going to keep it."[30] With that, Nixon delivered a sharply worded rebuke of the Democratic ticket before finishing the broadcast with a plea for viewers to telegraph, telephone, or write the RNC in Washington, D.C., with their own opinions as to whether he should remain as the running mate on the Eisenhower ticket.

"Wire Deluge Follows Nixon TV-Radio Plea," the *Los Angeles Times*, Wednesday morning, September 24, 1952, front-page headline reported the morning after the coast-to-coast broadcast with a special "How to Direct Messages to G.O.P. Chiefs," item on the paper's front page.[31] "Messages Pour in Backing Nominee," the *New York Times* front-page headline reported on Thursday, September 25, 1952, just two days after Nixon's thirty-minute broadcast. "Wires at Rate of 4,000 an Hour Overwhelmingly in Favor of Retaining Californian."[32] "Deluge of Nixon Mail Forces G.O.P. Headquarters into Lobby," the *Washington Post*'s Saturday, September 27, 1952, headlines told readers as the RNC staff reported some 125,000 letters and 136,000 telegrams from Western Union. Nixon's broadcast from the El Capitan Theatre, Culbert writes, "demonstrated television's potential for intimate, direct, emotional communication at a stage of technical development when the very idea of coast-to-coast transmission still made headlines."[33] With an audience estimated at some 9,000,000 television viewers, its preeminence as a broadcast medium seemed finally and fully established in the black-and-white glow of television screens in the living rooms of American households.

Coast-to-coast television broadcasts by the candidates and their supporters the night before the Tuesday, November 4, 1952, election day is considered another historic first in television broadcasting. Eisenhower and Nixon spoke in a television broadcast airing at 10:00 PM EST from Boston while from 10:30 PM to 11:00 PM EST Stevenson and his running mate, Senator John J. Sparkman, televised their own broadcast from Chicago. Months later, Eisenhower's 1953 inauguration was seen on television by an estimated 20,000,000 viewers. Weeks later still on Capitol Hill, television correspondents were granted access for the first time to the press galleries in the House of Representatives and the Senate, a historic moment that marked television's arrival in Washington, D.C.

The airing of the first televised broadcast of Austin's KTBC-TV station on Thursday, November 27, 1952, brought yet another chapter in the history of television's connection with elected officials and figures at the highest levels of the nation's political establishment. Claudia Alta Taylor Johnson's purchase of KTBC's radio station in January 1943 with a family inheritance and her husband's close involvement in the management of the station when it aired its first television broadcasts on Thanksgiving Day in 1952 ("TV Starts Here on Turkey Day," the *Austin Statesman* reported on its front page on Friday, November 21, 1952) interwove then-Representative Lyndon Johnson closely to one of Texas's newest and soon-to-be most influential television stations. The *Austin Statesman*'s special twenty-two-page supplement on Friday, November 21, 1952, featured a number of stories on the arrival of television broadcasting to Austin, the culmination of years of financial investments by the Johnson family and their Texas Broadcasting Company.

The first year that more than 50 percent of American households owned a television set was 1954. By 1955 that number had grown to 64 percent or more of households owning a television set and again to 78 percent of households by 1957. The hours of television viewing in the typical American household grew to an average of five-and-one-half hours a day by the end of the 1950s. So too did the ownership in a growing number of households of multiple television sets. Even families who could not yet afford to purchase their first television set reportedly installed antennas atop their homes prior to the purchase of a set.[34] Interestingly, television's acceptance as a favored news source compared to the still-influential newspapers in America's cities and towns was almost a decade away with one 1954 survey showing some 71 percent of the public reading a newspaper every day compared to just 39 percent who watched news on their television on a similar basis, yet indisputably, television became in every way a part of the daily life of Americans.

"President's News Conference Filmed for Television and Newsreels for 1st Time," the *New York Times*' front-page headline read on Thursday, January 20, 1955, reporting on the first time that television cameras were allowed to prerecord the president's remarks for a later broadcast by the nation's television networks and their affiliates. "Under six great lights," the *New York Times* reported of the Wednesday, January 19, 1955, press conference at 10:30 AM EST in the old State Department Building, "television and newsreel cameras recorded a Presidential press conference today for the 1st time."[35] From the old State Department Building, President Eisenhower answered reporter's questions while two television crews filmed the president's remarks from their cameras in the back of the room.

By the mid-1950s, Capitol Hill also had become the center of television broadcasting from the nation's capital, as members of the House of Representatives and the Senate, often joined by members of the president's cabinet and congressional leaders, recorded everything from four-minute segments to thirty-minute programs for broadcast on television stations in their states and congressional districts. "The expanding list of notables who appear with a Senator or Representative on a home-town show," Nona B. Brown reported, "is a simple measure of the vast and important business these airborne political reports have become."[36] Refurbished in 1956, the television studios for members of the House of Representatives and the Senate, located in the basement of the Capitol Building, were staffed by some twenty-five employees, "complete with pseudo-windows and a view of the Capitol, 3 radio studios, processing laboratories, and a small viewing room."[37] Over half of the members of the House of Representatives and nearly all of the Senate spent time in the basement studios taping short segments that were sent back to stations in their states and congressional districts. They were well aware of their constituent's television viewing and of its growing influence in their reelection campaigns.

When an audience estimated at some 100,000,000 viewers watched some portion of the 1956 Democratic and Republican conventions, over 70 percent of the country's households owned a television set and a coast-to-coast system of coaxial cables, microwave towers, relay transmitters, and long-distance boosting stations carried live television broadcasts into the homes of tens of millions of Americans immediately, instantaneously. Few Americans were surprised to learn that in that year's race for the White House, President Eisenhower and Democrat Adlai Stevenson, in his second bid for the White House, spent over 50 percent of their ad budgets on television. "We are in a new age, an electronics age," White House Press Secretary James C. Hagerty told the *New York Times* on Monday, May 14, 1956.[38] Having overcome some of his own reluctance to air television spots in his 1952 bid for the White House against Eisenhower, Stevenson appeared regularly in commercials on behalf of his 1956 candidacy, even airing a series of sharply worded ads against President Eisenhower's administration, ads that were christened by some observers as the first negative television ads in the history of television broadcasting, a portent and a prologue, to be sure.

Chapter 7

Television and the Transformation of Postwar American Politics

Monday, September 26, 1960. 9:30 PM EST. WBBM-TV. CBS Channel 2. Chicago, Illinois. 2 candidates. 1 moderator. 4 panelists. 75,000,000 Americans. That evening in Chicago an unforgettable event in the growth of television broadcasting in America's politics took place, an event captured in black-and-white photographs and television footage of that first televised debate from the studios of Chicago's WBBM-TV. With televisions owned by some 90 percent of the nation's families, America's broadcast networks and their affiliated stations brought up-to-the-hour news of the 1960 presidential race into the households of millions of American families. And, with tens of millions of household viewers and hundreds of broadcast stations connected through a coast-to-coast system of coaxial cables, microwave towers, and transmitters, television brought the American electorate in closer, more regular contact with the nation's political candidates.

With television's immediacy and the intimacy of its coverage of candidates and their campaigns, the growing importance of a candidate's appearance and in the voters' perceptions of candidates is well recorded in this 1960 race for the White House. Everything from a candidate's casual remark to their physical appearance, their facial expression, even their slightest, seemingly most imperceptible gestures, were now under the watchful eye of the nation's television audience. A prolonged sigh or yawn, a raised eyebrow, a rolling of the eyes, even an overheard joke or whisper picked up by television's cameras and microphones, now became part of the serious business of campaigning for elective office, not to mention a part of governing once elected.

The year 1960 is remembered as the time when the expressiveness of candidates, their ability to articulate authenticity, sincerity, and sympathy in relating to voters, their body language, even their clothing and other aspects of their physical appearances, became part of their persona on the black-and-white television screens of a nation that now *looked* at candidates as much as *listened* to them. Although more than fifty years had passed since terms like atmospherics and optics were the lexicon of campaigning, candidates and those advising them in 1960 certainly appreciated the immediacy and importance of the image, of the appearance, of the visual. The year 1960 is also remembered as a time when sharper political attacks on the black-and-white screens of the nation's television sets took a place of prominence. While television ads in the 1950s largely avoided sharp attacks on rival candidates, television ads beginning in 1960 and especially after 1964 were increasingly negative.

TELEVISION AND THE 1960s

By January 1960, 88 percent of households in the United States owned a television set and during that year campaigning for public office changed forever. Households spent longer hours of their day watching television, with household viewing averaging almost five hours a day. America's electorate grew more reliant on television for a larger portion of their news about candidates and races for elective office. Coast-to-coast broadcasts and breaking news stories carried live on television were taken for granted by most Americans. A vast infrastructure of images and information unlike anything in the nation's history, built in less than a decade's time, with thousands of miles of coaxial cables, construction of microwave towers, and satellite dishes with their arc to the horizon, brought additional breakthroughs in television broadcasting.

The 1960 presidential race between Senator John F. Kennedy and Vice President Richard M. Nixon was a turning point in how national campaigns for elected office were run. While Vice President Nixon was aware of television's influence from his 1952 race and from its growing importance during his tenure as vice president, the Massachusetts senator became acquainted with it during the 1956 Democratic convention and in subsequent years as he built his reputation as one willing to appear in televised interviews from his Capitol Hill office. "Senior Senators," Donald A. Ritchie writes of the Massachusetts senator's colleagues in the Senate, "did not take Kennedy's presidential ambitions seriously until they began to notice the coils of television cable outside his Senate office."[1] In his race for the Democratic nomination in 1960, Kennedy himself became even more aware of television when he saw antennas on some of the most remote houses while he was stumping in West Virginia and elsewhere.

The 1960 presidential race is remembered for the live televised debates between Kennedy and Nixon, but it is important to remember the part television played in the primary contests in that year's race for the White House. The Democratic primaries in 1960 saw television's impact not only in the contests *between* the political parties but also *within* the parties as the significance of the state primary elections for convention delegates grew in importance to the national nominating conventions. The 1960 primary elections in Wisconsin and West Virginia saw the airing of television commercials in those states as an important part of the dynamic in that year's race. Also important were the mounting financial pressures for candidates to raise larger sums of money to pay for the cost of advertising on the airwaves during their primaries.

In February 1960, months before the Democratic and Republican conventions, CBS became the first television network to express interest in airing live debates between the two major presidential candidates in that fall's presidential race. CBS executives, who would host the first of the four televised debates at their WBBM-TV studios in Chicago, expressed their willingness to bring the candidates to their network's television viewers in one or more televised debate. In April, NBC executives also announced their network's interest in airing presidential debates. NBC executive David Sarnoff offered to air televised debates between the Democratic and Republican nominees as a part of his network's weekly broadcast of *Meet the Press*.

For months during the 1960 presidential race, Kennedy and his advisors, including J. Leonard Reinsch, expressed their eagerness for a series of televised presidential debates. "All I want is a picture of you and Nixon on the same television tube," Reinsch is recalled to have told the Massachusetts senator. "We'll take it from there."[2] In contrast, Vice President Nixon's advisors disagreed as to whether or not the vice president should debate the senator, with some of Nixon's advisors urging the vice president not to take part in a televised debate that would elevate Kennedy to the vice president's national stature. To journalists reporting on the vice president's campaign, Nixon appeared by most accounts reluctant to take part in televised debates. Then, in the days before the 1960 Republican National Convention (RNC), Nixon was asked by newscasters Walter Cronkite and Edward R. Murrow during a CBS broadcast whether he would debate Kennedy. Nixon said that he would be agreeable to debate Kennedy in a "face-to-face debate on television," according to *New York Times* journalist Jack Gould on Monday, July 25, 1960.[3] "Debate Approved by Vice President," the *New York Times* headline reported that same Monday as the Republican convention gathered in Chicago to nominate Nixon as their presidential candidate.

In 1960, the first year when the "debate on the debates," as it is sometimes known, took place, Nixon's and Kennedy's aides settled into several weeks of meetings regarding the format for the nation's first live televised debates. Their first meeting took place on Tuesday, August 9, 1960, and they began to work out an agreement for the format and the scheduling of the televised debates as well as to set the number of debates and to come to an agreement on the topics to be discussed. Everything from the lighting and the temperature in the television studios to the formats for the panelists' questions, even the rules for the candidates' opening and closing remarks, were on the table for discussion. Weeks of meetings between the senior staffs of Senator Kennedy and Vice President Nixon led to their final agreement that the televised debates would take place over four evenings, with the first and second evenings limited to the topic of domestic policy and the fourth evening to foreign affairs. ABC, CBS, and NBC executives went to considerable lengths to ensure that the stages, studios, backgrounds, technical production, and equipment in all instances afforded no advantage to either of the candidates.

During these meetings, Nixon is recalled to have made the determination that the audience for the first of the four televised presidential debates would be smaller than the audiences in the third and fourth televised debates, a determination that included Nixon's insistence on scheduling the topic of foreign policy, an important issue for the vice president in his bid for the White House, as the topic for the fourth debate. Nixon believed the audiences would increase in size after each of the televised debates so that more viewers would tune in to the third and fourth televised debates as the Tuesday, November 8, 1960, election grew closer. Believing that the fourth and final televised debate would have the largest audience, Nixon's senior staff scheduled the issue of foreign policy to be the topic for the fourth televised debate, a miscalculation that Nixon himself variously attributed to his staff's inability to know at the time which of the four televised broadcasts would have the largest viewing audience ("We could only guess") or to his inability to persuade his staff ("I yielded to their judgment") of his own self-stated belief at the time that the viewing audiences would be largest in the first of the televised debates. Years later, Nixon insisted that he personally believed, in his own words, "interest would diminish as the novelty of the confrontation wore off," a belief that Nixon later insisted was overruled by his advisors who, in Nixon's telling of the story some time later, felt audiences would grow in the televised debates closer to election day.[4]

"Good evening. The television and radio stations of the United States and their affiliated stations are proud to provide facilities for a discussion of issues in the current political campaign by the two major candidates for the president. According to rules set by the candidates themselves, each man shall make an opening statement of approximately eight minutes duration and a closing statement of approximately three minutes duration. In between, the candidates will answer or comment upon answers to questions put by a panel of correspondents. In this, the first discussion in a series of four joint appearances, the subject matter has been agreed will be restricted to internal or domestic American matters. And now for the first opening statement by Senator John F. Kennedy." With that, 75,000,000 million Americans in more than 20,000,000 households watched as the first televised presidential debate got underway on Monday, September 26, 1960, from the Chicago WBBM-TV studios. CBS news correspondent Howard K. Smith anchored the first debate with a panel of four journalists, explaining to the viewing audience that, by agreement of the candidates, the first debate was limited to "internal or domestic American matters."

At 9:30 PM EST, as CBS cameramen and the production staff silenced those assembled in the studio, viewers in tens of millions of living rooms across the United States heard the opening remarks and saw the televised images of the candidates. On all three of the nation's television networks, the televised debates with their stark, somber black-and-white images went out across the nation by coaxial cable, by microwave relay, and by the airwaves. Millions of Americans listened to the debates on the radio, allowing for the oft-repeated belief that those Americans watching the televised debate felt the winner of the debate was Kennedy while those listening on the radio felt Nixon was the winner. Still, it was television's viewing audience that Monday evening, an audience of some 75,000,000 viewers, a viewing audience larger than the number of Americans who cast their ballots on Election Day, Tuesday, November 8, 1960, who saw before their eyes the power of the televised image to bring politics into their living rooms. No audience was in the WBBM-TV studios that Monday evening. The image was simple: two men standing at their podiums on a small stage. Today, televised cutaways that allow the audience to see facial expressions, reactions, and responses to moderators' questions and to the candidates' answers have become an important element of televised debates.

At the first debate, Vice President Nixon and Senator Kennedy both had ample time for their opening remarks, each having agreed weeks earlier to a format of eight minutes for their opening statements, which would allow both candidates to explain in some detail their respective campaign platforms during the first debate. In his opening remarks, Kennedy compared the conflict with Communist China and the Soviet Union to the 1860 American debate on slavery and the Civil War. The senator then connected his campaign platform on the domestic issues of the day to the larger concerns of the American public with the pressing foreign policy.

"The things that Senator Kennedy has said, many of us can agree with," Vice President Nixon responded in his opening statement. "I subscribe completely to the spirit that Senator Kennedy has expressed tonight, the spirit that the United States should move ahead." This statement almost immediately placed Nixon in a position of responding to Kennedy rather than defining his own platform. In his opening statement, in several instances, Nixon expressed his agreement with statements made just moments earlier by Kennedy. "Our disagreement is not about the goals for America, only about the means to reach those goals," Nixon said when concluding his opening remarks, just prior to Howard K. Smith's introduction of the four panelists who would ask questions for the remainder of the evening's debate. After the first question to Kennedy from the panel regarding Kennedy's experience and the record of the Democratic Party and after the senator's answer to the question, moderator Smith asked whether Nixon would reply. "I have no comment," Nixon remarked, thereby missing a chance to discuss at length his own experience and record as vice president as well as his own party's platform. During the evening, Nixon frequently expressed his "agreement" with the senator, later declining to use time in the debate given by Smith to answer or reply to statements made by Kennedy. Well documented, of course, was the perspiration on the vice president's forehead and upper-lip captured by television cameras in WBBM-TV's studios in the close-up shots. Kennedy's attentiveness to the answers to questions by Nixon and even the spring in his step as Kennedy stood up from his chair to answer questions at his podium is remembered in contrast to Nixon's conciliatory, more restrained demeanor and his less-sure posture as he steadied himself at the podium several times throughout the debate.

To the 75,000,000 Americans watching the Massachusetts senator's confident demeanor at his podium, the vice president appeared shaky. Television audiences did not know that an injury to Nixon's knee from an accident with an automobile door was the reason for his unsteadiness. First impressions were to matter in televised debates. A day earlier, Senator Kennedy and his staff had accepted the invitation extended to both campaigns to visit WBBM-TV studios to familiarize themselves with the layout, the lighting, and the overall setup of the studio. Vice President Nixon's campaign had scheduled events that Sunday and Monday, so he declined the invitation for the walk-through. Kennedy, however, spent time in the studio, acquainting himself with its lighting, its stage, and its podiums as positioned relative to the television cameras. In preparation for the televised debate that evening, Kennedy's staff scheduled no public events or speeches, instead allowing the senator to spend time in his hotel room where he was briefed on potential questions that might be asked during that evening's debate. For Kennedy, Monday was a day of preparation and rest. Before his appearance, Kennedy's staff was attentive to the details of his wardrobe, even looking at the color of the senator's shirt and how it looked in the studio television monitors and the length of his socks when his legs were crossed while sitting in his chair next to his podium.

When the second televised debate at the Washington, D.C., NBC affiliate WRC-TV took place on Friday, October 7, 1960, it was evident that there would be a smaller viewing audience than for the first televised presidential debate. When figures were finally available, an estimated 61,000,000 Americans tuned in to watch the second televised debate. This smaller audience was unfortunate for Nixon, as most headlines favored the vice president's performance over that of the senator in contrast to their first televised match-up.

On Thursday, October 13, 1960, 70,000,000 viewers tuned in to watch the third debate, which began at 7:30 PM EST, with its split-screen television shots of Vice President Nixon in Los Angeles and Senator Kennedy in New York City. "Identical Television Studios Are Put Up for the 3rd Debate Tomorrow, Nixon to Appear in California, Kennedy in New York, Both are Advised to Wear the Same Shade of Attire," the *New York Times*, Wednesday, October 12, 1960, headline reported. "Candidates 'Meet' a Continent Apart in 3rd TV Debate," read the *Washington Post*'s Friday, October 14, 1960, headline. The third of the four televised debates featured a format in which questions were asked from any subject area by the four panelists, with a large portion of the questions asked involving foreign policy and international affairs.

"Good evening, I'm Bill Shadel of ABC News," Wednesday's debate began. "It's my privilege this evening to preside at this, the third in a series of meetings on radio and television of the two major presidential candidates." "Like the last meetings," Shadel explained, "the subjects to be discussed will be suggested by questions from a panel of correspondents. Unlike the first two programs, however, the two candidates will not be sharing the same platform. In New York, the Democratic presidential nominee, Senator John F. Kennedy. Separated by 3,000 miles in a Los Angeles studio, the Republican presidential nominee Vice President Richard M. Nixon, now joined for tonight's discussion by a network of electronic facilities, which permits each candidate to see and hear the other." With that, Shadel opened the debate with the panel of journalists who asked their questions of Nixon and Kennedy from a third television studio in Los Angeles. Black-and-white, split-screen television images of the senator and the vice president appeared on millions of television sets with ABC executives estimating some five hundred of its employees involved in the coast-to-coast transmission from its studios in Los Angeles and New York City. With monitors in their respective studios, Nixon and Kennedy were able to watch their rival's questions and responses, itself something of a breakthrough in the coast-to-coast transmission of television, something that was all but impossible just a few years earlier.

The fourth debate took place at 10:00 PM EST on Friday, October 21, 1960, in New York City in the ABC studios. An estimated 63,000,000 viewers tuned in to the debate. This debate between Senator Kennedy and Vice President Nixon was the last time for another sixteen years that candidates running for the White House would again face one another in a live televised presidential debate. With no debate between vice presidential running mates, Lyndon B. Johnson and Henry Cabot Lodge Jr., the 1960 televised debates came to a quiet end that Friday evening just three weeks shy of Election Day, Tuesday, November 8, 1960.

The year 1960 is remembered for the televising of the first presidential debates, but it is also remembered as a year when television, its network news programs, and the paid commercial advertisements by the candidates all took on an ever larger role in the race for the White House. Senator Kennedy and Vice President Nixon both appeared as guests on *The Jack Paar Show*, one of the first times candidates for national office took their case to the popular NBC late-evening television program, which aired as late as midnight on some network affiliates, and it was the beginning of a well-worn path of candidate appearances on evening entertainment programs in the years to come. The popularity of sixty- and even thirty-second paid ads, including ads featuring motion picture actors, celebrity endorsements, and entertainers, also took a prominent role in 1960. Commercials featuring Jacqueline Kennedy aired in that year's race, including a Spanish-language television ad featuring the senator's wife who spoke fluent Spanish in an ad that aired on stations in Texas and elsewhere. Ads featuring former First Lady Eleanor Roosevelt expressing her support for Kennedy ("He is a man with a sense of history") aired on the nation's television networks as well.

In the weeks after the Tuesday, November 8, 1960, election, President-elect Kennedy exhibited a certain finesse and ease in front of television cameras. Cox radio and television executive J. Leonard Reinsch, a close advisor to Kennedy during his race for the presidency, remained a trusted advisor as the new president and his staff sought to build upon their earlier successful relationship with television. Reinsch was featured prominently at the 1961 Inaugural and can be seen just over the newly sworn-in president's shoulder in many pictures taken that historic day.[5] Kennedy and his family were well accustomed to the presence of television cameras on the campaign trail and were soon willing to allow the nation's television broadcasters into the White House to bring the country's television audience closer to the president's work and family life. Wednesday, January 25, 1961, just five days after his inauguration on the steps of the Capitol, President Kennedy stood before a crowded room of newspaper reporters and television cameras for the historic first live televised press conference by a U.S. president. Beginning at 6:00 PM EST, more than four hundred reporters sitting in a newly remodeled theater in the State Department building questioned the president about his first week in office. "In the old days," *New York Times*' Russell Baker reported, "one of the dramatic highlights of every conference was the thundering crash of bodies against the exit as newsmen fought to be the 1st to the telephone. There was no need for that tonight," Baker noted.[6] "The viewer sitting before his television set," Douglass Cater wrote later of the press conferences in the newly constructed State Department auditorium, "could see and hear much better than the participants."[7] Later estimates put the viewing audience of the president's first televised press conference at some 65,000,000.

In the year 1961, the Kennedy White House and the president's staff inaugurated the beginning of a transformation in television's prominence in the

White House. Even as FCC Chairman Newton N. Minow excoriated broadcasters for television's "vast wasteland" in his Tuesday, May 9, 1961, speech before the National Association of Broadcasters (NAB), the White House sought ever closer relationships with these very same broadcasters; broadcasters who had for the first time a president accustomed to the presence of television cameras on the grounds and in the hallways of the White House.[8] In February 1962, First Lady Jacqueline Kennedy invited CBS to broadcast her guiding a tour of the White House. With President Kennedy's use of television for his live televised press conferences as well as his broadcasts from the Oval Office, congressional leaders sought their own platform for reaching the country through television and began to air their televised press conferences from Capitol Hill.

The year 1963 was also a defining year for the nation's commercial television broadcasting inasmuch as television's reporting on the news and the stories of the day for the first time that year was more widely relied upon by a larger number of Americans surveyed in public opinion polls than any other source of news. Additionally, in 1963 the nation's television networks aired their first thirty-minute network news broadcasts with CBS first airing its expanded thirty-minute nightly news format over the Labor Day holiday weekend at 6:30 PM EST on Monday, September 2, 1963; in fact, Walter Cronkite interviewed President Kennedy from his summer home in Hyannis Port, Massachusetts, during that newscast. Days later, on Monday, September 9, 1963, NBC expanded its own nightly broadcast from a fifteen-minute to a thirty-minute evening broadcast. Network anchors of these nightly newscasts soon became some of America's most trusted figures. According to *Time* magazine, they were "the most important and influential molders of public opinion in the United States."[9] Television in the years after 1963 brought everything from broadcasts of Elvis Presley and the Beatles on *The Ed Sullivan Show* to the beginnings of U.S. exploration of outer space, culminating in one of the most spectacular moments in television history: live televised coverage of the Sunday, July 20, 1969, moon landing of Apollo 11.

A 1963 Elmo Roper and Associates survey yielded a historic first: network broadcasts became the most important and relied-upon source of news, surpassing newspapers and news magazines. The Roper and Associates survey coincided with the first nightly network newscasts that fall. Televised images from Birmingham, Alabama, in April 1963, when millions of Americans watched black-and-white images of civil rights marchers facing down police are some of the most defining moments of the twentieth-century civil rights movement. When President Kennedy told his aides that the television images of the physical assaults on the civil rights demonstrators in Birmingham "sickened him," the president no doubt spoke for millions of his fellow Americans. That Tuesday, June 11, 1963, when the president introduced his first bill for civil rights legislation to Capitol Hill, he turned to television to carry his message in an Oval Office broadcast to the American people. On Wednesday, August 28, 1963, the March on Washington, D.C., brought still more images of some 200,000 civil rights marchers at the Lincoln Memorial. Most chilling of all, the president's assassination in Dallas on Friday, November 22, 1963, most certainly brought tens of millions of Americans to their television sets for hour after hour and then day after day of television coverage.

When two bullets struck President Kennedy in the head, killing him moments later, while his motorcade traveled its route through downtown Dallas shortly after 12:30 PM on the afternoon of Friday, November 22, 1963, television became the nation's eyes during the anguished weeks and months to come. Within the hour, nearly the entire country learned of the death of President Kennedy in his Dallas motorcade; they watched hour after hour of television coverage as reporters in Dallas and in the network television studios updated Americans with the latest news in an uninterrupted live television broadcast unlike anything to date. The television coverage of the Kennedy assassination, Donald A. Ritchie tells us, "touched a nerve, brought the nation together, and seared some iconic moments into people's memories, from a parade of foreign dignitaries to a son's salute."[10] Sitting in front of millions of black-and-white television screens, Americans watched the network anchors report the news updates of that day's tragic events in Dallas, a day finally and forever establishing television's vast power in bringing the breaking events of the day into the quiet of America's bedrooms, family rooms, and living rooms.

1964: TELEVISION, PRESIDENT LYNDON B. JOHNSON, AND THE MAKING OF THE MODERN MEDIA PRESIDENCY

Sworn into office by Federal judge Sarah T. Hughes on Friday, November 22, 1963, with First Lady Jacqueline Kennedy standing at his side, President Lyndon B. Johnson's remarks just minutes later from a bank of microphones on the tarmac of Dallas's Love Field Airport underscored the extent to which television enduringly altered the nation's cultural landscape and its political life. President Johnson is remembered as an avid television viewer, having multiple television sets installed in the Oval Office and in his private study as well as in the residence in the White House and in the Johnson family home at their ranch in Texas. Even when hospitalized for overnight stays, President Johnson had his staff arrange for three television sets to be placed at the foot of his hospital bed. Johnson and his family also owned a multimillion-dollar television—and later cable—business centered on the Austin KTBC-TV station.

Financial investments by the Johnson family in Texas broadcasting began when Johnson's wife, while he was still a state representative, purchased Austin's radio station KTBC in January 1943 with $17,500 of her inheritance.[11] Running the station on a day-to-day basis, Lady Bird Johnson and her husband were a constant presence in the financial and broadcast operations of KTBC. What was later named the L.B.J. Broadcasting Company and still later changed back to the Texas Broadcasting Corporation after Johnson became president, KTBC became the first in a series of investments by the Johnson family in what became a commercially successful broadcasting business in the Texas capital and throughout the region.[12]

"TV Starts Here on Turkey Day," the *Austin Statesman*'s front-page headline announced on Friday, November 21, 1952, in a special issue of that day's paper, which featured a special twenty-two-page section on KTBC-TV's inaugural broadcast scheduled to begin at 1:00 PM on Thanksgiving Day, Thursday, November 27, 1952. When Austin's KTBC-TV aired its first television broadcast, the station began "an effective telecasting monopoly in a city of 186,000 and its environs," and entwined the Johnson family's financial investments in the broadcast business with the rising political fortunes of then-senator Johnson, whose own leadership in the Senate and the Democratic Party grew steadily over the next decade.[13] With an estimated net worth of some $14,000,000 to $15,000,000 in 1964, financial records suggested as much as 50 percent of the Johnson family's investment portfolio came from KTBC-TV broadcast operations as well as the family's investments in stations in Waco, Texas, Victoria, Texas, and in Ardmore, Oklahoma.[14] The Johnson family also made a series of investments in cable television businesses in Texas well into the mid-to-late 1960s during President Johnson's term in the White House.

Airing its first television broadcast on Thursday, November 27, 1952, Austin's KTBC-TV aired the programming of all four television networks, a lucrative financial arrangement for the Johnson family with ABC, CBS, NBC, and DuMont network programming all broadcast at different times of the day by the station. "Austin's Bringing in a Gusher, Set Makers Prepare for KTBC-TV'S Dec. 1 Debut," *Broadcasting* magazine enthused in its Monday, October 27, 1952, coverage of KTBC-TV just prior to its first broadcast. KTBC-TV's broadcasting operation yielded millions in profits, not to mention inestimable influence with business clients and network executives, for the Johnson family.[15] Beginning years earlier while in the House of Representatives and then during his tenure in the Senate and still later during his White House years, Johnson is known to have kept a close eye on the day-to-day operations of KTBC-TV as well as the financial operations of the station, its executives always available for frequent telephone calls. President Johnson also had an apartment suite built at the offices of KTBC-TV in downtown Austin where he and his family stayed when in the city.

President Johnson's penchant for watching hours of television in the White House is captured in the photographs of him peering over his desk in the Oval Office at a specially built console that was fitted for three television sets and installed a few feet from his desk. The cabinet that housed the console was built beneath a recessed set of bookshelves to the left of the president's desk. In many of these photographs, the president is shown talking on his desk telephone, leaning in to watch the three television sets. Photographs also show the president upstairs in the residence with the same type of cabinet also containing three television sets. One photograph depicts the Johnson family in the White House residence preparing for the Wednesday, January 20, 1965, inaugural with each of the three television sets in the foreground showing network coverage of the upcoming event.

"The President likes to get the news first from his own network," *Business Week* observed in a March 4, 1967, profile titled "How Johnson Brings the World to His Desk." The profile highlighted President Johnson's staff briefings and his gathering of information and news in the White House. "But when news is breaking," *Business Week* told its readers of President Johnson's television viewing habits in the White House, "he is apt to turn on the 3 TV sets in his office to see—all at once—what the 3 major networks are reporting."[16] Photographs of Johnson show the president at times sitting with his staff crowded around his desk or alone in the Oval Office, sometimes leaning across his desk watching the three television sets tuned to the nightly network news broadcasts or special broadcasts. Photographs also show President Johnson in his private study just off of the Oval Office where three television sets were perched on top of a small shelf in the study. Color photographs of Johnson watching his three television sets in the Oval Office show some of the television networks airing their network news programming in color.

President Johnson's habit of telephoning television network to correct items in their news broadcasts or otherwise express his agreement or disagreement with their coverage of a particular news story is well known among those television executives and network anchors who worked during the Johnson administration. The Oval Office's teletype machine (specially built for the president) is also visible in many of these photographs. The special case around the teletype machine and its glass window allowed him to have access to breaking stories from the Associated Press (AP) and the United Press International (UPI) wires at any time while still being able to talk on the telephone or have conversations with visitors in the Oval Office. In some photographs Johnson is seated on a wooden chair placed several feet away from the television sets, allowing him to lean in even closer to the television sets when watching them.

"Television Studio for Johnson's Use Will Be Built in the White House Basement," a *New York Times* headline reported on Wednesday, August 26, 1964. ABC, CBS, and NBC executives, working with White House staff, arranged for the studio to be constructed in the basement of the White House, allowing for almost immediate broadcasts of President Johnson's televised addresses on the networks and offering a state-of-the-art facility with seating for some thirty visitors and White House staff.[17] White House Press Secretary Bill Moyers explained to *Time* magazine in its Friday, October 14, 1966, issue, "President Johnson feels that television offers him the most direct, straightforward, and personal way to communicate with the people. It is not someone else's attitude or interpretation of what the President said," Moyers added. "It is the purest form of communication, and I think the most desirable."[18] Coverage of the 1964 Democratic and Republican national conventions by ABC, CBS, and NBC is recalled as yet a further sign of the growth in the influence of television in the nation's campaigning for elective office.

The 1964 race marked the advent of some of the most negative television commercials to date; commercials that broke from the plainspoken testimonials of candidates, their running mates, and their supporters and instead focused on the emotional intensity (and to a large extent the emotional manipulation) of imagery and the conspicuous absence of the candidates themselves. The most famous televised ad of the 1964 presidential race featured neither footage nor images of either of the candidates running that year, nor were candidates mentioned by name. It was a year when a single one-minute television ad that aired only once is remembered as a medium-making moment in the persuasiveness and pervasiveness of television's presence in America's political life.

Monday evening, September 7, 1964, is regarded as one of the watershed moments in the history of televised political advertising. On that Labor Day, *Monday Night at the Movies* had an audience estimated by CBS executives to be some 50,000,000 Americans when a sixty-second ad showing the image of a young girl pulling petals off a flower was followed by a full-screen image of a nuclear explosion that filled the television screen. The young girl, who is slowly counting down from ten as she pulls the petals off her flower, loses count and her quiet voice is replaced by a jarring one that counts down in echoing tones, "10–9–8–7–6–5–4–3–2–1–0." The countdown is followed by a deafening roar and the explosion of a nuclear bomb. Even as the bomb's explosion is still roaring in the ad's audio, the voice of Johnson is audible over the explosion, warning viewers: "These are the stakes, to make a world in which all of God's children can live, or to go into the dark. We must either love each other, or we must die." Following the president's message, an announcer insists, "Vote for President Johnson on November 3rd; the stakes are too high for you to stay home."

Airing for its first and only time on CBS, the ad, nicknamed the "Daisy ad," reached a vast audience of television viewers that Labor Day evening. While this ad aired only once, other ads by President Johnson's reelection campaign contained some of the same emotional intensity, including an ad showing a young girl eating an ice cream cone while the announcer discusses radioactive fallout from atmospheric nuclear testing, which appeared regularly in the closing weeks of the 1964 race. Accounts by people close to the president and his staff recall the president's public disapproval of the ad within hours of its airing even though some of those same accounts recall that the president privately praised the ad's impact and questioned his senior staff as to whether or not to air it again in the closing weeks of the 1964 race.

In 1964, television screens in households across the United States were filled with negative commercials in the race for the White House, as both President Johnson and Senator Barry Goldwater aired ad after ad attacking their rival. Black-and-white sixty- and thirty-second ads by Johnson aired with sharp rebukes of Goldwater, which sometimes included quoted passages from the senator's speeches as well as press accounts of his remarks on domestic and international issues. From civil rights to Social Security to the Tennessee Valley Authority, Johnson's commercial spots took on his Republican rival with an impact and an intensity never before seen on the nation's television screens—sometimes these ads did not even mention Goldwater by name.

The year 1964 is also remembered for the larger purchases of commercial television ad time not only on the nation's three network broadcasts, but also in the purchase of airtime for commercials from local markets in many different parts of the country. Senator Goldwater and the RNC aired their television ads not only on network broadcasts by ABC, CBS, and NBC but also during airtime purchased from television stations in as many as 130 of the nation's local television markets. This was the beginning of candidates' preference for the market-by-market ads, or so-called spot ads, that have become so familiar to campaigning in the early twenty-first century.

"White House Cool to Debates on Television," a *New York Times* front-page headline reported on Thursday, July 30, 1964, after their Wednesday, July 29, 1964, "Goldwater 'Ready' to Debate Johnson in Campaign on TV," front-page headline a day earlier. Johnson's unwillingness to debate Goldwater in nationally televised presidential debates led many, including former Vice President Nixon, to express their support for a televised debate in the 1964 race. Willing to spend millions of dollars on television commercials as well as thirty- and sixty-second ads that redefined television as a medium in America's political process, the president still refused to take part in televised debates with Goldwater. This was to echo Nixon's refusal to debate Vice President Humphrey during the 1968 presidential race.

In 1965, 94 percent of America's households owned at least one television set and a growing number of households owned two or more sets. Sales of color television sets grew in 1965 as millions of American households purchased them. On Sunday, July 11, 1965, the *New York Times'* Tom Wicker reported on the offices built in Austin's federal building for the president's use during his trips home to Texas, describing the familiar arrangement of three television sets directly in front of the president's desk. "Remote control," Wicker wrote of the three sets installed in a cabinet in front of the president's desk, "will make it easy to switch from Huntley-Brinkley to Cronkite, as he lounges in a blue, high-back swivel chair." And the office— with its tenth-story view of the Texas statehouse, the campus of the University of Texas, and Johnson's beloved Hill Country—afforded a view of KTBC-TV's East 10th Street building. "He can look out over the building housing KTBC-TV, the Johnson family television station," Wicker noted of the president's Austin office.[19]

President Johnson is also remembered as the first president to deliver the State of the Union during evening prime-time viewing hours rather than the midday broadcasts of previous presidential addresses. "Johnson Talk at Night Welcomed," the *New York Times*, Tuesday, January 5, 1965, headline reported. Knowing that larger audiences watched television in the prime-time hours of the evening rather than in midday, President Johnson's first televised evening State of the Union Address at 9:00 PM EST on Monday, January 4, 1965, is also recalled as prompting within one year's time the beginning of another well-established tradition: the first televised State of the Union response to the president's remarks by Republican leaders. On Wednesday, January 12, 1966, the first televised remarks in response to the president's State of the Union were delivered by the Republican Party's Senator Everett Dirksen of Illinois and Representative Gerald Ford of Michigan's Fifth Congressional District, most certainly further examples of television's powerful presence in America's political process.

TELEVISION IN 1968

Television viewing audiences were astonished on Sunday evening, March 31, 1968, to watch President Johnson announce his decision not to run for a second term in the White House. Weeks earlier, Walter Cronkite's Tuesday, February 27, 1968, remarks on CBS regarding the Vietnam War ("To say that we are mired in stalemate seems the only realistic, yet unsatisfactory, conclusion") underscored television's far-reaching power, moving public debate on the Vietnam War further than many hundreds of newspaper editorials and opinion columns were able to. Days later, television brought tragedy into America's living rooms and family rooms with the news of Reverend Dr. Martin Luther King Jr.'s assassination in Memphis. Weeks later, television viewers watched as Senator Robert Kennedy, the brother of the late President John F. Kennedy, was shot and killed in a hotel kitchen in Los Angeles. Riots, protests, and demonstrations in the wake of the murder of Reverend Dr. Martin Luther King Jr. and campus protests against the war in Vietnam and demonstrations at the Democratic National Convention (DNC) in Chicago saw television's viewers facing head-on the fissuring and the fracturing of the country's civic and political life.

The unrest on the nation's college campuses and the demonstrations, riots, and violence in the streets of some of the nation's largest cities in 1968 was the backdrop for that year's race for the White House, a race that further elevated the intertwining of campaigning for elected office with television news coverage and with the television ads purchased by the campaigns. Writers, television producers, pollsters, and strategists of all kinds became more prominent during the 1968 race, working to craft their phrases, wording, and imagery to appeal to voters through an ever-larger number of paid commercials airing in more costly, much shorter, and more sharply negative ads on the nation's television networks. Carefully managing television appearances and scripting and staging even the most seemingly impromptu remarks by the candidate are remembered as a centerpiece of Richard Nixon's 1968 race for the White House. This year also marked the unwillingness of Nixon to appear in televised debates yet one that also noted his own campaign's calculated crafting of his candidacy's imagery in thirty- and sixty-second television commercials and in thirty-minute paid panel programs aired on stations in many cities across the country.

With a reporter's instinct for behind-the-scenes detail well honed by his experience as a reporter with the *Philadelphia Inquirer*, Joe McGinniss brought his readers a glimpse of the ad production and television strategy of Nixon's 1968 campaign. Failing in his request for a meeting with the creative team and ad agency working for Vice President Humphrey, McGinniss contacted Nixon's ad agents in New York City. Nixon advisor Harry Treleaven invited McGinniss to meet with the producers and writers working on Nixon's ads, giving the reporter a look at the television-centered campaign of a candidate whose own storied career had been marked by his own triumphs and troubles with television.

McGinniss's book *The Selling of the President* opens in a New York City television studio on a morning when Nixon is cutting ad spots with his creative team. Refusing to read his lines from a script, Nixon cuts take after take, cleaning up or correcting his wording in each take, occasionally changing the wording slightly from one take to the next. That Nixon makes slight changes in the content and the wording of his spots for specific parts of the country, including an ad to be aired only New York City that references a teachers' strike in the city at that time, is recognition of the importance of different television markets across the country and the issues and phrasing most likely to appeal to the audiences in these markets.[20]

From the opening pages through the briefing papers and campaign memorandum reproduced in the closing pages, McGinniss describes the television-centered, image-driven, appearance-focused staging of even the most routine, seemingly extemporaneous appearances and remarks of Nixon in his second bid for the White House. "The situation should look unstaged even if it's not," Harry Treleaven Jr. advises Nixon. "Let's not be afraid of television gimmicks," another advisor urges the former vice president.[21] "The whole day was built around a television show," McGinniss writes of a trip by Nixon to Chicago to tape a television broadcast, a day when Nixon remained in his hotel room to prepare for his broadcast in contrast to his 1960 visit to that city when he did little to prepare for his first televised debate with Kennedy.[22]

"We are going to build this whole campaign around television," Nixon tells his campaign's advisors in the opening months of the 1968 presidential race in a line that is evident across nearly every page of McGinniss's book.[23] The 1968 campaign left almost nothing to chance as Nixon took an attentive hand in the details of all of his televised appearances while working closely with Harry Treleaven and Frank Shakespeare to produce and tape the thirty- and sixty-second commercials aired during his campaign. Roger Ailes, at the time a twenty-seven-year-old advisor to the former vice president and years later the president of Fox News Channel, is profiled by McGinniss as taking the lead in the production of ten televised panel broadcasts by Nixon in different television markets across the country. The year 1968 was the beginning of the carefully scripted informality and leave-nothing-to-chance attentiveness that are now the mainstays of successful campaigns.

"It is the purpose of my thesis to examine the growth of television in the White House and its replacement of newsprint as the President's primary means of communication," a Harvard College senior began his thesis, which he submitted to his faculty advisor weeks before his graduation and at the beginning of a career that took him from the newsroom of Nashville's *The Tennessean* to the floor of the House of Representatives, then the Senate, and eventually to the vice presidency of the United States. Written in the spring of 1969, Al Gore's senior thesis is an insightful look at television's impact on the nation's campaigning for office written by a soon-to-be-prominent figure on the national stage, elected for his first term in the House in November 1976, and whose own weak performance as a candidate on television is widely regarded as having damaged his 2000 candidacy for the White House. Gore's 103-page thesis, *The Impact of Television on the Conduct of the Presidency, 1947–1969*, evinced the family connections the Tennessee senator's son had as well as his familiarity with Washington, D.C., which included the younger Gore's interviews with former special assistant to the president Arthur M. Schlesinger Jr., former White House Press Secretary Bill Moyers, and the *New York Times*' James Reston. Writing on President Kennedy's ease with television broadcasting, President Johnson's grappling with his own "overexposure" in television broadcasts, and President Nixon's decision not to deliver a televised State of the Union Address in the first weeks of his administration in January 1969, Gore illustrated the pitfalls and the possibilities of television appearances for the presidency.

"Humphrey Offers to Purchase Time for 3-Way Debate on TV," the *New York Times* headline reported on Saturday, October 12, 1968, a front-page headline similar to any number of headlines made during that fall's race after Nixon refused to debate Vice President Humphrey. "Humphrey Taunts Nixon as 'Chicken'," the *New York Times* headline reported days later on Wednesday, October 16, 1968. Nixon's unwillingness to take part in televised debates against Humphrey led to a number of newspaper stories as well as editorials taking Nixon to task, editorials that not infrequently cited his earlier criticism of President Johnson's refusal to debate Senator Goldwater in the 1964 presidential race.

TELEVISION IN THE 1970s

"In no other Western democracy has television become so dominant a factor in politics," *Time* magazine told its readers in its Monday, September 21, 1970, issue, describing America's political process as having, "increasingly become a contest of bank accounts and artful contrivance . . . a unique way to bypass political party organizations and challenge entrenched incumbents," making candidates beholden to "the techniques of political image makers often [working] in the service of distortion."[24] With the popularity of a growing number of comedies, dramatic series, game shows, and television talk shows on the nation's television networks in the early 1970s, candidates for office began to adapt part of their time in running for office to guest appearances or cameo walk-ons on these popular programs, all a part of what *Time* called "the image game." The year 1970 is remembered as a time when television not only entwined itself fully into the nation's campaigning for elective office but also when candidates for elective office were more inclined to make appearances in television's many different programs, everything from situation comedies and network newscasts to prime-time and late-evening news specials and even game shows. Interviewers such as Merv Griffin, Barbara Walters, Mike Wallace, and others, as well as the growing popularity of Johnny Carson's *The Tonight Show* whose audiences grew in the early 1970s as his nightly monologues reflected the headlines of the day as well as sometimes making headlines themselves the next morning, emerged alongside of the network newscasters, establishing new venues for elected officials and for candidates running for office to reach television viewers. The first episode of CBS's *60 Minutes*, which aired on Tuesday, September 24, 1968, soon became a standard for broadcast television as other networks began airing their own programs with a format focused on the discussion of the issues of the day.

What by the mid-1970s was being called the permanent campaign, the seemingly ceaseless fund-raising of candidates, in everything from the scheduling of cross-country travel by candidates for events with their contributors and donors to the growth of direct-mail services, grew ever larger for elected officials given the larger viewing audiences tuning into the nation's television networks and the growing prominence of commercial products and advertising. Candidates faced greater pressures to spend larger amounts in the purchase of more costly television commercials, purchases often made on the nation's networks but increasingly made from network affiliates in markets across the country. Candidates for the House of Representatives and the Senate faced their own pressures to increase the amount of money raised to air television commercials in their congressional districts and states, money whose fund-raising steadily increased the influence of well-established interests and whose organizations and groups grew more influential in Washington, D.C. In this era, too, begins one of the important chapters in the nation's history of the regulation of the raising of financial support for candidates running for elective office at the federal level as larger sums of money needed to purchase television airtime led members of Congress as well as their challengers to invest larger amounts of their attention and time to raising this money.

President Nixon's 1972 reelection bid brought once again to the forefront the value of television ad spots by both the Democratic and the Republican tickets for the White House. Senator George McGovern of South Dakota, whose nomination by the Democratic convention in Miami came well after midnight, was the last presidential nominee to address his party's convention and the nation's television viewers in the early morning hours, detouring from the well-scripted dictates of prime-time television broadcasting. President Nixon and his campaign aired commercials extensively on the nation's television networks, an advertising schedule inevitably driving the formidable fund-raising of the president's reelection bid and establishing momentum in Congress for the soon-to-be-enacted campaign finance legislation. The 1972 race for the White House with its expanded schedule for caucus and primary elections in the Democratic and Republican nominations further melded campaigning with television broadcasting, as presidential candidates faced pressure to begin earlier and more extensive television ads in the caucus and primary states. Scheduling by the Iowa Democratic Party of its state's caucuses in 1972 to precede the first statewide primary elections in New Hampshire, joined by the state's Republican Party in 1976, leveraged significant television coverage of the nation's presidential nomination process in both states, turning both states by the end of the twentieth century into a full-blown inundation of television coverage not only by the broadcast networks but by cable television networks, Internet news sites, and even international television coverage.

The 1972 Democratic convention was the last nominating convention not to have its nomination acceptance speech delivered to a prime-time television viewing audience, typically from 10:00 PM to 11:00 PM EST on the final night of the convention. McGovern's acceptance speech, with its well-known "Come Home, America" theme, which became a refrain in that fall's election contest, was delivered well after 2:00 AM EST to one of the smallest viewing audiences for such a nationally televised address.[25]

With his family, friends, and party leaders crowded on the stage behind him, McGovern accepted his nomination and delivered his acceptance speech at 2:45 AM EST on Friday, July 14, 1972. It was to be the last time a major party nominee addressed the nation's television viewing audience at such a late hour.

"McGovern Would Pay for Debates, Offer Rejected," the *New York Times* headline reported on Thursday, October 19, 1972, one of many headlines that fall reporting on the unwillingness of the president to appear in televised debates with Senator McGovern. Nixon's refusal to debate McGovern prompted the same outpouring of newspaper editorials and headlines as a similar refusal had done four years earlier. McGovern and the DNC offered to purchase airtime from the nation's networks to air a televised debate with President Nixon. There were similar bids by Barry Goldwater in 1964 and Hubert Humphrey in 1968; the White House, however, declined to accept the offer and instead continued its heavy schedule of television ads. The *Washington Post*'s front-page headline, "FBI Finds Nixon Aides Sabotaged Democrats," on Tuesday morning, October 10, 1972, was the first publicly documented Nixon administration connection with the June 1972 break-in at the Washington, D.C., offices of the DNC. The House of Representatives' investigations of the alleged interference of White House staff in the FBI investigations of the break-in led months later to the historic televised coverage by the nation's networks of the investigative proceedings in the House of Representatives and in the Senate. The convening of special hearings on Thursday, May 17, 1973, by the Senate Select Committee on Presidential Campaign Activities, chaired by Senator Samuel J. Ervin Jr., began what became over a year's airing on the nation's television networks of the Senate's hearings that brought the House of Representatives and eventually the Senate closer to the permanent broadcasting of proceedings in the legislative branch.

"Senate Inquiry Will Begin Today," the *New York Times* front-page headline on Thursday, May 17, 1973, reported as the opening of the hearings of the Senate Select Committee whose live broadcasts carried by all three networks became a historic moment in the months of investigations into the Nixon White House. From its 10:00 AM first session on Thursday, May 17, 1973, in the Caucus Room of the Old Senate Office Building, the Select Committee and its broadcasts became a medium-defining moment as millions of Americans watched some three hundred hours of testimony in the hearings on the Nixon White House, including former Deputy Assistant to the President Alexander P. Butterfield's testimony on Monday, July 16, 1973, revealing the tape recording of Oval Office conversations between President Nixon and his staff. The House of Representatives voted on Wednesday, February 6, 1974, by a vote of 410 to 4 to begin hearings as to whether or not grounds existed for the initiation of impeachment proceedings against President Nixon. Television cameras again carried live broadcasts to the nation of hearings by members of the House Judiciary Committee, which, on the evening of Wednesday, July 24, 1974, began live televised coverage at 7:30 PM EST, culminating days later in the historic vote on Saturday evening, July 27, 1974, by the House Judiciary Committee by a vote of 27 to 11, with six Republicans joining the committee's twenty-one Democrats—to recommend the impeachment of President Nixon.

"The times demand this legislation," President Gerald Ford told reporters after signing the 1974 Federal Elections Campaign Act (FECA) in the White House's East Room only days after the televised prime-time address to the nation by President Nixon on the evening of Thursday, August 8, 1974, announcing his resignation ("Effective at noon tomorrow") to a nation watching on their televisions. It marked a serious and significant attempt to address the corrosive, if not corrupting, impact of money and of the constant fund-raising necessary by elected officials and candidates for elective office to meet television's price tag. "There are certain periods in our nation's history when it becomes necessary to face up to certain unpleasant truths," President Ford explained in his remarks to the press after signing the FECA legislation. "The unpleasant truth," Ford explained, "is that big money influence has come to play an unseeming role in our electoral processes." He continued, "By removing whatever influence big money and special interests may have on our federal electoral process, this bill should stand as a landmark of campaign reform legislation."[26] With the first federal statutes for the public financing of presidential campaigns (including funds for the national party conventions) as well as the establishment of a provision for voluntary public contributions (through a designation on federal income tax forms) to pay for this financing, the 1974 Federal Elections Campaign Act (FECA) was a step to address the mounting public criticisms of the ever-growing financial contributions and fund-raising of the day, contributions and fund-raising largely driven by the expense of the television commercials purchased by presidential candidates.[27] Coupled with legislation enacted by Congress in 1972 to establish the so-called lowest unit rate for paid political advertisements on the nation's television broadcasters, both legislative statutes expressed an effort on the part of elected officials to address the pressures of raising larger amounts of private contributions to pay for the soaring costs of television commercials and their production, legislation that ultimately did little if anything to disengage candidates from their efforts to amass larger coffers to pay for more costly television airtime.

The debut on Saturday, October 11, 1975, of a new late-night comedy show, NBC's *Saturday Night* (later *Saturday Night Live*), with its first guest host, comedian George Carlin, paved the way for another chapter in America's electoral life. *Saturday Night*, in its first episodes and during its first season, brought an irreverence ("The Unofficial Seal of the United States of America" appearing on podiums in some skits) to television programming and used satire to make fun of elected officials and of candidates for office during a time of public disillusionment and dissatisfaction with post-Watergate America.

When President Gerald Ford's press secretary Ron Nessen, a former Washington, D.C., NBC News correspondent, played as a character in some episodes by actor Buck Henry, appeared on NBC's *Saturday Night* as its guest host on Saturday, April 17, 1976, he was able to arrange the taping of a guest appearance on the program by President Ford, who opened the show with its famous line, "Live, from New York, it's *Saturday Night.*" Nessen's appearance on that episode included several skits making light of President Ford, including a skit on a stage-set of the Oval Office with Nessen playing himself and actor Chevy Chase playing President Ford. Nessen's appearance marked the beginning of the late-night comedy program's serious place in America's campaigns for elective office, and Washington, D.C., press corps, its journalists and reporters, and most certainly Nessen's own White House successors have kept their attention on *Saturday Night Live*, especially if the program's walk-on and guest-host appearances are by candidates for elective office.

Over the years, various candidates appeared on NBC's *Saturday Night Live*, including Representative John Anderson, Senator George McGovern, Senator Gary Hart, Senator Bob Dole, Reverend Jesse Jackson, Senator Barack Obama, and many more. Chevy Chase's popular impression of President Ford (which in Chase's first appearance as the character of President Ford included the television caption, "This is not the President of the United States"), Dan Aykroyd's Jimmy Carter, Phil Hartman's Bill Clinton, and Will Ferrell's George W. Bush (not to mention Tina Fey's Sarah Palin) left audiences laughing and shaped impressions for millions of Americans as they were frequently replayed in network newscasts.

9:30 PM EST. Thursday evening. September 23, 1976. Philadelphia's Walnut Street Theater. 2 presidential candidates. 1 moderator. 3 panelists. 69,700,000 television viewers. "Ford, Carter Clash on Fiscal Policy," the *Washington Post* front-page headline reported that Friday, September 24, 1976, of the previous evening's ninety-minute televised debate between President Ford and Georgia governor Jimmy Carter, the first of three televised debates in that year's presidential race and the first televised debate in almost twenty years. "One evening a few weeks ago," *Time* magazine reported in its Monday, September 27, 1976, issue—as if to underscore even more the historic connection to the 1960 debates—"Carter, in work clothes and boots, sat in the den of his Plains home. An old kinescope of the first Kennedy-Nixon debate had been set up for him, and he studied the two candidates closely." *Time* reported the governor's reaction after he watched the 1960 debate film: "At the end, [Carter] agreed that the images of the debate, the ways Nixon and Kennedy had looked and acted, had made more of an impression on him than the content of the questions and their answers."[28] Weeks later, with match-ups between the president and Governor Carter airing on the evenings of Wednesday, October 6, 1976, and on Friday, October 22, 1976, and with viewers tuning in on the evening of Friday, October 15, 1976, to watch the first ever televised vice presidential debate, the nation's television viewers saw yet again television's undeniable and undiminished presence as the driving dynamic in campaigning for the nation's highest offices.

The Tuesday, November 2, 1976, election of Jimmy Carter led to a series of statements from the president-elect and from his press spokespersons that his administration intended to regularly address the nation in televised addresses from the White House, an announcement that immediately led some in the press to make the connection to Roosevelt's Fireside Chats. President-elect Carter told *Time* magazine that his administration would still hold televised press conferences with reporters and that he also intended to host televised broadcasts from the White House as kind of "fireside chats to explain complicated issues" to the American public.[29]

"Good evening," President Carter remarked to television viewers on the evening of Wednesday, February 2, 1977, from in front of the fireplace in the White House Library. "Tomorrow will be two weeks since I became president. I've spent a lot of time deciding how I can be a good president. This talk, which the broadcast networks have agreed to bring to you, is one of several steps I will take to keep in close touch with the people of our country to let you know informally about our plans for the coming months." With these words on Wednesday evening at 10:00 PM EST, Carter began his twenty-five-minute live televised address (which opened with the caption "LIVE FROM THE WHITE HOUSE" and the image of Carter sitting in front of a fireplace over which hung the portrait of George Washington) from the White House Library, one of the first times in years that a prime-time televised address did not take place in the Oval Office or in the White House press briefing room. Addressing the nation's energy problems that evening, the president detailed a list of initiatives and plans his administration pledged to undertake in the months to come. President Carter's televised remarks, in which he wore a cardigan sweater rather than a suit and tie and was seated in a chair rather than behind a desk, immediately brought comparisons to Roosevelt's Fireside Chats and is most certainly a frequently cited as part of President Carter's early efforts to reach out to the American television viewers. Yet the president's presence at an often overlooked yet significant moment in television history in his home state of Georgia marked another chapter in television's changing dynamic.

CABLE TELEVISION AND THE REINVENTION OF TELEVISION IN AMERICAN POLITICS

Sunday, June 1, 1980. Atlanta, Georgia. 6:00 PM EST. President Jimmy Carter, the nation's thirty-ninth president of the United States, is traveling in Fort Wayne, Indiana, when Cable News Network (CNN) reports on his visit to the Midwest from its studio in Atlanta, coverage that included the interruption of a commercial for a breakaway to a live-remote from Indiana where President Carter spoke with reporters. That Sunday evening from Atlanta, cable subscribers watched the nation's first twenty-four-hour cable news network air its first broadcast as a network, beginning a reinvention of television that has since reverberated across the globe. Later that same evening as a part of its maiden broadcast, CNN's veteran journalist Daniel Schorr conducted an exclusive interview with President Carter. Reaching an estimated 2,500,000 cable television viewers on cable systems in some thirty states, this broadcast, Robert Goldberg and Gerald Jay Goldberg aptly tell us, "quite literally changed the way we look at the world." CNN's Ted Turner described his news channel as "a newspaper you can watch" and spoke with reporters of wanting to "deliver a newspaper electronically" to cable viewers.[30]

"Many small communities are entirely cabled now and others are following every day," *Popular Science* enthused to its readers in its June 1970 issue, heralding the possibilities for cable television a decade before CNN's first broadcast from Atlanta in June 1980. "Eventually," *Popular Science* told its readers, "a large part of the country will get its television programs from cables instead of antennas. Some experts are predicting, for less than the cost of the family car, a complete home communications terminal with access to computer libraries, two-way video, and hundreds of input channels. Cable TV could make it all come true," *Popular Science* explained at a time when only some 5 percent of the nation's television households subscribed to cable television services.[31] Enthusiastic accounts of cable services abounded in the early 1970s. "As cable systems are installed in major cities and metropolitan areas," Ralph Lee Smith wrote in his 1972 book, *The Wired Nation: Cable TV, the Electronic Communications Highway*, "the stage is being set for a communications revolution."[32] Cable television, *Time* magazine told its readers, "could change the country's way of life. Its copper coaxial cables, though larger than telephone cord, have 1,000 times the capacity. Washington-willing, the U.S. could be transformed into what some call 'the wired nation,'" *Time* magazine noted, envisioning possibilities for the delivery of television programming to households as well as the ability of television viewers to reply to and respond with the transmissions themselves.[33]

Well underway by 1970, cable television's history is an exceptional and extraordinary chapter in the history of television and in the delivery of broadband digital services to tens of millions of households by the end of the twentieth century. Of all of the breakthroughs in television since the advent of postwar broadcasting in the late 1940s, few are as important as the impact of cable television and direct-subscriber services, especially the growth of cable news channels and networks devoted to the coverage of Washington, D.C., events and news. With the growth of direct-satellite subscription services accompanying cable television's boom since the early 1980s, the reach of subscription television services into tens of millions of America's households is of far-reaching importance for political campaigning.

Cable television's early history is bound up with the expansion of America's postwar population into more dispersed suburban areas outlying America's largest metropolitan areas and even its smaller cities and towns. At almost the same moment in the early to mid-1950s that television broadcasting was bringing signals over the treetops and rooftops into America's homes, commercial investors were working to assemble the infrastructure and building the marketplace for the delivery of television through the installation of central antennas and the distribution of its signals through specially installed lines from house to house. Facing consumer demand and given the difficulty of receiving television signals as more and more Americans moved into areas farther away from the clear reception of the signals of broadcast stations, cable outfits began populating the suburban expanses of postwar America. The growth of suburban cable companies accompanied the arrival of interstate highways, which were being built in the mid- to late 1960s and continued into the 1970s and beyond.

In the late 1940s and early 1950s, cable's history is well recalled as beginning in the quiet, often rural areas where the lack of a clear television signal led local businessmen and entrepreneurs, "many of them appliance salesmen trying to sell television sets in areas with weak or non-existent signals," as George Mannes explains, to build their own local outfits with larger antennas for receiving broadcasts and with specially built wiring for sharing these signals with individual households.[34] John Walson, a Mahanoy City, Pennsylvania, appliance store owner, was one of the early innovators who started his own cable outfit in the late 1940s. Having had difficulty selling television sets in his appliance store due to the poor reception for most of his town's households, Walson took it upon himself to build a large antenna to receive television signals from Philadelphia, some ninety miles away.[35]

In 1949, a local cable company owned by Ed Parsons in Astoria, Oregon, built a large antenna to receive the signal from television station KRSC-TV in Seattle, Washington, a distance of some 125 miles away with mountains impeding the broadcast signal for most local residents, at a cost of $3 a month for households in the Oregon town. In 1950, Panther Valley Television Company, an outfit owned by Robert J. Tarlton operating in Lansford, Pennsylvania, built an antenna to bring in television signals from Philadelphia as well as from nearby Scranton. Reports of "community antennae television" in Arkansas, Maryland, and elsewhere by the end of the 1940s established the beginnings of a much larger commercial enterprise to unfold steadily over the next fifty years. By 1950, an estimated seventy cable companies served approximately 14,000 households, nearly all in either mountainous areas with poor television reception or in otherwise distant towns, a figure that would grow to some 560 local cable outfits by 1959.[36] Lyndon Johnson and his family's investments in broadcasting in Texas expanded to include several cable franchises in the years after 1960. With KTBC-TV's influence in Austin well established, the Johnson family's investments in cable television in the mid- to late 1960s proved a financially lucrative investment and firmly established the family's influence on broadcasting in the Lone Star State.

"The weakest thing about the prospering U.S. television industry is its broadcast signals," *Time* magazine reported on Friday, November 13, 1964. "Blocked by mountains, bothered by airplanes, bounced by hills and high buildings, they generate only ghosts on television screens in many parts of the country. Serving mostly outlying areas, cable television has grown into a $750 million business that includes 1,450 systems and 1,600,000 subscribers spread over all states except Alaska and Rhode Island." "Cable television companies optimistically foresee a system in which television will no longer depend on broadcast alone, but will be sent over a microwave-wire combination everywhere in the U.S."[37] Construction of the infrastructure for cable services continued from the mid-1960s well into the 1970s, building an infrastructure not just for carrying television signals but eventually the Internet and World Wide Web broadband digital services. At the beginning of the 1970s, cable television moved from being a scattered and selective service in markets across the United States to being a much more commercially lucrative and politically relevant actor in the media marketplace. By June 1971, some 2,750 cable companies were thought to be in business in the United States, reaching an audience of some 19,000,000 viewers. Households with subscriptions to cable services increased from approximately 19 percent at the end of 1979 to 29 percent in 1982 to 38 percent in 1983. The adoption of cable and other subscription services soon offered the beginnings of a shift in the interplay between television and the political campaigning.

Long discussed in the House of Representatives and the Senate, the arrival in March 1979 of the Cable Satellite Public Affairs Network (C-SPAN), at a time when some 12,000,000 American households subscribed to cable services (approximately 16 percent of the country's households), ushered in the regular coverage of legislation in the House of Representatives as the first television channel dedicated to continuous congressional coverage. With a House vote of 342 to 44 to approve the television coverage, C-SPAN and its Arlington, Virginia–based staff of four employees, with a budget of some

$500,000, a single telephone line that served both as a business line as well as a call-in line for its viewers, and a leased satellite feed that broadcast C-SPAN's programming only during daytime hours, began broadcasting proceedings from the House of Representatives at noon EST on Monday, March 19, 1979.

"First TV Broadcast of House Session Isn't High Theater," the *New York Times* Tuesday, March 20, 1979 headline reported. C-SPAN's first day of coverage lasted two hours and twenty minutes, on a day when deliberations on the floor of the House focused mostly on the so-called special order speeches typical of many sessions in the House. "It was," B. Drummond Ayres Jr. noted, "2 and ½ hours of the same routine that goes on day after day after day in the House. There were no shots of members snoozing or reading newspapers. There were no telephoto intrusions into corner caucuses. There was no feel for the high-ceilinged vastness of the House chamber, no sense that only about 25 of the 435 members were on the floor, the usual complement for a routine day."[38] Representative Al Gore of Tennessee explained in his remarks before the Houses of Representatives on that Monday afternoon, "Television will change this institution, just as it has changed the executive branch."[39] Of the approximately 3,500,000 homes subscribing to one of the 160 cable service providers delivering that first day of C-SPAN's programming, few viewers likely watched this historic broadcast of the proceedings of the House of Representatives.

After years of unwillingness by some Senate members to allow televised coverage of their chamber's deliberations, on Tuesday, July 29, 1986, by a vote of 78 to 21, the Senate allowed C-SPAN to air continuous coverage of its floor deliberations and proceedings. C-SPAN and its affiliated cable systems reached as many as 29,000,000 households on an estimated 2,200 of the approximately 9,500 cable outfits in the United States and, within a year's time, reached some 40,000,000 households with its coverage of congressional deliberations, hearings, floor votes, and related activities as well as press conferences and other events. Members of the Senate were now visible to many of their constituents during their deliberations on the floor of the Senate as well as in growing coverage by the network of congressional committee hearings, press conferences, and other meetings. Decades later, C-SPAN still provides uninterrupted live broadcasts of both the House of Representatives as well as the Senate chamber on C-SPAN 2 and its array of related programming, much of it increasingly streamed and viewed through the network's website. With its gavel-to-gavel continuous coverage of the deliberations on the floor of the House of Representatives and the Senate as well as its coverage of congressional committee hearings, major policy addresses, presidential candidate appearances, and innumerable programs of commentary on current events and history, C-SPAN, with its extensive television programming, its radio coverage, and its vast archive of programming on the World Wide Web, is far-and-away one of the most important institutions available to the press and holds prominence in the policymaking and political process in the United States today.

CAMPAIGNS, CANDIDATES, AND COMMUNICATIONS IN THE 1980s AND BEYOND

Television is the day-to-day, hour-to-hour, even minute-to-minute dynamic that drives nearly every aspect of campaigning for elected office at the beginning of the twenty-first century. Light-reflectors positioned by production crews and boom-microphones overhead in the scrum of reporters are familiar sights to candidates seeking office today. Today's candidates are accustomed to even the smallest production details of their television ads, often knowing well the market-by-market strategies for the purchase of their ads by their campaigns as well as the financial implications of running these ads. Because television advertising is so expensive, a considerable amount of their time is now devoted to attending meetings with donors, traveling to fund-raisers, and taking part in all aspects of contact with contributors. Writing and producing ads, testing them with their target audiences, purchasing time for their ads in select markets on particular television programs or shows, then tracking the audience responses to the ads and gauging the impact of their ad buys, monitoring the responses (if any) of rivals to their ads, and repeating this process, market-by-market, state-by-state in closely contested television markets in so-called battleground or swing states is the immovable imperative of campaigning for national office.

The airing of television ads is an unvarying constant in the strategies of candidates in every step of their candidacies from the first televised spots introducing them in early caucus and primary states to the fever-pitch airing of television spots in the hurried final days of the race. The workhorses of most campaigns for elected office remain the thirty-, twenty-, and even fifteen-second television ads. Staggering sums of money—a sizeable amount raised in online contributions, which, in turn, are spent on the purchase of broadcast television ads, or, as the *Los Angeles Times*, Friday, October 29, 2010, headline put it, "Candidates Raise Cash on the Internet but They Spend It on TV,"—wash into the sales offices of television stations in markets across the United States, especially in those closely contested television markets in swing states.

"TV," Joseph Lelyveld observed in the March 1976 *New York Times Magazine*, "has made political communication a matter of fleeting impressions." "It's a 30-second world," as Walter Staab, an ad executive "who has lately been buying TV time for President Ford," was noted as saying in the mid-1970s as increased costs of television airtime and the larger number of channels in a growing number of American households all meant the airing of shorter but more frequent campaign ads.[40] By the mid-1970s and early

1980s, television's central place in campaigning for elective office was well established. The cost of producing ads and the purchase of television airtime exceeded nearly all other campaign expenditures. Larger television viewing audiences coupled with the longer hours of the day spent viewing television by most Americans in the 1970s and afterward, not to mention the growth in the number of channels with the growth of cable, meant campaigns now reached their audiences with more ads aired more frequently on a greater number of channels and on a greater number of programs. Ads lasted from twenty to thirty seconds, a far cry from the thirty-minute commercials popular with candidates in the 1950s and even the one-minute ads still used by some candidates for office in the 1970s. With the increased cost of airtime, campaigns gave closer attention to the preair testing of their commercials with their desired audiences through the use of focus and dial groups to gauge audience responses to the effectiveness of the television ad before airing it.

The 1980 presidential race saw both President Jimmy Carter and Ronald Reagan adapt to and adept in television's near-constant presence in the campaign and in the coverage by nightly news broadcasts. Carter's insistence that he appear in the first of any televised presidential debates only with Reagan before he would agree unwillingly to appear in a three-candidate televised debate with Reagan and Representative John Anderson in his independent bid for the White House did little to alter the expectation that candidates face their rivals in live televised debates. Eventually, Carter and Reagan agreed to a single, ninety-minute televised debate with only the two major party candidates on Tuesday evening, October 28, 1980, just a week before the election. Even the familiar language of so-called blue and red states in the lexicon of campaigning for office is thought to have been first used in the 1980 network newscasts of that year's Election Night returns as the anchors used these colors on maps in their newsrooms to shade in states carried by President Carter and by Ronald Reagan.

Year after year, the interweaving of television's presence in campaigning for elective office is the driving dynamic of American politics, a dynamic well evidenced in 1980 and afterward. Ronald Reagan's election on Tuesday, November 4, 1980, brought further attention to the era of governance in the age of television. Journalists accustomed to the behind-the-scenes accounts of lawmaking in Washington, D.C., understood the prominence of television coverage in the governing process, penning accounts with a growing emphasis on the staging of seemingly routine announcements and the timing of these events to work with the dictates and schedules of television networks and their producers.[41] Well-publicized accounts by longtime Washington, D.C., journalists of the lengths to which the packaging of news conferences, policy announcements, and even seemingly impromptu remarks with an eye to the visual imagery of these events became the conventional wisdom of the work of media professionals in the 1980s and in the years since.

"Modern politics today requires a mastery of television," Walter F. Mondale explained in a St. Paul, Minnesota, press conference with reporters the day after his defeat in the Tuesday, November 6, 1984, presidential race, a race that saw some of the most extensive purchases to date of televised commercials aired by President Reagan's reelection campaign as well as that of his Democratic rival.[42] Mondale's observation is in some respects a milestone of a moment in America's political life near the end of the twentieth century, namely, the acknowledgment, according to Hedrick Smith, that television "has become the central battleground of American campaigns."[43] "I've never really warmed up to television," Mondale told reporters. "And in fairness to television, it never warmed up to me."[44] Mondale later conceded that he felt that he'd lost the 1984 race when he finished the second of his two televised debates with President Reagan on the evening of Monday, October 22, 1984, a debate in which Reagan, when asked by one of the panelists whether he was "too old to handle a nuclear crisis," famously answered, "I am not going to exploit for political purposes my opponent's youth and inexperience." Mondale later recalled, "When I walked out of there, I knew it was all over."

"The next President will have been chosen in a campaign dominated as never before by television," *New York Times*' Michael Oreskes explained days before that November election in his newspaper's Sunday, October 30, 1988, front page.[45] As Democratic strategist David Axelrod explained in November 1988, "TV reigns supreme in U.S. politics, making arguments more effectively and efficiently than the flesh-and-blood precinct captains of a bygone era."[46] The 1988 presidential race is remembered as a defining moment of sorts in the intertwining of television into the day-to-day decisions and dynamics of campaigns at the end of the twentieth century with everything from the carefully choreographed productions of the nominating conventions to the negative television ads (a significant number of which were aired by independent groups unaffiliated with the candidates themselves) to the declining purchase of airtime on the nation's networks (in favor of ad purchases from local affiliates in select markets as well as some cable airtime) to the importance of candidates responding in a timely fashion (sometimes in a matter of hours) to the televised ads of rival campaigns, especially those attacking their candidate. Made-for-television events and cinematic-like settings were well evident in the 1988 presidential campaign, yet even then, the emphasis on imagery—as with Michael Dukakis's famous helmeted tank ride—reminded campaigns that their focus on imagery and visuals (and most especially when these clips replayed on television news programs) still had the potential for mishap and misstep.[47] "There are three things that get covered," Roger Ailes, a longtime Republican strategist working in 1988 for Vice President Bush's campaign, told Oreskes in October 1988: "Visuals, attacks, and mistakes. You try to avoid mistakes and give them as many attacks and visuals as you can," Ailes added.[48]

Nearly continuous monitoring of the televised appearances of a campaign's rivals, not to mention the monitoring of the latest ads aired by their rivals, along with the monitoring of the television commentary and news coverage of the candidates and issues of the hour, all of this is remembered as taking a central place in the 1992 race between President Bush and Arkansas's governor Bill Clinton with that year's innovations in the production, in the delivery, and in the tracking and the polling of the effectiveness of these ads. Improvements in computer technology allowed Clinton's strategists in 1992 to focus on what they termed the "cost-per-persuadable-voter" in deciding where to air their television ads, a process described by David Lauter as "a ruthless form of political triage" involving "pouring money and energy into key states while leaving others almost untouched."[49] Color-coded maps of selected states and their media markets were a prominent feature in Clinton's campaign offices in Little Rock.

"Bush and Clinton Customize Their TV and Radio Ads in the Swing States," a *New York Times* headline reported on Thursday, October 22, 1992, in a race whose state-by-state and market-by-market ad buys, in the words of Elizabeth Kolbert, were guarded with "Pentagon-like secrecy" by the strategists advising President Bush and Governor Clinton.[50] Decisions by Clinton's campaign and that of President Bush to steer larger amounts of their advertising to these midsized markets, Martin F. Nolan reported, "changed the electoral map from familiar Rand McNally proportions to a Silly Putty sprawl of adjacent television signals."[51] *The Today Show, The Tonight Show*, MTV, Governor Clinton's appearance with his wife, Hillary Clinton, on the Sunday, January 26, 1992, CBS *60 Minutes* show immediately after Super Bowl XXVI, H. Ross Perot's guest appearances on CNN's *Larry King Live*, the first televised town-hall presidential debate from Richmond, Virginia, with an audience of some 250 voters on the evening of Thursday, October 15, 1992, and Governor and Mrs. Clinton's Wednesday, June 3, 1992, appearance on *The Arsenio Hall Show* all illustrate television's indisputable dominance as the decisive dynamic in the 1992 campaigns for president that remained unrivaled in the last decade of the twentieth century.

The race for the White House in 2000 mirrored the growth of television sales and the increasing number of hours of television viewership, a phenomenon that would see even larger growth through an array of broadband and multimedia Internet services that were becoming increasingly accessible to millions of households. Even with the growing presence of the Internet in the campaigns of Texas governor George W. Bush and Vice President Al Gore, television still held sway in the 2000 race—what the *Washington Post*'s Dan Morgan called "the most valuable commodity in American politics: advertising time on TV," especially the airing of ads in select television markets in the country's swing states.[52] Stations and network affiliates projected some $600,000,000 in ad buys in the 2000 race, almost 50 percent

more than the buys in the 1996 race and more than doubling airtime purchases in 1992. "Bush, Gore Ad Campaigns Steer Clear of National TV," an
Advertising Age headline announced in its Monday, August 7, 2000, issue.
"This year," reported Jeff Leeds on Wednesday, October 25, 2000, "the candidates each have spent nearly 100% of their ad war chests on local broadcast TV."[53] The market-by-market and state-by-state ad buys in 2000, Leeds
reported weeks earlier on Friday, September 29, 2000, "shows how party
and campaign strategists view the nation, not as a whole or even as 50 separate states but as a mix of 210 television media markets where the candidates' messages can vary depending on whose airwaves are carrying it."[54]
"Campaigns Fuel a Frenzy of TV Spots," the *Washington Post* reported in a
front-page story on Friday, October 27, 2000. "In Campaign 2000, Local
Stations Are Winning Big," reported the *Wall Street Journal* on Friday,
November 3, 2000, just days before Election Day on Tuesday, November 7,
2000.

"The road to the White House runs through me," David Letterman chided
George W. Bush on the evening of Wednesday, March 1, 2000, during Bush's
first guest appearance on the popular late-night show, a line that Letterman
repeated with some slight variation over the years, including in a Monday,
September 20, 2004, visit by Senator John Kerry and again in a Thursday,
October 16, 2008, appearance by Senator John McCain.[55] By 2000, Jay
Leno, David Letterman, Oprah Winfrey, and other television talk show
hosts became a familiar path on the campaign trail. When the *New York
Times'* Richard L. Berke and Kevin Sack reported that Vice President Gore's
staff arranged for Gore to watch a tape of a *Saturday Night Live* parody of
his performance in his first televised debate with Governor Bush in preparation for the vice president's appearance in the second televised debate on
Wednesday, October 11, 2000, it was a reminder of the influence wielded by
NBC's popular comedy program and programs like it in the dynamics of
campaigning for elective office.[56]

The 2004 reelection bid of President Bush in his race against Senator John
Kerry and four years later the contest between senators John McCain and
Barack Obama saw a familiar and further interweaving of television and
campaigning. With vast sums of money flowing into the coffers of the 2004
Bush and Kerry campaigns and even larger sums into the 2008 race, televi-
sion's driving dynamic remained at the center of the campaigns, with most
of the hundreds of millions of dollars raised by the candidates spent on what
David Carr of the *New York Times* in his Monday, October 27, 2008, column called "the sweet spot of political persuasion," namely the sixty- and
especially the thirty-second ads in select markets, "blitzing" viewers of *The
Oprah Winfrey Show, Dr. Phil, Live with Regis and Kelly, Wheel of Fortune,
Jeopardy,* and other programs in some of the country's most closely contested markets, especially in Cleveland, Columbus, Dayton, and Toledo as
well as in Kansas City and St. Louis.[57]

"Campaign Buying More Ads But Targeting Fewer States," the *Washington Post*'s Saturday, September 25, 2004, front-page headline reported, a headline that was to be familiar in 2004 and again in 2008. "The shifting state-by-state and city-by-city strategies," *Washington Post*'s Paul Farhi observed, "essentially affirm something that became apparent in 2000: the death of the national campaign ad."[58] The 2008 race most certainly underscored this in the airing of ads in select television markets with even greater attention to specific markets and to select programs airing in these markets by Senator John McCain and Senator Barack Obama. "Not since the Kennedy-Nixon race has television played such a significant role in a presidential election," *Los Angeles Times*' Mary McNamara explained just days before the Tuesday, November 4, 2008, election.[59] Appearances by the candidates on daytime and late-night programs took on even more prominence in 2004 and in 2008, especially the late-night programs hosted by Jay Leno, David Letterman, Stephen Colbert, and Jon Stewart, not to mention NBC's *Saturday Night Live*. Advertising in select markets in the 2008 race was typical to the same extent as in recent campaigns for the White House. Senator Obama's campaign also made the decision to purchase a series of thirty-minute commercials on three of the nation's four networks (CBS, Fox, and NBC), which prompted Major League Baseball to make a slight adjustment to the start time for that evening's World Series game. At 8:00 PM EST on Wednesday, October 29, 2008, viewers on CBS, Fox, and NBC, as well as BET, MSNBC, and Univision, an estimated 33,000,000 viewers in all, as reported by Nielsen Media Research, watched the simulcast of the thirty-minute commercial, a buy estimated to cost some $5,000,000 by the Obama campaign.

Even the most cursory of glances at some of 2012's headlines ("73,000 Political Ads Test Even a City of Excess," "Hundreds of Ads a Day Hit Ohio Airwaves," "Romney Tailors Ads by State," "Swing States to Weather Brunt of Deluge of Ad Spending," "Political Ads Boost Broadcasters," and "Obama's Campaign Uses Daytime TV Ads to Sell Reelection Bid") remind us of the immovable presence of television ads and appearances by the candidates in virtually every aspect of campaigning for the nation's highest office today. Campaigning that is more attentive to the growing digital dominance and pervasive Web presences of the candidates, their fund-raising, and their voter outreach. Whether in their fund-raising expectations, their state-by-state ad strategies, their targeting of even greater kinds of television programming for ad buys, and their now-familiar appearances of the candidates on daytime, late-night, and other television programming venues, the 2012 reelection bid of President Barack Obama and the campaign of Republican nominee Mitt Romney is a familiar chapter in the importance of television in presidential races. With 210 television markets in the United States and with some states having a dozen or more key television markets, the 2012 race reminds us that even in the data-driven, digital-dynamics of the twenty-first century, all politics is local *television*.

ATMOSPHERICS, OPTICS, AND THE TWENTY-FIRST-CENTURY TELEVISION CAMPAIGN

In the early years of the twenty-first century, even with the growth in direct satellite services, broadband digital streaming, and digital recording systems, campaigning for America's highest elected offices is still in almost every way a constant fight to find and fix the attention of television viewers in their bedrooms, their family rooms, their kitchens, and their living rooms in tens of millions of America's households, especially the broadcast affiliates in the most closely contested parts of the country and in the states and the parts of states being hard-fought by the candidates and their campaigns. Candidates hew close to their carefully crafted, well-rehearsed messages, staying on-message as much as possible in the high-stakes skirmishes that play themselves out hour-after-hour on the television screens of millions of American households. Candidates' facial expressions, grimaces, sighs, smirks, and stammers are as much fodder for the television cameras as their words.

"Television dominates each weekday," political scientist Martha Joynt Kumar writes of the hour-to-hour attention to the pulse and punctuations of television in the press offices of Washington, D.C., a process that extends into every aspect of the work of lawmakers and lobbyists alike who walk the halls and work the offices of Capitol Hill, and most especially to the candidates on the campaign trail.[60] White House hallways, meeting rooms, and offices, as with offices of members of Congress and in Washington, D.C.'s news bureaus throughout the capital feature flat-panel television sets, where lawmakers, staff, and even the president of the United States interrupt their routines and their work to watch the latest news stories as they break. Television appearances set the tempo of the day for many elected officials, beginning in the early morning hours and continuing throughout the day and into the late-evening hours on Stephen Colbert, David Letterman, Jon Stewart, Jimmy Fallon, and any number of late-night programs, not to mention the early-morning network shows that pick up almost exactly where the late-night comedians' programs sign-off. Well aware of the potential of even the most insignificant story or utterance to shake up and shape the news cycle as it is filtered through this dawn-to-dusk television cycle, campaign staffs do their utmost to monitor closely the coverage of the television networks and their correspondents on the campaign trail as well as prepare well in advance of potential lines of attack by rival campaigns. Dimly lit, monitor-filled rooms of flat-screen televisions and laptop computers are the new hubs of campaigning for elective office in the twenty-first century, the modern counterpart to the smoke-filled rooms of lore or of the editorial and newsrooms of the great nineteenth- and twentieth-century metropolitan newspapers.

"I run all my campaigns as if people were watching television with the sound turned down," strategist Karl Rove is known to have said over the years to his candidates and to the journalists who report on his work.[61] Whether it is the network broadcasts "from the President's ranch in Crawford, Texas," when, in fact, reporters who covered President Bush in his visits home to Texas aired their live-remotes from a field behind the Crawford Middle School miles away from his Prairie Chapel Ranch, or the driveway just to the side of the White House's north lawn where news networks maintain a near-constant presence of television cameras, or in the television interviews of members of Congress standing on the third-floor balconies with the marble columns and railings of the Cannon House Office Building and the Russell Senate Office Building rotundas across the street from the Capitol Building, television's coverage and reporting is still the very heart and heartbeat of the carefully choreographed, image-conscious, television-driven twenty-first-century campaign. Politics, in a figurative if not a literal sense, *is* television in the twenty-first century. The pulse and the pursuit of campaigns and their strategists in seeking the attention of viewers for whom the decision to linger with a candidate, their remarks, and their commercials is always a split-second click of the television remote-control away. Advance campaign staff, or "advance," as it is often known, select locations and venues for press conferences, speeches, and town-hall meetings and plan the details of every policy announcement by officeholders and by the candidates for these offices. The podiums, the lighting, the location, the clothing of audience members taking part in these events, the "extensive location-scouting, technical expertise, and attention to minute detail," as *Los Angeles Times*' Edwin Chen puts it, all become part of the attention paid by campaign strategists who work with painstaking details to prepare their candidate for how they will appear on television.[62]

"However unfairly," Katharine Q. Seelye tells us, "modern campaigns driven by television and personality . . . place a premium [on] an ease with language, a telegenic presence, a sunny countenance, a willingness to be packaged."[63] Advance teams, personal stylists, makeup artists, wardrobe consultants, lighting specialists, and others do much of the day-to-day work when it comes to what Julie Bosman describes as "the highly produced theatrical productions that pass for campaign events these days" and "advance teams that carefully prepare camera-ready appearances with professional lights, music and backdrops, and heavily stocked with vetted (and sometimes coached) supporters."[64] When Senator John F. Kennedy and his staff decided to arrive in Chicago days early to prepare for the first of his four televised debates with Vice President Nixon on the evening of Monday, September 26, 1960, it marked the first time a candidate elaborately prepared for a televised appearance; preparations that included the assemblage and study of briefing books, the practicing of answers to potential questions, the rehearsal of opening and closing remarks, even the careful selection of wardrobe. All of this attention to detail certainly strengthens the dynamic of television's imagery and its increased importance in winning over voters.

The immovable force of fund-raising and financial assets is the dictate of the twenty-first-century candidacy for elective office, whether in the thousands of dollars a week raised by most members of the House of Representatives and the Senate; the millions of dollars raised by candidates for the White House; the scramble for donors by national party leaders; the funds raised by thousands of advocacy associations, business, trade, and professional organizations, and membership groups in Washington, D.C.; or in the continuous coverage by the nation's journalists and reporters, not to mention the constant debate within the federal courts and in federal agencies such as the Federal Election Commission (FEC) and other agencies. Candidate's fund-raising commitments of time and travel, much of it driven by the demand to replenish campaign coffers for the insatiable expenses of television advertising, is an inevitable accompaniment to the day-to-day scheduling of candidates, their spouses, and their supporters at almost every level, especially with the expenses of time and of travel. What is known by candidates for the House of Representatives, the Senate, and especially those seeking the nation's highest office as "dialing for dollars," the day-in, day-out, week-after-week, month-after-month work of raising money face-to-face at fund-raising events and as often by telephone is, as Richard Berke puts it, "the real business of campaigns, one that takes place largely out of public view."[65] The purchase of television airtime and the scheduling of ever larger amounts of time in advancing, arranging, and attending the fund-raisers to pay for it, is the centerpiece of well-organized campaigns for office even as the Internet's social media grows ever larger in campaign outreach.

The purchase of time in sixty- and thirty-second bursts on the broadcast airwaves in television markets across the country is one of the most important dynamics in campaigns today, "the vehicle of choice to reach elusive swing voters in a polarized nation," as Nick Anderson puts it, as strategists skilled in the negotiation and purchase of ads in these television markets carefully select their states and the particular media markets within those states to air ads.[66] Effectively reaching smaller, more specific segments of the electorate, whether described as persuadables or "swings," as they are sometimes called, groups cross-referenced into analytical models with their data-points of television viewership profiles, audience measurements, and surveys of consumer preferences, lifestyle indices, and political affiliations are the reality of twenty-first-century campaigns. Writers and producers of television ads find themselves under ever greater pressure to script ad spots in shorter periods of time while campaign staff pour over the production of these commercials to determine if all the factual elements are met. They also prepare rebuttals to response ads while still more staff analyze the varied slivers of the electorate, using more carefully tailored ads to speak directly to specific groups through buys on programs determined to be the most likely to reach those voters.[67] Analysis of television audiences as they overlap with these sought-after segments of the voting electorate is at the heart of the strategy in production and placement of ads. It is the dynamic of today's data-driven campaigning. Audience analysis and so-called dial group technology take the twenty-first-century campaign strategist far beyond public opinion surveys to assess the individual response to television commercials (and prerehearsed debate lines, stump speeches, and other prepared statements) in a way that matches with and more realistically mirrors the individual's experience of watching television in the intimacy and privacy of the home instead of the detached response to public opinion surveys or to the contrivance of focus groups' idiosyncratic dynamics. Experienced purchasers of television airtime are accustomed to sifting through programming schedules, advertising rates, and weighing the demographics of television audiences and viewership as they relate to the segments of voters being targeted so that purchase of airtime can be as cost effective as possible.

"Where once the country was knit together by the collective experience of watching the same sitcom on one of the networks or having the meaning of a national tragedy interpreted by Walter Cronkite," Peter Marks explained on Sunday, July 30, 2000, "the I-can-do-it-myself ethos engendered by technology is on the verge of assuring that there will be no collective electronic experience."[68] Television no longer delivers what it once did in the eyes of any number of strategists. "It is harder and harder," one strategist explained to Los Angeles Times' Jeff Leeds, "to break through and communicate with voters."[69] The Los Angeles Times quoted Tad Devine, senior advisor to then–vice president Al Gore, "It is more difficult generally to deliver messages through television as viewers become more diffuse."[70] According to Adam Nagourney, "the proliferation of communications channels, the fracturing of mass media, and the relentless political competition to own each news cycle are combining to reorder the way voters follow campaigns and decide how to vote."[71] Still television, "augmented by 24-hour news stations and the eternal playback feature of the Internet," reports Mary McNamara of the Los Angeles Times, is a dynamic as important as ever. Television's indelible "campaign-defining moments," as the New York Times' Sheryl Gay Stolberg says, are "relentlessly replayed, resampled, and remixed" on the World Wide Web.[72] Even the proliferation of digital video recorders, broadband streaming, and Internet-to-television subscription services serve to underscore the enduring importance of television's presence in the households of tens of millions of Americans and in the disparate strands of campaigning for elective office. It is, to be sure, a far cry from the time when President Johnson and his custom-built console in the Oval Office with its three television sets offered a relatively up-to-the-minute grasp of what most of the nation's television viewers were watching at that time. Still, the ubiquity of television sets in most offices and workspaces in the White House today, their ubiquity too in congressional offices and in the Capitol Building, the nearly constant presence of television crews and network reporters in the cubicles of the West Wing press offices and the lighting, light-reflectors, microphones, and tarps stationed alongside the driveway outside the West Wing with the iconic view of the White House and its lawn in the background, all of this is a persuasive reminder of the pervasiveness, presence, and power of television in the hallways, press rooms, and offices in Washington, D.C.

Still, even with all of this, television's enduring and unique place in the American household is why it remains, all of its challenges and limitations notwithstanding, the medium of choice and the workhorse of the twenty-first-century political campaign. It is a connective force binding us together in everything from entertainment programs and sporting events to breaking news stories of the moment.[73] It is an undemanding media for an era where more and more Americans work in front of computers on their desks and type on keyboards. It is a screen at a distance, across the room from where we sit on our couches and in our chairs or in our beds; a screen that demands only the reflexivity of changing the channel or the occasional changing of the television's volume, otherwise allowing the largely undemanding grazing and gazing that is television's enduring and unique place and popularity with the American public and especially the nation's candidates for elective office.

Chapter 8

The Internet and Politics in the Digital Age

American political life in the twenty-first century is transformed every minute of every day with speed-of-light digital Internet and World Wide Web
(the Web) communications, especially in its broadband and wireless infrastructure that are quite literally redefining the underlying dynamics of our
most enduring political institutions and traditions. Similar to the way the
landscape of America's nineteenth century was altered by railroad tracks
that stretched across the Midwest and through the mountains of the West,
changing forever the lives of every American and forming the foundation for
America's commercial and communications infrastructure, the fiber-optic
filament in the buried-bundles and in the cellular transmission towers for
wireless and broadband services embodies a shift of the economy and a
change in the way Americans conduct their lives. Digital technology in the
twenty-first century places in the palm of one's hand and at the flick of a
fingertip a vast architecture of data, information, and news accessible anywhere, at any time, by anyone; a digital architecture reinventing almost by
the minute the dynamics of political campaigning in an era when television's
scripted, tightly managed broadcasts with their strategically selected backdrops, microphone-bearing booms, and camera operators, video engineers,
and production assistants still dictate much of the hour-to-hour scheduling
and nearly all of the dollar-for-dollar spending of these campaigns.

In Washington, D.C., today, in its hallways, its meeting rooms and offices,
its House of Representatives and Senate chambers, in state legislatures and
meeting rooms and offices across the United States, on the campaign trail
with candidates and their staff, in newspaper, radio, and television newsrooms and editorial meeting rooms, in White House conference rooms and
offices, and everywhere in between, the handheld digital devices with digital

streaming and access to the Internet with the tap of a finger, in the text messaging and telephone calls and voice mails, is the fulcrum of the political process and most especially political campaigning. The Internet and the World Wide Web are the connective-tissue of the day-to-day, hour-to-hour, minute-to-minute, even the second-to-second dynamic of twenty-first century campaigning and governance. Glancing into the palms of our hands everywhere from sidewalks and hallways to bank lines and crosswalks to office cubicles and classrooms, tens of millions of Americans effortlessly connect to a global communications infrastructure unmatched in its vastness and in its instantaneous accessibility. Equipped with higher-resolution cameras and video recorders, these handheld devices allow for the instantaneous posting and uploading of any overheard utterance. Unseen in this handheld, fingertip-driven reinvention of human conversation and expression is the vast architecture of data warehouses with their massive backup generators and their air-conditioning systems that house the architecture of the economy. Floor-to-ceiling stacks of servers and racks of routers, their lights continuously blinking away, sitting in air-conditioned, highly secured warehouse-sized facilities, are the hidden architecture of a twenty-first-century life of always-on, always-accessible, always-instantaneous digital global communications.

America's political campaigning at the beginning of the twenty-first century is consumed with the technologies of instant, digital communications unlike any seen at any time in history. Information technology's latest breakthroughs in archiving, dissemination, processing, and retrieval of vast quantities of information at often staggeringly fast times and at lower and lower costs, are rewiring and rewriting the dynamics of political campaigning. Data retrieval, desktop video conferencing, document archiving, and audio and video file downloads (and uploads) are but a few of the many hardware and software tools that bring together the streams of data of the World Wide Web to create a torrent of data and information available around the clock. Laptop-wielding journalists updating their Twitter accounts allow something of a real-time reading of the old-fashioned reporter's notebook, as reporters traveling with the president, presidential candidates, and other elected and public officials upload their own photographs from events and post up-to-the-minute updates and reports of the latest announcements and statements, not to mention the unfiltered observations and off-the-cuff streams of gleanings, gossip, and general observations from the campaign trail.

Data mining, the sifting and sorting and winnowing of vast amounts of information accessible through and retrieved from a growing number of databases maintained by the national party committees as well as by independent associations, organizations, and consulting firms, is one of the most formidable tools and without question one of if not the most important techniques used in contemporary campaigns. Volunteers equipped with smartphones, iPads, and electronic tablets are able to input and upload detailed information from the precinct—and even the doorstep—level, allowing information to be disaggregated in everything from direct mail, telephone messaging, and e-mail and Web-based appeals to the planning of campaign events to large-scale, low-dollar fund-raising. Armed with the latest flat-panel, touch-screen tablets, digitally connected with broadband wireless to the servers of their campaigns, today's precinct-by-precinct, street-by-street, door-to-door campaigning avoids even the momentary fumbling of opening a laptop computer by merely pressing fingertips on the flat-panel, touch-screen to log-in an unceasing torrent of bits and bytes of data logged from staff and volunteers on the campaign trail.

The impact of the Internet and the World Wide Web on political campaigning offers a glimpse of the likely transformation in future campaigning, as the delivery of more attention-grabbing, digitally narrowcast content to a variety of media platforms, especially handheld and mobile devices, is reinventing the art of campaigning for office in the age of information overload and message clutter. It is only a matter of time when some kind of electronic voting online is a reality, a proposition that in all certainty will reinvent the use of the Internet and the World Wide Web by elective office candidates in the ever more sophisticated targeting of voters. More elaborate digital fund-raising efforts on the World Wide Web, first used effectively in the 2000 presidential race and even more in 2004 and especially in the 2008 presidential race, is likely to adapt and evolve in the coming years as candidates and their campaign staff do their best to tap into the handheld personal electronic devices and digital platforms of a growing number of voters for instantaneous, large-scale, low-dollar appeals. In 2004, Massachusetts's senator John Kerry raised more than $82,000,000 through the World Wide Web, an astonishing sum compared to previous elections, yet also an amount well surpassed in 2008 and especially in the 2012 race. With large-scale, low-dollar appeals across the electorate in a variety of media platforms, websites and digital content delivery are likely to be the engines that propel much of the strategy of campaign fund-raising for the foreseeable future.

AN EARLY HISTORY OF THE INTERNET

From its origins in the early 1960s as a part of the Department of Defense and its Advanced Research Projects Agency (ARPA), the Internet and its graphics-driven component, the World Wide Web, are very much the product of government initiative, government infrastructure, and government investment. Historical accounts have exaggerated its infrastructure as a data delivery device deliberately constructed to withstand the devastation of a nuclear attack from the former Soviet Union. This account is "a myth," Katie Hafner and Matthew Lyon tell us in their 1996 book, *Where Wizards Stay Up Late: The Origins of the Internet*; a myth "that [has] gone unchallenged long enough to become widely accepted as fact."[1] ARPA's creation of a distributed data-sharing infrastructure, according to Hafner and Lyon, "embodied the most peaceful intentions, to link computers at scientific laboratories across the country so that researchers might share computer resources."[2] Hafner and Lyon insist that "the ARPANET and its progeny, the Internet, had nothing to do with supporting or surviving war, never did." Innovations born in wartime's urgency are most certainly the hallmark of some of the most important breakthroughs in the earlier history of the computer and information technology, yet the ARPA infrastructure is a data-sharing network initiated less because of the immediacy of wartime's threat of nuclear annihilation than the interest of the Department of Defense and its affiliated researchers in building a data-sharing infrastructure for mainframe computers to serve the Department of Defense and allow it to communicate with and exchange substantial amounts of data with faculty and graduate students working on defense-related research initiatives at some of the nation's leading research universities.

The University of Pennsylvania's Electronic Numerical Integrator and Calculator (ENIAC) was the most famous of the early experiments funded by the federal government during World War II. These computers were developed too late to aid in the war effort, but nonetheless built the foundation for electronics and computer innovation in postwar twentieth-century America. "Today," Jane Abbate tells us, "we take it for granted that information can travel long distances instantaneously."[3] When the first large-scale mainframe computers in the 1940s were assembled and tasked with everything from the calculations of artillery firing trajectories to the breaking of cryptographic codes used by the Germans and the Japanese during World War II, it is remarkable to think that within twenty years, astonishing as those early mainframe computers were in their complex calculations and computations, it is the story of the networking of computers, their digital connections across the globe in desktop and eventually handheld devices, that is the truly remarkable story of the digital era.

By 1959, International Business Machine (IBM) Corporation's research in the networking of mainframe computers together in so-called time-sharing networks—networks built, in part, by the work of faculty and graduate students at Stanford University, MIT, and elsewhere—became something of a blueprint for the eventual expansion of these networks into the Internet. UCLA's Paul Baran began his work with the RAND Corporation in 1959, envisioning what he termed "distributed-networks" and "survivable-networks" for the distribution of data. Baran's sketches of a decentralized ("distributed") system of networked computers with multiple interconnections between one another led to an important idea for the eventual architecture of the Internet, namely, the breaking up or disaggregation of large amounts of information or data files into "message switching," "store-and-forward switching," or "packet-messaging"—that is, smaller packets of data to be distributed in a variety of pathways across the network and reassembled at the recipient computer, irrespective of the different routes or pathways taken by the smaller packages or packets of data.

"Of all the ARPANET's technical innovations," Abbate tells us of the groundbreaking prototypes and networking envisioned in the mid-1960s by the Department of Defense's Advanced Research Projects Agency, "perhaps the most celebrated was packet switching."[4] By breaking up large data files into smaller packets of data, embedding these packets or packages with special codes to allow for their routing and their reassembly across networks and their eventual arrival at the same destination, likely out-of-sequence and traveling by a variety of different delivery destinations, where their original configuration or sequence would allow them to be reassembled into the original, larger data file, packet-messaging laid the engineering and the intellectual foundation for the eventual construction of the largest, most complicated machine ever built on the planet, namely, the Internet and its World Wide Web graphic interface.

While the Internet's founding venturers and visionaries began to more widely publicize the idea of a distributed infrastructure connecting larger mainframe computers together as shared networks in the early- to mid-1960s, their work most certainly met some unwillingness along the way by some of the largest telecommunications and telephone companies and their executives. In the early- to mid-1960s, AT&T executives hesitated to back what ARPA administrators described as a distributed-switching network, the first in a long series of disconnects between AT&T's analog, circuit-switching, and the packet-switching networks being proposed by the RAND Corporation and others.[5] AT&T's hesitance, as described by Hafner and Lyon, to innovate beyond the status quo of its circuit-switched telephone lines is in contrast to Paul Baran and his RAND Corporation colleagues who together collaborated in a series of technical papers over the next four years, culminating in a distributed network with specifications and technical protocols for the transmission of packets of data between mainframe computers to be disassembled, distributed, and reassembled across the network.[6]

In the mid- to late 1960s, ARPA and its administrators took still further steps in assembling a far-flung network of university faculty, computer programmers, and software designers to envision the networking of a national and even global system of interconnected computers. Bolt, Beranek, and Newman (BBN), a firm based in Cambridge, Massachusetts, built some of the earliest prototypes for message-switching terminals. By 1966, ARPA senior administrative staff had computer terminals in their offices connected to mainframe computers at MIT in Cambridge, the University of California at Berkeley, and at the RAND Corporation in Santa Monica, California. ARPA's Robert W. Taylor undertook a project in late 1966 to design and build a distributed network to share data and messaging between the various universities and researchers working with ARPA.

In October 1967, ARPA's Lawrence Roberts authored the first technical paper in which he coined the term "ARPANET," his name for the proposed ARPA network of terminals connecting mainframe computers and translating commands between these mainframes built by Burroughs, Digital, Honeywell, IBM, and other manufacturers. ARPA administrators envisioned installation of BBN's store-and-forward machines, known as Interface Message Processors (IMP), in four computer centers later that year to eventually take the first steps in connecting with mainframe computers across the country.[7] ARPA administrators envisioned expanding their network to connect together mainframe computers at some dozen or more different campus and research facilities, one of the first and most significant steps forward in building the Internet and its World Wide Web graphic interface.

On Tuesday, September 2, 1969, faculty and graduate assistants at the University of California in Los Angeles, working with BBN employees, installed a specially modified Honeywell DDP-516 shipped across the country from the BBN offices in Cambridge, Massachusetts, to its UCLA Boelter Hall destination. Installation of the Honeywell DDP-516 marked the first step in the construction of ARPA's first large-scale packet-switching architecture, essentially the first node of what is today the Internet. "Creation of the network represents a major step forward in computer technology and may serve as the forerunner of large computer networks of the future," explained a September 1969 UCLA press release shortly after UCLA faculty and students began their preliminary testing of the Honeywell DDP-516 as the first node of the newly established ARPA-financed network. Weeks later, Stanford University's Douglas Engelbart and his colleagues established ARPA's second node from the Stanford Research Institute (SRI)—a terminal operational by Monday, October 20, 1969, and prepared within a week's time to make history by connecting its terminal with an identical refrigerator-sized terminal set up weeks earlier in Los Angeles by UCLA's Leonard Kleinrock and his faculty colleagues and students.

Working from an IMP terminal in Boelter Hall's Room 3420, Kleinrock and his faculty and graduate students at 10:30 PM PDT on Wednesday, October 29, 1969, successfully sent the first ARPA transmission ("22:30 TALKED TO SRI HOST TO HOST," reads the handwritten note in UCLA's logbook) to an identical IMP terminal some 359 miles away at SRI in Menlo Park, California, this after having crashed the network in attempting to make its first connection with the Stanford terminal.[8] "We knew what we were doing was important but not nearly the magnitude of what it became," Kleinrock later recalled.[9] "Nobody," Ben Barker, then a twenty-one-year-old engineer for Cambridge, Massachusetts–based BBN in the UCLA computing center that October evening, recalls, "had any clue how important it was." BBN programmer David Walden remembers, "It didn't feel like being on the frontier." A group of some fifteen faculty and graduate students were in Boelter Hall Room 3420 when UCLA's Scientific Systems Sigma 7 successfully logged into the network, having earlier received an error message after their first unsuccessful login.

By December 1969, ARPA's network had grown to BBN-built IMPs at some four different locations on the West Coast. "The geographic bias wasn't an accident," Andrew Blum writes in *Tubes: A Journey to the Center of the Internet*, as a "burgeoning technology culture" of businesses and computer firms near several of the four universities—UCLA, Stanford, the University of Utah, and the University of California at Santa Barbara, those who had the first ARPA-financed IMPs—found a familiar footing in the West Coast "cultural appetite for new ideas."[10] The Cambridge, Massachusetts, BBN offices became the first node on the East Coast in 1970. Harvard University and MIT both established their terminals in 1970, as the network's nodes grew.

By the early 1970s, the Department of Defense's Information Processing Techniques Office, now under the direction of Robert E. Kahn, held a series of meetings in Cambridge, Massachusetts, and elsewhere to begin planning the first demonstration of the DARPA network, its administration renamed the Defense Advanced Research Projects Agency (DARPA) in March 1972. For over a year, Kahn and his staff prepared for the first public demonstration of the coast-to-coast computer network and its distributed packet-switching, a demonstration to take place at the first International Conference on Computer Communication (ICCC), held by the Institute of Electrical and Electronics Engineers (IEEE) Computer Society, the Association for Computing Machinery, and the IEEE Communications Society—at the Hilton Hotel in Washington, D.C., in October 1972.

For three days in the Washington, D.C., Hilton Hotel ballroom, beginning on Tuesday, October 24, 1972, attendees at the first ICCC were able to retrieve files from IMP terminals at the BBN, route them across the country through an IMP at UCLA, and then have the files transmitted back across the county to print them in the Washington, D.C., hotel ballroom. Hundreds of conference attendees, including a group of still-skeptical AT&T executives, took part in this first public demonstration of DARPA packet-switching, with some thirty-six DARPA-connected computer terminals and with staff members to assist attendees in accessing the Cambridge and Los Angeles network computer connections. DARPA staff and attendees at the October 1972 conference recall the enthusiasm of the hundreds of attendees who glimpsed the long-distance packet-switching for the first time, with some attendees staying in the ballroom well past midnight asking questions and logging onto the terminals.[11]

With the DARPA infrastructure of packet-switching in the transmission of data-packets at computer terminals from Cambridge, Massachusetts, to Palo Alto, California, faculty and graduate students in the early 1970s experimented with networking programs and protocols for the sharing and the transmission of data across the network. In the mid-1970s, these experiments culminated in the proposal by DARPA administrators of the Transmission Control Protocol/Internet Protocol (TCP/IP) system, a system for transmitting packets of data designed by Stanford University's Vinton G. Cerf and DARPA's Robert Kahn. Officially adopted network-wide by DARPA administrators in January 1983, TCP/IP protocols allowed each message transmitted by DARPA terminals to be broken into literally hundreds if not thousands of smaller-sized packets, with headers indicating which message each packet was a part of, where the message originated, and its final or terminal destination. At the terminal or node of the message's destination, the TCP protocol collected the packets as they arrived (sometimes by different routes over the network) and assembled them in the proper sequence, requesting any missing packets be retransmitted across the network. Essentially the same framework guides the transmission of literally billions of such messages to this day—every day—on the Internet and the World Wide Web.

"Between the 1960s and the 1980s," Abbate tells us in her 1999 book *Inventing the Internet*, "computing technology underwent a dramatic transformation: the computer, originally conceived as an isolated calculating device, was reborn as a means of communication."[12] With the earliest terminal-nodes of what is today known as the Internet located at computer laboratories in some of the nation's leading universities, private firms, and government agencies, the nation's first computer-based communications infrastructure unfolded at a steady pace. Each month after the first terminals came on line in 1969 and 1970, new computing centers, research institutions, and university and college campuses were brought on to the coast-to-coast network. The expense of an institution or research laboratory's joining DARPA cost from $55,000 to as much as $100,000 in 1972.[13] Faculty, graduate assistants, and systems analysts tasked with bringing new campuses into the network soon began writing a variety of software programs allowing systems operators to share a host of data files with one another. New computer protocols and improvements in modems emerged as the DARPA network grew steadily throughout the early 1970s. File transfer programs and more sophisticated protocols for data sharing were some of the earliest innovations by the technicians running the DARPA infrastructure, and many of their early technical decisions on data transmission protocols remain at the center of today's World Wide Web.

In April 1971, the ARPA affiliated terminals had grown to twenty-three computer centers, as computer scientists and researchers used the packet-switching and transfer protocols of the network to archive and transfer files. The strung-together network of computer terminals in the corners of university classrooms and offices, Andrew Blum writes, "existed in spare classrooms of university computer science departments, within outbuildings on military bases, and across the copper lines and microwave links of the existing telephone network by always-on phone connections provided under special terms by AT&T."[14] Discussion boards and the posting of everything from recipes and computer games to copies of the Declaration of Independence and other historic documents were posted by scientists, technicians, and faculty and graduate students all using DARPA's network. In 1973, the DARPA network became an international network with its first network connection to London's University College. Terminals and network connections to DARPANET in some 110 different computing centers on university campuses and research firms across the country grew the network still further.

In August 1975, with the financial investment of BBN and with the executive leadership of its president, former ARPA administrator Lawrence Roberts, Telenet Communications Corporation became the first commercial packet-switching network in the United States, allowing its customers to have dial-up telephone-modem access (at a cost of $1.40 per hour) to its computer network service for users in seven U.S. cities.[15] Months earlier, in January 1975, *Popular Electronics* featured a front-cover photograph ("Project Breakthrough! World's 1st Minicomputer Kit to Rival Commercial Models, Altair 8800") of Micro-Instrumentation Telemetry Systems (MITS) Altair 8800 Computer, a personal computer sold by the Albuquerque, New Mexico–based business.[16] With Apple Computer's sales of the Apple II personal computer beginning in May 1977 for some $1,300 as well as the first sales that same month of the Commodore Personal Electronic Transactor (PET) personal computer and Tandy's TRS-80 personal computer weeks later in August 1977, the era of the personal computer and soon the computer modem ("modulator/demodulator"), commercially retailed to computer owners for the first time in the 1977 Hayes Microcomputer Modem, marked the first steps in a global infrastructure unrivaled for its impact on the world.

In 1979, USENET became one of the largest of the growing number of private, dial-up telephone-modem computer networks, a loosely structured, collaborative network of electronic bulletin boards and newsgroups first established by graduate students at the University of North Carolina at Chapel Hill and Duke University. The first of several dial-up telephone-modem networks not affiliated with DARPANET and its computing centers, USENET grew rapidly in the early 1980s. Described as a "poor cousin" to DARPANET, the North Carolina–based USENET, as Edwin Diamond and Stephen Bates recall, "used auto-dialers to exchange messages late at night when phone rates were low."[17] CSNET, a forerunner of the National Science Foundation's NSFNET, as well as BITNET were formed in the late 1970s as consortiums of computer centers and research facilities. With as many as thirty regional computer networks emerging in the late 1970s and the early 1980s, including California's CERFNET, FIDONET, and San Francisco's PRNET, hundreds of thousands and soon millions of Americans suddenly had access in their homes to these coast-to-coast computer networks. CompuServe, Prodigy, the Source, and the popular California-based computer network, The Well, all flourished in the 1980s as personal computers became more affordable to a growing number of Americans.

The adoption by DARPA administrators of the TCP/IP protocols in January 1983 made it even easier for research facilities to access the network, by now the backbone of a coast-to-coast network of computer centers and access terminals for faculty, graduate students, private sector researchers, and government employees. By 1984, DARPA boasted terminals at some five hundred or more research universities, private consulting firms, Department of Defense computer centers, and DARPA administrative offices in Arlington, Virginia. Some DARPA network administrators and users for the first time in 1984 began calling the expanding network the Internet, a term that became more popular over the next decade. Finally, following years of investment by administrators, the Department of Defense officially took the first steps to close its connection with the network, beginning the transition of the network affiliates and its network connections to a National Science Foundation (NSF) network. Known to its users as NSFNET, the term "Internet" became steadily more popular to describe the growth of the network as it spliced in with other smaller networks.

In the mid- to late 1980s, millions of Americans logged on to the nation's private computer dial-up telephone-modem computer networks and bulletin board services on a regular basis, taking part in the largest expansion yet of the Internet and its affiliated networks.[18] Estimates are that some 800,000 modems were sold in 1983, with another 1,000,000 bought by computer owners in 1984. Routers commercially available for the first time in 1986 and privately owned routing services opening for the first time in 1987 led the way to a still further growth of electronic mail and networking services in the late 1980s, with MCI Mail well established by this time as one of the leaders in a soon-to-be crowded field of private subscription services for personal computer owners with dial-up telephone modems. MCI Mail was approved by the Federal Research Internet Coordinating Council (FRICC) to connect its commercial e-mail services with NSFNET in 1988, with the MCI Mail-NSFNET connection becoming publicly accessible for the first time in June 1989 as the first commercial connection with NSFNET. It soon led to similar connections with NSFNET by America Online, CompuServe, Prodigy, and Sprint's Telemail.

CompuServe, Prodigy, and other dial-up services brought thousands and soon millions of Americans into these networks. These networks were, however, still largely text-based.

The 1990 innovations by the European Particle Physics Laboratory (CERN) in Geneva, Switzerland, with Hypertext Transport Protocol and Hypertext Markup Language (HTML), developed under the direction of CERN computer scientist Tim Berners-Lee, brought an accessible architecture of graphics, imagery, and, soon enough, video and sound to the largely text-based postings on the Internet. The passage of the High Performance Computing and National Research and Education Network Act by the House of Representatives and the Senate in September 1991 brought further investment in the infrastructure of the Internet—with financial resources from the National Research and Education Network (NREN) and its consortium of private-sector investors and public-sector researchers and computer scientists responsible for breakthroughs in high-capacity, high-performance data circuits and in high-bandwidth, fiber optic networking. The April 1993 release of the first Internet browser software by the University of Illinois National Center for Supercomputing Applications (NCSA), the so-called Mosaic browser preceding the April 1995 release of Netscape Navigator 1.0 and the August 1995 launch of Internet Explorer 1.0 by the Seattle, Washington–based Microsoft Corporation, forever changed the face of the Internet and ushered in the popular use of the World Wide Web. Also, the April 1995 closing of the National Science Foundation's NSFNET, the culmination of years of work by government-funded researchers and their private-sector counterparts in the "booming Web of electronic networks" with some 20,000,000 users in more than sixty countries, marked the continued growth of the Internet and the World Wide Web as an even more accessible media.

The familiar dial-tone of the dial-up modem was a commonplace sound in the millions of households with personal computers and access to dial-up networks in the early to mid-1990s. Robert Wright reported in September 1993, "Though [the Internet has] suddenly become affordable, about $20 a month through no-frills access providers, it remains a realm mainly of hackers, scientists, and assorted others with some institutional link to it."[19] Still, entrepreneurs, financial investors, software innovators, start-up firms, and non-profit outfits of all sizes, not to mention newspapers and the campaign staffs of candidates for elective office, scrambled by the mid-1990s to adapt to and adopt the latest developments of the Internet and its digital, multimedia possibilities. The announcement on Sunday, May 7, 1995, by the *New York Times* of its "national on-line information service on the Internet's World Wide Web"—a page D7 story in its Monday print edition—is still regarded as the most important, innovative, and influential investment in website technology to be created in the twentieth century.[20] Innovations in desktop publishing, flat-panel displays, larger computer memories, laser printing, audio and graphic-based user interfaces, and word processing all drove the personal computer industry still further by the end of the 1990s, laying the foundation for the growth of Internet services over the next decade, a time when candidates for elective office for the first time grew more serious in their use of the Internet and especially its graphic-interface, the World Wide Web, to post their campaign materials, to keep in contact with journalists and reporters, to raise funds, and to reach out to their supporters.

COMPUTERS, CYBERSPACE, THE INFORMATION HIGHWAY, AND CAMPAIGNING FOR ELECTIVE OFFICE IN THE DIGITAL AGE

Political campaigning in the nineteenth and twentieth centuries is always and in every way a history of the efforts by candidates and their strategists and their staff to disseminate the latest, most accurate, most up-to-date information and news as it develops. Newspapers in the nineteenth and early twentieth centuries published multiple editions throughout the day, with some larger-circulation papers publishing as many as a dozen different editions or stars on Election Day or other important days and certainly epitomized the insatiability of candidates, officeholders, and the American public for the latest, most up-to-date news and reports whether it be financial, sports, or politically related. The telegraph, the teletype, and then the telephone, not to mention the news and stock-quote ticker, especially favored by financial and business executives, elevated the unceasing efforts to secure the latest news or breaking stories. By the late nineteenth century, as many as twenty telegraph lines had been installed in the Executive Mansion, allowing presidents, including President William McKinley, to monitor the latest news from the news-wires and even, on more than one occasion, to walk into cabinet meetings with the latest dispatches and stories off the telegraph or ticker-tape. Inventions in the delivery of news and information frequently became adapted to and used in any number of ways by the candidates for elective office of the time. Early-morning newspaper clippings assembled by White House staff, especially at the end of the nineteenth and the early twentieth centuries, kept presidents and their cabinets apprised of the latest stories while extensive record-keeping and filing cabinets kept by party leaders from the national level to neighborhood precincts certainly kept attention on the acquisition of information.

Teletype machines reshaped the gathering of information and news in the late nineteenth and the early twentieth centuries. Teletype machines were in the Capitol as well as in the White House, where presidents and their staff were posted on the latest, up-to-the-minute stories as they broke.

From the ticker-tape machine installed in the White House by President Theodore Roosevelt to the Oval Office cabinet with the Associated Press (AP) and United Press International (UPI) bulletins installed by President Lyndon Johnson to the personal computers and laptops used by presidents since, including the computers in the private study next to the Oval Office and in the White House residence used by President Barack Obama, the latest in computer and information technology has been a constant in contemporary politics. With the prevasive presence of desktop and laptop computers and the constant updating of websites in any and every office on Capitol Hill, in the White House, and elsewhere in Washington, D.C., it is difficult to recall a time when computer and digital technology has not been the driving dynamic and the constant presence in the lives of elected officials, policymakers, and candidates for office.

The 1976 presidential race saw computer technology take a more prominent role with candidacies for the nation's highest office. Commercial, dial-up e-mail and bulletin board services became more affordable by the mid- to late 1970s allowing campaigns to use the newly accessible dial-up services to reach not just their own staff and volunteers on their campaigns but the public itself. The candidacy of Jimmy Carter in 1976 used an early variant of dial-up modems to share and transfer files on the computers between Carter's staff and his running mate, Walter Mondale. A *Washington Star* headline on Sunday, November 21, 1976, "Computer Tied Carter, Mondale Campaigns Together," allows an early glimpse into campaigning for the White House and the use of the still-emerging personal computers and their connection by dial-up modem to so-called time sharing mainframes (Carter's 1976 computer operation was based in Bethesda, Maryland, and cost a total of $5,000 for that year's campaign) in the mid-1970s.[21]

With hourly, even by-the-minute and by-the-message charges and commercial rates from private dial-up electronic services, few voters, especially few undecided voters, likely spent much time online in the late 1970s reading and viewing the text-only postings of the candidates and their campaigns. Political campaigns in the 1980s saw further strides in the adaptation of computer technology. Well-known consultants, pollsters, and strategists, including Karl Rove, were early adopters of the networking of mainframe computers for direct-mail and automated-telephone services as well as the regular use of the lightweight, more-affordable personal computers in the early to mid-1980s. Frank Luntz devoted a chapter of his 1988 book *Candidates, Consultants, and Campaigns: The Style and Substance of American Electioneering* to the state-of-the-art, leading-edge application of mainframe and personal computing in campaigning for elective office.[22] Jeffrey B. Abramson, F. Christopher Arterton, and Gary R. Orren's 1988 book *The Electronic Commonwealth: The Impact of New Media Technologies on Democratic Politics* is another masterful work with insight on the still-emerging application of computers in the day-to-day work of campaigning for office and for governance by elected officials.[23]

The 1992 race for the White House is the first campaign where the candidates and their staff broke new ground in the use of the Internet and e-mail as a way not only of maintaining regular contact with their field staff and volunteers in offices across the country but also in the posting of information and materials on electronic services and so-called bulletin board services on the Internet. The campaign headquarters in Little Rock of then-governor Clinton featured a small but sophisticated computer network regularly updated throughout the day to campaign field offices and staff across the country.[24] With CompuServe, Prodigy, and other services investing ever larger resources in advertising and marketing, the 1992 race is the first election where the campaigns took their first steps toward regular posting of text-only documents and materials not just to their staffs and journalists but also to the public.[25]

Within weeks of the Wednesday, January 20, 1993, inauguration, President Bill Clinton and his White House staff showed an enthusiasm for the expansion of computer technology in the White House as well as federal information technology policy.[26] "White House: A Computer Nerdville," a *New York Times*, Saturday, February 20, 1993, headline told its readers in an in-depth profile of the Clinton administration's "high-tech Presidency" on what it called the "data superhighway."[27] White House staff upgraded the computer system, as well as the telephone and voice-mail system, in the White House, especially using the Internet early in President Clinton's first term to deliver documents to journalists to the public. E-mail addresses through America Online (clintonpz@aol.com), CompuServe (75300.3115@compuserve.com), and MCI Mail were established in the White House, with president@whitehouse.gov and vice.president@whitehouse.gov formally announced by the White House Office of Presidential Correspondence on Tuesday, June 1, 1993.[28] Jonathan P. "Jock" Gill, director of Special Projects in the White House Office of Media Affairs, equipped his office and his staff with some of the newest electronic communications for the Clinton administration in his earliest months in office. Jeff Eller, director of the White House Office of Media Affairs, worked closely with Gill and his staff to implement many of the first digital and electronic communications initiatives in the history of the White House.[29]

"For the 1st time ever," Richard L. Berke reported in a front-page story on Monday, April 5, 1993, "even people with little knowledge of computers can send a message to the White House through electronic mail."[30] Vice President Al Gore, whose own background in the House of Representatives and then in the Senate, established his early leadership in the federal government's initiatives in information technologies and took part in several live, online computer chats during his tenure as vice president, including a well-publicized online, real-time question-and-answer session he hosted from the

White House ("the conversations actually took place in one of several mainframe computers in Columbus, Ohio, operated by the CompuServe Information Service," the *New York Times* reported) on Thursday, January 13, 1994.[31] The Clinton administration, via http//www.whitehouse.gov, posted the first White House World Wide Web ("Welcome to the White House") on Thursday, October 20, 1994.[32] "More and more," Graeme Browning reported the day after the White House's first website went on-line, "the volunteers who've long been the lifeblood of grass-roots organizations, the envelope-lickers, the poster-hangers, and the precinct-walkers, are being replaced by machines that whirr, ring, and blink their way into the American political consciousness."[33] Whatever its designation—cyberspace, the data highway, the information highway, the information superhighway, the net, or simply, the Internet—the digital age of electronic, instantaneous information arrived in the Clinton White House to immediately transform government and governance itself in far-reaching ways.

On Tuesday, November 8, 1994, the elections in the House of Representatives and the Senate saw some of Washington, D.C.'s longtime lawmakers, including then-senator Edward M. Kennedy of Massachusetts, one of the first members of the Senate with an Internet presence and World Wide Web site, as well as their challengers adapt to and adopt e-mail and the posting of campaign-related documents, photographs, texts, and even video through the Internet. In 1995, THOMAS Internet service, under the administration of the Library of Congress at http://thomas.loc.gov and formally unveiled on the second day of the 104th Congress on Wednesday, January 5, 1995, by the newly elected Speaker of the House, Representative Newt Gingrich of Georgia's 6th Congressional District, established a wide array of electronic access to federal documents and pending Congressional legislation.[34] Edmund L. Andrews reported on Friday, January 6, 1995, "The Clinton administration offers everything from White House announcements to news about Jupiter observations on the Internet." (Andrews's report on the inauguration of the Library of Congress THOMAS Website noted that only seven of the 100 members of the Senate and just 36 out of 435 members of the House of Representatives even had e-mail addresses publicly available at the time.) "The number of people using the Internet is growing daily, and as new software makes the tangled maze of services easier to navigate, lawmakers are bound to join in," Andrews observed just months prior to the beginning of the first race for the White House to feature widely available electronic materials and resources on the Internet and especially the World Wide Web.[35]

"Technicians have laid 3,500 miles of copper cable and 31 miles of fiber-optic wire in Capitol Hill offices in the last 2 years," Eric Schmitt reported on Wednesday, July 10, 1996, "snaking the lifeline to the Internet through air ducts, steam tunnels, and early 19th century chimneys."[36] He continued, "That is a small part of the total technological investment, estimated at several hundred million dollars over the next few years required to bring Congress into the modern computing age."[37] On Friday, March 28, 1996, at the Computers, Freedom, and Privacy Conference in Cambridge, Massachusetts, lawmakers in the House of Representatives and the Senate formed the Congressional Internet Caucus, as a growing number of pending and proposed bills touched upon the growing commercial and communications impact and influence of the Internet and the World Wide Web.[38]

The year 1996 is remembered as the first presidential race where candidates Bill Clinton and Bob Dole embraced the World Wide Web as a way of interacting with voters beyond simply posting text-only documents of their speeches and other text-only materials. New graphics-based interfaces, including audio and video files, as well as improvements in Internet fundraising allowed the 1996 White House candidates to make their websites far more innovative and interactive. Also in 1996 President Clinton and former Senate Majority Leader Dole improved their websites in the months prior to the November election. Improved browser software and the improvements in full-color monitors for personal and desktop computers led to far more interactive, visually engaging websites than simply the posting of text-only position papers, press releases, and speech transcripts. When Dole mentioned his campaign website in the nationally televised debate with President Clinton from Hartford, Connecticut, on the evening of Sunday, October 6, 1996, it marked the first time that a candidate directed television viewers to their website.

The *New York Times*, the *Wall Street Journal*, the *Washington Post*, and dozens of newspapers, news magazines, television networks, and other news organizations felt for the first time the far-reaching impact of the public's growing interest in their Web coverage. Websites, including the Drudge Report, increasingly set the tempo and the terms of the nation's political debate and campaign discussion in the late twentieth century. Still, widespread skepticism regarding the Web's ability to reach older, less well-engaged voters, or "finding a target audience of likely voters on the Web is nearly impossible," Rebecca Fairley Raney warned in July 1998.[39]

By the end of the twentieth century, everything from the growing commercialization and the disparate accessibility of the Internet to the piracy and the theft of intellectual property and of Internet copyright-protected material to concerns with the Internet's erosion of face-to-face social interactions, its challenges to newspaper circulation and readership, and its threats to the confidentiality and the privacy of individuals all clouded, to some extent, the enthusiasm for the still-emerging digital landscape. Piracy and privacy, entwined issues for a growing number of Americans using the Web in larger areas of their life—from education to financial transactions to entertainment and friendship and even romance—drove a host of debates on the Web and its reach into our daily public and private lives. Terms like "information overload," "the data glut," "data smog," and "digital exhaust" dominated the growing discussion of our reliance or over-reliance on e-mail and digital communications. Issues of anonymity, and to some extent the reliability of Web documents and the transitory nature of digital information, became an issue of greater interest to many of its users. Spam, viruses, worms, and other maladies of the information age certainly drew still more expressions of concern. Issues of the so-called digital divide, the seemingly ineradicable inequities and inequalities in access to the Internet and its high-bandwidth services, emerged by the end of the twentieth century as yet another issue of interest among many lawmakers and policymakers, most especially the Clinton administration.

SOCIAL NETWORKING, THE WORLD WIDE WEB, AND TWENTY-FIRST-CENTURY CAMPAIGNING

The World Wide Web is the twenty-first century's interface of video, audio, text, and data technologies, a media much-anticipated by future-oriented visionaries who had long dreamed of the delivery of facsimile-type electronic newspapers to personal computers in the home and who had imagined fully interactive cable systems allowing streams of televised content and data from broadcasters to the homes of viewers and then streamed back with comments and selections from viewers to the broadcasters. Newspapers, *Chicago Tribune*'s Clayton Kirkpatrick envisioned in 1971 when cable television franchises began to stretch their services out into the suburbs surrounding his city of Chicago and other cities across the country, "might eventually be reproduced on screens which could be read in the home."[40] Decades later, the Internet and the Web are at once more modest than and, as often as not, far exceed many of the far-reaching possibilities imagined in the early decades of digital culture.

The Internet and its World Wide Web graphical interface are driven by the high-bandwidth, fiber-optics routers and servers of the nation's Internet service providers and especially its cable television franchises and its direct-satellite subscription services. Breakthroughs in personal computers and their operating and software systems, in the production and sales of higher-resolution full-color monitors, and in the digital modems and wireless routers available for home are bringing more and more households to the Web's ever-changing possibilities. It is the digital infrastructure of the twenty-first century, a broadband network built on a sprawling, vast backbone of wireless transmissions and buried fiber-optic bundles that allows literally tens of billions of packets of data to stream through a dense latticework of routers and servers maintained by Internet service providers, cable television franchises, telephone companies, government agencies, and colleges and universities. It is a system of servers, routers, and satellite dishes that together transmit streams of data at rates of tens of millions of bits per second, making possible a host of electronic mail services, World Wide Web browsing, instantaneous interactivity—"the nation's growing, technologically abetted obsession with getting what you want when you want," in the words of Peter Marks—and the individualization of information and news, massive transfers of numerical and textual data, and digitalized audio and video files of all kinds.[41] By the 2000 presidential race, the accessibility, affordability, and convenience of the Internet and the World Wide Web in delivering a torrent of commentary, debate, information, news, and opinion to tens of millions of American households was well established.

"During my service in the United States Congress, I took the initiative in creating the Internet," then-vice president Al Gore told CNN's Wolf Blitzer in a live, nationally televised interview on Tuesday, March 9, 1999, an aside in an otherwise routine televised interview destined to remain an oft-replayed utterance in the 2000 campaign for the White House. Gore's comments to Blizter brought ridicule from the vice president's Republican rivals but also bespoke an undeniable certainty, namely the leadership by Gore in the House of Representatives and later in Gore's tenure in the Senate and still later as vice president of the United States in the Clinton White House to foster innovation and research in information technologies as well as to transition the federal government's administration of NSFNET to research universities, telecommunications firms, and emerging data networking businesses building the Web's post-ARPANET infrastructure and its day-to-day operations. "No Father of Computing, But Maybe He's an Uncle," the *New York Times* headline reported days later on Thursday, March 18, 1999, in a story by Katie Hafner, with some of the World Wide Web's most well-respected innovators praising Gore's work to "[help] lift the Internet from relative obscurity and turn it into a widely accessible, commercial network.[42]

The 2000 presidential campaign marked the first race where the World Wide Web offered an indispensable and pivotal new way for candidates and their campaigns to connect with a much larger and more diverse array of voters. Although the 1996 presidential race, in the words of *Washington Post*'s Terry M. Neal, "used the Internet mostly as an afterthought for brochure-like biographies and occasional updates from the campaign trail," the 2000 race for the White House and the campaign websites of Vice President Al Gore and Texas governor George W. Bush saw new multimedia formats, not to mention a growing emphasis on encouraging website visitors and viewers to post their own content, especially multimedia such as photographs and video. "The Internet, a technology that is inherently individualistic and interactive, is rapidly growing in prominence in the political process," Marks explained on Sunday, July 30, 2000, reporting improvements in Internet fund-raising and even the potential for casting votes electronically on the World Wide Web, a potentiality still unrealized in the unfolding digital age.[43]

The 2004 reelection bid by President George W. Bush and his challenge by Senator John F. Kerry of Massachusetts saw still more of a presence of the Internet and the World Wide Web in that year's race as the candidates routinely directed their audiences to their campaign websites in their nationally televised debates and in their day-to-day speeches and events on the campaign trail. Voters were increasingly spending larger amounts of time on the social networking sites of Facebook, Friendster, MySpace, and other websites. Websites by President Bush and Senator Kerry and their campaigns included up-to-the-minute updates submitted by their campaign spokespersons and staff on breaking news with extensive archives of digital photographs and high-quality digitalized videos of the candidates, their appearances and remarks, their policy addresses and their speeches, and numerous other multimedia. Yard signs, billboards, bumper stickers, and television ads, the familiar mainstays of political campaigns, were all now prominently adorned with the digital addresses of campaign websites. Websites maintained by most state secretaries of state and similar offices allowed voters the chance to access official election information and materials, previously only available through the mail or through in-person visits to local election offices or state agencies. Extensive fund-raising from large-scale, small-dollar donors also took hold in the 2004 race with well-documented reports by the *New York Times*' Glen Justice and other reporters of the vast sums of money raised in the large number of online web contributions to the campaigns of both President Bush and Senator Kerry.[44] "The emergence of the Internet as a major fund-raising tool is arguably the largest single change to the campaign finance system to come from this year's presidential race," Justice reported on Saturday, November 6, 2004, an innovation to be mirrored in subsequent election cycles with the large-scale, small-dollar online contributions that tracked closely the events of the campaign trail and with the frequent mentions and references to the candidates of their website addresses in major addresses, press conferences, and speeches to televised audiences.[45]

The 2008 campaigns of Senator Barack Obama and of Senator John McCain led to still further innovation in the World Wide Web's place in the twenty-first-century campaign. Large-scale, low-dollar online fund-raising, online social networking, innovations in tailoring websites to handheld, wireless digital platforms, instant messaging, and the hour-by-hour, even minute-by-minute networking of micro-blogging websites led by the San Francisco, California–based Twitter, all took hold of the candidacies in the 2008 presidential race. With an estimated 1,000,000,000 e-mails sent by Senator Obama's campaign to its supporters in the 2008 race, e-mail, online contributions, social networking "likes" and "re-tweets," search-engine ads and analytics, and millions upon millions of text-messages all swept across the year's electoral landscape.

The election of Barack Obama on Tuesday, November 4, 2008, entwined the Internet and the World Wide Web still further into the day-to-day executive governance of the United States with his determined efforts to continue using his BlackBerry and his electronic access to e-mail and various documents and materials from his staff.[46] With advice from some of the leading corporate executives in the digital economy, including the late Steve Jobs of Apple Computers, Google's Eric Schmidt, and others, President-elect Obama and his White House transition team took the lead in pressing for still-further expansion of a digital presence by the White House, executive agencies, federal officials, and offices on all levels.

The Internet at the beginning of the twenty-first century provides more immediate, instantaneous access to the latest news, press briefings, candidate news conferences, and policy statements. Never before in the nation's history have so many different technologies been used to reach the public in so many different ways, untethered as never before by Wi-Fi, cellular, and wireless broadband networks. Unedited, unfiltered information, news, commentary, opinion, not to mention innuendo, gossip, and rumor, all grew steadily in the early years of the twenty-first century. Exaggerations, gaffes, mistakes, and misstatements of all manner, of seemingly otherwise insignificance, now live on in the digitally captured and endlessly replayed digital videos and 140-character posts on Twitter and elsewhere on the Web. Innovations in the use of the Web to build face-to-face meetings and organizing in everything from Governor Howard Dean's use of the Meetup Website in the 2004 race for the Democratic presidential nomination to the popularity of so-called flash-mobs orchestrated both online and through cellular telephones certainly undercut to some extent the criticisms that the Internet and the Web are irreversibly eroding and weakening face-to-face interactions. The Internet is transforming campaigning for elective office by offering the ability for voter involvement at any time of the day or night with the simplest click of a mouse and a few keystrokes. Fund-raising is without a doubt a driving dynamic in the twenty-first-century's campaigning on the Web, the large-scale, low-dollar fund-raising now integral in every way to the fund-raising strategy of campaigns for the nation's highest office, campaigns ever more likely to raise extraordinary sums almost every hour of the day. Exhaustive, seemingly inexhaustible amounts of biographical material on the candidates, their backgrounds, financial statements, voting records, and donors and financial contributions are accessible 24/7 to any voter with even the most rudimentary expertise in navigating and surfing the Web. Inexhaustible, too, are the sites uploading digitalized video files of utterances of candidates that are endlessly replayed, remixed, and resurrected by the public, not to mention ridiculed and relentlessly replayed by rival campaigns. Digitalized tracking of viewers and visitors to websites and the cross-referencing and cross-tabulation of these views and visits is a vast trove of data to be mined in the more sophisticated targeting of specific segments of the electorate.

The twenty-first century is appreciated already for the interactive, customized, self-selected, self-directed media of the day, a media of keyboards and touch-screens, of instantaneous customization and the bunkering and hunkering down of millions upon millions of Americans in their information silos of self-directed, self-selected information streams. The customization of news and the self-specified delivery of individualized content on the Internet and the Web in the early years of the twenty-first century is a much more user-driven interface than at any other time in the history of media, an interface eagerly embraced not just by smartphone-wielding voters but by candidates themselves, their staff, their strategists and press spokespersons, and the legions of journalists and reporters following (and tweeting) their every move and utterance and encounter with audiences and crowds on the campaign trail. Engaging and exciting as the twenty-first century's self-selected, self-directed media are for a generation accustomed to instant messages, status updates, text messages, and tweets, the use of these more customized and individualized digital platforms for the delivery of ads and message content for candidates running for elective office is still likely for some time to be overshadowed by the larger, older-skewing audiences of commercial broadcast television. The Internet and the World Wide Web is a medium where the keyboard, the mouse, and habit govern the rhythms and the routines of its users, unlike the radio or television where the individual is more likely to have a (somewhat) smaller selection of programs, is more likely to be doing something else (like listening to the radio while driving or doing chores in the house while watching television) while the program is on, and is more likely to take in everything (including commercial ads) that is being broadcast at a particular time on a particular channel. It is understood by most strategists who advise candidates running for elective office that the Internet and the World Wide Web is a medium more effective for regular outreach to existing supporters than the cultivation of contacts with so-called persuadable voters or swings, as they are sometimes known. With individual-centered, user-driven customization of news feeds and delivery of content, with the self-selection of websites and the need for constant user input in everything from Google searches to the pointing and clicking at endless prompts and website requests, and with the likelihood that often-visited websites amass their own data and information to customize advertising and related content to the individual, the overall experience of the Web tends to be one of reinforcing preexisting beliefs and opinions (and habits of returning to particular websites) and of reaffirming already-evident sympathies rather than the potential, as in television's two- or three-minute bursts of commercial breaks, to be exposed to commercials from multiple candidates (or multiple officeholders running for different offices) where the particular focus of these ads tends to be more attention-capturing bursts of information and visual imagery than the typically more text-driven realm of the Web and its digital environment.

With reliance on digital media, candidates for elective office and especially their staff, reliant as they are on e-mail, instant messaging, text messaging, status updates, and tweets, are advised to avoid using it too often. The digital detritus of the day in the unedited, uninhibited e-mails, instant messages, statuses, and tweets and re-tweets that swirl in the fast pace of the twenty-first-century campaigns is often now the source of controversy. The 140-character and shorter bursts of text, or "micro-press releases," now have the potential to flitter uninhibitedly from thumbs typing on a handheld device to dominate that day's news cycle. Contemporary campaigns are awash with innumerable stories of errant text messages, status updates, tweets, even digital photographs and YouTube digital videos virally resurfacing from candidates' long forgotten late-night parties or from texts or tweets or on social media websites' profile-pages posted days, weeks, months, or even years earlier.

Washington, D.C.'s elected officials, staff, lobbyists, journalists, reporters, and their counterparts across the United States, from governors and state legislators to mayors and city council members, all find themselves spending longer hours of their week using their smartphones, iPhones, iPads, and other handheld and portable digital devices, cultivating an always-connected, always-commenting, always-reacting, always-updated culture. Members of the House of Representatives, the Senate, their staffs, the lobbyists who work the hallways and offices on Capitol Hill, and the journalists reporting on the nation's lawmakers all conduct larger parts of their day working on their handheld digital devices. Predawn news summaries, Mike Allen's Playbook for Washington, D.C.–based Politico, which is the most widely read of these, set much of the tempo and the tone for the day's unfolding stories. Google News Alerts, texts, tweets, and customized, user-selected updates blip in throughout the day, hour-by-hour, minute-by-minute, the pulse of unceasing, unfiltered, unyielding information, itself always and in all ways the currency of influence in the hallways and meeting rooms and offices of a capital and a campaign-trail wired—figuratively and literally—as never before to the age-old maxim that knowledge is power, especially when it is better, earlier, and faster. Headline-making stories of President Obama's persistence in working with White House advisors and staff to keep his BlackBerry is emblematic of the ever-closer focus of lawmakers, candidates, and their staff on the use of these electronic devices. Obama's use of an iPad2, given to him by Apple's co-founder, the late Steve Jobs, as well as the use of an iPad and iPhone by 2012 Republican nominee, former governor Mitt Romney, is still further evidence of the reliance of elected officials and candidates on these electronic devices.

From its bustling offices at the corner of one of the busiest intersections in downtown Arlington, Virginia, Politico, nestled next to the broadcast studios and production facilities of Washington, D.C.'s WJLA-TV, has the most influential website of the digital era, a website that sets the pace for much of the day in our nation's capital. With its bright, open-design workspace and glass-walled offices, Politico is the twenty-first-century equivalent of the newsrooms of the great metropolitan newspapers of the nineteenth and early twentieth centuries; its staff of writers keep abreast of the latest stories from flat-panel monitors throughout the Politico newsroom as well as from their computer screens and handheld devices. Politico senior editors and staff from their row of windowed offices alongside its large newsroom little resemble the editorial and publishing personalities of the nineteenth- and early twentieth-century newspapers, yet their offices shape most of the reporting dynamics and coverage of Washington, D.C., stories.

The growth and expansion of data, information, and knowledge itself has expanded beyond anything imaginable to the authors of science fiction classics and the authors and illustrators of popular magazines from the early years of the twentieth century who envisioned an age of information abundance far, far exceeded by the realities of digital information in the twenty-first century. Still, even with the billions of e-mail messages, text messages, and instant-messages each day churning through the servers and routers of the nation's Internet service providers, the newspapers in driveways and on doorsteps, the chattering and conversation of the nation's radio airwaves, and the breaking reports and stories in the newsrooms and the live-remote broadcasts of the country's television networks and stations remain a constant presence and a familiar part of the lives of millions of Americans and of the candidates for elective office seeking to reach these Americans. In the rich history of America's press and its political life, it is the intermingling of the nation's still-vibrant newspapers and the still-voluminous broadcasts on the nation's radio and television airwaves with the vast technologies of the digital age that still defines and still drives debates and discussions by candidates and their campaigning for elective office.

Notes

CHAPTER 1: THE PRESS AND AMERICAN POLITICS, 1787–1800

1. John Bach McMaster, *A History of the People of the United States from the Revolution to the Civil War* (New York: D. Appleton and Company, 1891), 436.

2. Kate Mason Rowland, *The Life of George Mason, 1725–1792* (New York: G. P. Putnam's Sons, 1892), 171–172.

3. Max Farrand, ed., *The Records of the Federal Convention of 1787, Volume 3* (New Haven, Conn.: Yale University Press, 1911), 73–74.

4. Charles L. Mee Jr., *The Genius of the People* (New York: Harper and Row, 1987), 284.

5. Elaine F. Crane, "*Publius* in the Provinces: Where Was *The Federalist* Reprinted Outside of New York City?," *William and Mary Quarterly* 21, no. 4 (October 1964): 590.

6. Richard B. Morris, *Witnesses at the Creation: Hamilton, Madison, Jay, and the Constitution* (New York: Holt, Rinehart and Winston, 1985), 21.

7. "No wonder," Robert Allen Rutland writes, "we have not one Madison or Hamilton document from this episode in the great newspaper debate, for the printers apparently took the scribbled notes and, after their composing chores, tossed the smudged sheets into a scrapheap." Robert Allen Rutland, "The 1st Great Newspaper Debate: The Constitutional Crisis of 1787–1788," *Proceedings of the American Antiquarian Society* 97, no. 1 (April 1987): 53.

8. Ralph Ketcham, *James Madison: A Biography* (Charlottesville: University of Virginia Press, 1990), 239.

9. George Henry Payne, *History of Journalism in the United States* (New York: D. Appleton and Company, 1920), 205.

10. Joseph Gales, *The Debates and Proceedings of the Congress of the United States, Volume 1* (Washington, D.C.: Gales and Seaton, 1834), 456.

11. Ibid., 441.

12. Ibid., 442.

13. Ibid.

14. Ibid., 443.

15. Ibid.

16. Ibid.

17. Ibid., 459.

18. Ibid., 459, 462.

19. John P. Kaminski, "Congress Proposes the Bill of Rights," in *Well Begun: Chronicles of the Early National Period*, ed. Stephen L. Schechter and Richard B. Bernstein (Albany, NY: New York State Commission on the Bicentennial of the United States Constitution, 1989), 100.

20. Thomas C. Leonard, *The Power of the Press: The Birth of American Political Reporting* (New York: Oxford University Press, 1986), 7.

21. Joseph J. Ellis, *Founding Brothers: The Revolutionary Generation* (New York: Alfred A. Knopf, 2002), 126.

22. Noble E. Cunningham Jr., *The Jeffersonian Republicans: The Formation of Party Organization, 1789–1801* (Chapel Hill: University of North Carolina Press, 1957), 14–15.

23. Jeffrey L. Pasley, "The Two National Gazettes: Newspapers and the Embodiment of American Political Parties," *Early American Literature* 35, no. 1 (March 2000): 68.

24. Willard Sterne Randall, *George Washington: A Life* (New York: Henry Holt, 1997), 491.

25. "Yesterday, the doors of the House of Representatives were thrown open for the admission of the citizens," the *New York Daily Gazette* reported on Thursday, April 9, 1789. Charlene Bangs Bickford, "Throwing Open the Doors: The First Federal Congress and the Eighteenth Century Media," in *Inventing Congress: Origins and Establishment of the First Congress*, ed. Kenneth R. Bowling and Donald R. Kennon (Athens: United States Capitol Historical Society and Ohio University Press, 1999), 166.

26. Gerald L. Grotta, "Philip Freneau's Crusade for Open Sessions of the U.S. Senate," *Journalism Quarterly* 48, no. 4 (Winter 1971): 669.

27. As vice president, Thomas Jefferson is recalled to have had a complete set of Bache's *Aurora and General Advertiser* bound at a bindery and sent to his library at his home in Monticello.

28. "It appears to have been thought that, in a paper calculated to descend to posterity, allusions to temporary causes of irritation had better be suppressed," biographer Edward Everett recalls of the disappearance of the paragraph from the president's final published letter. Edward Everett, *The Life of George Washington* (New York: Sheldon and Company, 1860), 220.

29. James Madison, *Letters and Other Writings of James Madison, 4th President of the United States, In 4 Volumes, Volume 2, 1794–1815* (Philadelphia: J. B. Lippincott and Company, 1865), 141.

30. David McCullough, *John Adams* (New York: Simon and Schuster, 2001), 496.

31. Ibid., 501.

32. Donald H. Stewart, *The Opposition Press of the Federalist Era* (Albany: State University of New York Press, 1969), 467.

33. Paul Leicester Ford, ed., *The Works of Thomas Jefferson, Volume 8* (New York: G. P. Putnam's Sons, 1904), 450.

34. Ibid.

35. McCullough, *John Adams*, 506.

36. James Morton Smith, *Freedom's Fetters: The Alien and Sedition Laws and American Civil Liberties* (Ithaca, NY: Cornell University Press, 1956), 389.

37. James Morton Smith, "President John Adams, Thomas Cooper, and Sedition: A Case Study of Suppression," *Mississippi Valley Historical Review* 42, no. 3 (December 1955): 439.

38. Thomas Cooper, *A Treatise on the Law of Libel and the Liberty of the Press* (New York: G. F. Hopkins and Son, 1830), 78.

39. Ibid.

40. James Morton Smith, "Sedition in the Old Dominion: James T. Callender and *The Prospect Before Us*," *Journal of Southern History* 20, no. 2 (May 1954): 182.

41. John Clyde Oswald, *Printing in the Americas, Volume 1* (Port Washington, NY: Kennikat Press, 1937), 272.

42. George L. Montagno, "Federalist Retaliation: The Sedition Trial of Matthew Lyon," *Vermont History* 26, no. 1 (January 1958): 4.

43. Smith, *Freedom's Fetters*, 237.

44. "As no one got a majority," James Fairfax McLaughlin recalls, "there was no election in September and another trial of strength at the polls took place in December, while Lyon was in the Vergennes jail in close confinement. The President of the United States and his whole party were actively engaged on one side, Matthew Lyon in his cell, backed by his old associates, the Green Mountain Boys, on the other." "The result," McLaughlin recounts, "was an overwhelming victory for the prisoner, who proved more powerful in shackles than John Adams in the Presidency." James Fairfax McLaughlin, *Matthew Lyon, The Hampden of Congress: A Biography* (New York: Wynkoop Hallenback Crawford Company, 1800), 375.

45. Ibid., 377.

46. "The vast multitude that welcomed Lyon as he emerged from his cell, and who followed him on his rejoicing way, 'reached,' says a Vermont writer, 'from Vergennes, as they traversed Otter Creek upon the ice, nearly to Middlebury.'" McLaughlin, *Matthew Lyon*, 377–378.

47. Smith, *Freedom's Fetters*, 359.

48. John Spargo, *Anthony Haswell: Printer, Patriot, Ballader* (Rutland, Vt.: The Tuttle Company, 1925), 52.

49. Spargo, *Anthony Haswell*, 86.

50. Gordon S. Wood, *Empire of Liberty: A History of the Early Republic, 1789–1815* (New York: Oxford University Press, 2009), 250.

CHAPTER 2: THE NINETEENTH-CENTURY PRESS AND AMERICAN POLITICS

1. Olga G. Hoyt and Edwin P. Hoyt, *Freedom of the News Media* (New York: The Seabury Press, 1973), 7.

2. Donald H. Stewart, *The Opposition Press of the Federalist Era* (Albany: State University of New York Press, 1969), 30.

3. Frank Luther Mott, *American Journalism* (New York: Macmillan, 1962), 167.

4. Michael E. McGerr, *The Decline of Popular Politics: The American North, 1865–1928* (New York: Oxford University Press, 1986), 22.

5. Lynn L. Marshall, "The Strange Stillbirth of the Whig Party," *The American Historical Review* 72, no. 2 (January 1967): 451.

6. Judith R. Blau and Cheryl Elman, "The Institutionalization of U.S. Political Parties, Patronage Newspapers," *Sociological Inquiry* 72, no. 4 (Fall 2002): 595.

7. Michael Schudson, *Discovering the News: A Social History of American Newspapers* (New York: Basic Books, 1978), 15.

8. Mott, *American Journalism*, 190.

9. Hoyt and Hoyt, *Freedom of the News Media*, 18.

10. Reuben Gold Thwaites, *The Ohio Valley Press before the War of 1812–1815* (Worcester, Mass.: The Davis Press, 1909), 44.

11. Noble E. Cunningham Jr., *The Jeffersonian Republicans in Power, 1801–1809* (Chapel Hill: University of North Carolina Press, 1963), 241.

12. J. E. D. Shipp, *Giant Days, or the Life and Times of William H. Crawford* (Americus, Ga.: Southern Printers, 1909), 182.

13. Alexis de Tocqueville, *Democracy in America*, trans. Henry Reeve (New York: George Adlard, 1839), 182–183.

14. Ibid., 178.

15. Ibid., 180.

16. Charles G. Steffen, "Newspapers for Free: The Economies of Newspaper Circulation in the Early Republic," *Journal of the Early Republic* 23, no. 3 (Fall 2003): 396.

17. Frank Luther Mott, "Newspapers in Presidential Campaigns," *Public Opinion Quarterly* 8, no. 3 (Autumn 1944): 351.

18. Michael Schudson, *Discovering the News: A Social History of American Newspapers* (New York: Basic Books, 1978), 4.

19. Gerald J. Baldasty, *The Press and Politics in the Age of Jackson* (Columbia: University of South Carolina College of Journalism, 1984), 14.

20. Donald A. Ritchie, *Press Gallery: Congress and the Washington Correspondents* (Cambridge, Mass.: Harvard University Press, 1991), 54.

21. Gerald J. Baldasty, *The Commercialization of the News in the Nineteenth Century* (Madison: University of Wisconsin Press, 1992), 23.

22. Ritchie, *Press Gallery*, 23.

23. Doris Kearns Goodwin, *Team of Rivals: The Political Genius of Abraham Lincoln* (New York: Simon and Schuster, 2005), 141.

24. David M. Ryfe, "News, Culture, and Public Life: A Study of Nineteenth-Century American Journalism," *Journalism Studies* 7, no. 1 (February 2006): 65.

25. Michael E. McGerr, *The Decline of Popular Politics: The American North, 1865–1928* (New York: Oxford University Press, 1986), 15.

26. George Henry Payne, *History of Journalism in the United States* (New York: D. Appleton and Company, 1920), 334.

27. William F. Gienapp, "Politics Seemed to Enter into Everything: Political Culture in the North, 1840–1860," in *Essays on Antebellum American Politics, 1840–1860*, ed. Steven Maizlish and John Kushma (College Station: Texas A&M Press, 1982), 41–42.

28. Richard Allen Heckman, *Lincoln Versus Douglas: The Great Debates Campaign* (Washington, D.C.: Public Affairs Press, 1967), 42.

29. Few specific details are known of the *Illinois Staats Anzeiger* and its circulation or readership, though historical records indicate Illinois's General Assembly members used state funds, as allowed at the time, to subscribe to the paper. No copy of the paper is known to exist to this day.

30. Robert S. Harper, *Lincoln and the Press* (New York: McGraw Hill, 1951), 101.

31. Harold Holzer, *Lincoln at Cooper Union: The Speech That Made Abraham Lincoln President* (New York: Simon and Schuster, 2004), 60.

32. Richard Carwardine, "Abraham Lincoln and the Fourth Estate: The White House and the Press during the Civil War," *American Nineteenth Century History* 7, no. 1 (March 2006): 2–3.

33. Mott, *American Journalism*, 414.

34. George Juergens, "Theodore Roosevelt and the Press," *Daedalus* 111, no. 4 (Fall 1982): 116.

35. Ryfe, "News, Culture, and Public Life," 6, 73.

CHAPTER 3: NEWSPAPERS AND TWENTIETH-CENTURY AMERICAN POLITICS

1. Peter Benjaminson, *Death in the Afternoon: America's Newspaper Giants Struggle for Survival* (Kansas City, Mo.: Andrews, McMeel and Parker, 1984), vii.

2. George Juergens, "Theodore Roosevelt and the Press," *Daedalus* 111, no. 4 (Fall 1982): 116.

3. Chester S. Lord, *The Young Man and Journalism* (New York: Macmillan, 1922), 44.

4. Woodrow Wilson, *The New Freedom: A Call for the Emancipation of the Generous Energies of a People* (New York: Doubleday, Page and Company, 1921), 115. Speaking to a January 1911 dinner at the National Press Club, Wilson told reporters "what we are really after in the field of politics is to drive everything into the field of facts, drive everything into the open." "Take Politics from Ambush Says Wilson, Tells National Press Club Guests His Hobby Is Publicity in Business and Politics," *New York Times*, February 1, 1911, A8.

5. George Juergens, "Theodore Roosevelt and the Press," *Daedalus* 111, no. 4 (Fall 1982): 119.

6. Ibid., 118.

7. Nathan Miller, *Theodore Roosevelt: A Life* (New York: HarperCollins, 1992), 421.

8. William W. Price, "How the Work of Gathering White House News Has Changed," *Washington Evening Star*, December 16, 1902, A32–33.

9. H. W. Brands, *T. R.: The Last Romantic* (New York: Basic Books, 1997), 515–516.

10. Patricia O'Toole, *When Trumpets Call: Theodore Roosevelt after the White House* (New York: Simon and Schuster, 2005), 362.

11. Oswald Garrison Villard, *The Disappearing Daily: Chapters in American Newspaper Evolution* (New York: Alfred A. Knopf, 1944), 36.

12. James M. Cox, *Journey through My Years* (New York: Simon and Schuster, 1946), 231.

13. Sherman A. Cuneo, *From Printer to President* (Philadelphia, Penn.: Dorrance and Company, 1922), 57.

14. Ibid., 102–103.

15. Cox, *Journey through My Years*, 387.

16. "No Sale," *Time* 18, no. 1 (July 6, 1931): 26.

17. Graham J. White, *FDR and the Press* (Chicago: University of Chicago Press, 1979), 15.

18. Villard, *The Disappearing Daily*, 3.

19. Ibid., 4–5.

20. "The 10 Best American Dailies," *Time* 103, no. 3 (January 21, 1974): 58.

21. Cox executive J. Leonard Reinsch was retained for several months to advise President Harry S. Truman. Franklin D. Mitchell, *Harry S. Truman and the News Media: Contentious Relations, Belated Respect* (Columbia: University of Missouri Press, 1998), 168–169.

22. Douglass Cater, *The Fourth Branch of Government* (Boston: Houghton Mifflin Company, 1959), 4.

23. James L. Baughman, "Wounded but Not Slain: The Orderly Retreat of the American Newspaper," in *A History of the Book in America, Volume 5: The Enduring Book, Print Culture in Postwar America*, ed. David Paul Nord, Joan Shelley Rubin, and Michael Schudson (Chapel Hill: University of North Carolina Press, 2009), 119.

24. A. J. Liebling, *The Press*, 2nd rev. ed. (New York: Ballantine Books, 1975), 31–32.

25. Ibid., 30.

26. Jack Lyle, *The News in Megalopolis* (San Francisco: Chandler Publishing Company, 1967), 27.

27. Leo Bogart, *Press and Public: Who Reads What, When, Where, and Why in American Newspapers* (Hillsdale, N.J.: Lawrence Erlbaum Associates, 1981), 55.

28. Alex S. Jones, "At Many Papers, Competition Is at Best an Illusion," *New York Times*, September 22, 1991, D18.

29. Alfred McClung Lee, "Trends Affecting the Daily Newspapers," *Public Opinion Quarterly* 3, no. 3 (July 1939): 499–500.

30. Baughman, "Wounded but Not Slain," 122.

31. Ibid., 126.

32. Richard Perez-Pena, "Big News in Washington, but Far Fewer Cover It," *New York Times*, December 18, 2008, A1, A29.

CHAPTER 4: RADIO AND THE RISE OF BROADCAST POLITICS

1. "Smith Hails Microphone as Mouthpiece of Nation, Governor Tells What He Thinks about Radio, Managers Plan Record Hook Up to Carry His Key Speeches to All America, Hoover's Plan Not Announced," *New York Times*, July 8, 1928, XX12.

2. "'It Is a Success,' Says Moore of a New System of Wireless Telegraphy Developed by Weather Bureau," *Toledo Blade*, February 8, 1901, A6.

3. "Marconi System Is Excelled, Pittsburgh Scientist Has Invented Wireless Telegraph That Can Pierce Oceans of Distance, Works Clear as Wire, Ocean Cables Now Near Their Passing, Federal Committee Decides Prof. Fessenden's Methods Are Perfect, Revolutionizes International Intercourse," *Pittsburgh Press*, April 27, 1901, A1, A4.

4. Helen M. Fessenden, *Fessenden: Builder of Tomorrows* (New York: Coward-McCann, Inc., 1940), 92.

5. Lawrence W. Lichty and Malachi C. Topping, *American Broadcasting: A Source Book on the History of Radio and Television* (New York: Hastings House Publishers, 1975), 465.

6. "Nation to Take Over Tuckerton Plant, President Orders Navy to Use Station for Sending All Radio Code Messages Abroad, May Try to Buy It Later, Government Will Not Allow Missives in Code to Be Forwarded from Any Other Place," *New York Times*, September 6, 1914, A14.

7. "Check on Wireless to Keep Neutrality, Sweeping Order by the President Prohibits Messages to Aid Belligerents, Navy Will Enforce It," *New York Times*, August 6, 1914, A4.

8. "20,000 American Watchdogs, How Our Boy Wireless Operators Are Forming a Great Army of Defense, Uncle Sam Realizing How Easily a Hostile Force Could Approach Our Long, Badly Patrolled Coasts, Looks to Amateurs For Signal Duty in Detecting Its Approach, and for Quick Transmission of Military Intelligence, Youths, in Joining the New Radio League, Pledge Themselves as Modern Paul Reveres in Periods of War, Riot and Disaster," *San Francisco Chronicle*, January 30, 1916, A4.

9. "Wireless Owners Band for Defense, The 300,000 Amateurs Having Equipment to Aid in National Preparedness, Naval Experts Co-Operate, Organization Called Radio League of America, Plan and Its Aims Are Explained," *New York Times*, November 21, 1915, A22.

10. "A Formidable Defense Weapon," *Electrical Experimenter* 3, no. 8 (December 1915): 381.

11. "Government Seizes Whole Radio System, Navy Takes Over All Wireless Plants It Needs and Closes All Others," *New York Times*, April 8, 1917, A2.

12. "Seizure of all radio stations in the United States and its possessions, operation of those needed for naval communications, and closing of others, was authorized yesterday by President Wilson," the *Washington Post* reported that Saturday morning. "It is understood that all plants for which no place can be found in the Navy's wireless system, including amateur apparatus, for which close search will be made, are to be put out of commission immediately." "Wilson Orders All Radios Seized, Amateur Stations Will Be Closed," *Washington Post*, April 7, 1917, A4.

13. "Government Seizes Whole Radio System, Navy Takes Over All Wireless Plants It Needs and Closes All Others," A2.

14. "Federal Agents Seek All Wireless Outfits, Several in Atlanta Under Surveillance Probably Be Closed by U.S.," *Atlanta Constitution*, April 11, 1917, A11.

15. "War!" *QST* 2, no. 6 (May 1917): 3. QST was touted as "a magazine devoted exclusively to the wireless amateur."

16. "How the Government Seals Radio Apparatus," *Electrical Experimenter* 5, no. 3 (July 1917): 188.

17. "A Brief Account of What Happened at Buffalo When Orders Were Received to Disconnect All Radio Apparatus and Dismantle All Aerial Wires, and the Means Used to Enforce the Orders," *QST* 2, no. 8 (July 1917): 26.

18. "Another Season Opens but–," *QST* 2, no. 10 (September 1917): 16.

19. "More Stringent Than Supposed," *QST* 2, no. 10 (September 1917): 16.

20. "Wilson Approves Making Wireless a Navy Monopoly, Administration Plans Permanent Purchase and Operation of All Plants, Bill Goes to Congress, Single Control Necessary to Make Radio Profitable, Based on War Experience," *New York Times*, November 25, 1918, A1, A5.

21. "Federal Control of Radio Stations Sought by Wilson, Administration Pushing Measures for Acquisition and Operation by Navy of All U.S. Shore Wireless Stations, Stations to Be Open to Public Business, Secretary of Navy to Fix the Rates, It Is Denied That Measure Seeks to Establish a Government Monopoly," *Atlanta Constitution*, November 25, 1918, A1, A5.

22. "Federal Control of All Wireless Stations Urged," *Atlanta Constitution*, December 13, 1918, A1.

23. "Mexican Wireless Depicted as Peril, Controlled by Germans and Will Hamper Our Trade, Nally Tells Committee, Oppose Ownership Bill," *New York Times*, December 18, 1918, A17.

24. "Burleson Presses Ownership Plan, Writes Moon That Wire Systems Can Be Paid for in 25 Years without Cost to Treasury, Economies Would Do It, These Could Be Effected by Eliminating the Duplication in Plant and Operating Expenses," *New York Times*, December 17, 1918, A15.

25. "Navy Department, Naval Communication Service, Office of the Director, Washington, D.C., April 14, 1919," *Electrical Experimenter* 7, no. 2 (June 1919): 131.

26. Hugo Gernsback, "Amateur Radio Restored," *Electrical Experimenter* 7, no. 2 (June 1919): 131, italics in original.

27. The text of the navy's Friday, September 26, 1919, statement read as follows: "The Secretary of the Navy authorizes the announcement that effective October 1, 1919, all restrictions on amateurs and amateur radio stations are removed. This applies to amateur stations, technical and experimental stations at schools and colleges, and to all other stations except those used for the purpose of transmitting or receiving commercial traffic of any character, including the business of the owners of the stations. The restrictions on stations handling commercial traffic will remain in effect until the President proclaims that a state of peace exists. Attention is invited to the fact that all licenses for transmitting stations have expired and that it will be necessary for the amateurs to apply to the Commissioner of Navigation, Department of Commerce, for new licenses. In so far as amateurs are concerned, radio resumes its pre-war status under the Department of Commerce." The American Radio Relay League, *Fifty Years of ARRL* (Newington, Conn.: The American Radio Relay League, 1965), 27.

28. *Washington Post*, September 27, 1919, A6.

29. Woodrow Wilson, *Addresses of President Wilson: Addresses Delivered by President Wilson on His Western Tour, September 4 to September 25, 1919, On the League of Nations, Treaty of Peace with Germany, Industrial Conditions, High Cost of Living, Race Riots* (Washington, D.C.: Government Printing Office, 1919), 60.

30. *The New York Times*, December 26, 1919, A3.

31. Catherine L. Covert, "'We May Hear Too Much': American Sensibility and the Response to Radio, 1919–1924," in *Mass Media between the Wars: Perceptions of Cultural Tension, 1918–1941*, ed. Catherine L. Covert and John D. Stevens (Syracuse, NY: Syracuse University Press, 1984), 205.

32. *New York Times*, February 9, 1922, A1.

33. *Washington Post*, February 9, 1922, A2.

34. "Bryan Hails Radio as Aid to His Party, Wireless Broadcasting Will Give Democrats More Publicity, Says Commoner Here, Again Attacks Evolution, but Declines to Comment on the Supposed Moral Breakdown of the Youth," *New York Times*, September 3, 1922, A3.

35. Randall Patnode, "Path Not Taken: Wired Wireless and Broadcasting in the 1920s," *Journal of Broadcasting and Electronic Media* 49, no. 4 (December 2005): 385.

36. "Nation's Radio Fans Listen to Coolidge, St. Louis Hears the Rustle of the Pages as the President Reads His Message, New York Gets Each Word, Thousands in Homes, in Equipment Stores and Offices Hear His Voice Distinctly," *New York Times*, December 7, 1923, A3.

37. "Maine 'Looks Good,' Friends Tell Davis, They Say Republican Split on Klan Issue May Elect Democratic Governor, Cummings Visits Nominee, Candidate Believes Use of the Radio Has 'Completely Changed Campaign Methods,'" *New York Times*, July 23, 1924, A3.

38. "Radio Politics," *Time* 4, no. 4 (July 28, 1924): 22.

39. "Political Spellbinding by Radio," *Popular Mechanics* 42, no. 6 (December 1924): 879.

40. Edward W. Chester, *Radio, Television, and American Politics* (New York: Sheed and Ward Publishers, 1969), 23.

41. Stephen Ponder, *Managing the Press: Origins of the Media Presidency, 1897–1933* (New York: St. Martin's Press, 1998), 123.

42. "Smith Hails Microphone as Mouthpiece of Nation, Governor Tells What He Thinks about Radio, Managers Plan Record Hook Up to Carry His Key Speeches to All America, Hoover's Plan Not Announced," *New York Times*, July 8, 1928, **XX**12.

43. David G. Clark, "Radio in Presidential Campaigns: The Early Years, 1924 to 1932," *Journal of Broadcasting* 6, no. 3 (Summer 1962): 230.

44. "Governor Smith Heard by Radio Millions, 100,000 Miles of Circuits with 111 Stations Carry Speech All Over Country, Applause Comes Clearly, Only Two Minor Breaks Occur in Huge Network and are Quickly Repaired," *New York Times*, August 23, 1928, A8.

45. "Smith Hails Microphone as Mouthpiece of Nation, Governor Tells What He Thinks about Radio, Managers Plan Record Hook Up to Carry His Key Speeches to All America, Hoover's Plan Not Announced," *New York Times*, July 8, 1928, **XX**12.

46. "Broadcasters to Canvas for Greatest Vote Ever, Hoover, If Nominated, Plans to Campaign on the Air, Essentials of Successful Political Speeches Are Outlined, Broadcasts Expected to Attract Record Number of Voters to Polls," *New York Times*, May 13, 1928, **XX**13.

47. "Radio Listeners Eavesdropped on 1st Convention in 1924," *New York Times*, June 10, 1928, **XX**16.

48. Louise Overacker, *Money in Elections* (New York: Macmillan, 1932), 28.

49. Orrin E. Dunlap Jr., "Praise Amid Complaints, Broadcasters Study Results of Inaugural Program, Microphones Were Invisible, No Television on the Scene," *New York Times*, March 12, 1933, **X**10.

50. Lawrence W. Levine and Cornelia R. Levine, *The President and the People: America's Conversation with FDR* (Boston: Beacon Press, 2002), 16.

51. David Halberstam, *The Powers That Be* (New York: Knopf, 1975), 16.

52. Ibid., 15–16.

53. Edward W. Chester, *Radio, Television, and American Politics* (New York: Sheed and Ward Publishers, 1969), 33.

54. Francis Chase Jr., *Sound and Fury: An Informal History of Broadcasting* (New York: Harper and Brothers, 1942), 113–114.

55. William C. Ackerman, "The Dimensions of American Broadcasting," *Public Opinion Quarterly* 9, no. 1 (Spring 1945): 3.

56. David McCullough, *Truman* (New York: Simon and Schuster, 1992), 624.

57. Raymond L. Carroll, "Harry S. Truman's 1948 Election: The Inadvertent Broadcast Campaign," *Journal of Broadcasting and Electronic Media* 31, no. 2 (Spring 1987): 121; McCullough, *Truman*, 624.

CHAPTER 5: TELEVISION IN THE EARLY TWENTIETH CENTURY

1. Gary R. Edgerton, *The Columbia History of American Television* (New York: Columbia University Press, 2007), xi.

2. Michael Winship, *Television* (New York: Random House, 1988), 4.

3. Ibid., 4.

4. Cartoon character Dick Tracy's "2-way wrist radio," which became the "2-way wrist television," is a popular example.

5. R.W. Burns, *John Logie Baird, Television Pioneer* (London: The Institution of Engineering and Technology), 75–76.

6. Ibid., 75–76.

7. O. G. Hutchinson, "Radio Images Are Glimpsing across the Atlantic, Scotsman's Road to Television Fraught with Many Obstacles, Poverty and Adversity Tugged at Baird as He Toiled toward His Goal, His Efforts Now Crowned with Success," *New York Times*, February 19, 1928, **XX**17.

8. "Radio Shows Far Away Objects in Motion, Washington Officials See Test of Invention," *New York Times*, June 14, 1925, A1.

9. "First Motion Pictures Transmitted by Radio Are Shown in Capital, Government Officials and Scientists, Summoned Quickly by Telephone, View Successful Experiment in Laboratory of C. Francis Jenkins, Small Apparatus Functions Perfectly," *Washington Post*, June 14, 1925, A1, A2.

10. "Far Off Speakers Seen as Well as Heard Here in a Test of Television, Like a Photo Come to Life, Hoover's Face Plainly Imaged as He Speaks in Washington, The 1st Time in History, Pictures Are Flashed by Wire and Radio Synchronizing with Speaker's Voice, Commercial Use in Doubt, but AT&T Head Sees a New Step in Conquest of Nature after Years of Research," *New York Times*, April 8, 1927, A20.

11. "Radio Television to Home Receivers Is Shown in Tests, Pictures and Voices Clearly Seen and Heard in 3 Schenectady Residences, Sent Out from Laboratory, New General Electric Device Records Every Move and Remark of Broadcaster, for Public in 5 Years, Prediction Made That Machine Will Supplant the Loud-Speaker in That Time," *New York Times*, January 14, 1928, A1, A5.

12. "Radio Vision Takes Another Step toward the Home, Device for Seeing by Radio Is Easily Attached to Sets, Televisor Connection Is Similar to That of Loud-Speaker, Present Receivers Will Not Be Made Obsolete by Television," *New York Times*, January 22, 1928, **XX**14.

13. "Jenkins' Television Laboratories Here Get Radio License, Federal Commission Recognizes Potential Value of Movie Pictures, Another Is Granted to Lexington Station, Officials Also Announce Many Assignments, Numbers and Wave Lengths," *Washington Post*, July 21, 1928, A16.

14. "Sight Tubes Aid Image Broadcasts, Bulbs Filled with Neon Gas Are Called Oramatrons, Electricity Is Converted into a Pink Glow Visible to the Eye," *New York Times*, June 24, 1928, **XX**13.

15. "Television Waves Pass Unnoticed, No One Reports Seeing Images Broadcast by WGY, Sales of Aluminum and Neon Lamps Reveals Great Activity in Boston," *New York Times*, May 20, 1928, X21.

16. "Improved Television Sought as Scientists Work Overtime, Amateurs Build Receivers," *Atlanta Constitution*, June 3, 1928, A18.

17. Charles Francis Jenkins, *Radiomovies, Radiovision, Television* (Washington, D.C.: National Capital Press Publishers, 1929), 18.

18. "WRNY to Start Daily Television Broadcasts, Radio Audience Will See Studio Artists," *New York Times*, August 13, 1928, A19.

19. "Smith Rehearses for Camera Men, as Accommodation, He Gives Gestures in Advance on Notification Platform," *New York Times*, August 22, 1928, A3.

20. *Time* magazine's Monday, August 27, 1928, issue reported the latest developments in television transmissions: "[Eight] U.S. radio stations last week were broadcasting pictures. Two were operating regularly, four irregularly. The last were testing out their frequencies. The stations: WGY, Schenectady, New York (General Electric), KDKA, East Pittsburgh, Pa. (Westinghouse), WRNY, New York (Experimenter Publishing Co.), 3XK, Washington (Jenkins Laboratories), 2XAL, New York (Experimenter Publishing Co.), 1XAY, Lexington, Mass. (Donald R. Lafflin), 4XA, Memphis, Tenn. (WREC, Inc.), 9XAA, Chicago (Chicago Federation Of Labor)." "Visual Broadcasting," *Time* 12, no. 9 (August 27, 1928): 39.

21. Ibid., 39–40.

22. Ibid., 40.

23. K. A. Hathaway, "Thousands See 1st Television Program Here, Crowds Watch W9XAP Program on Sets Operated by Dealers," *Chicago Daily News*, August 28, 1930, A26.

24. "Television Placed on Daily Schedule, RCA Now Broadcasting Images Regularly From 7 to 9 o'clock from 411 5th Avenue, Purpose Is Experimental, Dr. Goldsmith Says Fading, Picture Quality and Other Problems Are Being Studied," *New York Times*, March 22, 1929, A20.

25. "Six Visual Stations on the New York Air, Peak of Skyscraper Selected as Aerial Site, New Image Broadcaster in Debut This Week," *New York Times*, July 19, 1931, XX13.

26. Erik Barnouw, *Tube of Plenty: The Evolution of American Television,* rev. ed. (Oxford: Oxford University Press, 1982), 86.

27. Ray Barfield, *A Word from Our Viewers: Reflections from Early Television Audiences* (Westport, Conn.: Greenwood Publishing Group, 2008), 3.

28. In January 1934, to cite one of many examples, Kansas City's First National Television, Inc. featured an ad in *Popular Mechanics* for training at its station, W9XAL. "Learn Televion with Radio—Now!" First National Television, Inc.'s ad told its readers. "You learn radio and television from the beginning to end in our marvelously equipped labs and studios." "Television now perfected and ready for the market ON THE NEXT BIG BUYING WAVE," the ad enthused. "GET IN NOW and 'build up' with the world's next billion dollar industry." First National Television, Inc.'s ad prominently featured the National Recovery Administration's American

eagle logo as a reminder of the difficult times. *Popular Mechanics* 61, no. 1 (January 1934): A19.

CHAPTER 6: TELEVISION IN THE 1930s AND IN WARTIME AMERICA

1. Orrin E. Dunlap Jr., "Telecast of President at the World's Fair to Start Wheels of New Industry," *New York Times*, April 30, 1939, X12.

2. Orrin E. Dunlap Jr., "Ceremony Is Carried by Television as Industry Makes Its Formal Bow, President Screened for First Time, Scenes at Grounds Shown, Mayor Is 'Most Telegenic' of Notables Viewed," *New York Times*, May 1, 1939, A8.

3. John Cabot Smith, "Television Reaches Capitol and What Seemed Magic Becomes a Fact, Hundreds See Historic Telecast, Interviews on Mall Suggest the Shape of Many Things That Are to Come," *Washington Post*, January 29, 1939, B4.

4. Carter Brooke Jones, "Mobile Television Unit Brings New Magic to Washington, Camera Picks Up Street Scenes in 1st Demonstration in Capital," *Evening Star*, January 27, 1939, B11.

5. "Television's 1st Roadshow Proves a Hit, Federal Officials Much Impressed by NBC-RCA," *Broadcasting* 16, no. 4 (February 15, 1939): 21.

6. "Too Early for Television?" *Time* 35, no. 16 (April 15, 1940): 81.

7. Orrin E. Dunlap Jr., "Ears and Eyes on the G.O.P., Microphones and Tele-Cameras to Pick Up Keynote Speech, Convention Expected to Be Televieved 200 Miles Away," *New York Times*, June 23, 1940, 10.

8. "Convention City," *Time*, 36, no. 2 (July 8, 1940): 16.

9. "Roosevelt Rally Sent by Television, First Use of New Medium as 'Vote Getter' Is Made at Gathering in Garden, Reception Called Poor, Images 'Fuzzy' and Faces Are Hard to Discern, Willkie Telecast on Saturday," *New York Times*, October 29, 1940, L14.

10. "It was the 1st time in history that any Congressional event has been broadcast pictorially," the *New York Times* noted. "Television Is Used at House Opening, Truman at His Desk Observes 1st Radio Picturization of a Congress Session," *New York Times*, January 4, 1947, A2. "Congress made its bow in television today," the *Washington Post* reported on Saturday, January 4, 1947. "The opening session of the House of Representatives was placed on the air for 2 hours," "This 1st Congressional program was carried in black-and-white television pictures to one Washington station, WWTG, and by television cable to Philadelphia and New York," "House Makes Television Debut, Martin Portrayed in Address," *Washington Post*, January 4, 1947, A1.

11. "Television of President Is Acceptably Clear Here," *New York Times*, January 7, 1947, A18.

12. "The Infant Grows Up," *Time* 51, no. 21 (May 24, 1948): 73–74, 77.

13. Larry Wolters, "WGN-TV Makes Debut Tonight with Big Show, 2 Hour Salute Begins at 7:45 P.M," *Chicago Daily Tribune*, April 5, 1948, A4.

14. Sonia Stein, "D.C. a Gold Mine of Copy for Kid Brother of Radio," *Washington Post*, April 14, 1948, C1.

15. Larry Wolters, "Midwest TV Net Makes Intercity Shows Possible, Illini Games Relayed to WGN-TV Viewers," *Chicago Daily Tribune*, October 31, 1948, C14.

16. Harold J. Bock, "Until Coast Gets Coax, It Must Use Plenty Film," *Billboard* 61, no. 3 (January 15, 1949): 12.

17. Winifred Mallon, "Television Permits Are Halted by FCC, Action Hits 302 Pleas Pending Technical Studies, Use of Sets in Operation Unimpaired, New Conference Called, Engineers Will Consider Rules and Standards and Possibly Channel Allocations," *New York Times*, October 1, 1948, A22.

18. Erik Barnouw, *Tube of Plenty: The Evolution of American Television*, 2nd rev. ed. (Oxford: Oxford University Press, 1990), 113.

19. "TV's C-Day, Industry Marks Notable Growth in Opening of New Midwest Cable," *Billboard* 61, no. 3 (January 15, 1949): 9.

20. William S. Hedges, "Video Facing Mountainous Economic Problems but Will Lick Them, Hedges Is Sure," *Billboard* 61, no. 3 (January 15, 1949): 10.

21. William L. Bird Jr., "A Spate of New Toys Invades America's Living Rooms," *Smithsonian Magazine* 20, no. 3 (June 1989): 82.

22. "U.S. television, . . . continues to snowball ahead at the rate of 1,000 new sets installed every 24 hours." "Young Monster," *Time* 53, no. 1 (January 3, 1949): 31.

23. Jack Gould, "10,000,000 Viewers See the Ceremony, Television Audience Is Able to Note Close-Up Detail as If from a Front-Row," *New York Times*, January 21, 1949, A6.

24. Bird, "A Spate of New Toys Invades America's Living Rooms," 82.

25. Jack Gould, "President on New Coast-to-Coast Video Hook-Up, Television Spans United States for the 1st Time as President Talks at Parley," *New York Times*, September 5, 1951, A7.

26. George Mannes, "The Birth of Cable TV: Half-a-Century Ago, a Few Small-Town Tinkerers Brought Some Simple Equipment and Accidentally Founded a Multi-Billion Dollar Industry," *American Heritage of Innovation and Technology* 12, no. 2 (Fall 1996): 43.

27. "The Eye of the Nation," *Time* 60, no. 2 (July 14, 1952): 22. *Time*'s cover image for the Monday, July 14, 1952, issue was a map of the United States with a large eye looking down on the convention floor of one of the party conventions, with three television cameras labeled USA-TV.

28. David Culbert, "Television's Nixon: The Politician and His Image," in *American History, American Television: Interpreting the Video Past*, ed. John E. O'Connor (New York: Frederick Ungar, 1983), 186.

29. "The existence of a 'millionaire's club' devoted exclusively to the financial comfort of Sen. Nixon, G.O.P. Vice Presidential candidate, was revealed today," *New York Post*'s Leo Katcher reported that Thursday—of an account at the First Trust and Savings Bank of Pasadena, California, administered by Dana C. Smith, an

attorney chairing California Volunteers for Eisenhower. Leo Katcher, "Secret Rich Men's Trust Fund Keeps Nixon in Style Far beyond His Salary," *New York Post*, September 18, 1952, A3, A26.

30. Nicknamed the "Checker's Speech" for this reference, Nixon himself came to describe his televised remarks as the "Fund Speech."

31. "Wire Deluge Follows Nixon TV-Radio Plea, Facilities Swamped with Messages Favoring Nominee," *Los Angeles Times*, September 24, 1952, A1, A14.

32. Clayton Knowles, "Messages Pour in Backing Nominee, Wires at Rate of 4,000 an Hour Overwhelmingly in Favor of Retaining Californian," *New York Times*, September 25, 1952, A1, A24.

33. "Were it not for television," Culbert tells us, "he probably would have been dropped from the Republican ticket in September 1952." Culbert, "Television's Nixon," 184.

34. "In some neighborhoods," James L. Baughman tells us, "TV became so popular that some status-conscious residents, forced to put off the purchase of a 1st TV set, had antennas installed atop their homes so to seem part of the enveloping trend." James L. Baughman, "Television in the 'Golden Age': An Entrepreneurial Experiment," *The Historian: A Journal of History* 47, no. 2 (February 1985): 179.

35. "President's News Conference Filmed for Television and Newsreels for 1st Time," *New York Times*, January 20, 1955, A1, A13.

36. Nona B. Brown, "Willing Guests in Washington, Headliners Cheerfully Join Congressmen for Broadcasts," *New York Times*, June 14, 1959, X13. "The incumbents' Election Day benefit from his regular appearances in his constituents' living rooms between elections," *New Republic*'s Walter Goodman writes in May 1953, "is incalculable." "On their trips home nowadays," Goodman adds, "photogenic Senators are greeted on the street by alert TV fans." Walter Goodman, "Candidates and the Camera," *New Republic*, 132, no. 19 (May 9, 1953): 14–15.

37. Ibid., 13.

38. "Talmadge for Stevenson, President Plans TV Drive," *New York Times*, May 14, 1956, A1, A15.

CHAPTER 7: TELEVISION AND THE TRANSFORMATION OF POSTWAR AMERICAN POLITICS

1. Donald A. Ritchie, *Reporting from Washington: A History of the Washington Press Corps* (New York: Oxford University Press, 2005), 194.

2. Mary Ann Watson, *The Expanding Vista: American Television in the Kennedy Years* (Durham, NC: Duke University Press, 1990), 9.

3. Jack Gould, "Nixon's Willingness to Meet Kennedy in Debate Seen Enlivening Campaign," *New York Times*, July 25, 1960, A47.

4. John W. Self, "The 1st Debate Over the Debates: How Kennedy and Nixon Negotiated the 1960 Presidential Debates," *Presidential Studies Quarterly* 35, no. 2 (June 2005): 366.

5. "The Architect of a Triumph on Television, Broadcaster Reinsch Planned Kennedy's Use of Television," *Broadcasting* 59, no. 47 (November 14, 1960): 32.

6. Russell Baker, "Kennedy and Press Seems a Hit, Star Shows Skill as Showman," *New York Times*, January 26, 1961, A12.

7. Douglass Cater, *Power in Washington: A Critical Look at Today's Struggle to Govern in the Nation's Capitol* (New York: Vintage Books, 1965), 111.

8. Lawrence Laurent, "F.C.C. Chief Beards Broadcasters, Vows to Make Them Serve Public," *Washington Post*, May 10, 1961, A1, A9.

9. "The Most Intimate Medium," *Time* 88, no. 16 (October 14, 1966): 56.

10. Ritchie, *Reporting from Washington*, 195.

11. "Because KTBC was purchased in his wife's name and she became President of the company and was active in its affairs," biographer Robert A. Caro writes of the Johnson family's purchase of KTBC, "Lyndon Johnson was able to maintain for the rest of his life that the company, which was eventually to consist of a galaxy of radio and television stations, was not his but hers, all hers and only hers." Robert A. Caro, *The Years of Lyndon Johnson: Means of Ascent* (New York: Alfred A. Knopf, 1990), 88.

12. "The Multimillionaire," *Time* 84, no. 8 (August 21, 1964): 16. "Up from Poverty," *Time* 83, no. 25 (June 19, 1964): 19. Keith Wheeler and William Lambert, "How L.B.J.'s Family Amassed Its Fortune," *Life* 57, no. 8 (August 21, 1964): 64. Louis M. Kohlmeier, "The Johnson Wealth, How President's Wife Built $17,500 into Big Fortune Television, Firm Is Only TV Broadcaster in Austin, Turns a Profit on Other Texas Ventures," *Wall Street Journal*, March 23, 1964, A1, A12.

13. Wheeler and Lambert, "How L.B.J.'s Family Amassed Its Fortune," 64.

14. "The Multimillionaire," 16. "Up from Poverty," 20. President Johnson's longtime aide and White House press secretary, Bill Moyers, began his work with the Johnson family as a reporter with Austin's KTBC-TV. "L.B.J.'s Young Man 'In Charge of Everything,'" *Time* 86, no. 18 (October 29, 1965): 26.

15. "Austin's Bringing in a Gusher, Set Makers Prepare for KTBC-TV's Dec. 1 Debut," *Broadcasting* 43, no. 17 (October 27, 1952): 90.

16. "How Johnson Brings the World to His Desk," *Business Week* 38, no. 1957 (March 4, 1967): 180.

17. "White House to Get Its Own TV Studio," *Atlanta Constitution*, August 26, 1964, A2.

18. "The Most Intimate Medium," *Time* 88, no. 16 (October 14, 1966): 56.

19. Tom Wicker, "New Austin Offices Fit for a President," *New York Times*, July 11, 1965, A50.

20. "No one, unless he traveled a lot, would hear any statement but the one designed for him," McGinniss wrote. "A question about law and order might evoke one response in New England and a slightly different one in the South," McGinniss noted of the ads. "Nothing big enough to make headlines, just a subtle twist of inflection or the presence or absence of a frown or gesture as a certain phrase was spoken." Joe McGinniss, *The Selling of the President* (New York: Trident Press, 1969), 63.

21. Ibid., 37.

22. Ibid., 62.

23. Ibid., 81.

24. "Electronic Politics: The Image Game," *Time* 96, no. 12 (September 21, 1970): 43.

25. "A Fumble at the Hour of Triumph," the *New York Times*' front-page headline reported on Friday, July 14, 1972, of McGovern's televised address to his convention and his early-morning remarks to the nation's waning and weary television viewing audience. "Even the night watchmen on the Pacific Coast were going to bed before Mr. McGovern could make the most important speech of his career," James Reston reported from the Democratic convention in Miami. James Reston, "A Fumble at the Hour of Triumph," *New York Times*, July 14, 1972, A1, A12.

26. John Herbers, "Bill to Reform Campaign Funds Signed by Ford Despite Doubts," *New York Times*, October 16, 1974, A31.

27. Gaylord Shaw, "Ford, Referring to Watergate, Signs Campaign Spending Reform Measure," *Washington Post*, October 16, 1974, A12.

28. "Jostling for the Edge," *Time* 108, no. 13 (September 27, 1976): 12.

29. "Carter: 'I Look Forward to the Job,'" *Time* 109, no. 1 (January 3, 1977): 23.

30. Robert Goldberg and Gerald Jay Goldberg, *Citizen Turner: The Wild Rise of an American Tycoon* (New York: Harcourt Brace, 1995), 2.

31. Walter G. Salm, "Once Just a Way to Get Signals to Distant Places, Cable TV Is Now Growing Fast Even in Big Cities, Here's Why CATV Is Coming to Your Town," *Popular Science* 196, no. 6 (June 1970): 120

32. Ralph Lee Smith, *The Wired Nation: Cable TV, the Electronic Communications Highway* (New York: Harper and Row, 1972), 1.

33. "To Wire a Nation," *Time* 95, no. 22 (June 1, 1970): 71.

34. George Mannes, "The Birth of Cable TV: Half-a-Century Ago, a Few Small-Town Tinkerers Bought Some Simple Equipment and Accidentally Founded a Multi-Billion Dollar Industry," *American Heritage of Innovation and Technology* 12, no. 2 (Fall 1996): 44.

35. "TV: Biggest Boom Ahead, Unfreezing, Then Red Tape, Then Growth," *U.S. News and World Report* 32, no. 15 (April 11, 1952): 69.

36. Jack Gould, "Neighborly Lines, Rise in Community Antenna Systems May Open Back Door to Pay TV," *New York Times*, April 5, 1964, X13.

37. "The Big Wire," *Time* 84, no. 20 (November 13, 1964): 110–111.

38. B. Drummond Ayres Jr., "First TV Broadcast of House Session Isn't High Theater," *New York Times*, March 20, 1979, B13.

39. Frank Kane, "House Opens Its Doors to Camera's Stern Eye," *Toledo Blade*, March 19, 1979, A23. "

40. Joseph Lelyveld, "The Selling of a Candidate: Carter's Image Is a Vision, or a Con, or a Little of Both, in Any Case, His Media Man Maintains, 'It's Jimmy,'" *New York Times Magazine*, March 28, 1976, 16.

41. James David Barber, *The Pulse of Politics: Electing Presidents in the Media Age* (New York: W.W. Norton, 1980); W. Lance Bennett, *News: The Politics of*

Illusion, 1st ed. (New York: Longman, 1983); Austin Ranney, *Channels of Power: The Impact of Television on American Politics* (New York: Basic Books, 1983); Mark Hertsgaard, *On Bended Knee: The Press and the Reagan Presidency* (New York: Farrar Straus Giroux, 1988); Kathleen Hall Jamieson, *Packaging the Presidency: A History and Criticism of Presidential Campaign Advertising* (New York: Oxford University Press, 1984); Michael Parenti, *Inventing Reality: The Politics of the Mass Media* (New York: St. Martin's Press, 1986).

42. Bernard Weinraub, "Mondale Farewell, Viewing Loss, He Asserts Time to Do Something Else Has Arrived," *New York Times*, November 8, 1984, A24.

43. Hedrick Smith, "For Democrats, the Medium's a Mess," *New York Times*, December 10, 1984, B10.

44. Weinraub, "Mondale Farewell," A24

45. Michael Oreskes, "TV's Role in '88, The Medium Is the Election," *New York Times*, October 30, 1988, A1, A30.

46. David Axelrod, "Broadcast Views, Since 1952, TV Advertising Has Changed the Way Politicians Run for Office," *Advertising Age 59*, no. 45 (November 9, 1988): 92.

47. Governor Bill Clinton's much-mocked speech at Atlanta's Democratic convention on Wednesday, July 20, 1988—a misstep at that moment when the Arkansas governor was taking his first steps onto the national stage—was mended, in part, by his appearance on Johnny Carson's *The Tonight Show*. The governor's appearance a week later on the Johnny Carson show is remembered as one of the first of Clinton's skillful use of appearances on evening and late-night television programs. When Clinton came out from behind the curtain on Carson's Burbank, California, television set and took his seat next to Carson's desk, the host brought out an old-fashioned hour-glass to make light of the governor's speech. "As sand trickled through an hour-glass on Johnny Carson's desk," *Los Angeles Times*' journalist Deborah Christensen reported, "Arkansas Governor Bill Clinton conceded to *Tonight Show* viewers that his widely ridiculed nomination speech for Democratic presidential nominee Michael S. Dukakis at last week's Democratic National Convention in Atlanta was not his finest hour—or, more accurately, his finest half-hour." "Carson," Christensen noted, "introduced Clinton with a long-winded speech of his own that included minute details from Clinton's educational background. He added: 'Not to worry, we have plenty of black coffee and extra cots in the lobby.'" Deborah Christensen, "If You've Got the Time, Heeere's Johnny—and Bill," *Los Angeles Times*, July 29, 1988, A2.

48. Michael Oreskes, "TV's Role in '88, the Medium Is the Election," *New York Times*, October 30, 1988, A30.

49. David Lauter, "Clinton's Strategy of Triage, 'Don't Be Greedy Little Pigs,' Remarked an Advisor, Abandoning Some Big States as Probably Hopeless, Those That Got Immediate, Massive Attention Were Key to Winning White House," *Los Angeles Times*, November 5, 1992, A1, A6.

50. Elizabeth Kolbert, "Secrecy over Television Ads, or the Peculiar Logic of Political Combat," *New York Times*, September 17, 1992, A21.

51. Martin F. Nolan, "Electoral College Bowl, with the Decline of Network TV, the Key to Electoral Success Is Now 'Areas of Dominant Influence,'" *Boston Globe*, October 25, 1992, A71.

52. Dan Morgan, "A Made-for-Television Windfall, Candidates' Air Time Scramble Fills Stations' Tills," *Washington Post*, May 2, 2000, A1, A6.

53. Jeff Leeds, "Both Campaigns Scrambling for Votes, and for TV Ad Spots, Bush and Gore Backers Are Preparing a Blizzard of Commercials, with Volume Expected to Be about Even on Both Sides, but Air Time Is Scarce," *Los Angeles Times*, October 25, 2000, A14.

54. Jeff Leeds, "Switching to a Tailor-Made Ad Campaign Strategy, after Soaking the Airwaves for 15 Weeks with Generic Messages, the Democrats Start 'Selective Audience Appeals' in Markets Most Critical to the Election," *Los Angeles Times*, September 29, 2000, A26.

55. Caryn James, "Bush Flunks Letterman's Late-Night Examination," *New York Times*, March 2, 2000, A22. "The road to the White House runs right through here," the CBS *Late Show with David Letterman* host again told his viewers in Thursday, October 16, 2008's appearance by Senator John McCain. Robert Lloyd, "McCain Trial by Letterman's Fire," *Los Angeles Times*, October 18, 2008, E1.

56. Richard L. Berke and Kevin Sack, "In Debate 2, Microscope Focuses on Gore," *New York Times*, October 11, 2000, A1, A28.

57. David Carr, "Campaign Gravy Train at an End," *New York Times*, October 27, 2008, B7.

58. Paul Farhi, "Campaigns Buying More Ads but Targeting Fewer States," *Washington Post*, September 25, 2004, A8.

59. Mary McNamara, "It's Still All about How They Look on TV," *Los Angeles Times*, October 24, 2008, E1.

60. Martha Joynt Kumar, *Managing the President's Message: The White House Communications Operation* (Baltimore: Johns Hopkins University Press, 2007), 202.

61. James C. Moore, "The Man with the Plan, How Karl Rove Won the Election for Bush," *Boston Globe*, November 7, 2004, D12. In a May 2002 interview with political scientist Martha Joynt Kumar, then-advisor to President George W. Bush expanded on his well-known dictum—invoking the Reagan White House's Michael Deaver and his advice of "building stories visually"—in what Kumar describes as "winning the picture." "Karl Rove traces the high point of media sophistication in this regard to the Reagan administration: 'I think in the post-1980 era, we all owe it to [Michael] Deaver, who said, "Turn off the sound of the television, and that's how people are going to decide whether you won the day or lost the day: the quality of the picture."'" "He [Rove] explains, 'That's what they're going to get the message by, with the sound entirely off. And I think that's simplistic, but I think it's an important insight. There is a reason why that old saw, a picture is worth a thousand words— how we look, how we sound, and how we project—is important. So winning the picture is important, and [so is] having a President with the right kind of people to drive and hone the emphasis of the message, [so he will] be seen in a positive, warm,

and strong way.'" Interviewing then–White House Communications Assistant Scott Sforza—a figure known in the Bush White House for his advance-work and design of backdrops ("wallpaper"), locations, and settings for President George W. Bush, Kumar offers Sforza's own words: "I sort of use the rule of thumb, if the sound were turned down on the television when you are just passing by, you should be able to look at the TV and tell what the President's message is. If you are passing by a store-front and see a TV in the window, or if you are at a newspaper stand and you are walking by, you should be able to get the President's messages in a snapshot, in most cases." Kumar, *Managing the President's Message*, 100.

62. Edwin Chen, "New Strides in Presidential Stagecraft, Bush's Venue-Scouting, Step-Counting Advance Team Has Set Standards in Image-Making," *Los Angeles Times*, July 6, 2004, A15.

63. Katharine Q. Seelye, "Bob Dole's Done There, Been That," *New York Times*, July 21, 1996, D4.

64. Julie Bosman, "When Campaigning Strays off Script," *New York Times*, November 25, 2007, E5.

65. Richard L. Berke, "A Senate Candidate's Refrain: 'Could You Stretch It to $500?'" *New York Times*, June 8, 2002, A1, A13.

66. Nick Anderson, "Ad Experts Not Sold on Campaign Commercials," *Los Angeles Times*, May 10, 2004, A12.

67. "So many of these commercials are made by sleep-deprived, over-caffeinated consultants sitting in dark Washington, D.C. studios using the same tired tech-niques," Republican media strategist Mark R. Weaver explained to the *Columbus Dispatch*.

68. Peter Marks, "A Convention for Everyone, One at a Time," *New York Times*, July 30, 2000, D3.

69. Jeff Leeds, "Stay Tuned for Political Advertising Prime Time, Presidential Candidates Reach Most California Voters via Airwaves, Poor Choices Can Be a Financial Drain," *Los Angeles Times*, March 4, 2000, A16.

70. Jeff Leeds, "Strategists Say TV Ads Are Losing Their Punch, the Bush, Gore Camps Are Spending Record Sums of Money on Advertising, but They Say the 30-Second Commercial Has Lost Much of Its Appeal," *Los Angeles Times*, November 2, 2000, A22.

71. Adam Nagourney, "Carefully Shaped Message Now a Campaign Relic," *New York Times*, September 16, 2008, A22.

72. McNamara, "It's Still All about How They Look on TV," E1; Sheryl Gay Stolberg, "Containing Themselves, the Whoop, Oops, and the State of the Political Slip," *New York Times*, January 25, 2004, D1, D3.

73. Television's nowness, its ever-insatiable insistence on the coverage of the breaking, the latest, the newest, the most up-to-date news is as poignant and as powerful as any part of the medium. The ability of the television screen with the caption "BREAKING NEWS" or "DEVELOPING" or "HAPPENING NOW" or "JUST IN" or simply "LIVE" to arrest us in our tracks, to quiet conversation and to gather around the screen to hear—and to read, thanks to all manner of banners,

"crawls," "flippers," and headlines on the screen—is unlike any other news medium. Interrupting a broadcast or breaking in to a program, in a moment such as that vividly recalled by millions of viewers in the late Sunday evening interruption of television broadcasts on May 2, 2011, with the breaking news of the death of Osama Bin Laden, is a reminder of the indelible place of television and its power and presence in our lives. Television screens interrupted by newscasters convey an urgency almost unparalleled in its ability to catch our attention and connect us in shared moments.

CHAPTER 8: THE INTERNET AND POLITICS IN THE DIGITAL AGE

1. Katie Hafner and Matthew Lyon, *Where Wizards Stay Up Late: The Origins of the Internet* (New York: Simon and Schuster, 1996), 10. In a *Wall Street Journal* op-ed, L. Gordon Crovitz takes issue with the government's role in the creation of the Internet. He—at not inconsiderable length—makes an argument against the Internet's being built to withstand a nuclear attack by the former Soviet Union. "The myth," Crovitz writes, "is that the Pentagon created the Internet to keep its communications lines up even in a nuclear strike." Crovitz argues that "the federal government was involved, modestly, via the Pentagon's Advanced Research Projects Agency network. Its goal was not maintaining communications during a nuclear attack, and it didn't build the Internet." "Robert Taylor, who ran the ARPA program in the 1960s, sent an e-mail to fellow technologists in 2004 setting the record straight: 'The creation of the ARPANET was not motivated by considerations of war.'" L. Gordon Crovitz, "Who Really Invented the Internet?" *Wall Street Journal*, July 23, 2012, A11. Andrew Blum's 2012 book *Tubes: A Journey to the Center of the Internet* claims that "the grim notion that the nascent ARPANET might evolve into a communications network that could survive a nuclear war [is] a popular myth about the origins of the Internet." Andrew Blum, *Tubes: A Journey to the Center of the Internet* (New York: Harper Collins, 2012), 40.

2. Hafner and Lyon, *Where Wizards Stay Up Late*, 10.

3. Janet Abbate, *Inventing the Internet* (Cambridge, Mass.: MIT Press, 1999), 1.

4. Ibid., 7.

5. AT&T executives, Hafner and Lyon tell us, refused to share their long-distance technical specifications for AT&T's circuit-switched telephone lines with the RAND Corporation. AT&T executives also expressed doubts about the feasibility of packet-messenging systems: "Vulnerability notwithstanding, the idea of slicing data into message blocks and sending each block out to find its own way through a matrix of phone lines struck the AT&T staff members as totally preposterous. Their world was a place where communications were sent as a stream of signals down a pipe. Sending data in small parcels seemed just about as logical as sending oil down a pipeline one cupful at a time." Hafner and Lyon, *Where Wizards Stay Up Late*, 62.

6. Ibid., 63.

7. As Hafner and Lyon tell us of the recollections of ARPA's Lawrence G. Roberts and others of the skepticism of some colleagues: "I [Roberts] remember one guy turning to the other and saying 'What have you got on your computer that I could use?' Engelbart recalled, and the other guy replied, 'Well, don't you read my reports?' No one was taken by the idea. People were thinking, 'Why would I need anyone else's computer when I've got everything right here?' recalled Jon Postel, then a graduate student at UCLA. 'What would they have that I want and what would I have that I want anyone else to look at?'" Hafner and Lyon, *Where Wizards Stay Up Late*, 72. In a December 1999 interview with *New York Times*' John Markoff, Taylor recalled a similar reluctance: "I had to go around and talk to our contractors to see if I could get their cooperation," "and some of them were enthusiastic, and some of them saw it as an infringement on their computing facilities. They said, 'I don't want to share my [computing] cycles with some guy across the country. I don't have enough cycles as it is. Now you're going to build something that allows people to come in and use my machine?' That took awhile to bring people together." John Markoff, "An Internet Pioneer Ponders the Next Revolution," *New York Times*, December 20, 1999, C38.

8. "As a historical event," *Boston Globe*'s Aaron Zitner writes upon the occasion of a September 1994 reunion of participants in Wednesday, October 29, 1969's UCLA-to-Stanford University connection, "it had none of the excitement of a moon landing or even of Alexander Graham Bell's famous 1st telephone call." "But 25 years ago this Autumn, when Ben Barker and Marty Thrope sent an electronic message from Los Angeles to Menlo Park, California, the computer era took a major leap forward." "Baker and Thrope," Zitner explains, "were part of a government-sponsored team charged with linking computers at 4 research centers." "When they were done, they had created a network that eventually became the Internet—the humming web of computers that serves as an international mail system, and which could soon be a major delivery channel for movies, store catalogs, educational programs, and business data." "Neither [Ben] Barker nor [Marty] Thrope remembers what words they exchanged over the early version of the Internet," Zitner notes. "They can't even decide who sent the message to whom." "But they and other computer scientists acknowledge their transmission as the 1st to go over the network using a technology called 'packet switching' which made complex networks possible." "Those transmissions were the 1st in which a communication was broken into packets by an IMP, then reassembled by a 2nd IMP in another city." Aaron Zitner, "A Quiet Leap Forward in Cyberspace, 25 Years Ago, the Internet Was Born—and Not Many People Noticed," *Boston Globe*, September 11, 1994, A1, A96.

9. "We did not know it would be 20,000,000 people doing e-mail and library access and bulletin boards," UCLA's Kleinrock recalled years later. "In fact," Zitner recounts quoting Kleinrock, "on the day UCLA's piece of the Internet was born, 'we did not even think to bring a camera.'" Zitner, "A Quiet Leap Forward in Cyberspace," A96.

10. Blum, *Tubes*, 43.

11. "More than 1,000 people came," *Washingtonian Magazine*'s John Adams writes. "Recalls ARPA's [Lawrence] Roberts: 'It was difficult for many professionals to accept that well over a hundred pieces of equipment could function together reliably.' The 3 day demonstration proved they could." John Adams, "Geek Gods: How Cyber-Geniuses Bob Kahn and Vint Cerf Turned a Pentagon Project into the Internet and Connected the World," *Washingtonian Magazine* 32, no. 11 (November 1996): 108.

12. Abbate, *Inventing the Internet*, 1.

13. Ibid., 84.

14. "It had no special places, no monuments," Blum tells us. "By the end of the [1970s], the network's geography was fully-entrenched around 4 regions: Silicon Valley, Los Angeles, Boston, and Washington. Only a few scattered nodes dotted the middle of the United States." "It was," Blum recalls, "a series of isolated outposts strung together by narrow roads, like a latter-day Pony Express." Blum, *Tubes*, 50.

15. Telenet's first seven cities with its so-called switching-notes for dial-up modem access in August 1975 included Washington, D.C., Boston, New York City, Chicago, Dallas, Los Angeles, and San Francisco. "These networks began to offer the general public the kind of reliable, cost-efficient data communications that the ARPANET had provided for a select few." Abbate, *Inventing the Internet*, 80.

16. "For all practical purposes," *InfoWorld*'s Thom Hogan writes in August 1981, "there were no significant sales of microcomputer equipment before the *Popular Electronics* article on how to build an Altair 8800 computer was published in January 1975." Thom Hogan, "From Zero to a Billion in 5 Years, Trends in the Hardware Marketplace," *InfoWorld: News for Microcomputer*, August 31, 1981, 6. Some 5,000 Altair 8800s were sold by the New Mexico–based retailer by the end of 1975. Ed Edelson, "Fast-Growing New Hobby, Real Computers You Assemble Yourself: Low-Cost Microcircuits Bring Tremendous Computing Power to Thousands of Homes," *Popular Science* 209, no. 6 (December 1976): 83. *Byte: The Small Systems Journal*, which published its first issue in September 1975, featured a story on the Albuquerque manufacturer and retailer in its second issue in October 1975 as well as ads by Altair for its computers ranging from the $439 kit to the $621 "assembled and tested Altair." *Byte*'s October 1975 story included a photograph of MITS's Altair computers and their assembly in the company's workshop. "Are They Real?" *Byte: The Small Systems Journal* 1, no. 2 (October 1975): 81.

17. Edwin Diamond and Stephen Bates, "The Ancient History of the Internet: Though It Appears to Have Sprung Up Overnight, The Inspiration of Free-Spirited Hackers, It in Fact Was Born in Defense Department Cold War Projects of the 1950s," *American Heritage* 46, no. 6 (October 1995): 38.

18. "Today," *Los Angeles Times*' William C. Rempel reported in a Sunday, February 24, 1985, story, "information that might otherwise require costly long-distance calls or delays for postal delivery can be exchanged across town or around the world virtually in an instant via 'electronic mail,' a computer-to-computer communications system regarded as the most revolutionary since the telegraph and telephone replaced horseback couriers more than a century ago." "Although still a

fledgling industry, with revenues last year estimated at $200,000,000, electronic mail use is growing at an annual rate of nearly 60%, faster than any other segment of the industry," Rempel reported. An estimated 1,000,000 e-mail accounts or "electronic mailboxes," as Rempel described them, were reportedly in use in February 1988. William C. Rempel, "Electronic Mail, a Revolutionary Courier Aims to Become Routine," *Los Angeles Times*, February 24, 1988, F1, F8. Lawrence J. Magid, "Revolutionary Software Expands Capabilities for Electronic Mail Users," *Los Angeles Times*, May 4, 1987, D3, D4.

19. Robert Wright, "Voice of America: Overhearing the Internet," *New Republic* 209, no. 11, September 13, 1993, 20, 24.

20. "The *Times* Is Joining New On-Line Service," *New York Times*, May 8, 1995, D7.

21. The *Washington Star* is worth quoting at length to appreciate the early applications of this still-emerging technology: "Jimmy Carter was sometimes described as the 'computer-driven candidate' during his determined quest for the presidency. Along with the computerized cost controls, the Democratic candidate had terminals humming in both his and running mate Walter Mondale's airplanes as they criss-crossed the country. It was the computer that kept track of each other's schedules and—more important—kept tabs on what each was saying to avoid embarrassing contradictions. If Mondale wanted to know what Carter was saying on tax reform, all he had to do was have an aide punch a few keys and the machine would come up with all his speeches on the subject. Similarly, if Carter wanted to get a message to Mondale, the fastest way often was to punch it into the computer. As soon as the chartered campaign plane landed, it could connect with the computer and all incoming messages would be printed out. As far as the staff on the planes were concerned, they were checking in with Atlanta headquarters. Actually, everything in the system—from the Atlanta operation to the candidates themselves anywhere in the country—was being funneled through a very powerful computer located on the 3rd floor of the Suburban Trust building in Bethesda." Carter's 1976 computer operation was known as Mailbox, a hardware and software interface allowing for messages to be typed at a terminal ("a modern electric typewriter with some extra keys") and then sent by modem to be "deposited," with messages "addressed to one other person, several, or everybody on the system." John Holusha, "Computer Tied Carter, Mondale Campaigns," *Washington Star*, November 21, 1976, A3.

22. Frank I. Luntz, *Candidates, Consultants, and Campaigns: The Style and Substance of American Electioneering* (New York: Basil Blackwell, 1988), 199–217.

23. Jeffrey B. Abramson, F. Christopher Arterton, and Gary R. Orren, *The Electronic Commonwealth: The Impact of New Media Technologies on Democratic Politics* (New York: Basic Books, 1988).

24. "The [Clinton] field media operation is sophisticated and ruthless," Michael Kelley reported on Wednesday, September 30, 1992. "The computer that sits on [Clinton's National Field Director Craig] Smith's desk is connected to computers on 50 other desks around the country and sends each state operation fresh 'talking

points,' and documentation for defensive and offensive efforts 4 or 5 times a day." Michael Kelly, "Those Chicken Georges and What They Mean," *New York Times*, September 30, 1992, A21. Edward Walsh in a report from then-governor Clinton's campaign offices in Little Rock, Arkansas, in September 1992 estimated that some 275 computers along with an estimated 50 facsimile machines, some 600 telephones, and "wire service machines from 3 news services plus dozens of television sets that are watched 24-hours a day to monitor the daily skirmishes of the presidential campaign," were used by the staff of some 350 along with more than 100 volunteers. Edward Walsh, "Remote Control: A Nerve Center Wired for Action, Technology Keeps Message Flowing from Little Rock," *Washington Post*, September 21, 1992, A10.

25. "At Clinton headquarters in Little Rock, Arkansas," Michael K. Frisby reported on Monday, June 1, 1992, "[then-Governor Bill Clinton's Director of Field Communication Jeff] Eller works on devising ways to get the message out. He noted that through CompuServe, which sends Clinton's speeches to its nearly 1,000,000 subscribers, he gets an average of 20 electronic messages a day from voters seeking more information about policies or asking how to make contributions." Michael K. Frisby, "Clinton Camp Weighing 30-Minute Broadcasts Once a Week," *Boston Globe*, June 1, 1992, A9. "In the area of public email, the Democrats in 1992 had the field virtually to themselves." Thomas W. Benson, "The 1st Email Election: Electronic Networking and the Clinton Campaign," in *Bill Clinton On Stump, State, and Stage: The Rhetorical Road to the White House*, ed. Stephen A. Smith (Fayetteville, AK: University of Arkansas Press, 1994), 318. clinton-hq@campaign92.0rg was one of the main e-mail addresses maintained in the 1992 race by then-governor Clinton's campaign.

26. "The Clinton White House [will] connect directly to voters via electronic mail sent by personal computers, [aide to then-President-elect Bill Clinton Jeff] Eller says," Frisby reported on Tuesday, January 12, 1993. "Presidential orders, speeches, and other communications could be transmitted directly to the public, or at least those with PCs, through electronic 'bulletin boards,' giving the White House another way to bypass the news media in reaching the public—an electronic Larry King." Michael K. Frisby, "Clinton's Recipe for Communication: High Tech and a Few Shots of Reagan," *Wall Street Journal*, January 12, 1993, A16.

27. "On the campaign trail," Steve Lohr reported of President Bill Clinton's campaign staff, "his people regarded laptop personal computers as casual tools of everyday life, plugging them into computer bulletin boards and firing off electronic mail messages around the country. And through electronic town halls and electronic mail, President Clinton pledges to bring the government to the people." "Perhaps," Lohr adds, "but the White House itself seems trapped in the technological dark ages." Lohr documented "a chronic shortage of personal computers" in the White House noting that the computers in place at the beginning of the administration were "arrayed in a hodgepodge of 21 networks that cannot talk to one another." "One result," Lohr observed, was that "the President's daily schedule is still printed on paper and distributed by hand, instead of by computer, so some people get it a couple of

hours late." "The Clinton staff," Lohr reported, "got used to high-speed technology on the campaign trail, scouring the news wires constantly by computer and reacting almost instantly with statements, position papers, and rebuttals to charges or controversies. These messages were distributed through an elaborate electronic mail system linked to campaign offices in all 50 states. 'Our motto on the campaign was that speed kills,' explained Jeff Eller, the White House director of media affairs." Steve Lohr, "White House: A Computer Nerdville," *New York Times*, February 20, 1993, A33.

28. "Hundreds of computer messages, or e-mail, are sent to the White House each day," Richard L. Berke reported in a Monday, April 5, 1993, story on the White House's computer initiatives. "The technology," Berke added, "has not reached the point where people can routinely get electronic messages back. Until the White House tools up its computer operation, people who send electronic messages to the President and Vice President will get a written, albeit slower, response via the United States Postal Service (snail mail, computer users call it)." Richard L. Berke, "'Hey, Prez!' Computers Offer New Line to Clinton," *New York Times*, April 5, 1993, A14. Carla Lazzareschi, "White House Starts Losing Its ZIP," *Los Angeles Times*, March 11, 1993, D1. Lawrence J. Magid, "White House Is Definitely Plugged In," *Los Angeles Times*, March 19, 1993, D3. Joel Achenbach, "Plugging In to E-Mail, from Your House to the White House, It's Leaving a Stamp on the Way We Communicate," *Washington Post*, March 22, 1993, B1, B4. T. R. Reid, "Writing Letters to the White House, the High-Tech Way," *Washington Post*, August 16, 1993, F16. "Today," President Bill Clinton and Vice President Al Gore announced in their Tuesday, June 1, 1993, statement released by the White House Office of Presidential Correspondence, "we are pleased to announce for the 1st time in history, the White House will be connected to you by electronic mail. Electronic mail will bring the Presidency and this Administration closer and make it more accessible to the people." "The White House will be connected to the Internet as well as several online commercial vendors, thus making us more accessible and more in touch with people across the country." "However," the statement added, "we must be realistic about the limitations and expectations of the White House electronic mail system." Thomas W. Benson, "The 1st Email Election: Electronic Networking and the Clinton Campaign," in *Bill Clinton on Stump, State, and Stage*, 334–335. John Burgess, "Clinton Goes On-Line with E-Mail, His Electronic Address Plugs Computer Users into White House," *Washington Post*, June 2, 1993, F3. "E-Mail to the Chief: Clinton in Computer Net," *Los Angeles Times*, June 2, 1993, A19.

29. "Mr. Clinton," Richard L. Berke reported, "does not have a computer in the Oval Office (he prefers legal pads) but he has surrounded himself with a new generation of aides who are steeped in the latest technology." "They are," Berke added, "marketing Mr. Clinton (his computer name is clintonpz) in ways that a President has never been presented before." Richard L. Berke, "'Hey, Prez!'," A1, A14.

30. "Subscribers to major online computer services like America Online, CompuServe, MCI Mail, and Prodigy can get information put out by the White House on their computers within hours after it is processed," Berke reported. "After

punching the command 'GO WHITEHOUSE,' users of CompuServe see this greeting flash on their computer screens: 'Welcome to the White House forum!' They can then retrieve speeches from the President, Vice President, or First Lady on dozens of subjects. They can also view photographs of the President striking any number of patriotic poses. In classrooms around the country, students and teachers can retrieve by computer the daily White House news briefings and schedules, and Mr. Clinton's speeches." "That is only the beginning," Berke added, "administration aides are tinkering with things like digital photography that would allow the President's image to be transmitted almost instantaneously to people around the country, and building the President's own cable television network to show government at work. There is even talk of a live, online 'town meeting' with Mr. Clinton." Ibid., A1, A14.

31. Peter H. Lewis, "Gore Preaches, and Practices, the Techno-Gospel," *New York Times*, January 17, 1994, D1, D4. Peter H. Lewis, "Live, Via CompuServe, It's On-Line with Al Gore," *New York Times*, January 14, 1994, D2. Amy Harmon, "Al Gore and 900 Others in Virtual Conversation, the Vice President Demonstrates Communications to Come, a Magazine and an On-Line Service Sponsored the Meeting," *Los Angeles Times*, January 14, 1994, D1, D2.

32. The White House Webpage was first posted to the public on Thursday, October 20, 1994. "People often think the White House is a web of intrigue," John Schwartz wrote on Thursday, October 20, 1994. "And as of today, it has a Web—a World Wide Web site." John Schwartz, "White House Unveils Internet Web, Computer Link Eases Access to Government Information, Services," *Washington Post*, October 20, 1994, A19. Peter H. Lewis, "Socks Can't Be Mistaken for a Dog Now," *New York Times*, November 2, 1994, D6. By January 1995, http://www.whitehouse.gov featured some 3,400 publicly viewable documents.

33. Graeme Browning, "Zapping the Capitol: Computers, Faxes, and Their Progeny Are Revolutionizing the Way Americans Marshal Their Forces on Important Issues and Make Their Opinions Known to Lawmakers," *National Journal* 26, no. 43 (October 22, 1994): 2448.

34. "Today," Edmund L. Andrews reported, "Mr. Gingrich proudly unveiled a new system that will allow Congress to match electronic wits [with the White House]. Operated by the Library of Congress, the new service is available over the World Wide Web, the hottest growth area of the Internet." "A person who taps into the service, called THOMAS in honor of Thomas Jefferson, can call up the full-text of any bill introduced in Congress since 1992 and will soon be able to get all new issues of the *Congressional Record*, which contains every speech made on the House and Senate floors." "The World Wide Web allows people to use a new generation of software to jump from site to site and subject to subject just by clicking on icons or words." In unveiling the THOMAS website, Speaker Gingrich and other government officials were reminded of the costliness of the computer hardware, modems, and monitors needed to view the site—as well as the slowness of the telephone-modem connections used by most American households at the time. "Even assuming every citizen could afford the equipment," Andrews noted, "if they use regular telephone lines and modems, they will find the service very slow." "You could take a shower

while you wait for some of this to come in over a regular line," one official with the Library of Congress told the *New York Times*. Edmund L. Andrews, "Mr. Smith Goes to Cyberspace, Coming Soon to Internet: Every-Word@Uttered.In.Congress," *New York Times*, January 6, 1995, A22. Robert Thomason, "A New Window on Congress," *Washington Post*, January 12, 1995, C7.

35. Andrews, "Mr. Smith Goes to Cyberspace," A22.

36. "Legislative aides," Eric Schmitt reported from Washington, D.C., in July 1996, "now spend minutes online rather than hours or days on the phone researching questions on topics as varied as welfare benefits and proposed food and drug rules." Eric Schmitt, "Capitol Hill Takes to Cyberspace, Though in Fits, Starts and Stumbles," *New York Times*, July 10, 1996, A12.

37. Schmitt, "Capitol Hill Takes to Cyberspace," A12.

38. "On Friday [March 28, 1996]," Peter H. Lewis reported from the Cambridge, Massachusetts, conference, "a bipartisan group of 'wired' lawmakers addressed the conference by telephone and Internet to announce the formation of a Congressional Internet Caucus." Peter H. Lewis, "Pioneers of Cyberspace Move into Wider Arena," *New York Times*, April 1, 1996, A14. "YourCongressman.Gov," *Washington Post*, April 15, 1996, F17.

39. Rebecca Fairley Raney, "Politicians Woo Voters on the Web, On-Line Stumping, Video Clips, Dirty Tricks, and a Chat with Marvin the Dog," *New York Times*, July 30, 1998, G1.

40. Jerrold Oppenheim, "The Coaxial Wiretap: Privacy and the Cable," *Law and Social Action* 2, no. 3 (Spring 1972): 287.

41. Peter Marks, "A Convention for Everyone, One at a Time," *New York Times*, July 30, 2000, D3.

42. Katie Hafner, "No Father of Computing, but Maybe He's An Uncle," *New York Times*, March 18, 1999, G3.

43. Marks, "A Convention for Everyone," D3.

44. Glen Justice, "Kerry Sets Web Record in Donations," *New York Times*, July 2, 2004, A14. Glen Justice, "Even with Campaign Finance Law, Money Talks Louder Than Ever," *New York Times*, November 8, 2004, A16.

45. Glen Justice, "Kerry Kept Money Coming with Internet as His A.T.M," *New York Times*, November 6, 2004, A12.

46. Peter Baker, "New Symbol of Elite Access: E-Mail to the Chief," *New York Times*, February 1, 2009, A1, A18.

Index

Abbate, Jane, 178–179, 182
ABC, 129, 140, 143, 147, 148, 149, 150
Abrahamson, Jeffrey B., 187
Ackerman, William C., 99
Adams, Abijah, 18
Adams, John: administration of, 18, 20; newspaper coverage of, 22; Sedition Act and, 17–18, 23; as vice president, 8, 11; War Speech of, 15
Adams, John Quincy: in election of 1824, 29–30; use of *Publicola* (pseudonym) by, 11
Adams, Samuel, 12
Adams, Thomas, 18
Advanced Research Projects Agency (ARPA), 177–179
Aero Products Incorporated, 112
Ailes, Roger, 166
Albany Evening Journal, 35
Albany Register, 20
Alexanderson, Ernst Frederik Werner, 107
All-electronic television, 115
Allen, Ethan, 20
Allen, John, 16
Allen, Mike, 196
Altair 8800 Computer, 183
America Online, 185, 188
American Boy, 78
American Daily Adviser, 12, 15

American Radio Relay League (ARRL), 78, 79–80, 82, 84
Anderson, John: in election of 1980, 165; as member of House of Representatives, 158
Anderson, Nick, 172
Andrews, Edmund L., 189
Apollo 11, 145
Apple Computers, 183, 194
Arkansas Gazette, close of, 67, 68
Army Signal Corps, 76
ARPANET, 180
Arsenio Hall Show, 167
Artgerton, F. Christopher, 187
Articles of Confederation, 1
Aspen Daily News, 68
Aspen Times, 68
Associated Press, 148; establishment of, 36
Association for Computing Machinery, 181
Atlanta, capture of, 41
Atlanta Constitution, 56, 80, 108; wireless transmissions and, 81
Atlanta Georgian, 56, 57
Atlanta Journal, 56; radio broadcast station of, 86
AT&T, 88, 89–90, 106, 112, 127, 131
Audience analysis, 173
Audio file downloads/uploads, 176

Aurora and General Advertiser, 14, 15, 16, 17, 21, 22
Austin Statesman, 135, 147
Automobiles, radios in, 99
Axelrod, David, 69, 166
Aykroyd, Dan, 158
Ayres, B. Drummond, Jr., 163

Bache, Benjamin Franklin, 12, 13, 14–15, 16, 17
Bache, Richard, 14
Bache, Sally, 14
Baird, John Logie, 107; shadowgraphs of, 103, 104–105; television system of, 111
Baker, Russell, 144
Baldasty, Gerald J., 33
Baltimore American, 20
Baltimore Sun, 65, 67; close of, 68
Baran, Paul, 178–179
Barfield, Ray, 114
Barker, Ben, 180–181
Barnoux, Erik, 114, 130
Bates, Stephen, 183
Battlefield photography, 40
Baughman, James L., 63, 68, 69
Beatles, 145
Bell Telephone Laboratories, 110
Benjaminson, Peter, 47
Berke, Richard L., 168, 172, 188
Berners-Lee, Tim, 185
Bernstein, Carl, 65–66
BET, 169
Bill of Rights, 4, 7–10, 23
Bird, William J., Jr., 130
BITNET, 183
Blackberry, 194, 196
Blair, Francis Preston, 25, 31–32, 33
Blair House, 33
Blau, Judith R., 25
Blitzer, Wolf, 192
Blum, Andrew, 181, 183
Bolt, Beranek, and Newman (BBN), 179
Booster relay stations, 121
Bosman, Julie, 171
Boston, newspapers in, 1, 16, 23, 57, 63, 66, 68
Boston American, 57
Boston Centinel, 16
Boston Daily Adviser, 57
Boston Gazette, 23
Boston Globe, close of, 68
Boston Herald Traveler, close of, 66

Boston Post, 63, 107
Boy's Life, 78, 84, 86
Bradford, John, 7
Bradlee, Benjamin C., 65
Brady, James S., Press Briefing Room, 70
British Broadcast Corporation (BBC), 111
Broadcasting, 121, 147
Broadcasting, growth of, 56–57
Brooklyn Eagle, 99; close of, 68
Brown, Nona B., 136
Bryan, William Jennings, 87, 89
Buffet, Warren, 71
Bulletin board services, 188
Buren, Martin Van, 33
Burgess, George K., 105
Burke, Aedanus, 9
Burleson, Postmaster, 82–83
Burroughs, 180
Bush, George H.W.: in election of 1988, 166; in election of 1992, 167
Bush, George W.: in election of 2000, 167–168; in election of 2004, 168, 193; portrayal of, on *Saturday Night Life,* 158; television coverage of, 171; website of, 192
Business Week, 148
Butcher, Harry, 96
Butler, Pierce, 13
Butler, William M., 89
Butterfield, Alexander P., 156

Cable Satellite Public Affairs Network (C-SPAN), 162–163
Cable television: introduction of, 64; reinvention of television in American politics and, 160–164
Californian, 35
Callender, James T., 19–20
Candidates, Consultants, and Campaigns (Luntz), 187
Canisius, Theodore, 39
Cape Hatteras, 74–75
Cape Henry, 74–75
Capra, Frank, 99
Carlin, George, 158
Carr, David, 168
Carson, Johnny, 154
Carter, Jimmy: debate with Ford, 158; debate with Reagan, 99; in election of 1976, 159, 187; in election of 1980, 165; portrayal of, on *Saturday*

Night Life, 158; television coverage of, 160; use of television by, 159
Carwardine, Richard, 40
Cater, Douglass, 63, 144
CBS (Columbia Broadcasting System), 92, 95, 129, 140, 147, 148, 149, 150
Centinel of the Northwestern Territory, 11
CERFNET, 184
Chain broadcasting, 88
Charles, Joseph, 28
Charleston, South Carolina, Civil War in, 40
Chase, Chevy, 158
Chase, Francis, Jr., 98
Chase, Samuel, 20
Chen, Edwin, 171
Chicago, newspapers in, 37, 38, 39–40, 41, 42, 43, 49, 57, 60, 62, 63, 65–66, 68–69, 112, 128, 129, 191
Chicago American, 57
Chicago Daily News, 60, 63, 112; close of, 68
Chicago Daily Tribune, 37, 128, 129
Chicago Examiner, 57
Chicago Herald and Examiner, 57
Chicago Herald Examiner, 65
Chicago Press and Tribune, 37, 39–40
Chicago Sun Times, 66; close of, 68
Chicago Tribune, 41, 43, 49, 60, 62, 65, 66, 69, 191; radio broadcast station of, 86
Cincinnati, newspapers in, 11, 29, 35, 42, 52, 55, 63, 68–69
Cincinnati Advertiser, 29
Cincinnati Commercial Gazette, 52
Cincinnati Enquirer, 29, 55
Cincinnati Gazette, 35
Cincinnati Post, 63; close of, 68–69
Cincinnati Times Star, 52, 63; close of, 68
Citizen Kane, 57
Civil rights movement, TV coverage of, 145–146
Clark, David G., 92
Clay, Henry: in election of 1824, 29–30; selection of, as secretary of state, 30
Claypoole, David C., 2, 3, 5, 15
Cleveland, Grover, 95; administration of, 45
Cleveland, newspapers in, 37, 41, 43, 63, 67, 68
Cleveland Leader, 37

Cleveland News, close of, 63, 68
Cleveland Plain Dealer, 63, 67
Cleveland Press, 41, 43; close of, 67
Clinton, Bill: administration of, 189; in election of 1992, 67, 167, 188; in election of 1996, 190; inauguration of, in 1993, 188; portrayal of, on *Saturday Night Life,* 158
Clinton, Hillary, 167
Clymer, George, 9
CNN (Cable News Network), 160
Cobb Island, 74–75
Cobbett, William, 14
Codel, Martin, 120
Colbert, Stephen, 169, 170
Coleman, William, 26
Columbian Centinel, 20
Columbian Observer, 30
Commerce, U.S. Department of: applications for new commercial broadcasting licenses, 86–87; Radio Division of, 77
Commodore Personal Electronic Transactor (PET) personal computer, 183
CompuServe, 184, 185, 188
Computer Society, 181
Computers, Freedom, and Privacy Conference, 190
Congress, U.S. *See also* House of Representatives, U.S.; Senate, U.S.: meeting of first, 7–8, 13
Congressional Internet Caucus, 190
Connecticut Courant, 20
Conrad, Frank, 84–85
Constitution, U.S.: First Amendment to, 10, 23; need for Bill of Rights, 8–10; newspapers and debate over ratification of, 5–7; Seventeen Amendment to, 54
Constitutional Convention of 1787: Committee of Detail at, 3; newspapers and, 2–5
Coolidge, Calvin: administration of, 91; in election of 1924, 89–91; inauguration of, 91; State of the Union address of, 88
Cooper, Thomas, 18–19
Corteyou, George, 50
Covert, Catherine L., 86
Cox, James M., 63, 72; in election of 1920, 55–56
Coy, Wayne, 130

Crawford, William H., in election of
    1824, 29–30
The Crisis (Paine), 98
Croatian Sound Bridge, 75
Cronkite, Walter, 139, 145, 151, 173
CSNET, 183
Culbert, David, 132, 134
Cuneo, Sherman A., 55–56
Cushing, William, 22

Daily Adviser, 6
Daily Democratic Press, 37
Daily National Intelligencer, 27, 30
Daisy ad, 149–160
Dallas Morning News, 67
Dallas News, radio broadcast station
    of, 86
Dallas Times Herald, 63, 67; close of,
    68
Daniels, Secretary, 82
Dare County Parks and Recreation
    Department, 75
DARPA, 184
Data glut, 190–191
Data retrieval, 176
Data smog, 190–191
David, Jefferson, 41
Davis, Elmer, 99
Davis, Harry P., 85
Davis, John W., in election of 1924,
    89–90
Davis, Stephen B., 105
Dayton Evening News, 55
Dayton Journal Herald, 63
Dean, Howard, 194
Debates: Carter-Ford, 158; Carter-
    Reagan, 99, 165; Clinton-Dole, 190;
    debate on the, 139–140; Kennedy-
    Nixon, 138–146, 158–159, 171;
    over ratification of Constitution, 5–7
Defense, U.S. Department of: Advanced
    Research Projects Agency of,
    177–178; Information Processing
    Techniques office, 181
Defense Advanced Research Projects
    Agency (DARPA), 181–184
DeForest, Lee, 76–78
DeForest Radio Telephone and
    Telegraph company, 78, 112, 113
Delaware, ratification of Constitution
    by, 6
Democracy in America (Tocqueville),
    31

Democratic National Committee, 65,
    66, 88
Democratic National Conventions,
    87, 89, 149, 151, 155–156
Democratic Republicans, 12, 25
Des Moines Register, 69
Des Moines Tribune, close of, 67
Desktop video conferencing, 176
Detroit Free Press, 63
Detroit Times, 57; close of, 63
Devine, Tad, 173
Dewey, Thomas E., in election of
    1948, 61–62, 100
Dial group technology, 173
Dial-up modems, 185
Diamond, Edwin, 183
Digital, 180
Digital divide, 191
Digital exhaust, 190–191
Dirksen, Everett, 151
The Disappearing Daily (Villard),
    60–61
Distant electric vision, 103
Distributed-switching network,
    179
Document archiving, 176
Dole, Bob: in election of 1996, 190;
    as Senator, 158
Douglas, Stephen, 40
Dr. Phil, 168
Drudge Report, 190
Du Mont, 129
Dukakis, Michael, 166
DuMont Laboratories, 118, 124, 128
Duncan, Matthew, 29
Dunlap, John, 2, 3, 5
Dunlap, Orrin E., Jr., 95–96, 117–118,
    122
Durrell, William, 17–18

Early, Stephen T., 59
Ebbitt House Hotel, 52
The Ed Sullivan Show, 145
Eddy, Henry, 29
Edgerton, Gary R., 102
Eisenhower, Dwight D.: in election of
    1952, 132–133; in election of 1956,
    136; inauguration of, in 1953, 134;
    press relations and, 64; television
    commercials of, 133
Electrical Experimenter, 81, 83
Electrical Experiments (Gernsback),
    79, 80

The Electronic Commonwealth (Abramson et al), 187–188
Electronic Numerical Integrator and Calculator (ENIAC), 178
Electronic tablets, 177
Electronic World, 78
Eller, Jeff, 188
Ellis, Joseph, 11
Elman, Cheryl, 25
Empire State Building, 114, 115, 118
Engelbart, Douglas, 180
Ervin, Samuel J., Jr., 156
European Particle Physics Laboratory (CERN), 185
Express riders, 31

Facebook, 193
Fair Haven Gazette, 21
Fallon, Jimmy, 170
Famous-Barr department store, 119
Farhi, Paul, 169
Farmer's Library, 21
Federal Communications Commission (FCC), 123, 129–130
Federal Election Commission (FEC), 172
Federal Elections Campaign Act (1974), 157
Federal Galaxy, 22
Federal Radio Commission (FRC), 87, 107
Federal Research Coordinating Council (FDICC), 184
Federalist papers, 5–6
Federalists, 25
Fenno, John, 7–8, 11, 14, 15, 16
Ferrell, Will, 158
Fessenden, Helen, 75
Fessenden, Reginald Aubrey, 74–75, 76
Fey, Tina, 158
Fiber optics in driving World Wide Web, 191–192
FIDONET, 184
File transfer programs, 182
First Amendment, 10, 23
Ford, Gerald, 151, 158; debate with Carter, 158; signing of Federal Elections Campaign Act by, 157
Fort Hancock, 76
Fort Pitt, 2
The Fourth Branch of Government (Cater), 63

Franklin, Benjamin, 14; Bill of Rights and, 4; print shop of, 21, 28
Free Soil Party, 36, 37
Freed Eisenmann Radio Corporation, 112
Fremont, John C., 33
Freneau, Philip, 12, 13
Friendster, 193
Frontier settlement, newspapers and, 2, 11

Gales, Joseph, Jr., 27
Gallatin, Albert, 16–17
Gannett, Frank E., 59, 72
Gascoigne, Paul, 92–93
Gazette of the United States, 11–12, 16, 20; Hamilton's financial support for, 7–8, 11, 12; influence of, 13
General Advertiser, 12, 13
General Adviser and Political, Commercial, Agriculture, and Literary Journal, 14–15
General Electric, 92, 103, 107, 108, 110, 112, 122–123, 124, 125
Genius of the People (Mee), 5
Gernsback, Hugo, 78, 79, 80, 83, 110
Gerry, Elbridge, 4
Gienapp, William F., 38
Gifford, Walter F., 106
Gill, Jonathan P. "Jock," 188
Gingrich, Newt, 189
Goldberg, Gerald Jay, 160
Goldberg, Robert, 160
Goldwater, Barry: debates and, 150, 154, 156; in election of 1964, 150
Google searches, 195
Gore, Al, 173; in election of 2000, 167–168; Internet and, 192; as member of House of Representatives, 163; as newspaper reporter, 69; senior thesis of, 153; as vice president, 188–189
Gould, Jack, 131, 139
Graham, Katharine, 65
Gray, Frank, 110
Great Depression: start of, 58; television and, 111–114
Great Lakes Broadcasting Company, 112
Greeley, Horace, 35, 37, 39
Green, Duff, 31–32
Green Mountain Boys, 20–21
Griffin, Merv, 154

Griggs, John W., 82

Hafner, Katie, 178, 179, 192
Hagerty, James C., 136
Halberstam, David, 97
Hall, Joseph, 2
Hamilton, Alexander: collaboration
  with Madison and Jay, 5–6; financial
  support for *Gazette of the United
  States,* 7–8, 11, 12; press and, 26–27;
  as secretary of the treasury, 8, 11, 14;
  on Washington's decision for second
  term, 13; writings of, 26–27
Hancock, John, 12
Hangge, Pete, 62
Harding, Warren: early work in
  journalism, 55–56; in election of
  1920, 55–56; press conferences of,
  56; radio broadcasting and, 86
Harison, Richard, 18
Harper, Robert S., 39
Harris, Benjamin, 70
Hart, Gary, 158
Hartford Evening Post, 50
Hartman, Phil, 158
Haswell, Anthony, 12, 22–23
Hatteras-Roanoke line, 75
Hayes Microcomputer Modem, 183
Hearst, William Randolph: newspaper
  ownership by, 49, 55–56, 58, 59, 72;
  political ambitions of, 57; radio
  station ownership by, 56–57
Heckman, Richard Allen, 38
Hedges, William S., 130
Henry, Buck, 158
Herndon, William, 39
High Performance Computing and
  National Research and Education
  Network Act (1991), 185
Hill, 70
Holt, Charles, 20
Holzer, Harold, 39–40
Honeywell DDP-516, 180
Hoover, Herbert: in election of 1928,
  92–93; in election of 1932, 94; as
  Secretary of Commerce, 92, 106
House of Representatives, U.S. *See also*
  Senate, U.S.: C-Span coverage of,
  162–163; Gingrich, Newt, as speaker
  of, 189; Judiciary Committee and
  Nixon impeachment and, 157;
  Merchant Marine and Fisheries
  Committee of, 82; newspaper

coverage of, 13; O'Neill, Thomas
  P. "Tip" as speaker of, 66, 69; press
  galleries in, 70; radio coverage of,
  99; television cameras in, 125–126;
  television studios for members of,
  136
Houston Chronicle, 63
Houston Post, close of, 68
Houston Press, 63; close of, 68
Hoyt, Edwin P., 24, 28
Hoyt, Olga G., 24, 28
Hughes, Sarah T., 146
Humphrey, Hubert: debates and, 156;
  in election of 1968, 150, 152, 154
Hutchinson, O. G., 104
Hypertext Transport Protocol and
  Hypertext Markup Language
  (HTML), 185

IEEE Communications Society, 181
Illinois, newspapers in, 28, 29, 38, 39
Illinois Daily State Journal, 39
Illinois Emigrant, 29
Illinois Herald, 29
Illinois Staats Anzeiger, 39
Illinois State Register, 39
*The Impact of Television on the
  Conduct of the President, 1947-1969*
  (Gore), 153
IMPs, 181
Independent Chronicle, 17, 18
Independent Journal, 5, 6
Indiana, newspapers in, 28
Indiana Gazette, 29
Indianapolis Times, close of, 68
Information overload, 190–191
Institute of Electrical and Electronics
  Engineers (IEEE), 181
Inter-Departmental Board of Wireless
  Telegraphy, 75–76
Interface Message Processors (IMP),
  180
International Business Machine (IBM),
  178, 180
International Conference on Computer
  Communication (ICCC), 181
International Electricity Congress, 103
Internet, 162; fund-raising on the, 192;
  history of, 177–186; politics and,
  175–197
Inventing the Internet (Abbate), 182
Investigative reporting, 44, 46, 54, 56,
  65–66

iPads, 177, 196
iPhones, 196
Israels, Joseph, 92–93
Ives, Herbert E., 110

The Jack Paar show, 144
Jackson, Andrew: administration of,
    31–32, 34–35; in election of 1824,
    29–30; in election of 1828, 31–32;
    inauguration of, 31; newspaper
    editors as advisors of, 31–32;
    supporters of, 25
Jackson, James, 8–9
Jackson, Jesse, 158
Jay, John, collaboration with Hamilton
    and Jay, 5–6
Jefferson, Thomas, 27; in election of
    1800, 24; inauguration of, 24; press
    relations and, 26–27; private
    correspondence of, 14; purchase of
    Louisiana territory and, 27–28; as
    secretary of state, 12; Sedition Act
    and, 15, 16, 17
Jenkins, Charles Francis, 103,
    105–106, 107, 108, 111, 113,
    119–120
Jenkins Television Corporation,
    110–111, 112
Jeopardy, 168
Jobs, Steve, 194, 196
Johnson, Claudia Alta Taylor, 135,
    146–147
Johnson, Lyndon B., 135; as avid
    television watcher, 146, 147–148;
    decision not to run for second term,
    151; in election of 1960, 143; in
    election of 1964, 149–160; family
    investments in television, 162; habit
    of telephoning television network,
    148; installation of UPI bulletins by,
    187; overexposure of, in television,
    153; swearing in of, 146; televised
    addresses of, 148–149, 151;
    unwillingness to debate Goldwater,
    150, 154, 156
Jones, Alex S., 67
Jones, Carter Brooke, 120
Juergens, George, 43, 48–49, 50–51
Junior Wireless Club, 77
Justice, Glen, 193

Kahn, Robert E., 181, 182
Kaltenborn, Hans V., 99

Kansas City, newspapers in, 38, 44,
    51–52, 68
Kansas City Journal Post, close of, 68
Kansas City Star, 44, 51–52; radio
    broadcast station of, 86
Kansas City Times, close of, 68
KDKA, 85, 100
Kennedy, Edward M., 189
Kennedy, Jacqueline: advertisements
    featuring, for election of 1960, 144;
    at swearing in of Johnson, Lyndon,
    146; tour of White House by, 145
Kennedy, John F.: assassination of, 41,
    146; awareness of television by, 138;
    debate with Nixon, 138–146, 158–
    159, 171; in election of 1960, 63,
    138–143, 171; newspaper readership
    and, 65; press conferences of, 65;
    prominence of television in
    administration of, 65, 144–146
Kennedy, Robert, assassination of, 151
Kentucky, newspapers in, 7, 28, 29
Kentucky Gazette, 7
Kentucky Reporter, 29
Kerry, John: in election of 2004, 168,
    193; raising of money via World
    Wide Web, 177
Ketcham, Ralph, 6
Kimmel, Peter, 29
King, Martin Luther, Jr., assassination
    of, 151
Kirkpatrick, Clayton, 191
Kleinrock, Leonard, 180–181
Knox, Frank, 60
Knoxville Gazette, 11
Kolbert, Elizabeth, 167
KRSC-TV, 161
KSD-TV, 88, 126–127
KTBC-TV, 135, 146–147
Kumar, Martha Joynt, 170

Landon, Alfred M., 60; in election of
    1936, 99
Larry King Live, 167
Lauter, David, 167
Lee, Alfred McClung, 68
Leeds, Jeff, 168, 173
Lelyveld, Joseph, 164–165
Leno, Jay, 168, 169
Leonard, Thomas C., 11
Letterman, David, 168, 169, 170
Levine, Cornelia, 97
Levine, Lawrence W., 97

Lexington, Kentucky, newspapers in, 7, 29
Liberty Party, 36–37
Libling, Abbott Joseph, 63–64
Lightning presses, 36
Lincoln, Abraham: assassination of, 41; Civil War and, 40–41; editorials written by, 39; in election of 1860, 38, 39–40; inauguration of, 40; newspapers read by, 37, 38–39; relationship with newspaper editors/ publishers, 41; work as postmaster, 38–39
Lippmann, Walter, 62
Little, Donald, 85
Live with Regis and Kelly, 168
Lodge, Henry Cabot, Jr., in election of 1960, 143
Log Cabin, 35
Log Cabin Advocate, 35
Log Cabin Farmer, 35
Lord, Chester S., 49
Los Angeles, newspapers in, 38, 42, 49, 57, 63, 64, 65, 66, 67, 68, 123, 164, 171
Los Angeles Daily News, 68; close of, 68
Los Angeles Evening Mirror, close of, 63, 68
Los Angeles Examiner, 49, 57
Los Angeles Herald Examiner, 67; close of, 68
Los Angeles Star, 38
Los Angeles Times, 42, 64, 65, 66, 67, 68, 123, 164, 171
Louisiana, newspapers in, 28
Louisiana territory, U.S. purchase of, 27–28
Louisville, Kentucky, newspapers in, 29, 35, 39, 63, 86
Louisville Courier Journal, 63; radio broadcast station of, 86
Louisville Journal, 35, 39
Louisville Public Advertiser, 29
Luntz, Frank, 187
Lyle, Jack, 64
Lyon, James, 21, 28, 179
Lyon, Matthew, 28, 178; Sedition Act and, 20–23

Madison, James, 27; administration of, 19; Bill of Rights and, 4, 8–10; collaboration with Hamilton and Jay, 5–6; as member of House of Representatives, 8, 12; Sedition Act and, 15, 16; unsigned essays of, in National Gazette, 12–13; on Washington's decision for second term, 13
Mallon, Winifred, 129–130
Manchester Leader, 60
Manchester Union Leader, 69
Mannes, George, 132, 161
Map Speech, 98
March on Washington (1963), 146
Marconi, Guglielmo, 73–74
Marconi Publishing Company, 78
Marconi Wireless Telegraph and Cable Company, 82
Marion Daily Star, 55
Marks, Peter, 173, 192
Marshall, Lynn L., 25
Marshall Field department store, 118
Martin, Alexander, 13
Martin, Joseph W., Jr., 126
Marx, Groucho, 100
Maryland, ratification of Constitution by, 7
Mason, George, 3–4
Mason, Stevens Thomson, 17
Massachusetts, ratification of Constitution by, 6–7
Matthews, Chris, 69
Maxim, Hiram Percy, 82
McAdoo, William Gibbs, in election of 1924, 89
McCain, John: in election of 2004, 168; in election of 2008, 168, 169, 193–194
McClure's Magazine, 73–74
McCormick, Robert R., 49, 59
McCosker, Alfred, 95
McCullough, David, 16, 17, 100
McGerr, Michael E., 25, 36
McGill, Ralph, 56, 62
McGinniss, Joe, 152–153
McGovern, George, 158; in election of 1972, 155–156
MCI Mail, 184, 188
McKinley, William: death of, 50; in election of 1896, 49–50; monitoring of news-wires by, 186; relationship with journalists, 49–50
McLaughlin, James Fairfax, 22
McLean, Edward Beale, 58
McLean's Edition, 6

McMaster, John Bach, 3
McNamara, Mary, 169, 173
Medill, Joseph, 37, 38, 39
Mee, Charles L., Jr., 5
Meet the Presa, 128, 139
Meetup Website, 194
Message switching, 179
Metropolis (film), 106
Metropolitan Opera, wireless
   transmission from, 77
Meyer, Eugene, 63
Miami Daily News, 56
Miami Metropolis, 56
Michelson, Charles, 93–94
Micro-Instrumentation Telemetry
   Systems, 183
Microsoft Corporation, 185
Middletown Signal, 55
Miller, Arthur, 62
Miller, Nathan, 51
Minnesota Star Tribune, close of, 67, 68
Minow, Newton N., 145
Missouri Gazette, 28
Modern Electrics, 78
Mondale, Walter F.: in election of 1976,
   187; in election of 1984, 166
Monday Night at the Movies, 149
Monticello, 17
Moore, Willis S., 74
Morgan, Dan, 167–168
Morris, Richard B., 6
Morse, Samuel F. B., 34
Morse code transmissions, 77
Morton, Alfred H., 123
Mosaic browsers, 185
Mott, Frank Luther, 25, 27, 31, 43
Mount Pleasant Register, 17–185
Moyers, Bill, 149, 153
Mr. Smith Goes to Washington (film),
   99
MSNBC, 69, 169
MTV, 167
Murrow, Edward R., 99, 139
Mutual Broadcasting Company, 95
MySpace, 193

National Amateur Wireless Association,
   78
National Association of Broadcasters
   (NAB), 87–88, 95, 145
National Center for Supercomputing
   Applications (NCSA), 185
National Gazette, 12–13

*National Intelligencer and Washington
   Advertiser,* 25, 26, 27
National Mall, 120, 121
National Press Club, 56, 58–59, 64,
   120–121; establishment of, 52
National Research and Education
   Network (NREN), 185
National Science Foundation, 185
National Wireless Association, 82
Naval Communication Service, 83
NBC (National Broadcasting
   Company), 92, 95, 113, 117, 122,
   123, 124–125, 128, 129, 130, 139,
   140, 142, 144, 145, 147, 148, 149,
   150, 157–158, 168, 169
NBC-RCA, 120
Neal, Terry M., 192
Nelson, William R., 51–52
Nessen, Ron, 158
New Deal, Newspapers and, 58–62
New Hampshire, ratification of
   Constitution by, 7
New Hampshire Union Leader, 69
New London Bee, 20
New Orleans, newspapers in, 38
New Windsor Gazette, 17, 18
New York American, 35
New York City: advertising in, 48;
   establishment of Associated Press in,
   36; founding of Radio Club of
   America in, 77; growth of, 11;
   meeting of First Congress in, 7–8;
   newspapers in, 1, 5, 6, 17, 20, 24–27,
   30–31, 34, 35–36, 37, 38, 39, 41, 42,
   43, 44, 48–49, 50, 54, 57, 60, 63, 64,
   65, 66, 68, 153, 190; Printing House
   Square in, 40
New York Commercial Advertiser, 17,
   20
New York Daily Advertiser, 30–31
New York Daily News, 68
New York Daily Times, 37
New York Evening Post, 26–27
New York Express, 35
*New York Gazette and General
   Advertiser,* 20
New York Herald, coverage of Lincoln
   assassination by, 41
New York Herald Tribune, 60, 63, 64,
   65; close of, 63, 68
New York Journal, 49
New York Mirror, 57
New York Observer, 50

New York Packet, 6
New York Post, 68
New York Stock Exchange, collapse of, 58, 111
New York Sun, 34
New York Times, 43, 44, 49, 65, 68, 87, 107, 124, 153, 190; investigative reporting by, 65; radio stations and, 91; short feature items in, 108–109; wireless transmissions and, 75, 79, 81
New York Times Magazine, 164
New York Tribune, 39, 43, 50
New York World, 41, 49, 54, 63
New Yorker, 64
Newark Evening News, close of, 68
The News in Megalopolis (Lyle), 64
Newspaper Women's Club, 60
Newspapers: broadcasting as challenge to, 56; circulation of, 47, 70–71; Constitutional Convention of 1787 and, 2–5; content of, 48; debate over ratification of Constitution and, 5–7; delivery of, 48; in the 1830s, 31–34; electoral reform and, 43–44; New Deal and, 58–62; political influence of, 41–46, 47, 62–63; readership of, 47–48; rise of the Whigs and, 34–36; in the 1790s, 10–14
Newsweek magazine, 55
Nineteenth century, newspapers and politics in, 41–46
Nixon, Richard M.: Checkers' speech of, 133–134; debate with Kennedy, 138–146, 158–159, 171; in election of 1960, 138–143, 171; in election of 1968, 152–153, 154; in election of 1972, 155–156; in House of Representatives campaign, 64; impeachment and, 157; press relations and, 65; refusal to debate Humphrey in 1968, 150, 154; resignation of, 65, 157; State of the Union address of 1969, 153–154; support for televised debates, 150; television coverage of, 133–134; Watergate break-in and, 65–66, 156–157
Nolan, Martin F., 167
North Carolina, ratification of Constitution and Bill of Rights in, 10
NSFNET, 183, 184–185, 192

Oakland Post Enquirer, 57

Obama, Barack, 70, 158, 187; in election of 2008, 168, 169, 193–194; in election of 2012, 169; use of Blackberry, 194, 196
Ochs, Adolph S., 37, 49
Ohio, newspapers in, 28
O'Neill, Thomas P. "Tip," 66, 69
The Oprah Winfrey Show, 168
Oreskes, Michael, 166
Orren, Gary R., 187
Outer Banks, 75

Packet-messaging, 179
Packet switching, 181, 182
Paine, Thomas, 98
Palin, Sarah, 158
Panther Valley Television Company, 161–162
Parsons, Ed, 161
Paterson, William, 21
Patnode, Randall, 87
Payne, George Henry, 37
Pearl Harbor, attack on, 60, 125
Pearson, Drew, 62
Pennsylvania Evening Post and Daily Advertiser, 1–2, 3, 4, 5
Pennsylvania Gazette, 12
Pennsylvania Packet and Daily Adviser, 2
Penny Press, 34
Perot, H. Ross, appearance on *Larry King Live,* 167
Perskyi, Constantin, 102–103
Philadelphia: Constitutional Convention in, 2–5; move of U.S. capital to, 11; newspapers in, 1–2, 3, 12–13, 24, 34, 41, 42, 67, 68, 152; Pewter Platter Alley in, 2; print shops in, 21, 28
Philadelphia Bulletin, close of, 67, 68
Philadelphia Evening Bulletin, 41
Philadelphia Inquirer, 152; close of, 68
Philadelphia News, 41
Philadelphia Public Ledger, 34
Philco, 121, 125
Pickering, Timothy, 17–18
Pilot Laboratories, 112
Pinckney, Charles, 3
Pittsburgh, newspapers in, 2, 29, 34, 35, 41, 63, 68, 85
Pittsburgh Daily American, 35
Pittsburgh Gazette, 2, 29
Pittsburgh Post, 85

Pittsburgh Press, close of, 68
Pittsburgh Statesman, 29
Pittsburgh Sun Telegraph, close of, 63
Political influence, of newspapers, 62–63
Politico, 70, 194–195
Politics: Internet and, 175–197; radio and the rise of broadcast, 72–101; television in transformation of postwar American, 137–174
Polk, James, administration of, 27
Popular Electronics, 183
Popular Mechanics, 91, 107, 114
Popular Radio, 105
Popular Science, 160
Porcupine's Gazetter, 14
Porter, John Addison, 50
Presley, Elvis, 145
Price, William W., 45, 51, 53
Print shops, 1
Printing presses: improvements in, 25, 34, 41–42, 45–46; steam-driven, 30–31, 34, 36
PRNET, 184
Prodigy, 184, 185, 188
Publick Occurrences Both Foreign and Domestick, 70
Publicola (pseudonym), 11
Publius (pseudonym), 5, 6
Pulitzer, Joseph, 41, 49, 54

QST, 80–81, 84

Radio Age, 78
Radio Amateur News, 78
Radio Broadcast, 78, 86
Radio City, 113–114, 116
Radio Club of America, 77
Radio Digest, 78
Radio League of America, 78, 79–80
Radio movies, 103, 105
Radio News, 78, 104, 110, 113
Radio Radio Commission, 112
Radio Telephone Company, 76
Radio Visors, 106, 107
Radiomovies, Radiovision, Television (Jenkins), 107, 108
Radio(s): Americans owning, 100; in automobiles, 99; in the early 1900s, 73–78; emergence of commercial broadcasting, 84–88; growth of commercial, 73; immediacy of, 101; rise of broadcast politics and,

72–101; transformation of American politics and, 88–94
Radioscopes, 103
Radiotelegraphy, 77
Radiotelephonic television, 106
Radiotelephony, 77
RAND Corporation, 178, 179, 180
Randolph, Edmund, 4
Raney, Rebecca Fairley, 190
Rayburn, Samuel T., 126
RCA (Radio Corporation of America), 107, 110, 112, 115–116, 118, 124, 125
Reagan, Ronald: debate with Carter, Jimmy, 99; in election of 1980, 165; press relations and, 66; radio commercials featuring, 100
Redfield, William C., 82
Reinsch, J. Leonard, 100, 139, 144
Republican National Committee, 88, 89–90
Republican National Conventions, 122–123, 128, 139, 149
Republican Party, formation of, 33, 36–37
Republicans, 12
Reston, James, 153
Richmond Enquirer, 27
Richmond Examiner, 19–20
Ritchie, Donald A., 33, 35, 138–143, 146
Ritchie, Thomas, 27
Roanoke Island, 74–75
Roberts, Ray A., 64, 183
Robinson, William E., 64
Rochester Journal, 57
Rochester Post Express, 57
Rocky Mountain News, close of, 69
Roll Call, 70
Romney, Mitt: in election of 2012, 169; use of iPad and iPhone by, 196
Roosevelt, Eleanor: newspaper column written by, 60; press conferences of, 59, 60; support for Kennedy, 144; television interview of, 125
Roosevelt, Franklin D.: appearance on television, 115–122; editorials attacking, 60; editorials of, 59; in election of 1924, 89; in election of 1932, 94–95, 98; in election of 1936, 60, 98, 99; in election of 1940, 60, 98; in election of 1944, 98; Fireside Chats of, 73, 94–98, 123–124, 159;

first term of, 58–59; inaugurations of, 95–96; Map Speech of, 98; National Press Club and, 58–59; press conferences of, 59–60; second term of, 60; third term of, 60; World War II and, 60–61
Roosevelt, Theodore: death of, 51, 52; editorials of, 51–52; establishment of Inter-Departmental Board of Wireless Telegraphy, 75–76; friendship with the press, 50–51; installation of ticker-tape machines in White House by, 187; renovations in White House and, 50
Rosenberg, Leo, 85
Rotary press, improvements in, 38
Roulstone, George, 11
Rove, Karl, 170–171, 187
Rutland Herald, 21
Ryfe, David M., 36, 44

Sack, Kevin, 168
St. Louis, newspapers in, 28, 38, 39, 41, 43, 62, 63, 65, 67, 68, 100
St. Louis Globe Democrat, 62, 67; close of, 68
St. Louis Post Dispatch, 41, 43, 63, 65, 100
St. Louis Republican, 39
St. Louis Times Star, close of, 68
San Francisco, newspapers in, 41, 42, 68, 69, 76, 79
San Francisco Chronicle, 79; close of, 68
San Francisco Examiner, 41, 69
Sandy Hook, New Jersey, 76
Sangamo Journal, 39
Sarnoff, David, 116–117, 139
Saturday Night, 157–158
Saturday Night Live, 157–158, 168, 169
Schlesinger, Arthur M., Jr., 153
Schmitt, Eric, 189–190, 194
Schorr, Daniel, 160
Schudson, Michael, 25, 31
Scientific American, 76, 78
Scripp, E. W., 41
Scripps-Howard, 127
Scull, John, 2
Sears Roebuck Company, 112
Seaton, William Winston, 27
Seattle Post Intelligencer, 57; close of, 69

Sedition Act (1798): controversy over, 15–20; Lyon, Matthew, and, 20–23; signing of, 17–18
Seelye, Katherine Q., 171
Selling of the President (McGinniss), 152–153
Senate, U.S. See also House of Representatives, U.S.: C-Span coverage of, 162–163; investigation of Watergate break-in and, 156–157; newspaper coverage of, 13; press galleries in, 70; television studios for members of, 136
Seventeen Amendment, 54
Shadel, Bill, 143
Shadowgraphs, 103, 104
Shakespeare, Frank, 153
Shipp, J. E. D., 30
Shortwave and Television Laboratory Incorporated, 112
Silent nights, 73
Simon, Paul, 70
Sinatra, Frank, 100
60 Minutes, 154, 167
Smartphones, 177
Smith, Alfred E., 73; in election of 1928, 89, 92–93, 109–110
Smith, Hedrick, 166
Smith, Howard K., 99, 141–142
Smith, John Cabot, 119–120
Smith, Ralph Lee, 160
Smith, Samuel Harrison, 26
Smith, William, 9
Source, 184
South Carolina, ratification of Constitution by, 7
Spam, 191
Spargo, John, 22–23
Sparkman, John J., 134
Split ticket voting, 43
Spooner's Vermont Journal, 21
Springfield News, 55
Sprint's Telemail, 185
Staab, Walter, 164–165
Stanford Research Institute (SRI), 180
Stanford University, 181
Staten Island's Fort Wadsworth, 76
Steffen, Charles G., 31–32
Stein, Sonia, 128
Stevenson, Adlai E.: in election of 1952, 132–133; in election of 1956, 136
Stewart, Jimmy, 127
Stewart, Jon, 169, 170

Stolberg, Sheryl Gay, 173
Store-and-forward switching, 179
Stout, Elihu, 29
Stump speeches, 73
Sunbury and Northumberland Gazette,
    18–19
Sunday editions, 45
Swanson, C. A., & and Sons', 131
Syracuse Telegram, 57

T Days, 127–128
Taft, Robert, in election of 1952, 52
Taft, William Howard: relations with
    press, 53; as reporter, 52
Tames, George, 65
Tandy TRS-80 Computer, 183
Tarlton, Robert J., 161–162
Tayl, David W., 105
Taylor, Robert W., 180
Telegraph, 34, 42, 45
Telegraph Age, 73–74
Telenet Communications Corporation,
    183
Telephonoscopes, 103
Telephony, 78
Teleprompters, 133
Teletype machines, 186–187
Television: coining of word, 102–103;
    election of 1948 and, 127–130;
    election of 1952 and, 130–136;
    election of 1968 and, 151–154; Great
    Depression and, 111–114;
    introduction of cable, 64; in the
    1920s, 103–111; in the 1960s, 138–
    146; in the 1970s, 64, 154–159;
    political advertising on, 164–165;
    Republican National Convention of
    1940 and, 122–123; in
    transformation of postwar American
    politics, 137–174; World War II and,
    123–127
Televisors, 103
Telimco Wireless Telegraph, 76
Tennessean, 69
The Tennessean, 153
Texas Broadcasting Company, 135, 147
Theissen, Alfred H., 74
Thomas, Isaiah, 22
THOMAS Internet Service, 189
Thwaites, Reuben Gold, 28
Ticker-tape machines, 187
Time magazine, 55, 58, 121, 154, 162
Time-sharing mainframes, 187

Tocqueville, Alexis de, 31
The Today Show, 167
The Tonight Show, 154, 167
Towne, Benjamin, 2
Transmission Control Protocol/Internet
    Protocol (TCP/IP), 182, 184
Transportation, improvements in, 35
*A Treatise on the Law of Libel and the
    Liberty of the Press* (Cooper), 19
Treleaven, Harry, 152–153
Trenton Times, 68
Trentonian, 68
TRK-12 receivers, 116, 117, 118, 119
Truman, Harry S: in election of 1948,
    61–62, 100, 128–129; inauguration
    of, 130–131; remarks of, on
    television, 125; television viewing by,
    126
*Tubes: A Journey to the Center of the
    Internet* (Blum), 181
Turner, Ted, 160
TV Guide, 131
Twitter, 176, 193
2XAF, 92

UCLA, 181; Scientific Scientific System
    Sigma 7, 181
Unified system, 82–83
*Union or New Orleans Advertiser and
    Price Current,* 28
United Press International (UPI), 148,
    187
United Research Corp., 112, 113
United States, newspapers in, 24–25,
    31, 36, 42, 54, 55–56
United States Telegraph, 25, 31–32, 33
U.S. Navy, financing of wireless
    equipment, 74
Universal Gazette, 26
USENET, 183
Utah, University of, 181

Vergennes Gazette, 22
Vermont Gazette, 12, 22
Vermont Journal, 21
Video file downloads/uploads, 176
Vietnam War, television coverage of,
    151
Villard, Oswald Garrison, 53, 60–61
Virtual radio, 105
Viruses, 191
Visual broadcasting, 110
Visual radio, 103

Visual wireless, 103

WABD-TV, 124, 126
WAHG, 90
Walden, David, 181
Wall Street Journal, 68, 190
Wallace, Mike, 154
Walson, John, 161
Walters, Barbara, 154
War of Independence, print shops
   and, 1
War Production Board, 125
Warren, Earl, 61, 63
Washington, Bushrod, 18, 20
Washington, D.C.: establishment of
   National Press Club in, 52; Newseum
   in, 70; "Newspaper Row" in, 44;
   Newspaper Women's Club in, 60;
   newspapers in, 44, 45, 54, 63, 68;
   White House Correspondents
   Association in, 53
Washington, George: administration of,
   11–12, 13; anniversary of
   inauguration of, 116; cabinet of, 11;
   decision on second term, 13; decision
   to retire, 14–15; as presiding officer
   of Constitutional convention, 2–3
Washington, Harold L., 70
Washington Daily News, 58, 66; close
   of, 66, 68
Washington Evening Star, 44, 45, 51,
   58, 65, 66, 120; close of, 68
Washington Globe, 25, 31–32, 33
Washington Herald, 57, 58; close of, 68
Washington Post, 44, 63, 65, 66, 105,
   106, 119, 128, 167–168, 190;
   financial problems of, 58;
   investigative reporting by, 65–66
Washington Times, 57, 58
Washington Union, 27
Washinton, D.C. *Sunday Star*, 105
Watergate break-in, 65–66, 156
WBBM-TV, 137, 139, 141–142
WBHF, 90
WBKB-TV, 125, 129
WCAP, 88
WCBS-TV, 126
WDAF, 86
WEAF, 89
Weather Bureau, wireless innovation
   and, 74–75, 76
Weed, Thurlow, 35
Weekly Intelligencer, 20

Weir Point, 75
The Well, 184
Welles, Orson, 57, 100
WERN-TV, 129
West: rise of newspapers in, 27–29;
   settlement of, 28–29
Western Electric Company, 125
Western Television Corporation, 112
Westinghouse Company, 84–85, 103,
   110, 118
WEWS-TV, 127
WFAA, 86
WGN, 86
WGN-TV, 62, 128, 129
WGY, 92, 107, 108
WHAS, 86
Wheel of Fortune, 168
Where Wizards Stay Up Late (Hafner
   and Lyon), 178
Whig Rifle, 35
Whigs, 31; newspapers and rise of the,
   34–36
WHIO, 56
White, Graham J., 59
White House: Brady, James S., Press
   Briefing Room, 70; Diplomatic
   Reception Room in, 96; installation
   of wireless telephone receiver in, 86;
   Kennedy, Jacqueline's tour of, 145;
   Office of Media Affairs, 188; Office
   of Presidential Correspondence, 188;
   press corps of, 51; press room in, 50;
   prominence of television in, 144–146
White House Correspondents
   Association (WHCA), 53, 64
Wicker, Tom, 150–151
Wilbur, Charles D., 105
Wilson, Woodrow: in election of 1912,
   49; in election of 1916, 78; press
   conferences of, 52–53; on publicity
   and politics, 49; Roosevelt's editorials
   on, 52; wireless technology and, 80,
   81, 84; World War I and, 53, 79, 80
Winchell, Walter, 62
Winfrey, Oprah, 168
Winship, Michael, 102, 103
Wire services, 45
*The Wired Nation: Cable TV, the
   Electronic Communications Highway*
   (Smith), 160
Wireless, World War I and, 79–84
Wireless Age, 78
Wireless receivers, sales of, 85

Wireless Telegraph and Signal
Company, 73
Wireless telegraphy, Marconi's
experiments with, 73–74
Wireless Telegraphy for Amateurs, 77
Wireless telephone receivers, 86
Wireless transmitters, ban on, in World
War I, 72–73
Wireless World and Radio Review, 78
WJZ, 89, 90
WMAL-TV, 128
WNBQ-TV, 129
WNBT-TV, 123, 124, 125, 126
WNBW-TV, 128
WNMJ-TV, 129
Woodward, Bob, 65–66
Woodworth, E. B., 83
World War I: ban on wireless
transmitters in, 72–73; Wilson,
Woodrow and, 53; wireless and,
79–84
World War II: attack on Pearl Harbor
in, 60, 125; Television and, 123–127;

U.S. entry into, 60–61, 100
World Wide Web, 163–164; broadband
digital services of, 162; fiber optics in
driving, 191–192
World's Fair, 115–120
Worms, 191
WPTZ-TV, 122, 125
WRC-TV, 142–143
WRGB-TV, 125
Wright, Robert, 185
WSB, 86
WTMJ-TV, 127, 129
WTTG-TV, 126, 128
WWJ-TV, 127
W9XBK, 125
W3XK, 107, 108, 122

The Young Man and Journalism
(Lord), 49
YouTube digital videos, 196

Zworykin, Vladimir, 115

About the Author

Dr. Patrick Novotny has taught and written widely on the history of the American press and its relationship with political campaigns since the completion of his doctorate in the Department of Political Science at the University of Wisconsin-Madison in 1995. Having taught at Georgia Southern University since 1995, Dr. Novotny's scholarly work has included years of research on the history of the press in American political life, including publications in the *Harvard Journal of Press/Politics, Social Science Computer Review*, as well as in numerous articles and book chapters, including a study of the postwar emergence of television in the state of Georgia and its impact on political life in that state, featured in the *Georgia Historical Quarterly*. Dr. Novotny's books include *Where We Live, Work and Play: The Environmental Justice Movement and the Struggle for a New Environmentalism* (2000); *This Georgia Rising: Education, Civil Rights, and the Politics of Elections in Georgia in the 1940s* (2007); and *Listening, Looking, Living: Qualitative Research in Political Science* (2013).

0 1341 1661225 7

About the Author

Dr. Patrick Novotny has taught and written widely on the history of the American press and its relationship with political campaigns since the completion of his doctorate in the Department of Political Science at the University of Wisconsin-Madison in 1995. Having taught at Georgia Southern University since 1995, Dr. Novotny's scholarly work has included years of research on the history of the press in American political life, including publications in the *Harvard Journal of Press/Politics, Social Science Computer Review*, as well as in numerous articles and book chapters, including a study of the postwar emergence of television in the state of Georgia and its impact on political life in that state, featured in the *Georgia Historical Quarterly*. Dr. Novotny's books include *Where We Live, Work and Play: The Environmental Justice Movement and the Struggle for a New Environmentalism* (2000); *This Georgia Rising: Education, Civil Rights, and the Politics of Elections in Georgia in the 1940s* (2007); and *Listening, Looking, Living: Qualitative Research in Political Science* (2013).

0 1341 1661225 7